"The Learning of the Jews"

"The Learning of the Jews"

What Latter-day Saints Can Learn from Jewish Religious Experience

Edited by
Trevan G. Hatch and
Leonard J. Greenspoon

GREG KOFFORD BOOKS
SALT LAKE CITY, 2021

Paperback ISBN: 978-1-58958-499-0
Also available in ebook.

Greg Kofford Books
P.O. Box 1362
Draper, UT 84020
www.gregkofford.com
facebook.com/gkbooks
twitter.com/gkbooks

Library of Congress Control Number: 2021942550

In memory of two contributors
Rabbi Byron Sherwin and Rabbi Peter Knobel
Rest in peace

Contents

Introduction

Trevan G. Hatch and Leonard J. Greenspoon

The title of this book is taken from the opening passage in Latter-day Saints' foundational sacred text, the Book of Mormon. The author of this passage, a seventh-century BCE Manassehite living in Jerusalem, states that the record of his family consists in part of "the learning of the Jews" (1 Ne. 1:2). This book is about Latter-day Saints learning from Jews and the Jewish experience. Many Latter-day Saints seem to have approached their faith and their scriptures from a conservative Protestant perspective (which may be valuable in several aspects); however, what would the Latter-day Saint religious experience look like if they approached it from a Jewish perspective? We wonder what the Jewish experience can teach Latter-day Saints that may enhance their lived religious experience. After all, many Christians (including Latter-day Saints) have taught that during the Israelite period (what Christians call the "Old Testament" period), Jews struggled mightily at observing the Law, rejected and killed the prophets, and obsessively accepted and followed the "Letter of the Law" (the legal minutiae) over the "Spirit of the Law," and that they then rejected Jesus wholesale, killed Jesus, and have been punished by God ever since. Given that depressing interpretation, why would Latter-day Saints want to learn from the religious and lived experiences of Jews?

Why the Jews?

Today, the estimated global Jewish population is fifteen to twenty million, with about two-thirds living in the United States or Israel. Like Latter-day Saints, Jews seem to be overrepresented in certain key professions, such as academics, politics, technology, and entertainment. Regarding religious influence, which is most relevant for this volume, Jews produced what is arguably the most published book of all time—the Bible—which has been translated, in whole or in part, into 3,400 languages and dialects. Jews preserved the Hebrew Bible from their Hebrew and Israelite ancestors, and most of the New Testament is attributed to first-century Jewish writers.[1]

---

1. For a broad discussion, not only on the Jewish legacy of writing the books of the Bible but also on the Jewish legacy of preserving and translating the Bible,

The Book of Mormon, a volume of Latter-day Saint scripture, claims to be an ancient religious record written by sixth-century Jews and their descendants (2 Ne. 30:4, 33:8; Omni 1:14). Christianity, the religion of over two billion people worldwide,[2] was largely founded by Jews, regardless of whether the credit is given to Jesus of Nazareth, Paul of Tarsus, or Jesus's closest followers who headed the Jerusalem Church. Islam, the religion of 1.6 billion people,[3] was also heavily influenced by Hebrew thought. Islam's founder, Muhammad, claimed that his revelations were congruous with the teachings of the Hebrew prophets, who the Quran invites all believers to honor.[4] In short, half or more of the world's population identify with a religion that has Hebraic or Judaic foundations.

That the Jewish population has been so influential is remarkable considering the amount of persecution that they have experienced. They were persecuted and scattered by the Romans, were slaughtered by Christians during the Crusades, were expelled from multiple Christian countries in Europe, and faced extinction by Hitler's Nazi regime. Jews have also experienced and continue to experience anti-Semitism in the United States. Henry Ford, a beloved American icon, published multiple anti-Semitic writings that spanned an entire decade, beginning in the 1920s. His newspaper, *The Dearborn Independent*, contained articles about Jews and their alleged involvement in corrupting the financial system. A series of his articles were compiled into an anti-Semitic booklet titled, *The International Jew*, which accused Jews of conspiring to take over the world. By 1940, Henry Ford had claimed that Jews led the Bolshevik Revolution and accused Jews of starting World War II. Ford was eventually awarded a medal from Adolf Hitler and was praised in *Mein Kampf*.[5]

see Leonard Greenspoon, *Jewish Bible Translations: Personalities, Passions, Politics, Progress* (Philadelphia: Jewish Publication Society, 2020).

2. "Global Christianity–A Report on the Size and Distribution of the World's Christian Population. Pew Research Center," Pew Research Center, December 19, 2011, http://www.pewforum.org/2011/12/19/global-christianity-exec/.

3. "World's Muslim Population More Widespread than You Might Think," Pew Research Center, January 31, 2017, http://www.pewresearch.org/fact-tank/2013/06/07/worlds-muslim-population-more-widespread-than-you-might-think/.

4. Quran 2:135-136; 3:84; 4:163; see also Roberto Tottoli, *Biblical Prophets in the Qur'ān and Muslim Literature* (New York: Routledge, 2009).

5. See Spencer Blakeslee, *The Death of American Anti-Semitism* (Westport, CT: Praeger, 2000); William D. Rubinstein, "Anti-Semitism in the English-speaking world," in *Anti-Semitism: A History*, ed. A. S. Lindemann and R. S. Levy (New York: Oxford University Press, 2010), 150–65.

In the late 1930s, public polling revealed that anti-Semitism was as at its highest point in American history. *Fortune* magazine, for example, found that 50 percent of the respondents to their survey agreed that Nazi policies toward Jews were helping Germany's economy.[6] Another poll in 1938 asked, "Should we allow a larger number of Jewish exiles to come to the United States to live?" Seventy-seven percent of respondents answered "no."[7]

Despite such anti-Semitism, Jews are a highly influential cultural and religious minority that have experienced many complexities and paradoxes. Christians, and especially Latter-day Saints, have become increasingly interested in learning about Jews and Judaism because of their foundational influence in western civilization, their history of oppression, their rich religious and cultural heritage, and of course the Jewish connection to Jesus and early Christianity. This unprecedented experience can surely inform, inspire, and enlighten Latter-day Saints in relation to their own religious experience.

Origins of the Term "Jew"

The term "Jew" (*Yehudi* in Hebrew) is derived from the patriarch Abraham's great-grandson Judah (*Yehudah* in Hebrew), who migrated to Egypt with his eleven brothers approximately 1,600 years before the birth of Jesus of Nazareth. While it is commonly believed that Jews are descendants of the ancient Israelite tribe of Judah, this is not the case.

According to the book of Exodus, the descendants of Judah and his eleven brothers were enslaved and oppressed a generation or two after they had settled in Egypt. This enslavement continued for several hundred years until around 1250 BCE,[8] when God through Moses freed them by a series of miracles. The ancient text states that an entire nation called "Hebrews"—or Israelites because they were descendants of the twelve sons of Israel—fled Egypt and eventually settled to the northeast in the land of Canaan, which is in modern-day Israel and Palestine.

---

6. Arthur Hertzberg, *The Jews in America, Four Centuries of an Uneasy Encounter: A History* (New York: Touchstone Press, 1998).

7. Leonard Dinnerstein, *Antisemitism in America* (New York: Oxford University Press, 1994), 127.

8. Biblical and ancient history scholars have replaced BC ("before Christ") and AD (*Anno Domini,* a Latin phrase for "year of our Lord") with BCE (Before the Common Era or Before the Christian Era) and CE (Common Era or Christian Era). A couple reasons for this are: 1) Jesus was born anywhere from 5 BCE to 2 BCE, so BC and AD would not be accurate (Jesus was born two years before Christ?); and 2) to be more inclusive for non-Christian subjects and scholars.

The Israelites divided the land of Canaan into regions where descendants of each of the twelve sons of Israel lived together. The family of Judah, or tribe of Judah, settled in the southern portion of the land near the tribes of Simeon and Benjamin. The other nine tribal territories were located in the north and in the east across the Jordan River. Around 928 BCE, the Israelite nation divided into two kingdoms following the death of King Solomon. The southern kingdom was called Judah after the dominant tribe, and the northern kingdom was called Israel.

During the eighth century BCE, the Assyrians to the northeast of the two Israelite kingdoms had gained enormous power and sought to annex territories of neighboring kingdoms. In 732 BCE, the Assyrian king, Tiglath-Pileser III (commonly called "TP3" among biblical studies graduate students), annexed part of the northern kingdom of Israel and deported some of the population (2 Kgs. 15:29; 16:9). Over the next twelve years, Assyrian kings Shalmaneser V and Sargon II deported more people from neighboring territories, including the northern kingdom of Israel (17:3-6). Jews and Christians today speak of the "ten lost tribes" of Israel and often assume that all members of these northern tribes were exiled, never to be heard of again. However, the Bible states that Assyria did not deport every individual; rather, a portion of the population in the northern kingdom of Israel fled south into the kingdom of Judah (2 Chr. 15:9; 30:1-11; 34:3-9). Thus, by 720 BCE, only *some* members of all the northern tribes were exiled and became "lost" to their larger Israelite family who remained in the southern kingdom of Judah. Others from each tribe in the north were preserved when they escaped to the southern kingdom.

Roughly twenty years later, Assyria, under the leadership of King Sennacherib, invaded the southern kingdom of Judah. Five chapters in the biblical record describe Assyria capturing the walled cities of Judah and deporting much of the population (2 Kgs. 18-19; 2 Chron. 32; Isa. 36-37). Sennacherib's own account—recorded on two clay prisms now located in the Oriental Institute of Chicago and the British Museum—claim that Assyria took "46 . . . strong walled cities" and many "of the smaller towns which were scattered about . . . and plundered a countless number." Sennacherib boasted about expatriating "200,156 persons, old and young, male and female, together with horses and mules, asses and camels, oxen and sheep, a countless multitude."[9] Assyrian troops eventually surrounded Jerusalem, a city that had swelled to a population of perhaps 25,000 after Assyria's inva-

9. Anson F. Rainey and R. Steven Notley, *The Sacred Bridge* (Carta Jerusalem: Jerusalem, 2006), 243.

sion of the northern kingdom of Israel. Fortunately for those within, Assyria could not penetrate the fortified walls despite numerous attempts.

What, then, does this all mean for the origin of the term "Jew"? It means that by 700 BCE, after Assyria's invasion of both the kingdoms of Israel and Judah, members of *all* twelve tribes of the once-unified nation of Israel were deported, and members of *all* twelve tribes were spared and retained their identity. Therefore, technically, Christians and Jews should speak of "twelve *partially* lost tribes" instead of "ten lost tribes." In fact, the Bible never mentions "ten lost tribes." Instead, it indicates that the northern kingdom of Israel only contained nine of the twelve tribes—namely, Asher, Dan, Ephraim, Gad, Issachar, Manasseh, Naphtali, Reuben, and Zebulun. The southern kingdom included Benjamin, Judah, and Simeon.

The confusion, however, is related to the tribe of Simeon and whether it was included in the northern kingdom or southern kingdom. The book of Joshua places the tribe of Simeon directly within the land of Judah (19:1). Another passage, however, claims that five hundred men from the tribe of Simeon left their tribal territory and settled east of the Jordan River that was later controlled by the northern kingdom of Israel (1 Chr. 4:38-43). That the tribe of Simeon had been scattered among all the tribes of Israel (similar to the tribe of Levi) by the Assyria invasions is also possible. Evidence for this in found in Genesis, which states that the God of Israel will scatter the descendants of Levi and Simeon throughout all the tribes (49:5-7) because they took up a sword and murdered Canaanite men (34:25-31).

The support for "ten tribes" in the northern kingdom is located in the Book of Kings, which suggests that the God of Israel would split the kingdom into two separate entities, with Solomon's son Jeroboam being given "ten tribes" to rule over as king (1 Kgs. 11:31, 35). It is possible, however, that the tribe of Manasseh was counted twice, as it was divided in half by the Jordan River. Regardless of how many tribes comprised each kingdom, the fact remains that members of *all twelve tribes* were deported and members of *all twelve tribes* were spared. This is what James of the New Testament understood when he wrote his epistle to "the twelve tribes which are scattered abroad" (James 1:1).

The Israelites from *all twelve tribes* who survived the invasions and deportations of Assyria began to call themselves "Jews" (*yehudim*) after the name of the southern kingdom and its dominant tribe, Judah. (It is even possible that the inhabitants of the southern kingdom called themselves Jews before the Assyrian invasions.) The Book of Esther, which postdates the Assyrian deportations, provides a perfect example. Mordecai, a principal character in the Esther story, is the first person called a "Jew" in the Bible—even though he was from the tribe of Benjamin: "Now in Shushan the palace there was a certain Jew, whose name was Mordecai, the son of Jair, the son of Shimei, the son of Kish, a Benjamite" (Esth. 2:5). An authoritative Jewish text that postdates the Esther story by as much as nine hundred years comments on this passage as follows:

> Rabbi Yochanan said, As a matter of fact, Mordechai *descended from the* tribe of Benjamin. So why is *he called* a *Yehudi,* Jew, a man from *the* tribe of *Judah?* Because he repudiated idolatry "for whoever renounces idolatry is called a Jew, *Yehudi.*"[10]

In other words, according to Rabbi Yochanan, any individual who is a descendant of Israel and who observes Jewish law is a Jew—not just people who were literal descendants of the tribe of Judah.

Not only does the New Testament also affirm that tribal affiliation was retained for over seven hundred years after the Assyrian invasions, it also points out that all descendants of the ancient Israelites were considered "Jews" regardless of tribal descent. For example, Paul called himself a Jew even though he was also from the tribe of Benjamin (Acts 21:39; Rom. 11:1). Likewise, the Gospel of Luke describes the prophet Anna as a Jew who descended from the tribe of Asher (Luke 2:36), which was part of the northern kingdom of Israel during the Assyrian invasions.

In sum, despite what many may assume, contemporary Jews are not exclusively descendants of the ancient Israelite tribe of Judah—and not even primarily from the tribe of Judah. They descend from all thirteen tribes of Israel (including the landless, ubiquitous tribe of Levi), and many Jews may also descend from people outside of the House of Israel who converted to Judaism. The "ten lost tribes" (a term that does not appear in the Bible) was invented by later Christians and Jews to refer to *some* (not all) of the population from *all* twelve tribes that were deported by the Assyrians seven hundred years before the birth of Jesus.

We emphasize this point because too often Latter-day Saints talk about Jews as if they are descendants from one tribe of Israel. In addition, it is not uncommon for Latter-day Saints to claim that they are "Jewish" because their patriarchal blessing pronounces their lineage as being from the tribe of Judah. This misconception comes from a long-held belief that patriarchal blessings

10. Megillah 12b (Talmud), as quoted in Rabbi Yaakov Ibn Chaviv, comp. *Ein Yakov: The Ethical and Inspirational Teachings of the Talmud.* Translated by Avraham Yaakov Finkel (Jason Aronson Inc.: Lanham, MD., 1999), 266; emphasis added.

provide pronouncements of literal blood lineage. Given our knowledge of DNA science and population genetics in recent decades, patriarchal blessings cannot be pronouncements of literal biological heritage. They are spiritual pronouncements of the tribe into which one is adopted. It is nearly impossible for people from the Gentile nations of Europe, for example, to have a dominant DNA of an ancient Semitic people from over 3,000 years ago.[11]

Based on our more advanced knowledge of DNA and genetics, some in the Church have deemphasized claims of literal blood lineage and emphasized the spiritual blessings associated with tribal affiliation.[12] For example, Patriarch Eldred G. Smith, the last Church Patriarch before becoming an emeritus General Authority, explained, "Patriarchs . . . [are] giving blessings, [they're] not declaring lineage by terms of just genealogy. [They're] declaring lineage by terms of blessing. You go to a Patriarch to get a blessing."[13] Thus, a patriarchal blessing pronouncement from the tribe of Judah does not make one Jewish, and a person who is Jewish by ethnicity does not necessarily descend from the ancient tribe of Judah.

It also behooves Latter-day Saints to understand that one can be "Jewish" by conversion to the Jewish religion. The Jewish people are unique in that they have both a birth heritage and a religion. Not all ethnic Jews are adherents of the Jewish religion, and not all Jews by religious persuasion are ethnically Jewish. Some ethnic Jews may be Catholic, Protestant, Latter-day Saint, Buddhist, or even atheist. Moreover, some Jews by religion (not by ethnicity) may be Asian, African, Hispanic, or even Persian or Arab. Broadly speaking, an individual's claim of being "Jewish" usually refers to lineage and not necessarily religious traditions or beliefs.

----

11. This claim is based on personal correspondence with Latter-day Saint scientist and population geneticist Ugo Perego. See his presentation on this topic, "All Abraham's Children: A Genetic Perspective," at the 2016 Science & Mormonism Symposium: Body, Brain, Mind & Spirit, which took place on March 12, 2016 in Orem, Utah, https://interpreterfoundation.org/vid-ugo-a-perego-all-abrahams-children-a-genetic-perspective-2/. See also the Gospel Topics Essay, one of the authors of which was Ugo Perego, "Book of Mormon and DNA Studies," The Church of Jesus Christ of Latter-day Saints, updated April 2017, https://www.churchofjesuschrist.org/study/manual/gospel-topics-essays/book-of-mormon-and-dna-studies.

12. See Armand L. Mauss, *All Abraham's Children: Changing Mormon Conceptions of Race and Lineage* (Urbana, IL: University of Illinois Press, 2003), 34–35.

13. See the speech quoted in Irene M. Bates, "Patriarchal Blessings and the Routinization of Charisma," *Dialogue: A Journal of Mormon Thought* 26, no. 3 (Fall 1993): 5.

We should note here that as we have referred to "Jews" and "Judaism" in this introduction, we are not referring to all Jews everywhere. Like with most religious traditions and ethnicities, Jews are not a monolithic group. They are instead made up of diverse beliefs, traditions, and practices. Thus, we try to state clearly what aspects of Judaism we are discussing in a particular chapter and which Jewish group we are highlighting.

What this Book Is and Isn't

In the introduction to his *Mormon Christianity: What Other Christians Can Learn from the Latter-day Saints*, Stephen Webb, a Catholic scholar, writes that Christianity may be "on the verge of potentially radical transformations." According to Webb, "The rise of a truly global Christian community is breaking down not only geographical barriers but also doctrinal walls that have kept churches divided for centuries."[14] He posited that perhaps the best way to reenvision the future of Christianity in light of these transformations is to examine the Latter-day Saint religion, "one of the youngest branches on the Christian tree."[15]

Like Webb, we too seek additional inspiration from another religious tradition; however, unlike Webb we do not look to one of the "youngest branches" on the Christian tree; rather, we turn to the oldest branch on the western religious tree. Jews and Judaism have continued and stayed relevant through many centuries, periods of persecution, and wars. Like Jews who are the majority in Israel but a religious and ethnic minority in nearly all other countries, Latter-day Saints are the dominant group in Utah but a minority in almost every other state and country. As articulated by Harold Bloom, "The Mormons, like the Jews before them, are a religion that became a people."[16] Latter-day Saints have developed a unique identity and culture within the broader American culture (just visit Provo, Utah, as Exhibit A). It is only a minor surprise, then, to learn that the *Harvard Encyclopedia of American Ethnic Groups* included an entry on Mormons. Jews and Judaism, as both a "people" and religion, are ancient, and the Jewish experience is arguably unprecedented; therefore, we turn to the wisdom of Jews and Judaism to inform, inspire, and en-

---

14. Stephen Webb, *Mormon Christianity: What Other Christians Can Learn from the Latter-day Saints*, 1.

15. Webb, 2.

16. Harold Bloom, *The American Religion: The Emergence of the Post-Christian Nation* (New York: Simon & Schuster, 1992), 83.

hance the lived religious experience of Latter-day Saints. As the prominent twentieth-century Jewish thinker, Abraham Joshua Heschel, wrote, "'To be or not to be' is not the question. Of course, we are all anxious to be. How to be and how not to be is the question."[17] Likewise, the question for Latter-day Saints should not be whether they *are* or *are not* a Latter-day Saint; the question is, *what* do they do, *how* do they do it, and *why* do they do it precisely *because* they are a Latter-day Saint.

We emphasize that we do not seek inspiration and enlightenment for Latter-day Saint leadership on matters of Church administration and governance. Rather, our focus here is at the grassroots level in seeking to enhance the religious experience of individuals, families, and communities.

The nature of this book—one religious group inspiring and influencing another religious group—requires that we also explain what it is not. First, this book is not intended to be a type of "guide to Judaism" for Latter-day Saints. Books, blogs, and podcasts that serve the purpose of educating one group about another religious group's practices, beliefs, and history, particularly to increase religious tolerance, are numerous. Note, however, that a strong component of this book will incidentally serve the purpose of educating some readers about Judaism, but that is not our primary objective.

This book is also not meant to be an interfaith dialogue between Latter-day Saints and Jews—at least not in the traditional sense. Although this volume does have a kind of "back-and-forth" approach to each chapter, Jewish and Latter-day Saint contributors are not necessarily focused on establishing religious and cultural commonalities. Such an approach is usually employed between multiple groups to increase acceptance and understanding among its leadership and adherents. This book *is* one-sided in that Latter-day Saints *are* focused on commonalities with Jews and Judaism—not for increasing acceptance and tolerance, but rather to enhance their own religious experience. Jewish contributors, on the other hand, are not writing primarily in relation to the Latter-day Saint experience, and several may know very little about the Latter-day Saint tradition.

Furthermore, this book is not meant to be an exercise in religious appropriation. In other words, Latter-day Saints associated with this work do not seek to appropriate or adopt Jewish beliefs, religious practices, or cultural customs and repackage them for a Latter-day Saint audience. Some Christians who love Judaism and the Jewish people seem to do so for either theological reasons or because of Jesus's Jewishness; therefore, some

---

17. Abraham Joshua Heschel, *Moral Grandeur and Spiritual Audacity* (New York: Farrar Straus Giroux, 1996), 30.

have observed Christianized versions of various Jewish rituals. For instance, many Christian families have developed and observed a Christian version of the Jewish bar mitzvah ritual, and even renamed it using the Hebrew *Bar Barakah* ("Son of the Blessing"). Similarly, numerous Christian groups annually observe a Passover meal, and they turn the Passover meal into a discussion of symbols of Jesus, and so forth. Many Jews become suspicious of Christians who are zealous to adopt Jewish customs.

We are not interested in producing this volume because of the Hebrew roots of Christianity, nor because Jesus was Jewish. Although Jesus of Nazareth is mentioned in a few chapters, this volume does not contain a single chapter dedicated to the Jewishness of Jesus or the Jewish roots of Christianity. Our intent is to discuss and examine Jews and Judaism on Jews' terms (as best we can) and subsequently wrestle with how Latter-day Saints might benefit from 3,000 years of the Jewish experience. Again, our purpose here is not to suggest that Latter-day Saints must adopt various Jewish practices and beliefs. Rather, we hope that the discussions here may assist readers in adopting strategies, mentalities, and approaches to religious and cultural living as exemplified by Jews and Judaism.

Finally, this book is not meant to propose a definitive way that Latter-day Saints must learn from these Jewish approaches; rather, it is to show how Latter-day Saints might embrace, benefit, and learn from them. These chapters are meant to serve as catalysts for further introspection and learning, not as the end-all-be-all for how Latter-day Saints might learn from Jewish religious experience.

Why This Book?

Some may question the utility of this book and ask why they themselves should look for inspiration from another religious group. After all, the Latter-day Saint ideal is that living prophets guide the Church based on inspiration from God, so why should they look to Jews for additional inspiration? Before responding to this potential criticism, we acknowledge its legitimacy as a fair question. We also point out that it may be human nature to adopt a triumphalist approach to one's own religion. If, the argument goes, I have the "true" religion, then no other ("false") religion can possibly teach me anything of use that I don't already have.

As one anecdotal example, a Muslim—a friend of one of the editors of this volume—from Saudi Arabia conveyed that some members of her family in Saudi Arabia were perplexed that she chose to study religion and family life in America. The United States, they told her, is a godless, sexually promiscuous society, and so it seems counterproductive to learn about religion and family from them. Everything we need to know to have a good and spiritually fulfilling life, they argued, can be found in Islam and not in secular American academies. The response is that not all Americans are "godless and sexually promiscuous" and that "truth" and inspiration can be found in many faiths and cultures. This current volume was cited as an example of how Jews and Judaism may help inspire Latter-day Saints in certain aspects of their religion. After hearing about this project, the Muslim friend slowly shook her head and said, "That book and that approach to religion, or Islam, would never fly in Saudi Arabia. That kind of open-mindedness is remarkable."

Another brief example of this triumphalist attitude among many religious people is found in the comments section of an online article, "What Jews Can Learn from Mormons: Insights from the Church of Jesus Christ of Latter-day Saints."[18] The article discussed many similarities between Latter-day Saint religion and Judaism and what Jews can learn from Latter-day Saints on various topics. Note the first entry in the article's comments thread that appeared just after the article was posted online. Written by an Orthodox Jew, it said,

> I believe that OT stands for Only Testament :-)?
> Addressing the main theme of this article:
> How do you think I feel when it seems that Reform Jews are eager to learn from Mormons, but not from Orthodox Jews?[19]

Our response to these types of criticisms is that religious influence need not be a zero-sum game. In other words, looking to Jews and Judaism for inspiration and guidance for Latter-day Saint living does not diminish the role of prophets nor reduce the importance of their prophetic guidance. Inspiration does not *only* come from heaven in an ironclad fashion, and truth is found in every religion. In a July 1843 sermon, Joseph Smith taught: "One of the grand fundamental principles of Mormonism is to

---

18. Steven Windmueller and Mark S. Diamond, "What Jews Can Learn from Mormons: Insights from The Church of Jesus Christ of Latter-day Saints," Jewish Philanthropy, July 6, 2015, http://ejewishphilanthropy.com/what-jews-can-learn-from-mormons-insights-from-the-church-of-jesus-christ-of-latter-day-saints/.

19. This comment was from a Mr. Cohen on July 6, 2015, at 8:02 p.m.

xx   "The Learning of the Jews"

receive truth. Let it come from whence it may."[20] In another sermon two weeks later, he expanded on this idea by declaring:

> Have the Presbyterians any truth? Yes. Have the Baptists, Methodists, etc., any truth? Yes. . . . We should gather all the good and true principles in the world and treasure them up, or we shall not come out true "'Mormons."[21]

Likewise, the last line of the thirteenth Article of Faith instructs, "If there is anything virtuous, lovely, or of good report or praiseworthy, we seek after these things" (A of F 13). Smith's successor, Brigham Young, similarly maintained that being a Latter-day Saint means that "we believe in all good. If you can find a truth in heaven, earth, or hell, it belongs to our doctrine. We believe it; it is ours; we claim it."[22] Young's colleague in the Latter-day Saint Quorum of the Twelve Apostles and later successor, John Taylor, preached similar sentiments in an 1853 sermon:

> I was going to say I am not a Universalist, but I am, and I am also a Presbyterian, and a Roman Catholic, and a Methodist, in short, I believe in every true principle that is imbibed by any person or sect, and reject the false. If there is any truth in heaven, earth, or hell, I want to embrace it, I care not what shape it comes in to me, who brings it, or who believes in it, whether it is popular or unpopular. Truth, eternal truth, I wish to float in and enjoy.[23]

In the later twentieth century, President Spencer W. Kimball and his counselors reiterated this teaching by declaring:

> The great religious leaders of the world such as Mohammed, Confucius, and the Reformers, as well as philosophers including Socrates, Plato, and others, received a portion of God's light. Moral truths were given to them by God to enlighten whole nations and to bring a higher level of understanding to individuals.[24]

That Latter-day Saints have taken this to heart is evidenced by the popularity of several course sections every semester in both World Religions and Judaism & Islam offered by the Religious Education Department at

---

20. Joseph Smith et al., *History of the Church of Jesus Christ of Latter-day Saints*, ed. B. H. Roberts, 7 vols., 2nd ed. rev. (Salt Lake City: Deseret Book, 1948 printing), 5:499.

21. Smith et al., *History of the Church*, 5:517.

22. Brigham Young, April 24, 1870, *Journal of Discourses*, 26 vols. (London and Liverpool: LDS Booksellers Depot, 1854 86), 13:335.

23. John Taylor, June 12, 1853, *Journal of Discourses*, 1:155.

24. Spencer W Kimball, N. Eldon Tanner, and Marion G. Romney, "Statement of the First Presidency Regarding Love for All Mankind," February 15, 1978.

Brigham Young University. One would expect these types of courses to be offered by academic religious studies departments, but the Religious Education Department at Brigham Young University is not a traditional academic department—it advocates for a more devotional and applicative religious educational experience for students.

More pertinent to this volume, in recent years Latter-day Saint leaders have specifically pointed to Judaism as an example of where religious insight may be gained. In a sermon on the challenges facing the Latter-day Saints, Elder M. Russell Ballard mentioned Jews as an illustration of his point and concluded, "I think we could be more like this faithful Jewish family."[25] Three weeks later, in the biannual worldwide general conference for Latter-day Saints, Elder Quentin L. Cook shared his experience with Jews on the Sabbath as an illustration of meaningful Sabbath ritual.[26] Perhaps the most well-known sermon on Judaism from a Latter-day Saint prophet was Ezra Taft Benson's "A Message to Judah from Joseph," wherein he said (to an audience of both Jews and Latter-day Saints),

> We need to know more about the Jews, and the Jews ought to know more about the Mormons. When we understand one another, then perhaps you will understand *why* Ben-Gurion said, "There are no people in the world who understand the Jews like the Mormons."[27]

In this address, Benson not only articulated the importance of a relationship between Jews and Latter-day Saints, he emphasized that this relationship requires a more than superficial knowledge of Latter-day Saints about Jews and Judaism, and vice versa. This volume transcends the usual call to understand each other and seeks to gather truths from Jews and Judaism that inspire and motivate action on the part of Latter-day Saints in relation to their religious observance. Jews and the Jewish experience are the schoolmasters here.

---

25. M. Russell Ballard, "To the Saints in the Utah South Area," The Church of Jesus Christ of Latter-day Saints, September 13, 2015, https://www.lds.org/prophets-and-apostles/unto-all-the-world/to-the-saints-in-the-utah-south-area.

26. Quentin L. Cook, "Shipshape and Bristol Fashion: Be Temple Worthy—in Good Times and Bad Times," The Church of Jesus Christ of Latter-day Saints, October 4, 2015, https://www.lds.org/general-conference/2015/10/shipshape-and-bristol-fashion-be-temple-worthy-in-good-times-and-bad-times.

27. Ezra Taft Benson, "A Message to Judah from Joseph," *Ensign*, December 1976, https://www.lds.org/ensign/1976/12/a-message-to-judah-from-joseph.

Content and Structure

This volume brings together fifteen scholars, seven Jewish and eight Latter-day Saint, with a combined academic experience of over four hundred years. We have structured the volume around seven major topics with two chapters on each topic. A Jewish scholar first discusses the topic broadly vis-à-vis Judaism, followed by a response from a Latter-day Saint scholar. It must be noted that these Latter-day Saint scholars are trained in various fields of study and disciplines including history, sociology, family studies, religious studies, biblical studies, and literature. This wide array of experience and training illustrates the various approaches and perspectives of learning from another group. With the primary purpose of this volume being for Latter-day Saints to learn from Jewish religious perspectives and experiences, the essays are generally different from what you might normally expect in an interreligious dialogue. For the most part, the Jewish essays were not written with Latter-day Saints in mind but are simply broad overviews that could be helpful for any non-Jewish readership. Likewise, the Latter-day Saint responses are not trying to find commonalities as the primary goal; rather, their purpose is to explore any strategies, mentalities, motives, and so forth of Jews that might serve as a catalyst for Latter-day Saints to look introspectively and enhance their own lived religious experience. The seven topics include scripture, authority, prayer, women and modernity, remembrance, particularity, and humor. We hope that the reader will not only learn a great deal about Judaism and the Jewish experience while reading this volume but also use what they learn to enhance their own cultural and religious experience.

Acknowledgments

As editors, we are most grateful for all the contributors—for their enthusiasm regarding the project and for their time in writing and revising their essays. We also acknowledge the efforts of Greg Kofford Books, especially Loyd Isao Ericson, for their help along the way. We also thanks our various colleagues who have encouraged us.

Approaching Scripture:
Insights from Judaism

Gary A. Rendsburg

This essay divides into two parts. The first part treats the manner in which the regular Jewish attender of Shabbat services in the synagogue approaches scripture, while the second part addresses the question of how professional Jewish scholars of the Bible read the text and pursue their research.

The Regular Jewish Attender of Shabbat Services in the Synagogue[1]

The centerpiece of the Shabbat morning service in synagogues around the world is the weekly reading of the Torah. Let me begin, accordingly, with a survey of the history of this practice. Moreover, throughout this essay I will focus almost exclusively on the Torah, or Pentateuch, since it is so central to the Jewish experience, with nary a word about the other two main sections of the Jewish canon, Prophets and Writings.[2]

As is well known, in the biblical period the worship of God centered around the Temple cult. The book of Leviticus ordains the sacrifices that are to occur on a daily basis and on unique occasions (see especially chapters 1–7). The book of Numbers provides details for the additional sacrifices that are to be offered on the Sabbath, New Moon, and festivals (see especially chapters 28–29).

---

1. That is, "the Jew in the pew," as he or she is affectionately known in contemporary parlance.

2. After deciding on this approach, I read a very similar estimation by my colleague Benjamin Sommer of the Jewish Theological Seminary. See Benjamin D. Sommer, "Introduction," in *Jewish Concepts of Scripture: A Comparative Introduction*, ed. Benjamin D. Sommer (New York: New York University Press, 2012), 2–3. There is much of value in this edited volume, even if I will cite only one more item below (see fn. 22). The Torah, or Pentateuch, consists of Genesis, Exodus, Leviticus, Numbers, and Deuteronomy.

The original locus of the sacrificial cult was the Tabernacle, a large portable tent structure described in great detail in Exodus 25–31 and 35–40. While many scholars have doubted the historicity of this cultic center, there is no reason for such skepticism, especially in light of ancient Near Eastern parallels ranging from Mari to Egypt.[3] We cannot say with certainty when the Tabernacle first arose in ancient Israel, but I would argue for its central role in earliest Israel—say, the twelfth century BCE.[4] The Tabernacle would serve the people for about two centuries until it was replaced by the permanent structure built by Solomon in Jerusalem around 960 BCE—that is, the Temple (1 Kgs. 6–7). From that point on, for more than one thousand years (save for the seventy-year period between 586 BCE, when the First Temple was destroyed by the Babylonians, and 516 BCE, when the Second Temple was rededicated under Persian Rule), the Temple cult remained the center of Jewish religious life until the Second Temple was destroyed by the Romans in 70 CE. During that time, the flow of rams, goats, and bulls (or under some circumstances, doves and pigeons), along with the accompanying grains, olive oil, and wine offered to the God of Israel, was unceasing for more than one millennium.

Remarkably, however, in time a parallel stream of Jewish religious life developed, especially during the Second Temple period, wherein the Torah was elevated to a new status in early Judaism.[5] We may call this process the textualization of Judaism, with the concomitant canonization of the

---

3. See the second section of this essay.

4. Gary A. Rendsburg, "The Date of the Exodus and the Conquest/Settlement: The Case for the 1100s," *Vetus Testamentum* 42, no. 4 (1992): 510–27.

5. I leave open the question of whether the Torah as we have it, from Genesis through Deuteronomy, existed as a unified composition or a unified literary work before 586 BCE, or whether the various sources were melded during the Exile or early in the Persian period. That point aside, the linguistic profile of the text, including all its sources, is clearly Standard Biblical Hebrew of the monarchic period (1000–586 BCE). On this point, see the relevant essays in *Hebrew Studies*, vols. 46–47 (2005–2006). My own contribution in the latter volume is Gary A. Rendsburg, "Aramaic-like Features in the Pentateuch," *Hebrew Studies* 47 (2006): 163–76.

When I refer to sources in the first two sentences above, I do not intend the usual source-critical analysis which divides the Torah into J-E-D-P, but rather to "sources" more generally, which we may or may not be able to identify. For my basic statement, both on dating and on the sources, see Gary A. Rendsburg, *How the Bible Is Written* (Peabody, MA: Hendrickson, 2019), 443–90.

Torah.[6] The seeds of this development are to be seen in Nehemiah 8:1–8, where the religious leader Ezra conducts a ceremony at the piazza near one of the city gates of Jerusalem (c. 450 BCE), with a focus on the public reading of the Torah. Strikingly, numerous elements of the ceremony accord with the later synagogue service, and yet they are present already in the description of Nehemiah 8:[7] (a) the congregation consists of men, women, and children; (b) the Torah is read from a bespoke platform; (c) Ezra holds the scroll aloft for all to see; (d) Ezra blesses God; (e) the people respond "Amen, Amen"; and (f) the text is explained to the people.[8]

At least several centuries would pass before we would gain further evidence of the reading of the Torah from sources of the Greco-Roman period. Moreover, anyone who has attended a synagogue service in the twenty-first century CE will recognize the fact that all of these features are still present. Such is the historical depth of Jewish tradition, with what I have described here as but one illustrative feature within *la longue durée* of Jewish law, culture, liturgy, and religion that could be identified.

While the text of Nehemiah 8 does not refer to canonization per se, scholars associate that process, for the Torah at least, with the central figure of Ezra, as the Torah was on its way to becoming "the book of the

---

6. For a very readable survey, see William M. Schniedewind, *How the Bible Became a Book: The Textualization of Ancient Israel* (Cambridge: Cambridge University Press, 2004).

7. As pointed out by Moshe Weinfeld, "Israelite Religion," in *The Encyclopaedia of Religion*, ed. Mircea Eliade (New York: Macmillan: 1993), 7:494.

8. The Hebrew word *məvinim* in v. 7 means "cause to understand," hence "explain." The text of v. 8 provides further details, using the words *məforaš*, "clearly," *śom sekel*, "gave sense," and *yavinu*, either "explained" again (transitive) or "understood" (intransitive). Some scholars infer, based especially on the first word *məforaš*, that the Hebrew reading was accompanied by an Aramaic translation, based on the ever-increasing use of the latter language amongst the Jews of the Persian period. To my mind, however, the community of Jews in Jerusalem during the fifth century BCE would have been perfectly at home in the Hebrew language so as not to require a rendering into a foreign language. Explanation would have been required to elucidate some of the more archaic language, some of the technical language, and so on—no different than in the United States today, in which an average American may require help in understanding the precise meaning of the Declaration of Independence, the Constitution, or the Federalist Papers.

"Ezra holding a scroll of Torah," as depicted on the Dura Europos synagogue wall frescoes, to the upper right of the Torah shrine. Yale University Art Gallery, Dura Europos Collection.

people."[9] Later, Jews would recognize this point well, as demonstrated by the crucial placement of a panel portraying Ezra holding the scroll of the Torah in the magnificent artwork adorning the walls of the Dura Europus synagogue (Syria, third century CE).[10]

---

9. To use the felicitous term coined by William W. Hallo, *The Book of the People* (Atlanta: Scholars Press, 1991). The term has been re-used more recently by A. N. Wilson, *The Book of the People: How to Read the Bible* (London: Atlantic Books, 2015).

10. For the color image, see the front cover of Steven Fine, *Art and Judaism in the Greco-Roman World: Toward a New Jewish Archaeology* (New York: Cambridge University Press, 2005). The black-and-white version appears on page 180. Carl Kraeling, the original excavator of Dura Europos, debated whether the image of the man holding the scroll depicts Ezra (on the basis of Nehemiah 8) or Moses (based on Exodus 20, or at least its later interpretations). He elected the former,

Our earliest evidence for the synagogue comes from Hellenistic Egypt (c. 240 BCE), though at this point the institution was known by the Greek word *proseuche*, "prayer house." As the name indicates, the main function of the building was a place for prayer, as the Jews of Hellenistic Egypt (who comprised a large and thriving community away from Jerusalem) developed an alternative liturgical system, to wit, communal prayer. The synagogue inscriptions from this period do not refer to the reading of Torah per se,[11] but one may assume that such was practiced in the *proseuche*. Around 20 CE, Philo of Alexandria described this practice explicitly:

> Now these laws they are taught at other times, indeed, but most especially on the seventh day, for the seventh day is accounted sacred, on which they abstain from all other employments, and frequent the sacred places which are called synagogues,[12] and there they sit according to their age in classes, the younger sitting under the elder, and listening with eager attention in becoming order. (82) Then one, indeed, takes up the holy volume and reads it,[13] and another of the men of the greatest experience comes forward and explains what is not very intelligible, for a great many precepts are delivered in enigmatical modes of expression, and allegorically, as the old fashion was.[14]

Additional evidence for the reading of the Torah in the first century CE synagogue comes from the Theodotus inscription (Jerusalem) and the book of Acts (Diaspora). The former reads as follows:

> Theodotus, (son) of Vettenus, priest and *archisynagogos*, son of an *archisynagogos*, grandson of an *archisynagogos*, built the synagogue for the reading of the

---

and I agree—though Fine (p. 181) believes that the man should be identified with Moses.

11. For images of the dedicatory inscriptions and English translations, see a segment of the website created and organized by Donald D. Binder, "Egypt," Second Temple Synagogues, accessed April 13, 2020, http://www.pohick.org/sts/egypt.html. Note, however, that Binder uses "synagogue" in his translations of these inscriptions, though in all cases the Greek word is *proseuche*. While we are grateful to have these dedicatory inscriptions, not a single one was discovered in its original archaeological context, but rather all were found in secondary use (e.g., incorporated into the wall of a later structure). Which is to say, we have the dedicatory inscriptions, but we do not know what these *proseuche* buildings in Egypt looked like.

12. Note that Philo uses the word *synagogue*.

13. Almost undoubtedly the reading took place in Greek (by use of the Septuagint, which was produced c. 250 BCE in Alexandria), as opposed to in the Hebrew original.

14. Philo of Alexandria, *Every Good Man is Free*, book 12, para. 81–82.

law and the teaching of the commandments, and the guest-chamber and the rooms and the water installations for lodging for those needing them from abroad, which his fathers, the elders and Simonides founded. [15]

Several points are notable. First, the institution of the synagogue, which began in the Diaspora, reached the Land of Israel (including Jerusalem) by the first century CE, if not the preceding century. While the inscription dates to the first century CE, the text refers to Theodotus's grandfather already serving in the role of *archisynagogos*, that is, "head of the synagogue," which likely means he was active several decades earlier. Second, the reading of the Torah is mentioned explicitly as one of the activities that took place in the building. And third, prayer is conspicuously absent from the list of such activities. If people in Jerusalem wished to worship God, they visited the Temple. However, the reading of the Torah and other activities were already present in a different locus, to wit, the synagogue.

The book of Acts also refers to the reading of the Torah in the synagogue, providing additional evidence for this practice in first-century Judaism. Acts 13:15 refers to this custom in Antioch in Pisidia (Anatolia), while Acts 15:21 implies that the practice was well-nigh universal: "For the law of Moses has been preached in every city from the earliest times and is read in the synagogues on every Sabbath."

The origins of the reading of a section of the Prophets are obscure,[16] but again we may note the apparently widespread nature of this practice already by the first century CE. The key texts are again from the New Testament. The aforecited verse, Acts 13:15, actually refers to "the reading from the Law and the Prophets" (see also v. 27), and perhaps more famously, Luke 4:17–20 describes Jesus himself reading from a scroll of Isaiah (with specific citation of Isaiah 61:1–2 and Isaiah 58:6) in the synagogue at Nazareth.

---

15. See Donald D. Binder, "Jerusalem," Second Temple Synagogues, accessed April 13, 2020, http://www.pohick.org/sts/jerusalem.html.

16. Two proposals have been made by scholars. The first one holds that in order to distinguish themselves from the Samaritans (who canonized the Torah only), the Jews introduced the reading of a section of the Prophets to accompany the selection from the Torah, thereby demonstrating the centrality of Jerusalem, which dominates books such as Samuel, Kings, Isaiah, Jeremiah, and Ezekiel. The second suggestion proposes that during the persecutions of Antiochus IV, which included the prohibition of reading the Torah, the Jews introduced a portion of the Prophets which would evoke the theme of a particular section of the Torah, thereby retaining the centrality of scripture in liturgical practice without violating the prohibition explicitly. The truth is we simply do not know.

Reverse image of the virtually unrolled Leviticus scroll from Ein Gedi, Israel, c. 300 CE. Published in Segal, "An Early Leviticus Scroll from En-Gedi: Preliminary Publication," 33. Image courtesy of Seth Parker, Digital Restoration Initiative, University of Kentucky. (CC BY NC 4.0 attribution. See https://creativecommons.org/licenses/by/4.0/.)

Eventually we gain more information on the reading of scripture in Jewish tradition from the Mishna (c. 200 CE), with the major portion of an entire tractate, *Megilla* ("scroll"), devoted to the practice.[17] Among the points we learn are the following: the scrolls were kept in an ark (*Mishna Megilla* 3:1); the Torah was read according to a set order (*Mishna Megilla* 3:4, 3:6); and both the Torah and the Prophets were read (*Mishna Megilla* 4:1–5).

Fortunately, we have an archaeological discovery that speaks to the notion of Torah scrolls kept in an ark. A burnt scroll was found in the Ein Gedi synagogue during the excavations in 1970, in the niche that no doubt housed the ark, presumably made of wood. Due to its fragile nature, the scroll could not be opened—and indeed it still has not been opened. However, advances in technology, specifically micro-CT scanning, has made it possible for the text to be "virtually unwrapped" and shown to contain the beginning of the book of Leviticus.[18]

---

17. The tractate begins with the laws and traditions concerning the reading of the Scroll of Esther, but then segues into the laws and traditions concerning the reading of the Torah.

18. For the exemplary teamwork of archaeologists, biblical scholars, and technology experts, see Michael Segal et al., "An Early Leviticus Scroll from En-Gedi: Preliminary Publication," *Textus* 26 (2016): 29–58.

We gain no details in Mishna tractate *Megilla* about the set order (Heb. *seder*), but we know from later Jewish sources, starting with the Babylonian Talmud (*B. Megilla* 29a), that some communities (such as those in Babylonia) completed the lectionary cycle of reading Torah in one year, with the Torah divided into 54 *parashot* ("portions");[19] others in the Land of Israel took three to three and a half years to do so, with the Torah divided into somewhere between 141 and 175 *sedarim*, or "segments." These two systems coexisted into the Middle Ages, until eventually the former system ousted the latter, so that the annual cycle became the norm for all of world Jewry, as is the case until the present day.[20]

The foregoing may provide more historical detail than is necessary,[21] but to my mind it is important to understand this background as we now move to a discussion of how Jews today approach scripture.

Before proceeding, I provide here a word about the very word "scripture," derived from Latin *scriptura*, "writing," in turn derived from the verb *scribere*, "to write."[22] This term comes from Christian usage,[23] in which the Bible is (at least for the last 450 years) the printed book, an artifact in writing, and something that is often read silently, especially in devotion.[24] This is not to deny the fact that biblical texts serve as the basis for lectionary cycles within Christian liturgy, but the term "scripture" remains very telling.

This stands in contrast to the Jewish experience, in which the sacred text is not "scripture" per se, but rather the "Reading." In Judaism, while the text is indeed written and has been transmitted for millennia through careful scribal activity, the Hebrew term for "Bible" is *miqra'* ("the reading"

---

19. The similar-sounding words *parashot* and "portions" make for a convenient equivalency. I have attempted to create the same with *sedarim* and "segments" below.

20. This includes Karaite Jews as well, though see also below fn. 31.

21. After I completed this article, I came across Lawrence H. Schiffman, "The Early History of Public Reading of the Torah," in *Jews, Christians, and Polytheists in the Ancient Synagogue: Cultural Interaction during the Greco-Roman Period*, ed. Steven Fine (London: Routledge, 2002), 44–56, which covers much of the same territory.

22. Once more, after writing the words which follow, I discovered the same ideas in Sommer, "Introduction," 6–8.

23. The word has a long pedigree: It is first attested in the Northumbrian poem *Cursor Mundi*, c. 1300, already with the spelling *scripture*. See *OED*, s.v. "scripture."

24. Several paintings of Gerard Dou (1613–1675) come to mind, including "Portret van een lezende oude vrouw" ("Portrait of an Old Woman Reading") and "Het lezen van de Bijbel" ("Reading the Bible"), with an individual or a couple engaged in private reading of scripture.

or "that which is read"), derived from the verb *q-r-'* ("read, call aloud").[25] Note that the same verb means both "call" and "read," so that in the Jewish tradition "reading" is an oral-aural act.[26] The text of the Torah is chanted aloud each Shabbat day in the synagogue by a trained reader, and it is heard by the congregation.[27] Most people today sit with the printed text in their laps, following along, but this is a recent development, made possible in the last two centuries by easier modes of printing.[28] In antiquity and throughout the Middle Ages, before the age of printing, one person read from the Torah scroll, and everyone else simply listened, there being no other choice.[29]

I mention all this because this system of reading the Torah—aloud and in a set order, week after week—remains the centerpiece of the synagogue service. While Judaism does not have a communion or a Eucharist or any similar ceremony to serve as a sacrament or even an ordinance,[30] in

---

25. The Arabic word *qur'an*, "Qur'an, Koran, Reading," derives from the same Semitic root. In general, what I state here about Judaism regarding the recitation of the sacred text is equally true about Islam.

26. This was true of all ancient societies. As one demonstration thereof, see Isaiah 29:18, where the deaf, and not the blind, are the ones unable to "read"— that is, "hear the words of the book." Recall also the oft-cited comment by Augustine (354–430 CE) regarding his senior colleague Ambrose, bishop of Milan (340–397 CE): "When he read, his eyes scanned the page and his heart sought out the meaning, but his voice was silent and his tongue was still. Anyone could approach him freely and guests were not commonly announced, so that often, when we came to visit him, we found him reading like this in silence, for he never read aloud."—Augustine, *Confessions*, Book 6, ch. 3, quoted in Alberto Manguel, *A History of Reading* (New York: Viking, 1996), 42. From Augustine's observation, it is patently clear that Ambrose's ability to read silently was something at which to marvel, even as late as the fourth century CE—for the norm, as indicated, was to read a text aloud.

27. It is somewhat ironic, accordingly, that Martin Buber and Franz Rosenzweig, who greatly emphasized the orality of the biblical text, called their great translation project *Die Schrift* (1926–1938).

28. Perhaps for this reason, then, I continue to use the word "scripture" in this essay, indeed even in the title, for the term has a certain meaningful resonance in today's society, including within English-speaking Jewry.

29. This point may bring us back to the term "lectionary," which derives from Latin *legere*, "to read," which in fact is cognate to Greek *legein*, "to speak," once again reminding us of the oral-aural nature of ancient reading.

30. The ceremony known as *qiddush* (frequently spelled *kiddush* in popular circles), lit. "sanctification," involves wine and bread, and their appropriate

10 *"The Learning of the Jews"*

its stead, the centerpiece of the synagogue service is the Torah service, including the processional of the scroll through the congregation, its placement on the reading table, and then most importantly the chanting of the particular *parasha*.

Thus, when a Jew approaches scripture, he or she almost always looks to the Torah, in fact, on a weekly basis, as the cycle proceeds through the calendar year.[31] For example, as I write these words on Saturday evening, June 10, 2017, the reading in the synagogue earlier this morning was Numbers 8–12, known as *Be-ha'alotekha* ("when you mount"—that is, the lamps on the menorah), which is the first distinctive word in Numbers 8:2.[32]

The question before us, then, is how the average congregant engaged with these five chapters of the book of Numbers. This is an especially pertinent question because, unlike the other books of the Bible, Numbers lacks a unified theme or narrative as it zigzags back and forth between law and cult (some of it quite arcane) and narrative (though not as famous as the stories in Genesis or Exodus).[33] Note the wide-ranging subjects of

---

blessings, but this is a home ritual for Shabbat and festival meals, in the evening at the commencement of the day and at lunch after the morning synagogue service. Moreover, there is a crucial difference: In the Christian eucharist or communion, the wine and the bread are blessed; whereas in the Jewish *qiddush* God is blessed, as the blessings pronounced begin with the words *barukh 'atta 'Adonay 'elohenu*, "Blessed are you, O Lᴏʀᴅ our God."

31. Said cycle commences in the autumn, on the holiday of Simḥat Torah, "Rejoicing over the Torah," a celebration which developed only in the Middle Ages, once the annual reading cycle gained greater ascendancy. The holiday is marked by reading the concluding section of Deuteronomy (33–34) from one scroll and then immediately commencing with the opening section of Genesis (1:1–2:4) from another scroll.

In earlier days, the Karaite annual reading system commenced in the spring, but since the reforms introduced by Eliyahu Bashyachi (c. 1420–1490), the Karaite annual lectionary has aligned with the rabbinic one. Hence, all Jews begin the cycle with Genesis, chapter 1, on the first Shabbat after Sukkot (or, to be more precise, Shemini 'Atzeret)—although the Karaites do not observe the holiday of Simḥat Torah since it is not a biblical festival.

32. Indeed, all the *parashot* bear incipits as their names, using the first distinctive word. In the present instance, for example, note that "The Lord spoke to Moses saying" (v. 1) and "Speak to Aaron and say to him" (start of v. 2) are generic statements without a specific distinguishing word.

33. For the reasons for this arrangement, see Rendsburg, *How the Bible Is Written*, 547–48.

Numbers 8–12: the lighting of the menorah (8:1–4), the ritual purification of the Levites (8:5–26), the additional laws of Passover on the occasion of the one-year anniversary of leaving Egypt (9:1–14), the silver
trumpets (10:1–10), the departure from Mount Sinai (10:11–36), the
murmuring in the wilderness (11:1–35), and the complaint of Miriam
and Aaron against Moses's wife (12:1–16)—quite an assorted set of topics.

I would submit that when a synagogue-attending and Torah-listening
Jew encounters the text, he or she may ask three questions, each of a
different sort: What was the original setting of the material within its
historical context of circa three thousand years ago? How has the text been
interpreted and understood by Jews during the millennia? What meaning
does it have for me today?[34]

To guide the congregant with these questions, one typically looks to
the Ḥumash[35] volume one is holding in one's lap, whereby one follows
along with the reading. One of the most popular of all such volumes
is *Etz Hayim*, published by the Rabbinical Assembly and the United
Synagogue organization (two arms of the Conservative movement), which
includes the Hebrew text, an English translation, and commentary.[36] The
major part of this volume in turn is based to a great extent on the *Jewish
Publication Society (JPS) Torah Commentary* series, about which I will say
more in the second part of this essay. (I say "the major part" because the
historically-based material is indeed digested from the much larger JPS
commentary series. There is also a *derash* section in the *Etz Hayim* volume,
which engages in homiletics and ethical teachings, much of which is not
inherent in the biblical text but has been read into the text by Jewish sages
throughout the ages.[37])

---

34. For these three questions, albeit in a more succinct form, see W. Gunther
Plaut, *The Torah: A Modern Commentary*, rev. ed., ed. David E. S. Stein (New
York: Reform Judaism Publications, 2015), xlii.

35. A term which originally meant "one-fifth," with reference to a single book
of the Torah, but whose connotation morphed over time to mean "the five," with
reference to the five books of the Torah.

36. David Lieber et al., *Etz Hayim: Torah and Commentary* (New York: The
Rabbinical Assembly, 2001).

37. This section stems from the pen of Harold Kushner, well-known author
and congregational rabbi.

Using the *parasha* of *Be-haʻalotekha* as our sample and the *Etz Hayim*
volume as our guide,[38] let us explore how the average person present in
the congregation this morning approached the scriptural reading.[39] I do
so by providing one example relevant to each of the themes listed above.

The Lighting of the Menorah. The reader is reminded by *Etz Hayim* that
this familiar symbol of Judaism "is featured in a carving on the Arch of
Titus in Rome, which celebrates the defeat of the Jews in 70 CE; nineteen
centuries later, the seven-branched *m'norah* [*sic*] became the seal of the
State of Israel" (p. 816). Note how the biblical text, a well-known meme
from post-biblical Jewish history, and the evocation of modern Israel—
which together span three millennia—all speak to the Jewish congregant.

The ritual purification of the Levites. Without the Temple, one will admit
that the activity of the Levites relevant to the ancient sacrificial cult has
little resonance for the contemporary Jew. The details here, however, serve
to remind the reader to what extent Judaism was led by a priestly class
throughout the ancient period until the destruction of the Second Temple
in 70 CE.

Additional laws of Passover. This section reminds the reader about the
centrality of Passover to the Jewish tradition—both ancient and modern.
While the eating of the Passover sacrifice together with unleavened bread
(*matzot*) and bitter herbs receives much more attention in Exodus 12:1–10
(especially verse 8) than it does here in the book of Numbers, the same
ritual is nevertheless mentioned in Numbers 9:11. As is well-known, the
observance of Passover remains one of the most widely celebrated of all
Jewish customs, so that once more a bridge is made between the ancient
and the modern. True, the Passover sacrifice is no longer part of Jewish
ritual (presumably it died out with the destruction of the Temple in 70

---

38. In what follows the page numbers refer to the *Etz Hayim* volume mentioned
in fn. 36.

39. For a similar and enlightening treatment, see James S. Diamond,
Stringing the Pearls: How to Read the Weekly Torah Portion (Philadelphia: Jewish
Publication Society, 2008). In the current internet age, another valuable resource
is TheTorah.com, created, organized, and edited by Marc Z. Brettler, Zev Farber,
and David D. Steinberg. This website, which seeks to bring the world of biblical
scholarship to interested laypersons, follows the Jewish liturgical reading cycle,
adding new columns written by (mostly, though not exclusively, Jewish) biblical
scholars each week, *parasha* by *parasha*.

CE),[40] but the eating of bitter herbs and unleavened bread (*matzot*) remains a central part of the home ritual for Passover known as the Seder meal.

The silver trumpets. Every once in a while, one must admit, there is something in the text that lacks a modern resonance. The narrative of the silver trumpets is one of these. At this point the Jewish reader goes to the historical, with the reminder that silver trumpets were part of the ancient Israelite musical instrumental repertoire. It should be noted that these trumpets are not the more familiar *shofar* ("horn"—typically a ram's horn, though from other animals too) but rather a much less-known element of Israelite society.[41]

Departure from Mount Sinai. Numbers 10:13–36 is a rather mundane text, offering details on how the Israelites organized themselves as they marched through the desert. According to verse 25, the rear guard was led by the tribe of Dan, a point which led one traditional source to suggest that this tribe "was chosen for this role because, even though its members were weak in religious faith, . . . they were strong in their love for their fellow Israelites" (p. 825).[42] This comment is set in the past, but *Etz Hayim* provides for a relevant teaching for today: "There is a need in today's community for people who express their religious faith by caring for the left-behind."[43]

For this particular section of the *parasha*, I include a second comment. Numbers 10:35–36 are two verses that became a core part of Jewish liturgy. The first of these reads, "And when the Ark set out, Moses said, 'Arise, O Lord, And may your foes be scattered, And may your enemies flee before you'"; the second verse reads, "And when it rested, he would say, 'Return O Lord, (the one of) the myriads of the thousands of Israel.'" The actual Ark of the Covenant is a relic of Israel's distant past, barely mentioned in the Bible after its repositioning from the Tabernacle to the Temple (1 Kgs. 8:6), but

---

40. The Samaritans, however, continue to offer the Passover sacrifice. See Reinhard Pummer, *The Samaritans: A Profile* (Grand Rapids, MI: Eerdmans, 2016), 260–63 (including photographs).

41. Note that sixteen of the twenty-nine occurrences of the word *ḥaṣoṣra*, "trumpet," occur in Chronicles, one of the least read and least studied books of the Bible.

42. Unfortunately, the *Etz Hayim* volume does not disclose the source, and I have not been able to track it down.

43. While most of my remarks here address the first of the three questions listed above, this example speaks to the third of the questions: "What meaning does the text have for me today?"

the ark that houses the Torah scrolls in the synagogue evokes that earlier Ark that was kept in the Tabernacle. In fact, the same Hebrew word, *'aron*, is used for both furnishings.[44] In the synagogue liturgy, when the ark is opened to remove the Torah scroll in preparation for its public reading, Numbers 10:35 is recited; when the Torah is returned to the ark after the lectionary reading, Numbers 10:36 is recited. I mention all this because any regular attender of the synagogue service will readily identify the verses being read aloud when the reader reaches Numbers 10:35–36. One hears these words chanted from the Torah scroll only once a year (in the annual reading cycle), but one hears them every Shabbat morning in the congregational singing that brackets the Torah reading.

Murmuring in the wilderness. This section and the next one remind us that the Torah does not present a perfect Israel, nor does it present perfect individuals. Hagiography is for the medieval period, when the biblical luminaries would be elevated to saintly status. The Bible provides a different picture altogether, for it is a thoroughly human document. As such, we watch the travails and successes of God's people. As with all human existence, there are plenty of both. The murmuring motif that appears repeatedly in the books of Exodus and Numbers (and is then reflected upon in Deuteronomy) is a reminder of the human condition. God may have brought the people out of Egypt, and He may have revealed Himself to the people at Mount Sinai—but as they wander aimlessly in the desert with little to eat, it does not take long for those testimonies to God's hand in human history to recede to the back of one's memory bank.

Complaint of Miriam and Aaron against Moses's wife. We end not with answers, but with questions. The Torah is a terse text throughout, leaving much unsaid, and often raising more questions than providing answers. This section is introduced with the verse, "Miriam and Aaron spoke against Moses, on account of the Cushite woman whom he had married." Who? What? When? Where? Who is the Cushite woman? Is she the same woman as Zipporah (Ex. 2:21), who is earlier described as a Midianite (see Ex. 2:15; 3:1)? Or is she a different person? If the former, with a nod to Habakkuk 3:7, where Cushan and Midian appear in parallel poetic stichs

---

44. To be more accurate, I should note that the term *'aron*, "ark," for the synagogue structure that houses the Torah scrolls is used mainly by Ashkenazim. Most Sephardim use either *tevah*, "coffer," or *hekhal*, "sacred place." The former term seems to be the most original, since it is used in *Mishna Ta'anit* 2:1.

(as noted on p. 833), then our other questions are answered—except for one important one: what was the substance of the complaint? If the Cushite woman is not Zipporah, but rather a second wife, with possible reference to Cush (Nubia or Ethiopia), then when and where did Moses marry her (for the text never mentions a second wife)? The reader may have all of these questions in mind as he or she reads this passage, but, as indicated above, the Torah does not allow definitive answers—and truth be told, in this instance *Etz Hayim* offers little guidance.

This survey of some key features in the weekly Torah reading known as *Be-haʾalotkha* (Num. 8–12) hopefully offers an opportunity to experience how a Jewish reader of the Torah engages with the text while sitting in the pew in the synagogue service. My examples have been selected more or less at random. They represent places where I think the average reader might pause to consider a point, read the comment in *Etz Hayim*, and have the material inform his or her present. To be sure, not all of these illustrations have the same force or the same ability or the same potential (for example, the silver trumpets do little in this regard), but taken as a whole, the main point is this: the weekly Torah reading continues to inform the life of the contemporary Jew, as the text both transports one back in time over the course of millennia and yet at the same resonates with one's ongoing religious life, ritual observance, and commitment. If I have focused this material on the human, with less attention to God, that is because, as I intimated above, the Torah (and the Bible generally) focuses its attention on the human. It is often said that Jews do not discuss God in the same manner as Christians might.[45] If there is any truth to this, then I would propose that this is so because the Jewish Bible does not do so.

This may be a shocking comment for one who hears these words for the first time, but I believe that it holds true. We get a lot of "And God said to Moses" (or some other figure) clauses in the Bible, and occasionally God performs a miracle—but even in our *parasha*, for example, the manna (Num. 11:6–9; see earlier Ex. 16:14–36) and the quail (Num. 11:31–34; see earlier Ex. 16:13) are rather ordinary events, especially as explained by modern scientists.[46]

---

45. With the possible exception of Jews influenced by Kabbalah—that is, the mystical tradition.

46. The *Etz Hayim* volume provides relevant information in its comments to Exodus 16 on p. 416 (for the quail) and on p. 418 (for the manna).

If I may expand on this thought, I present here my definition of the Bible (that is, the Jewish Bible): "The Bible is the record of God's relationship with humanity, with an especial focus on one subset of humanity—the people of Israel. But that record is presented in a very imbalanced manner, for we get very few glimpses of God in heaven; rather, the camera remains tenaciously on earth." When the camera, as it were, does transport the reader to heaven, the scene is either part of a legendary account, as in Job 1–2, or the scene is so numinous, as in Ezekiel 1, that the language is virtually incomprehensible.[47]

My characterization of the Bible explains to a great extent, I believe, why Jews read the Bible as a record of the Jewish people, with a focus on that narrative and with less concern about the divine hand or the divine presence. Clearly, God's role as the providential guide of Israel's destiny is acknowledged, for the Bible itself proclaims this throughout, but the text, to repeat, focuses tenaciously on the human actors. The Jew, accordingly, sees his or her national heritage in the Bible, especially its ancient past. As that narrative still speaks to Jews today, in their position as the biological, cultural, and religious descendants of the people of Israel, the Bible remains a living text.[48] That life is nowhere seen more fully and more forcefully than in the public reading of the Torah in the synagogue each Shabbat morning.

---

47. Indeed, the later rabbis cautioned against reading Ezekiel 1 unless one had achieved a particular sagacious level; see *Mishna Ḥagiga* 2:1 and *B. Ḥagiga* 13a–13b.

48. At first glance, one might think that converts to Judaism do not share the biological descent, and of course this is true *sensu stricto*. But this question already was addressed by Moses Maimonides (1135–1204 CE). When a certain Obadiah, who had converted to Judaism, asked Maimonides whether he could recite the prayers—which include the phrases "God of our fathers," "Who has commanded us," and so on (since the proselyte's ancestors did not worship the true God, were not commanded by God, and so on)—the great sage responded, "Yes, you may say all this in the prescribed order and not change it in the least. In the same way as every Jew by birth says his blessing and prayer, you, too, shall bless and pray alike, whether you are alone or pray in the congregation." As such, Maimonides downplayed the biological linkage and instead stressed the spiritual connection. For the full text, see *A Maimonides Reader*, ed. Isidore Twersky (Springfield, NJ: Behrman House, 1972), 475–76.

The Professional Jewish Scholar of the Bible

We now turn to the manner by which the professional Jewish scholar of the Bible approaches the text that he or she studies.[49] Now I must admit that to some extent I am a bit uncomfortable with making a distinction between a Jewish or a Christian or a Muslim or a Hindu or a Buddhist or an atheist reader of the Bible. After all, in theory we all should seek the same truth: how did the original author intend his words, and how did his original audience perceive them? These two questions, which constitute two sides of the same coin, should remain front and center in the field of biblical studies—even as I recognize why this is not always the case.

In order to approach the text in such a manner, modern readers are at a clear disadvantage, because they cannot fully place themselves in the world of ancient Israel. And yet try we must in order to pursue, in Marc Brettler's words, "the challenge of reading like an ancient Israelite."[50] We are able to take steps in this direction by reading the Bible against the backdrop of the ancient Near East—that is, the broader cultural world that ancient Israel inhabited. To our good fortune, after almost two centuries of archaeological fieldwork, we have an enormous wealth of material from Egypt, Canaan, Assyria, and Babylonia, and so much of it in turn has shed considerable light on the biblical text.

For just one illustration out of literally hundreds that I could use, I point to the example of the Tabernacle, which keeps us within the weekly *parasha* of *Be-haʾalotkha* surveyed above. (The Hebrew word *miškan*, "Tabernacle," is used eleven times in Numbers 9–10—even if the most detailed description of the Tabernacle derives from Exodus 25–31, 35–40.)

---

49. In addition to my sketch here, along with several relevant bibliographic items below, see also the following more sustained treatments: Jon D. Levenson, *The Hebrew Bible, the Old Testament, and Historical Criticism* (Louisville: Westminster/John Knox Press, 1993); and Alan T. Levenson, *The Making of the Modern Jewish Bible* (Lanham, MD: Rowman & Littlefield, 2011). Frederick E. Greenspahn has written a series of germane essays over the years, including this one: "Jewish Theologies of Scripture," in *Jewish Bible Theology*, ed. Isaac Kalimi (Winona Lake, IN: Eisenbrauns, 2012), 13–29. Professor Greenspahn (Florida Atlantic University) informs me that he is working on a book on the subject.

50. Marc Z. Brettler, *How to Read the Bible* (Philadelphia: Jewish Publication Society, 2005), 16. For general introduction, see also Marc Z. Brettler, "Episode 13: On Being a Jewish Biblical Scholar," October 16, 2019, in *The Bible for Normal People*, produced by Pete Enns, podcast, https://www.peteenns.com/b4np-podcast-episode-13-jewish-biblical-scholar-marc-brettler/.

Once upon a time, biblical scholars questioned the veracity of the entire tradition, but information forthcoming from the ancient world in either direction of Israel now confirms the reality (or at least the possibility of the reality) of the biblical tradition. I refer to the large public tent at Mari in Mesopotamia, as studied by Daniel Fleming,[51] and to the ceremonial tent of Rameses II, as described by Egyptologists.[52]

Obviously, there is nothing specifically Jewish in the task that I have outlined here, and in fact the luminaries of the field have been both Jewish and Christian (Cyrus Gordon, Benjamin Mazar, Yigael Yadin, Moshe Weinfeld, et al., among the former; W. F. Albright, G. R. Driver, Roland de Vaux, John Emerton, et al., among the latter). That said, the use of ancient Near Eastern sources is very much characteristic of Jewish biblical scholarship. As one major indication thereof, I highlight here the five-volume *JPS Torah Commentary* series, mentioned earlier. Four prominent scholars produced the series between the years 1989 and 1996: Nahum Sarna (Genesis, 1989; Exodus, 1991), Baruch Levine (Leviticus, 1989), Jacob Milgrom (Numbers, 1990), and Jeffrey Tigay (Deuteronomy, 1996).[53] These volumes are replete with data emanating from the study of the ancient Near East, though as we will see below, there is much more as well.

Incidentally, this is an appropriate place to mention the oft-repeated comment of Moses Maimonides. This greatest of all Jewish medieval thinkers wrote as follows: "I say that my knowledge of the belief, practice, and worship of the Sabeans has given me an insight into many of the divine precepts, and has led me to know their reason. You will confirm it when I shall give the reason of commandments which are seemingly purposeless."[54] The term Sabeans (or Sabians) refers to an elusive sect or group of sects, apparently with gnostic tendencies, that retained various ancient polytheistic

51. Daniel E. Fleming, "Mari's Large Public Tent and the Priestly Tent Sanctuary," *Vetus Testamentum* 50, no. 4 (2000): 484–98.

52. Kenneth A. Kitchen, "The Desert Tabernacle: Pure Fiction or Plausible Account?" *Bible Review* 16, no. 6 (December 2000): 14–21; Michael Homan, "The Divine Warrior in His Tent: A Military Model for Yahweh's Tabernacle," *Bible Review* 16, no. 6 (December 2000): 22–33, 55; and James K. Hoffmeier, *Ancient Israel in Sinai* (New York: Oxford University Press, 2005), 193–222.

53. In the years since 1996, the Jewish Publication Society has produced additional volumes on the shorter books of the Bible (Jonah, Song of Songs, Ruth, Qohelet, Esther), with others currently in production.

54. Moses Maimonides, *Guide for the Perplexed*, trans. M. Friedländer (London: Routledge & Kegan Paul, 1904), 318.

practices. The Sabeans served Maimonides well, for it was the great savant's view that many of the laws of the Torah are a reaction to ancient pagan practices.[55] One specific example that Maimonides mentioned is the prohibition of the sacrifice of honey (Lev. 2:11), which he believed was an ancient pagan ritual.[56] In fact, such has been strikingly confirmed by the ancient sources now at our disposal, as modern scholars have noted the use of honey in the sacrificial cult both at Ugarit and in Mesopotamia.[57]

But there is another important thrust among contemporary Jewish scholars of the Bible: in addition to mining the ancient Near Eastern sources, they have also moved in a separate direction altogether and indeed almost entirely on their own. I refer to their attention to the wealth of material present in post-biblical Jewish literature, especially rabbinic texts. Jewish scholars have been especially adept at "excavating," as it were, the treasures awaiting discovery in these voluminous compositions and compilations. While several important scholars could be mentioned, remaining once more with the section of Numbers 8–12, our attention is turned to Jacob Milgrom, who, as noted above, produced the volume on the book of Numbers in the *JPS Torah Commentary* series.[58] Space does not permit a long discussion, and thus I limit myself to a single observation based on a single word. A rare Hebrew word occurs in Numbers 11:8, namely *lašad*, used in the description of the making of the manna cakes, which tasted "like the . . . *lašad* of (olive-)oil."[59] Milgrom is able to move in both directions, back to Akkadian *lišdu*, "cream" (attested in the Old Babylonian period),[60] and forward to Abraham ibn Ezra's (twelfth

---

55. For a thorough treatment of the subject, with an especial focus on the afterlife of Maimonides's position in later medieval and early modern scholarship, see Jonathan Elukin, "Maimonides and the Rise and Fall of the Sabians: Explaining Mosaic Laws and the Limits of Scholarship," *Journal of the History of Ideas* 63, no. 4 (2002): 619–37.

56. Maimonides, *Guide for the Perplexed*, 360.

57. See Baruch A. Levine, *The JPS Torah Commmentary: Leviticus* (Philadelphia: Jewish Publication Society, 1989), 12.

58. Jacob Milgrom, *The JPS Torah Commentary: Numbers* (Philadelphia: Jewish Publication Society, 1990).

59. Elsewhere the word appears only in Psalms 32:4, though the context is slightly different, with the word bearing a more metaphorical connotation, as in "vigor, moisture."

60. A. Leo Oppenheim et al., *The Assyrian Dictionary of the Oriental Institute of the University of Chicago*, 21 vols. (Chicago: University of Chicago Press, 1956–2010), 9 [L], 215.

century) understanding of the word as "the upper layer of the first pressing of the olive oil."[61]

This example is undeniably a minor one, and yet it speaks to the two-pronged approach employed by Milgrom (and others). Magnify this minor key and a major theme emerges. I can do no better than to cite Benjamin Sommer, who devoted several pages to summarizing and characterizing Milgrom's work:

> By using insights he gleans from both types of literature, Milgrom places the Bible on a long trajectory that moves backward from the Bible to the ancient Near East and forward toward rabbinic Judaism. Milgrom shows that just as earlier literature is relevant for understanding the Bible (even though some of it predates the biblical texts by a millennium), so too rabbinic works edited a thousand years after the biblical era can enhance our understanding of the Bible. The Bible in many ways grew out of the literary and cultural traditions of ancient Canaan and Mesopotamia, so that tracing the connections from Canaan and Mesopotamia to Israelite literature helps us understand the later texts; by the same token, examining how biblical culture grows into later Jewish cultures also helps us to understand what was latent or potential in the Bible.[62]

I hasten to add, though, that the issue is not simply a matter of using both these sources and those sources, but rather what stems from the entire enterprise. As Sommer goes on to state, with an especial eye to Milgrom's work on the priestly material in the Torah,[63] Milgrom sees all this mate-

---

61. Milgrom, *Numbers*, 84, with p. 308, fn. 25. Incidentally, curious to know whether the word is attested in post-biblical sources, I checked at *Ma'agarim*, the online Historical Dictionary of the Hebrew Language, produced by the Academy of the Hebrew Language (http://maagarim.hebrew-academy.org.il/). The answer is no, or at least not until the word was revived by writers of *piyyuṭ*—that is, Hebrew liturgical poetry—in the eighth century CE, starting with Pinḥas ha-Kohen ben Ya'aqov mi-Kappara.

62. Benjamin D. Sommer, "Reclaiming the Bible as a Jewish Book: The Legacy of Three Conservative Scholars (Yochanan Muffs, Moshe Greenberg, and Jacob Milgrom)," *Zeramin* 1, no. 3 (Spring 2017), https://zeramim.org/current-issue/volume-issue-3/.

63. In addition to his Numbers commentary cited above, here one must mention Milgrom's *magnum opus*: Jacob Milgrom, *Leviticus*, 3 vols. (New York: Doubleday, 1991–2001), a work which reaches over 2700 pages spread over the three volumes. A more accessible treatment is Jacob Milgrom, *Leviticus: A Book of Ritual and Ethics* (Minneapolis: Fortress Press, 2004), based on the much larger work.

rial as patently Jewish, "expressing core humanistic and religious values through ritual."[64]

Finally, as adumbrated above, I conclude with a word about post-modernism, deconstructionism, and reader-response criticism—with apologies if I lump these terms together in a manner that would not meet with the approval of specialists. Notwithstanding my comment above regarding my own predilection toward uncovering authorial intent and original meaning, I realize of course that for generations of readers of the Bible, the trend has been just the opposite.

In fact, one could argue that the Bible is the ultimate "deconstructed" text! It has no rival, to my mind, in serving as the paradigm to Jacques Derrida's assertion that "texts outlive their authors, and become part of a set of cultural habits equal to, if not surpassing, the importance of authorial intent."[65] This is obviously the case for the Bible, for it continued to be turned and re-turned[66] and read and re-read and interpreted and re-interpreted with each generation, in every which way imaginable. But that is a whole other field of study, the history of biblical interpretation, amongst both Jews and Christians.[67]

---

64. Sommer, "Reclaiming the Bible as a Jewish Book."

65. For convenience I cite here the succinct wording at https://en.wikipedia.org/wiki/Deconstruction (accessed 19 June 2017). See further the standard treatment by Jonathan Culler, *On Deconstruction: Theory and Criticism after Structuralism* (25th Anniversary Edition) (Ithaca, NY: Cornell University Press, 2008).

66. I allude here to *Mishna 'Avot* 5:25: "Turn it over, and churn it over, for all of it is in you, and all of you is in it," reading with the most reliable of all Mishna manuscripts, to wit, Kaufmann A50 (Budapest).

67. See the comprehensive resource, Constance Furey, et al., ed., *Encyclopedia of the Bible and Its Reception*, 17 vols. (Berlin: de Gruyter, 2009-present).

Maturing Latter-day Saint Approaches to Scripture

Ben Spackman

I am pleased to offer a brief response of sorts to Professor Rendsburg's historical exposition of Jewish approaches to scripture. My own academic and personal studies have profited greatly from exposure to Judaic approaches, including those of Rendsburg's mentor Cyrus Gordon[1] and of Rendsburg himself.[2] Herein, I provide a parallel but shorter overview, followed by reflections on how my own exposure to Jewish professors, scholarship, and sources has benefited me. My positive experiences with Jewish approaches—an outsider's narrow exposure to the whole of the tradition—inform this essay.[3]

Founded in 1830, Mormonism[4] is a young religion and remains underdeveloped in many ways. On the one hand, it means many of our traditions are not deeply rooted or refined by the passing of centuries, though the inertia of tradition develops very quickly. On the other hand, it means that when confronting the complexity of scripture, we do not have to reinvent the wheel. Our Jewish (and Christian) cousins have wrestled

---

1. I read Gordon's autobiography during the first semester of my graduate work in Semitics: *A Scholar's Odyssey* (Biblical Scholarship in North America, 2000).

2. See, for example, Gary A. Rendsburg and Cyrus H. Gordon, *The Bible and the Ancient Near East* (New York City: W. W. Norton, 1998); Rendsburg, *The Redaction of Genesis* (University Park, PA: Eisenbrauns, 2017); various technical papers, and Rendsburg, "The Book of Genesis," *The Great Courses*, audio lecture series, accessed April 27, 2020, https://www.thegreatcourses.com/courses/book-of-genesis.html.

3. I have had a variety of Jewish professors, studied in Israel, attended Torah study for sixteen months, have read Jewish texts in Hebrew, Aramaic, and Judeo-Arabic, and read broadly both from Jewish scholars and about Jewish approaches to scripture.

4. I use the term deliberately and inclusively here to include all denominations that descend from the Church founded in 1830. Hereafter, I use "Latter-day Saints" to refer more narrowly to members of The Church of Jesus Christ of Latter-day Saints.

productively with many scriptural issues that also confront Latter-day
Saints. Indeed, borrowing Krister Stendahl's phrase, I have "holy envy"
for the mature tradition of Jewish approaches to scripture, which has
shaped my own scholarship and faith in positive ways. Consequently, this
essay will reflect my personal (and therefore idiosyncratic) experiences and
views on what Latter-day Saints can learn from Judaism about scripture
and scripture study, with some historical notes on LDS tradition.

Within Christianity, The Church of Jesus Christ of Latter-day Saints
has a unique ecclesiological authority structure, which, combined with
some inherited historical attitudes, strongly influences how its members
read scripture. It may be useful to make explicit what some of these are and
the role they have played in shaping approaches to scripture. In looking
for core differences between Latter-day Saints and Evangelicals, Richard
Mouw has insightfully identified several of these structures, characterizing
them as Israelite patterns:

> It is important to underscore here the way in which the Mormon restora-
> tion of these ancient offices and practices resulted in a very significant de-
> parture from the classical Protestant understanding of religious *authority*. . . .
> [Evangelicals] often proceed as if the central authority issue to debate with
> Mormons has to do with the question of which authoritative *texts* ought to
> guide us. . . . We Evangelicals accept the Bible alone as our infallible guide
> while, we point out, the Latter-day Saints add another set of writings, those
> that comprise the Book of Mormon, along with the records of additional
> Church teachings to the canon—thus we classic Protestants are people of the
> Book while Mormons are people of the Books. . . . What we also need to see
> is that in restoring some features of Old Testament Israel, Mormonism has
> also restored the kinds of *authority patterns* that guided the life of Israel. The
> Old Testament people of God were not a people of the Book as such—mainly
> because for most of their history, there was no completed Book. Ancient Israel
> was guided by an open canon and the leadership of the prophets. And it
> is precisely this pattern of communal authority that Mormonism restored.
> Evangelicals may insist that Mormonism has too many books. But the proper
> Mormon response is that even these Books are not enough to give authorita-
> tive guidance to the present-day community of the faithful. The books them-
> selves are products of a prophetic office, an office that has been reinstituted
> in these latter days. People fail to discern the full will of God if they do not
> live their lives in the anticipation that they will receive new revealed teachings
> under the authority of the living prophets.[5]

---

5. Richard Mouw, "What Does God Think about America? Some Challenges
for Evangelicals and Mormons," *BYU Studies* 43, no. 4 (2004): 10–11.

Thus these Latter-day Saint structures and attitudes would include, among others, an open canon, an expanded canon, continuing prophetic status of Church leadership, and as a central hierarchy and populism or anti-elitism. How they interact to affect Latter-day Saint approaches to scripture is complex.

Like Catholicism, the Church operates with a central hierarchy charged with interpreting and determining the official teachings and doctrine of the Church (i.e., a *magisterium* charged with providing authoritative policies and interpretations of past revelation)—though the analogy is not perfect. However, unlike the Catholic Church, the Latter-day Saint hierarchy is imbued with prophetic status, which raises another Christian comparison. Seventh-day Adventists hold their founder Ellen White to be a prophet, just as Latter-day Saints hold their founder Joseph Smith to be a prophet. However, for Adventists, Ellen White's prophethood is limited to providing proper understanding of past scripture, not bringing forth new scripture. Moreover, her prophetic status was charismatic, not sacerdotal. In other words, Seventh-day Adventists present Ellen White as a founding prophet who used her prophetic gift to provide the correct understanding of the Bible, but that gift and authority ceased with her. By contrast, while Joseph Smith interpreted the Bible, he also brought forth new scripture and embedded the prophetic gift and authority within a sacerdotal hierarchy. Consequently, subsequent Latter-day Saint prophetic leadership has sometimes added new revelations to the already-expanded canon, which remains open.[6] (This all constitutes, of course, a robust rejection of *sola scriptura*.)

Since in The Church of Jesus Christ of Latter-day Saints the authoritative meaning of scripture[7] as it applies to and binds believers is mediated through living prophetic interpreters, the focus shifted primarily to those living interpreters, not to what they interpret. (This had an unintended effect on Latter-day Saint reading, which I enumerate below.) That is, since *sola scriptura* Protestants hold the Bible to be the ultimate authority, determining exactly what it means is of the utmost importance, which in turn motivates the study of Greek, Hebrew, and Aramaic; classics, ancient history, exegetical methods, and systematic theology. Since canonized scripture is not the highest authority in the Church, the necessity of adopting

---

6. These additions are rare. While the canon is officially open, in practice it is open merely a crack.

7. Since Mormonism has an expanded canon, I will speak more generally of "scripture" rather than "the Bible."

or developing such methods of interpretation was never felt. Differing ecclesiological structures incentivize different relationships to scripture, and Latter-day Saints were effectively discouraged from pursuing formal or informal exegetical education because the message of scripture did not belong to educated elites but to God's prophets. The received tradition of the Church, then, is distinctly non-exegetical.

Although it hews closer to Catholicism in its ecclesiological structure and accompanying implications for interpretation, The Church of Jesus Christ of Latter-day Saints retains a strong nineteenth-century Protestant inheritance in several ways, surviving through tradition, continuing cultural osmosis (at least in North America), and the lack of exegetically trained members who might call attention to and refine inherited assumptions. For example, the primacy and centrality of scripture is preached frequently, although with some unresolved tensions.[8] Children today are taught a song called "Scripture Power" in which they brandish their leather-bound scriptures while singing, "Scripture power keeps me safe from sin. Scripture power is the power to win." A 2001 Barna study revealed that "Mormons are *more* likely to read the Bible during a week than Protestants."[9] Daily reading, Sunday School lessons, and sermons typically disregard context in favor of utilizing scripture pragmatically toward personal application and building Christlike attributes, morals, and ethics.

Another inherited characteristic of Latter-day Saint approaches to scripture is populism. In this sense, populism means that scripture was conceived of as belonging to laypeople, not experts or clergy, and its meaning required no specialized training to understand. Philip Barlow writes that "the Saints were not anxious to replace a professional clergy, which they had earlier banished, with bookish academics."[10] Combined with the

---

8. That is, the tension between canonized scripture and living authority is not always hammered out clearly. See David Frank Holland, "The Triangle and the Sovereign: Logics, History, and an Open Canon," in *The Expanded Canon: Perspectives on Mormonism and Sacred Texts*, ed. Blaire G. Van Dyke, Brian D. Birch, and Boyd J. Peterson (Greg Kofford Books, 2018), 21–24. Brian Birch, "Beyond the Canon: Authoritative Discourse in Comparative Perspective," in ibid., 26–46.

9. "Protestants, Catholics and Mormons Reflect Diverse Levels of Religious Activity," *Barna Group*, July 9, 2001, https://www.barna.com/research/protestants -catholics-and-mormons-reflect-diverse-levels-of-religious-activity/. I suspect this poll was taken during one of the two years in which the Bible was the focus of Gospel Doctrine study, and the results would differ during the other two.

10. *Mormons and the Bible* (New York: Oxford University Press, 1991), 151.

prophet-centric nature of Latter-day Saint authority, this inherited populism means that Latter-day Saints have traditionally been suspicious of Bible scholars and their interpretations, particularly when they run against tradition. This suspicion manifested itself in liturgy, formal preaching, educational pursuits, the record of publications, and the tensions about creation and evolution at Brigham Young University. I illustrate these last three below.

Educational Pursuits

Sidney B. Sperry was one of the first Latter-day Saints to receive graduate degrees in fields related to Hebrew Bible. Little more than one hundred years passed between the organization of the Church and this first in its history, Sperry's reception of his PhD (University of Chicago, 1931). The first PhD related to New Testament—Russel B. Swensen, University of Chicago in 1934—came out of the same short-lived push for religious education, the so-called "Chicago Experiment"; not until several decades later did a practicing Latter-day Saint with such a degree—Stephen Robinson, a New Testament PhD from Duke in 1978—achieve tenure at a non-LDS school. Latter-day Saint understandings of scripture thus developed for a century without the influence of those trained in examining scripture and hermeneutical assumptions. This allowed the unconscious adoption of culturally popular interpretations, sometimes harmlessly incorrect but other times terribly damaging (e.g., the idea that Africans were cursed descendants of Cain).[11]

Record of Publications

Lack of expertise has never restrained Latter-day Saints from writing about scripture, because such expertise wasn't seen as necessary. In my own area of interest, the book of Genesis, I am aware of nearly ninety Latter-day Saint treatments of Genesis, creation, evolution, and reconciling science with scripture. The vast majority are written by intelligent non-specialists,

---

11. See "Race and the Priesthood," *The Church of Jesus Christ of Latter-day Saints*, accessed April 27, 2020, https://www.churchofjesuschrist.org/study/manual/gospel-topics-essays/race-and-the-priesthood; and Paul Reeve, *Religion of a Different Color: Race and the Mormon Struggle for Whiteness* (New York: Oxford University Press, 2015). See also "The Curse of Cain," in David M. Goldberg, *The Curse of Ham: Race and Slavery in Early Judaism, Christianity, and Islam* (New Jersey: Princeton University Press, 2005).

often lawyers, dentists, and accountants. As such, however well-meaning, they tend to commit the errors and perpetuate the assumptions of non-specialists; they, thus, often unknowingly express quasi-fundamentalist views. For example, they suppose that *they* are not interpreting the text and are instead just providing the plain and obvious meaning of scripture (although read in English and without full attention to historical, textual, or text-critical context). In doing so, they presume that scripture presents divinely revealed (and therefore accurate) historical and scientific information—although perhaps in symbolic or metaphorical terms—all of which is harmonious and consistent from beginning to end.

Creation and Evolution at Brigham Young University

The strength of this non-exegetical tradition carried over to the Church's flagship Brigham Young University (BYU), where formal scriptural expertise was lacking. During a tumultuous period from 1970 to 1992, some faculty in the Religious Education Department warred with science faculty in biology, zoology, and paleontology over biological evolution.[12] However, there was a relative imbalance of expertise between these departments. Whereas the science faculty had earned respectable PhDs in their respective fields, the Religious Education faculty who argued against them did not. One vocal anti-evolution Religious Education faculty member earned an EdD from BYU, with a dissertation on the subject of homeschooling; another earned a BS in Civil Engineering and compiled an anti-evolution pamphlet that he distributed to thousands of students each year, even after BYU administration warned him to stop. Non–Latter-day Saint scholars since the 1950s had been using recently discovered ancient Near Eastern texts to argue that Genesis was never intended as a natural history of the earth and thus had little to say about evolution. Since few BYU Religious Education faculty were getting any-

---

12. I pull here from numerous interviews, archival work, and other dissertation research. My dissertation treats the hermeneutical roots of post-1950 creation and evolution conflict in the LDS Church. I presenteded some of this data at the 2021 Mormon History Association, with my paper titled "The Fundamentalist Enthronement of Science: Seventh-day Adventist Influence on LDS Creationism, from Joseph Fielding Smith to Ezra Taft Benson." Some relevant history through 1986 can be found in Thomas W. Simpson, *American Universities and the Birth of Modern Mormonism, 1867–1940* (Chapel Hill: University of North Carolina Press, 2016); and Gary James Bergera and Ronald Priddis, *Brigham Young University: A House of Faith* (Salt Lake City: Signature Books, 1985).

thing like this training, the most vocal anti-evolution faculty at BYU had little knowledge of these materials, and their arguments relied primarily on selective authoritarianism, face-value interpretations of scripture, and fundamentalist Christian literature like John C. Whitcomb and Henry M. Morris's *The Genesis Flood*.

The status quo among Latter-day Saints appears to be changing quickly in some respects. Various Church leaders and publications have begun to acknowledge, for example, both the existence of different kinds of scriptural interpretation[13] and the religious utility of expertise granted by "advanced degrees in ancient history, biblical studies, and other fields."[14] English-speaking Latter-day Saints are beginning to read translations other than the King James Version, encouraged both by Church leadership citations of other translations[15] and study Bibles,[16] and even by the publication of a New Testament Study Bible by the Church-owned Deseret Book.[17] Moreover, the number of Latter-day Saint scholars trained in Hebrew Bible, Biblical studies, theology, philosophy, and related fields (among whom I find myself) is greatly increasing. As we collectively teach, write, speak about, and model the way formal training in these fields can enhance Latter-day Saint encounters with scripture, the enthusiastic reception has sometimes surprised me.

For example, I have spoken in various formal Latter-day Saint settings on the existence of different genres in scripture and have been interviewed on a Latter-day Saint podcast about that topic. For many Latter-day Saints,

---

13. For example, see the comments by Gaye Strathearn on contextual interpretation in "2 BYU religion professors weigh in on why 'Come, Follow Me' should be just the beginning of your gospel study," *Church News,* February, 25, 2019, https://www.thechurchnews.com/living-faith/2019-02-25/new-testament-come-follow-me-2-byu-religion-professors-october-2018-general-conference-weigh-in-on-personal-gospel-study-49036.

14. Elder M. Russell Ballard, "Questions and Answers," BYU Devotional, November 14, 2017, https://speeches.byu.edu/talks/m-russell-ballard/questions-and-answers/.

15. See the examples and discussion in Ben Spackman, "Why Bible Translations Differ: A Guide for the Perplexed," *Religious Educator* 15, no. 1 (2014): 30–65.

16. See Elder D. Todd Christofferson, "Saving Your Life," fn. 25, CES Devotional Broadcast of September 14, 2014; and Joshua M. Sears, "Study Bibles: An Introduction for Latter-day Saints," *Religious Educator* 20, no. 3 (2019): 26–57.

17. See Daniel O. McClellan, "'As Far as It Is Translated Correctly': Bible Translation and the Church," *Religious Educator* 20, no. 2 (2019): 53–83.

the idea that scripture might consist of different genres—including non-historical ones—proves novel, disconcerting, logical, liberating, and finally edifying, as it opens scriptures to their eyes and frees them from the false and confusing "literal verses figurative" dichotomy. One friend, a Harvard-trained lawyer, shared this insightful response to my podcast with friends on social media:

> Imagine how different your experience with Latter-day Saint Scripture would've been growing up if someone had explained this to you early on, if it had been integrated into the curriculum in a formal way—in seminary, in church, at BYU, wherever. It seems tragic to me that this has never happened. That generations of Latter-day Saint students—even very smart and educated ones—[thus] fixate on the wrong questions and the wrong preoccupations about the text because they've never been taught to do differently.

However, for one such presentation, I received a brief note from a relatively high Church authority, strongly implying that assigning certain parts of the Old Testament to non-historical genres was tantamount to undermining scripture's validity and causing doubt; I had presented the genre markers of Jonah which point to "satirical parable," along with both LDS tradition and the reasons, why committed Christians like C.S. Lewis and Raymond E. Brown, S.S. saw Jonah as non-historical. This small incident served as a reminder that many of the tensions involving scripture, authority, and interpretation arise because Latter-day Saint laypeople, scholars, and members of the hierarchy vary in exposure to and weighting of populist inheritance, tradition, familiarity, and comfort with mainstream scriptural scholarship.

While I remain a committed and believing Latter-day Saint, I am deeply indebted to my Jewish exposure for helping my approaches to scripture grow and mature in a number of ways. I am, for example, beholden to James Kugel for his focus on making invisible interpretive assumptions visible with interpreters ancient and modern. This helped me recognize my own inherited assumptions and think through them, which influenced my dissertation topic choice.

Perhaps the most important thing I have absorbed from my Jewish experiences was learning to become comfortable with tension, with contradiction, and with unresolved and sometimes unresolvable questions. Such tensions and questions exist in scripture, in religious tradition, and in scholarship. Tension can be very productive—for example, brakes require tension to function productively—but Latter-day Saints tend to manifest extreme discomfort with interpretive tension and unanswered questions.

Whereas Jewish tradition "end[s] not with answers but with questions," Latter-day Saints sometimes seem to start with answers and skip the questions altogether.

One aspect of the centralized Latter-day Saint curriculum that both reflects and reinforces this discomfort with ambiguity, tension, or unresolved questions is that the Church's manuals written for youth (Seminary), young adults (Institute), and adults (*Come Follow Me*) rarely present more than one view or interpretation. Typically, a scriptural citation is accompanied by a quotation from a Latter-day Saint leader (usually a non-contextual interpretation, though this distinction is not consciously made) and presents only one perspective. This singularity creates the impression that the interpretation presented represents the collective view of the governing bodies of the Church, that other views do not exist, that such a view came through revelation, and that it is therefore authoritative in every sense.

However, the history of manuals shows this is problematic. For example, one manual (1979) cited a venerated apostle and a president of the Church as well as authoritative rhetoric to emphasize one particular position (in this case, the date of Jesus's birth). The next revision of the manual (2014) cited two different authorities (a member of the First Presidency and a different venerated apostle) to the effect that the Church had *no* position![18] The citations for both of these latter authorities were for things they had spoken and written long before 1979; the singular position offered in the 1979 manual thus represented a historical and interpretive choice by the anonymous writers who presented it as if it were the only historical option. This encourages a sense of the monolithic, a lack of awareness of competing schools of thought. It also contributes to discomfort when one does learn about those different strains of Latter-day Saint thought, even among Church leadership.

During my roughly sixteen months attending Torah study at a local synagogue, I became acquainted with the Torah commentary *Etz Hayyim*. What struck me about it was how the scriptural text was framed by two tiers of commentary. The first came from traditional Talmudic commentary by ancient and medieval rabbis. The second represented the best of recent, academic Jewish scholarship. At times, these contradicted each other in their interpretations of the passage, as to what it meant and what

---

18. The Church of Jesus Christ of Latter-day Saints, *New Testament Institute Manual* (1979), 22. This source cites James E. Talmage and President Harold B. Lee. Compare with The Church of Jesus Christ of Latter-day Saints, *New Testament Institute Manual* (2015), 14–15. My thanks to Jared Patch for this example.

it implied or commanded for ethics, liturgy, and ritual. Like the two creation accounts in Genesis, the accounts of Samuel/Kings and Chronicles, and the four Gospels, these contrasting and sometimes contradictory authorities were allowed to coexist, each recognized and valued for its own contributions. Judaism thus builds on the broader biblical model that presents ambiguity, tension, and contradiction as productive even without resolving them. Learning to be comfortable with ambiguity, tension, and contradiction is both an academic necessity and a spiritual survival skill.[19]

For Latter-day Saints who wish to take advantage of Jewish scholarship, I have provided a short bibliography of authors and books illustrating the breadth of the Jewish interpretative tradition. All of this is accessible to laypeople.

Authors

Amy-Jill Levine, Benjamin Sommer, Cyrus Gordon, Gary Rendsburg, James Kugel, Jeffrey Tigay, Jacob Milgrom, Joel Baden, Jon D. Levenson, Marc Zvi Brettler, Nahum Sarna, Tikva Frymer-Kensky.

Books

Shai Cherry, *Torah Through Time: Understanding Bible Commentary from the Rabbinic Period to Modern Times* (Jewish Publication Society, 2007).

Brettler, *How to Read the (Jewish) Bible* (Oxford University Press, 2007).

Levenson, *Creation and the Persistence of Evil—The Jewish Drama of Divine Omnipotence* (Princeton Press, 1994).

Kugel, *How to Read the Bible: A Guide to Scripture, Then and Now* (Simon and Schuster, 2007).

Telushkin, *Jewish Literacy: The Most Important Things to Know About the Jewish Religion, Its People, and Its History,* Revised Ed. (Morrow, 2008).

Chaim Potok, *The Chosen* and *The Promise.* (These novels about two young Jewish men in Brooklyn in the 1940s and 50s explore the nature and tensions of scripture, interpretation, tradition, religious identity, and orthodoxy (in the general sense). Multiple rereadings have helped me become comfortable in my own intellectual and religious place.).

---

19. In a Latter-day Saint context, see Elder Bruce Hafen, "On Dealing with Uncertainty," *Ensign* (August 1979).

Commentaries/Reference

The JPS Torah Commentary/ The JPS Bible Commentary. (A multivolume series that has expanded beyond the Torah/Pentateuch, which presents the Hebrew and JPS translations in parallel along with extensive commentary drawing on both Jewish tradition and modern scholarship.)

The Jewish Study Bible, 2nd ed. (Oxford University Press, 2014).

The Jewish Annotated New Testament, 2nd ed. (Oxford University Press, 2017). (These one-volume works present the JPS translation of the Hebrew Bible and the New Revised Standard Version of the Greek Testament, with essays and commentary from scholarly Jewish perspective.).

The Eerdmans Dictionary of Early Judaism, Collins and Harlow, eds. (Eerdmans, 2010).

Neither Prophet nor Priest: Authority and the Emergence of the Rabbis in Judaism

Peter Haas

The formation of what we now call Western religions (including primarily Rabbinic Judaism, Catholic Christianity, and early Islam) grew out of the confrontation between the ancient traditional Near Eastern religions on the one hand and the intellectual legacy of Classical Greece on the other. The resulting amalgamation, summarized in the term "Hellenism," gave birth to whole new modes of religious discourse and institutions. This process of amalgamation was, to be sure, hardly a monolithic or monolinear process. It unfolded in diverse fits and starts over several centuries such that by the end of what has been called Late Antiquity (third century CE) there had emerged a very broad cultural understanding of how people in the late and post-Roman worlds would relate to the Divine. Over this time, the older models of religious institutionalization, based on the inherited teachings and practices of dynastic priesthoods, gave way to new chains of discipleship, based on select and maybe paradigmatic figures who achieved supernal knowledge though some combination of revelation, insight, and reasoning. The end result is the conviction that in exercising our minds as we reflect on our traditions, experiences, and insights, we achieve some access to transcendent—that is to say, divine—truth.[1]

In this regard, both the early Church and formative Rabbinic Judaism offer remarkable examples of how this process of change in religious authority brought about by the Hellenization of the Ancient Near East worked itself out. Both early Christianity and early formative Rabbinic Judaism shared common roots in the religious heritage of Biblical Israel as laid out by the Biblical texts. Even though the text itself in its received form is likely somewhat later than the religious community it describes, having been compiled probably in the sixth century as a response to the

---

1. See Jacob Neusner, *The Glory of God is Intelligence* (Salt Lake City: Bookcraft), 4–5, 197.

so-called Babylonian Exile, it nonetheless preserves in some large part the viewpoint of a traditional priestly line still largely unaffected by Hellenic thought. In the Roman world of a few hundred years later, however, we find that the priestly world described in the texts was disappearing. Texts from the region, such as the Books of Maccabees and the Dead Sea Scrolls, show us a religious culture that has already undergone profound changes and redefinitions. To be sure, there are still references to priests and temple and sacrifices, but these references take place in a very different intellectual framework. In the Community Rule of Qumran, for example, the leaders are still technically a priestly clan (the Zadokites), but they are without a temple and therefore do not perform actual sacrifices. Their role is now symbolic. Further, the intellectual foundation of the community is not the inherited esoterica of the priesthood, but rather the revelations of the "Moreh HaTzedek" ("Righteous Teacher" or "Teacher of Righteousness") about the end times. And just as profoundly, the main communal worship has been transformed into a sort of Roman banquet. In fact, as I have argued elsewhere, one could read the ritual life of the Qumran community as a kind of Greco-Roman mystery religion in which the foundation story of the community is centered around the central figure of Moses, and the communal liturgy is fashioned as a kind of recapitulation of the founding events—the idea being to achieve here and now the insight attained back then.[2] In this regard, it is probably suggestive that the texts are written in a Hebrew that was likely no longer a spoken language; instead, it was fashioned to be reminiscent of Biblical Hebrew, as though the scrolls were themselves a kind of Biblical revelation. This repackaging of Biblical religion in Greco-Roman forms is true in its own particular ways also in the early Jesus movement and in the Mishnah, as we shall see below. Each sees revelation as not just something from the past, but something that continues to happen in their own day.[3]

The point is that we can see that what is being described in the Dead Sea Scrolls fits into a larger pattern—namely, the erosion of traditional priesthoods in favor of more Greco-Roman models. We see this process of transformation going not just in Judaism, of course, but in the entire region and long before the first century CE. Our knowledge of what was transpiring in Judaism, however, is much more available than is true of

---

2. "Was the Judaism of the Dead Sea Scrolls a Mystery Religion?" in *Focusing Biblical Studies: The Crucial Nature of the Persian and Hellenistic Periods*, ed. Jon Berquist and Alice Hunt (New York: T and T Clark, 2012) 229–39.

3. See Neusner, *Intelligence*, 51.

other religious traditions. We in fact know of several groups in Roman Judea that were exploring ways to accomplish this Hellenistic transformation: Pharisees, Essenes, and Therapeutae, among others. We also assume that the Judean exile community in Babylonia, dating back to the mid-sixth century BCE, must also have had some way to preserve its identity for several centuries without access to the temple. These initiatives, undertaken while the Jerusalem Temple was still in operation, indicate how influential Hellenistic religious thinking was. Such developments also meant, of course, that when the Jerusalem Temple was actually destroyed by the Romans in 70 CE, there were already models available for building alternatives. Many, of course, remained convinced that "Judah-ism" could only survive with its sacrificial system intact; hence, for example, the revolt of Simon Bar Kochba in the 130s CE, which clearly had the rebuilding of the temple in mind. But the collapse of his revolt signaled to the more traditionalists that even "Judaism" would have to learn to function without the temple for at least the time being. In any case, it is out of the catastrophic series of events of the first century CE that both early Rabbinic Judaism and the early Catholic Church emerged as mainstream movements.

As these traditions coalesced out of the cataclysms of the first century (Crucifixion of Jesus, destruction of Jerusalem), one feature they turned to in common was the reconceptualization of religious leadership. Clearly the traditional role of the Aaronide priesthood was abolished, or at least suspended. The existential question was, what was to take its place? As mentioned earlier, the model was that of discipleship from some founding leader. This notion of leadership goes back to Classical Greece in which Plato, for example, established a group of disciples. His school, called "the Academy," was the model for his most famous pupil (or disciple), Aristotle, whose own teaching circle was called the "Lyceum." Circles of disciples who gathered around a teacher became an almost standard feature in Late Antiquity and well into the Middle Ages. We have already alluded to the Dead Sea Scrolls, which seem to have had in mind this sort of arrangement around the Righteous Teacher, and of course there is the circle of disciples gathered around Jesus. Chains of discipleship, and so of authoritative teaching and learning, became a built-in feature of both early Rabbinic Judaism and of Early Catholic Christianity.

This Greco-Roman model of religious leadership raises a number of questions. One, of course, is its sheer foreignness. Certainly traditionalists, not to mention hereditary priesthoods, resisted this model. But as the communities spread throughout the Hellenistic world and as the influence of the temples and their priesthoods receded, disciple-based communities, often resembling mystery religions, gained adherence and credibility. The proliferation of these groups, however, gives rise to a second problem— namely, the appearance of several circles of prophet-disciples who were in competition with each other. The religious marketplace became crowded with different, and sometimes mutually exclusive, claims to truth and authority. This raises a third question: how each group could push forward its own claim against rival claims. We see these tensions and struggles clearly in the shaping of the early Church and in Rabbinic Judaism.

One of the more well-known Talmudic passages that illustrates the debates behind the move to a discipleship-type line of authority is in the Babylonian Talmud, tractate Baba Metzia 59b. The story is as follows:

A Tannaite statement:

> On that day R. Eliezer produced all of the arguments in the world, but they did not accept them from him. So he said to them, "If the law accords with my position, this carob tree will prove it."
>
> The Carob was uprooted from its place by a hundred cubits –
>
> They said to him, "There is not proof from a carob tree."
>
> So he went and said to them, "If the law accords with my position, let the stream of water prove it."
>
> The stream of water reversed flow.
>
> They said to him, "There is no proof from a stream of water."
>
> So he went and said to them, "If the law accords with my position, let the walls of the school house prove it."
>
> The walls of the school house tilted towards falling.
>
> R. Joshua rebuked them, saying to them, "If disciples of sages are contending with one another in matters of law, what business do you have?"
>
> They did not fall on account of the honor owing to R. Joshua, but they also did not straighten up on account of the honor owing to R. Eliezer, and to this day they are still tilted.
>
> So he went and said to them, "If the law accords with my position, let the Heaven prove it!"
>
> An echo came forth, saying, "What business have you with R. Eliezer, for the law accords with his position under all circumstances!"
>
> R. Joshua stood up on his feet and said, "'It is not in heaven' (Deut. 30:12)."
>
> What is the sense of "It is not in heaven?"
>
> Said R. Jeremiah, "[The sense of Joshua's statement is this:] For the Torah has already been given from Mount Sinai, so we do not pay attention to echoes, since you have already written in the Torah at Mount Sinai, 'After the majority you are to incline' (Ex. 23:2)."

R. Nathan came upon Elijah and said to him, "What did the Holy One, blessed be he, do at that moment?"

He said to him, "He laughed and said, 'My children have overcome me, my children have overcome me!'"[4]

The context of this story is a complex discussion about how to purify a particular kind of oven which has contracted ritual uncleanness. The details of the legal question do not need to detain us. What is important is that the arguments back and forth seem to have reached an impasse. The discussion reported here is a final attempt to establish what the halacha (i.e., the law) should be. What is at stake is not merely how to resolve the case of "Akhnai's Oven" but more profoundly how one should go about establishing one's case altogether. The two antagonists, Rabbis Joshua (ben Hananiah) and Eliezer (ben Hyrcanus), were members of the formative generation of early Rabbinic Judaism. Both were disciples of Yohanan ben Zakkai, a contemporary of Jesus and the putative founder of the chain of discipleship that led to the formation of the Mishnah (the earliest rabbinic writings of the late second century) and who is held to have died in the year 90 CE. The debate before us thus would have taken place in the aftermath of the destruction of the temple in 70 CE, a period in which defining an alternative to the traditional priestly leadership had become urgent. It may be of interest to note that the traditional literature has R. Eliezer being a "Kohen"—that is, of priestly lineage.

The outline of the debate is simple. R. Eliezer in frustration turns to wonders or miracles to prove his case. Maybe this grows out of his priestly heritage which claims a more immediate relationship to the Divine than would be true of commoners. In any case, his invocations of miracles are time after time rebuffed by Joshua, who claims that supernatural events cannot be used to prove anything, and only testimony (that is, rational argumentation) has standing. Finally, in frustration, Eliezer goes so far as to produce a direct revelation from heaven announcing that he (Eliezer) is in fact correct. Joshua is unfazed and even cites scripture telling the divine echo to butt out. The thrust of his argument now becomes clear. The written Torah has been given to us and it is now up to us humans, and us alone, to sort out what the Sinaitic revelation means and how to apply it to daily life. For Joshua, it is discussion and debate that are our vehicles for realizing Torah in community life, not this, that, or the other claim to intuitive or supernatural insight, no matter how apparently compelling.

---

4. Jacob Neusner, *The Babylonian Talmud: A Translation and Commentary*, vol. 14 (Peabody, MA: Hendrickson, 2011), 286–87.

After all, anyone can claim to have had a revelation, but it is only through open discussion in the marketplace of ideas that communal consensus can achieve legitimacy. In the end, Joshua wins the day, even though he may be objectively wrong. We know what we know only if we can articulate it and argue for it in a way that convinces others.

The acceptance of this new model of authority in Judaism, as argued for by R. Joshua, was not immediately and widely accepted. First of all, there were many competing models, such as Eliezer's appeal to ongoing revelation of one kind or another. Another was, of course, what remained of the traditional priesthoods. While defeated and decimated, they did not entirely disappear. In this regard, it is notable that fragments of the so-called "Damascus Document" later found in the Dead Sea caves were first found in the Cairo Geniza by Solomon Schechter in 1897.[5] These documents center the ritual of the community around the Zadokite priesthood. Schechter dated the fragments he found to around the tenth or eleventh centuries CE.[6] That this kind of document was preserved for nearly a thousand years after the destruction provides striking evidence for how strong the pull of the traditional priesthood was. Besides revelation and the priesthood, a third contender for leadership was the royal family, that is, the House of David. We can catch a glimpse of this claim in the New Testament in which arguments are put forward that Jesus is a descendant of David and therefore has a legitimate claim to rulership over the land and people. John 19:19—which reports that over the cross of the crucified Jesus, Pontius Pilate had a sign attached announcing that the crucified was "Jesus of Nazareth, King of the Jews"—certainly reflects this tradition. We also seem to have evidence that the Davidic claim to authority was active in the Babylonian exile community as well. The leader of the Judean community appointed by the Persian authorities, the "exilarch" (or *resh galuta* in Aramaic), based their claim on their (reputed) Davidic descent.[7] A third alternative is provided by those who rejected the notion of any line of discipleship or hereditary authority altogether and claimed reliance only on

---

5. Solomon Schechter, *Documents of Jewish Sectaries: Fragments of a Zadokite Work* (Cambridge: Cambridge University Press, 1910).

6. Geza Vermes, *The Dead Sea Scrolls in English, Second Edition* (Harmondsworth: Penguin, 1975), 95.

7. An extended discussion of the office of Exilarch and its real or claimed Davidic connections can be found in Geoffrey Herman, *A Prince Without a Kingdom: The Exilarch in the Sasanian Era* (Tübingen: Mohr Siebeck, 2012), "Introduction."

the Written Torah itself. These groups coalesced in the most significant of anti-Rabbinite movements of the Early Middle Ages, namely the Karaites.

Even among those who accepted the notion of some sort of "rabbinic" discipleship, there was no consensus of which rabbinic line of intellectual discipleship was the correct one. The Mishnah, the earliest document of formative rabbinic Judaism, already seems to know of the existence of at least two rival "rabbinic" schools: those of Shammai and those of Hillel. The Dead Sea community, of course, pre-dated both Shammai and Hillel and relied on its own chain of transmission, as we have seen, going back to the Teacher of Righteousness. The early Church shows a similar pattern, beginning its chain of discipleship with Jesus (or maybe John the Baptist). And even those movements that share a common founder had disagreements and splits. We see this in the Baba Metzia story cited above. Although both Eliezer and Joshua were disciples of the same teacher, Yohanan ben Zakkai, they had fundamental disagreements over the very nature of what constituted "proof" of the acceptability of an argument.

What all this shows us is that the rise of logical argumentation as the fountain of rabbinic authority was not simple, monolithic, or inevitable. It was a long and twisting road for the Mishnaic and Talmudic rabbis to establish their vision over the Judaic communities of Late Antiquity and the Early Middle Ages. Nor were they ever fully successful. Various groups—Karaites, Kabbalists, various messianists, and later Reform movements—continued to rise and to challenge the classical rabbinic model. Nonetheless, it is clear that as we approach the end of the first millennium of the Common Era, the rabbinic model of open debate had largely won the day and became, and has remained, the defining characteristic of what we call Rabbinic Judaism.[8] Likewise, it is clear that over time the Rabbinic mode of logic and argumentation won out as a defining feature of rabbinic Judaism. In fact, as Jacob Neusner has demonstrated, a single type of argumentation and logical analysis can be seen to have asserted itself across the rabbinic literature. As he puts it, "What I show here . . . is that Rabbinic Judaism is exceptional in its commitment to coherent analytical inquiries that pertain everywhere and philosophically-rigorous types of argumentation that dictate the rules of engagement throughout."[9] To

---

8. A good, but brief description of the Karaite movement can be found in Robert M. Seltzer, *Jewish People, Jewish Thought* (NY: Macmillan, 1980) 337ff.

9. See his *Analysis and Argumentation in Rabbinic Judaism* (Lanham, MD: University Press of America, 2003), xvii. See also the conclusion of his *Introduction*, xxiii.

be sure, Neusner goes on to point out that his analysis and results are based only on those parts of the rabbinic corpus that actually present argumentation and so are not to be taken as characterizations of the literary corpus as a whole. His point is that the forms of argumentation he does find in the diverse documents of his database nonetheless all largely share a certain mode of logical discourse—namely the dialectic of statement, questions, response.[10]

It is reasonable at this point to ask why and how this mode of (dialect) logical argumentation emerged as characteristic of such a broad swath of literature. Surely one of the assertions that emerged and which surely bolstered the standing of rabbinic chain of discipleship was its claim that the ultimate founder of its "school" was none other than Moses himself. By making this assertion, the rabbis could claim that their tradition was indeed foundational for all Western religion, predating not only Jesus and Hillel and the Teacher of Righteousness, but certainly by implication even the Greek philosophical school attributed to Socrates. To be sure, the earliest layer of rabbinic Judaism, the Mishnah, does not make this claim; in fact it rarely cites anyone before Hillel and hardly ever quotes the Torah. Shortly after the publication of the Mishnah in the late third century CE, however, the "Chapters of the Fathers" (*Pirqe Avot)* appears, which for the first time describes a chain of (oral?) tradition that goes to Moses:

> Moses received Torah from Sinai and transmitted it to Joshua, and Joshua to the Elders and the Elders to the Prophets, and the Prophets transmitted it to the men of the Great Assembly. . . . Antigonos of Sokho received it from Simon the Just. . . . Shemayah and Avtalion received it from them. . . . Hillel and Shammai received it from them. . . . Rabban Yohanan ben Zakkai received [the tradition] from Hillel and Shammai. He used to say, "If you have learned much Torah, do not claim goodness for yourself because for this you were created." Rabban Yohanan ben Zakkai had five [notable] students. These are they: R. Eliezeer ben Hyrcanus, R. Joshua Ben Hananiah, R. Yosi HaKohen ["Joseph the Priest"], R. Shimon ben Netan'el, and R. Elazar ben Arach.

The above is a highly-abbreviated version of the first chapter of *Pirqe Avot*. Its point, however, is clear. The teachings of Hillel and Shammai did not start with those thinkers, whether by learning or revelation, but were already part of the patrimony of the "Fathers" that Shammai and Hillel received from their teachers and were now passing along to their disciples. Further, that very chain extends unbroken to the very authorities that now argue out the details of their intellectual heritage in the Mishnah. So as

---

10. For this see his explanation on page xxi and 177f.

we move into the Early Middle Ages (fifth through the tenth centuries CE), the emerging rabbinic estate is basing its authority on two different, albeit complementary, claims: first, that they are carrying forward the very revelation given to Moses at Sinai, and second, that this revelation has been transmitted through an oral tradition that has been passed on through a long line of scholars who were trained by this very tradition in how to read and interpret the text of the Written Torah and who pass this methodology on to their disciples. This notion that it is the intellectual study and analysis of the Oral Tradition that leads to divine insight is what stands at the heart of Rabbinism.[11] It is, then, on these two legs—received tradition and intellectual analysis of that tradition—that rabbinic Judaism stands.

The working out of these principles in practice can be illustrated by following the career of one topic to see how it unfolded across documents over time as the rabbinic tradition of argumentation matured. We will take as our example a piece of civil law of damages that begins in scripture: Exodus 21:33–36. It states,

> When someone opens a pit, or digs a pit and does not cover it, and an ox or an ass falls into it, the one responsible for the pit must make restitution; he shall pay the price to the owner, but shall keep the dead animal. When a person's ox injures his fellow's ox and it dies, they shall sell the live ox and divide its price and they shall also divide the dead animal. If, however, it is know that the ox was in the habit of goring, and its owner has failed to guard it, he must restore ox for ox, but shall keep the dead animal.[12]

The basic principle in these few verses is clear: if a person does an action either through commission ("open a pit") or omission (failure to cover an open pit), then they are responsible for any resultant damage. If there is no clearly responsible party (one ox unexpectedly gores to death another's ox), then no assignment of fiduciary responsibility is made and the two parties split the difference—each gets half the value of the living ox and of the dead ox. The last verse returns to the governing principle: if one has an ox known to be aggressive and fails to keep it under proper restraint, then indeed responsibility is assigned. This is in telegraphically short form a basic principle of civil law as received at Sinai.

After the destruction of the Second Temple in 70 CE, a pre-Rabbinic group undertook to reformulate the laws of Torah so as to make them conform to their new reality as urban dwellers in the Roman Empire.

11. This notion of study of Torah, "Talmud Torah," is the basis of Neusner's argument in *Intelligence*.

12. Author's translation, based on *The Torah* (Philadelphia: JPS, 1982).

We have already seen an example of how different visions of how this was to be achieved were argued out by Rabbis Joshua and Eliezer. Their efforts first achieved comprehensive written form in the Mishnah, generally thought to have reached its more or less received form and content in the second half of the third century CE, so maybe around 280 CE. This is how it rearticulates the principle behind Exodus 2:33–36 in Mishnah tractate Baba Kamma:

> [3:1] One who leaves a jug in the public domain and someone else came along and stumbled on it and broke it – [the one who broke it] is exempt [from having to pay for the broken jug] and if [the one who stumbled on it] is thereby injured, then the owner of the jug is liable for [paying damages] for the injury. If the jug was broken in the public domain and someone slipped on the water, or was hurt by the shards, [the one whose jug broke] is liable [for injuries sustained by others]. But R. Judah say, "[This is so] if he has intention; if not, then he is exempt."
>
> [3:2] One who pours water out in the public domain and someone else was injured by it, [the one who poured the water] is liable for the [later's] injuries. [Similarly,] one who put out thorns or glass, or who builds a wall with thorns in it, or whose wall falls down, into the public domain, and others are injured thereby, [the first one] is liable [for paying damages].[13]

The Mishnah goes on for several more pericopes elaborating on the various aspects of this legal principle as suggested in the Exodus verses. But the logical structure in this earliest layer of rabbinic writing is clear even from the snippet given above. The assignment of liability for injury is the same as in scripture, albeit translated by the authorities of Mishnah into urban Roman terms. It speaks not of pits and oxen, but of merchandise carried in the streets and roads of a town. In addition, it presupposes a legal distinction, as in Roman law, between a public domain (i.e., a street or road) and a private domain (where casual walkers-by are not expected to be). The Mishnah also spells out what may be implicit, but not so explicit, in the Torah text, namely that it is not just the jug and its shards (the "pit") that we are concerned with, but also such secondary effects as spilled content. Even further, Mishnah's teaching tells us that Scriptural liability applies even if one does not directly put the hazardous material (pit, jug) in the public way, but merely initiates a chain of events (builds a wall that later collapses) that leads to injury at some later point in time. As we proceed through the chapters of the Mishnah on this theme, we see

---

13. Author's translation based on Jacob Neusner, ed., *The Babylonian Talmud: A Translation and Commentary*, vol. 13 (Peabody, MA: Hendrickson, 2007), 107.

that the logical implications of the simple statement in scripture are being systematically laid out in rational and reasoned form.

The next step in the process is found in the great commentary on the Mishnah (the "gemara") which along with the Mishnah comprise the Babylonian Talmud. On the passage we have been discussing, we find the following:

> And someone else came along and stumbled on it and broke it—[the one who broke it] is exempt. Why should he be exempt? He should have been watching where he was going! They said in the school of Rab in the name of Rab, "We deal with a case in which the whole of the public domain was filled with barrels." Samuel said, "They were teaching if it happened in the dark." Rabbi Yohanan said, "We are dealing with a case in which the barrels were [tucked] in a corner." Said R. Papa, "A close reading of Mishnah must be according to either R. Samuel or R. Yohanan." . . . Said R. Abba to R. Ashi, "This is what they say in the West (i.e. Roman Judea), in the name of R. Ulla, 'The reason is that people do not ordinarily look out when they walk along the way.'" . . . Now there is no problem in understanding Samuel's ruling, since he acted in accord with his own tradition [that if the pitcher was visible, there would be liability]. But shall we then say that Rabbah concurred with Samuel? Said R. Pappa, "The damage was done at the corner of an oil factory, and, since it is entirely permitted to store barrels there, the defendant should have walked along with his eyes wide open."[14]

This is not the place to try a full explanation of the Talmudic text. In the interest of brevity and focus I have omitted some of the argumentation, as indicated by the ellipses. But the basic train of interpretation is clear. Why should someone who is walking in the public way and breaks a jug not be responsible for the damage he caused? After all, should he not be looking where he was going? One answer is that we cannot assume people are paying attention when walking on a public road since they are assuming that the public road, as public road, is passable. Other responses are that maybe the ruling before us applies only when there were so many barrels that one can hardly blame the passer-by for stumbling upon one, or that it was dark such that the pedestrian could not even see the unexpected barrel, or maybe it was in a place where a person should expect barrels to be stored outside and so they must be vigilant. My point in bringing this passage is to show how what might appear as a straightforward principle in scripture is first translated by Mishnah into Roman urban terms with its additional considerations, and then is brought by the

---

14. Author's translation based on Neusner, *The Babylonian Talmud*, 108.

gemara into all the complexities of actual day-to-day living. In all cases, the elaborations and innovations of the rabbis are not ascribed to revelation but are adduced by the application of reason and logic.

The next stage in this process of employing reason and rational argument to the task of aligning Torah concepts to the messiness of real life comes in the form of legal codes. The idea of a legal code is to arrange into some kind of coherent and accessible order the various legal decisions scattered throughout the Talmud, the midrashic literature, and the vast array of rabbinic response. The history of such codes goes back deep into the Middle Ages, one of the most famous being the code of Maimonides dating to around 1175 CE. The last comprehensive code, the Shulkhan Arukh ("Prepared Table"), was put together by Joseph Caro in around 1563. Here is what this code has to say on our topic.

> Who is responsible for a pit and what is its extent, and other ruling concerning the pit.
>
> 1. A pit is a major category of damage as it is written, "If one digs a pit. . . ." For after one digs it, that one is responsible for damage it causes, since he created something hazardous. . . . Therefore everything which one imagines is his and which remains in its place and causes damage—even spilling water in the public domain and on which another slips—he bears responsibility for.
>
> 2. The same is true of one who digs a pit and one who uncovers a pit that another dug and covered up appropriately and this one comes and open it—he bears responsibility.
>
> If one finds an open pit and covers it and subsequently uncovers it—the owner of the pit is responsible, and this last one is free. If he filled it with dirt and subsequently removed the dirt, this last one is responsible since by filling it in he erased the prior work.[15]

This chapter of Shulkhan Arukh goes on to discuss other details, but the short excerpt above is sufficient to elucidate two essential features. The first is that the code is built on the previous discussion that we have traced back to the Book of Exodus. The second is that it has summarized hundreds of years of discussion into some basic principles, which both stem from the sources and seem fully in accordance with common sense.

To explicate what has occurred here, I need to make a slight digression. In the Shulkhan Arukh, there are four classes of dangers that can cause damage and for which one is responsible. Maimonides has termed these "[goring] ox, grazing [animals], fire and the pit." The point of "ox"

---

15. Shulkhan Arukh: Hoshen Mishpat 410.

is that it refers to a living animal that moves on its own. "Grazing" encompasses damage that can be traced back to a human agent either directly or through negligence, such as sending animals out to graze without proper fencing. "Fire" refers to damage that is the unintended—or better, unforeseen—consequence of some action; for example, a farmer who starts a fire in his own field to burn stubble, and the fire "on its own" spreads to a neighbor's field. The "pit," which is our subject here, is distinguished from the others in that it is totally passive; it remains in place and the victim comes to it, as opposed to the others which move toward, or in some way actively attack the victim.

What is interesting in this code is that the law is now laid out as though flowing from pure reason. There is only the barest reference to scripture; other than that, there is no gesture toward revelation or really even to discipleship. It is as if the only communication from the Divine was to lay down the bare principles,: "If one dig a 'pit.'" There is also no reference to past authorities or chains of tradition. Once we have the foundational vocabulary (the "pit"), the rest of the matter unfolds in a straightforward and logical manner. It should be noted that this particular chapter of Shulkhan Arukh contains some thirty-two numbered paragraphs beyond the three cited above. The only justifications or validations of a view are stated as self-evident: "This last one is responsible since by filling it in he erased the prior work." So we see that by the sixteenth century, the time of the heights of classical Rabbinism, logic has become the sole standard for the elaboration of Jewish law.

This trend continues, of course, into the contemporary Jewish world. Legal rescripts from the more traditionalist communities regularly build on the legal legacy sketched out above with no reference to private revelation and only the barest nod to contemporary *poskim*—that is, legal decisors (the singular being *Posek*). The decision is always presented as a logical, reasoned extension of the received tradition.

One whole series of examples derives from automobile accidents, which offer a rich trove of material for considering damage and liability in today's world. An example comes from an article entitled, "Car Accidents in Halacha Classification and Application," published in *Din Online*.[16]

The generative situation is a car driven by "Reuven," who stops at a red light and is rear-ended by a car driven by "Simon." (Note that names

---

16. Harav Yehoshua Pfeffer, "Car Accidents in Halacha Classification and Application," *Din Online*, February 24, 2017, https://dinonline.org/2017/02/24/car-accidents-in-halacha-classification-and-application/.

of the sons of Jacob—Reuven, Simon, Levi, and so forth—are used in Jewish halachic discussions as place markers in much the same way as John Doe and Jane Doe are used in American law.) The first question to be sorted out is under which of the four damage categories the incident falls. The *Posek*, Rabbi Yehoshua Pfeffer, examines the four possibilities and arrives at the decision by a process of elimination that such a rear-end crash is an example of "grazing," since it is caused by a human agent (Simon), who either failed to brake, failed to notice that Reuven was stopped at a red light, or failed to keep proper distance. The offending car, after all, was in motion (so not "pit"), was not moving on its own volition or nature (so not a "goring ox"), and was always in the direct control of the driver (hence not "fire"). Thus, we are left with grazing (here also termed "Adam," or "human"). With the categorization of events having been determined, the *Posek* can proceed to determine various mitigating situations and consequent liabilities: whether it matters if Reuven stopped too suddenly, that there was an oil slick in the road, that Reuven chose the most expensive repair shop to determine damage payments, and so on. Here we see the culmination, as it were, to the rabbinic use of reason and logic to adduce new legal decisions out of standard principles.

The point of this quick tour of the history of classical rabbinic literature is to show how over time, debate and discussion—rather than revelation, inspiration, discipleship, or other modes of more private sources of legal postulation—rose to prominence. To be sure, there have always been trends opposing this mode of rabbinic jurisprudence. We noted that in pre-modern times the major locus of opposition was in the mystical communities, most notably in Lurianic Kabbalah and its offspring in eighteenth-century Hasidism. Here, public debate was not the source (or at least not the only source) of true wisdom and personal performance, but the source rather was mystical insight. There was also an element of discipleship in this, the foundational figure in Kabbalah being the second-century rabbi Shimon bar Yochai, who was the reputed author of the "Zohar" and so a guiding teacher of what would become "Kabbalah." Although he was a disciple of Akiba, and so had grounds to be a halachic authority on those grounds alone, he is maybe best known for hiding out in a cave from the Romans for thirteen years, during which time he and his son studied Torah and reached new insights into its hidden (that is, mystical) meanings. While there is no direct physical chain of discipleship from Shimon ben Yohai himself, kabbalists consider themselves in some sense or another, such as spiritually, to be a disciple of his. In later

Hasidism, the chain of discipleship goes through the eighteenth-century Rabbi Israel ben Eliezer (also known as the "Baal Shem Tov"), the teacher of several disciples who went on to establish their own sectarian Hasidic dynasties, many of which continue today.

Such extra rabbinical divine revelation has sometimes led to antinomian opposition to classical rabbinic law as mere legalism. One striking example is the false messiah Shabbtai Tzvi, a kabbalist, who in the mid-1660s actually led a movement that, among other things, sought to reoccupy Jerusalem as part of the beginning of the Messianic Age. Among his innovations were a number of changes in Jewish practice, often in direct and provocative disagreement with prevailing rabbinic halacha. This included calling women to read from the Torah scroll and eating festive meals on Jewish fast days. Ultimately, he converted to Islam, moving many of his most devoted followers to do so as well. But such radical antinomianism was rare once rabbinic discourse became normative. In fact, Hasidic Judaism has itself become "re-rabbinized" in many ways, and its adherents are often described today as Ultra-Orthodox, even though their devotion to their founder Rebbe and his dynastic heirs is far from what is usually deemed "Orthodox." Nonetheless, they have reengaged with Halacha and argue it out in ways similar to regular orthodox authorities, albeit with idiosyncratic references to principles and precedents derived from mystical insights.

The most severe challenge to traditional rabbinism and its way of conducting Judaism is the German Reform movement, which grew out of the Jewish emancipation taking place in early to mid-nineteenth century Western and Central Europe. In essence, the Reform movement claimed that while the Talmudic mode of discussion, debate, and argumentation was good and even useful for its time and age, the world had moved on with the Enlightenment and Judaism needed to do so as well. The result of this thinking was the call to, in essence, jump back to the original founding document of Judaism—namely the Tanach—and reinterpret it for modern times in light of Enlightenment rationality. This yielded its own brand of antinomianism, albeit derived from considerations of science and rationality rather than mystical insights. We find this stance articulated, for example, in the first significant statement of the underlying principles of Reform Judaism, the so-called Pittsburgh Platform of 1885. Among its stipulations is the following: "We recognize in Judaism a progressive religion, ever striving to be in accord with the postulates of reason."

On the surface, at least, traditional Talmudic argumentation was to give way to informed academic analyses. However, it was not long before the Reform movement in America established a "Responsa Committee" to deal with specific practices. The Committee was established as early as 1906 and began publishing its responsa (legal rescripts) around 1911.[17] As the movement developed especially in the North American continent after the Second World War, the writing of reasoned, rabbinic-like halacha for members of Reform Judaism grew in sophistication and importance. In fact, since the 1960s over a dozen collections of such response have been published by the Central Conference of American Rabbis, the professional organization of rabbis in the Reform movement. In form, if not always in substance, such writings engage in debate and discussion about Reform Jewish practice on a vast array of topics and in a way clearly reflective of traditional rabbinic discourse. These discussions do not call upon private revelations or on chains of discipleship but on reasoned and logical argumentation based on traditional Jewish sources as well as on accepted scientific and social scientific findings of the day. Thus a modern Reform response will comfortably cite the Talmud and the Shulkhan Arukh, as well as *The Journal of the American Medical Association* and the *Cambridge Quarterly of Healthcare Ethics*.[18]

What I have tried to show is that in the aftermath of the destruction of the Jerusalem Temple in 70 CE, the various Judaisms that survived struggled with how to maintain Jewish continuity in light of the loss of its greatest sources of legitimacy: the royal David family and the Aaronide priesthood. We noted that several alternatives presented themselves: the imminent return of the Davidic monarchy (possibly seen among some of the followers of Jesus), a continuation of priestly authority that may include the rebuilding of the Temple (as in the Bar Kochba rebellion), the establishment of schools with their teacher-student chains of discipleship (as seen in the early Schools of Shammai and Hillel in the pre-70 CE period), the invocation of chosen teachers who received special insight and revelations (such as the Dead Sea Scroll's Teacher of Righteousness and the early Hasidic tzaddikim/rebbes), and the deployment of public legal argumentation (as we saw in the debate on Baba Kamma, which started this essay). In the end, it is clearly the latter that won the day. While some

---

17. *American Reform Responsa: Collected Responsa of the Central Conference of American Rabbis 1889–1983*, ed Walter Jacob (NY: CCAR, 1983), xvff.

18. See, for example, "Hastening the Death of a Potential Organ Donor," *Central Conference of American Rabbis*, NYP No. 5763.3.

of the alternate modes of authority persisted, or tried to reassert themselves in various forms, none achieved widespread acceptance. In modern
times, both the Hasidic groups and the Reform movement have adopted,
each in its own way, the mode of public debate and discussion offered
to readers in the public realm. Clearly, then, this is the mode of Jewish
discourse that has become baked-in, that is, become part of the very DNA
of Judaism. Despite all the vicissitudes of history and changes in cultural
surroundings, the open debate and discussion of what constitutes Judaism
and its norms has proven to be both sustainable and productive. It is in
this mode, maybe, that we as humans can most closely echo the voice of
the divine in our religious communities.

What's the Church's Official Position on Official Positions? Grappling with "Truth" and "Authority"

Trevan Hatch

In the previous essay, Dr. Rabbi Peter Haas considered how some of our Jewish friends have approached the issue of authority in their search for truth. During my engagement with such approaches as a student at Baltimore Hebrew University, Hebrew University of Jerusalem, and the Spertus Institute of Jewish Studies in Chicago, I have wondered how this approach might inform my own quest for truth within the context of my faith tradition. As a Latter-day Saint, what authorities should I consult? Where do I turn for truth? How can I know whether a certain claim is an "official position" of the Church or where to find the "official position" if one exists? If the Church does not have an "official position" on a particular issue, then how do I proceed in formulating my own personal "official position"?

While some Latter-day Saints might believe the search for truth is as simple as figuring out the Church's current position on any given matter, this approach does not work for me, as I will explain. Instead, I am convinced that a dialectical approach that brings in a wide range of authorities is the responsibility of all Latter-day Saints. While there are certainly religious differences between Jews and Latter-day Saints, there is much we can learn from the way our Jewish friends have navigated this difficult aspect of the human experience.

I have sometimes worried about my students who seem to reduce their own search for truth to the question of what is "official doctrine" or the "official position." When they ask me the "official position" of any given topic, they usually imagine such a position can be found in the teachings of living prophets, with scripture following as an important but inferior source. From this standpoint, when they ask questions about the Church's official interpretation on a scriptural passage, women working outside the home, dating practices, guns, communism, or evolution and the age of the earth, they are conflating "truth" and "official positions." For them, the *perceived* "official position" of the Church is prophetic truth, and therefore divine truth, straight from the mind of God. There seems to be very little nuance in how many of them conceptualize truth, doctrine, "official positions," and general teachings of prophets.

My hope in this chapter is to demonstrate how much more complicated these issues of truth and authority are, and how much more agency and responsibility my students and others might assume for establishing their own "official positions" on many matters. My hope is also that this approach results in my students being fairer to Church leaders by not holding them to such an impossible standard. In order to avoid misunderstanding, I must state from the outset that I am *not* applying the following framework to the very few core and revealed doctrines of the Church. I am *only* comparing the non-revelatory aspects of our faith tradition with the non-revelatory aspects of Judaism.[1]

Official Positions are Complicated

Latter-day Saints in general seem to crave certainty, because we imagine that if we can identify an official position, then we can place our finger on a fundamentally and eternally "true" principle. Many Latter-day Saints do not respond well to ambiguity and complexity. Most of us have been conditioned to think that we have all the answers. It is often expressed that if any group on earth can answer life's questions, both big and small, it is the Latter-day Saints. Consequently, when many Church members realize that some of our answers are significantly more complex than previously thought, or have been overstated, we do not know how to deal with it. The quest for, and expectation of, certainty has led to the diminishing convictions of many Church members. Joseph Smith observed in 1844 that some Saints "fly to pieces like glass, as soon as anything comes that is contrary to their traditions."[2] My observation is that this remains a problem for many today. Given this context within the information age, many Latter-day Saint religious educators have weighed in on the subject of how to determine "truth," "doctrine," and "official positions" (a common phrasing among Latter-day Saints) of the Church. I offer a few examples

---

1. I appreciate and thank the nearly two dozen readers, reviewers, and interlocutors at BYU and elsewhere for their feedback and support regarding this essay.

2. "History, 1838–1856, volume E-1 [1 July 1843–30 April 1844]," p. 1867, The Joseph Smith Papers, accessed March 12, 2021, https://www.josephsmithpapers.org/paper-summary/history-1838-1856-volume-e-1-1-july-1843-30-april-1844/239.

to show that determining truth or an official position in our religious tradition is not simple on *all* matters.

In 2003—with similar versions published in 2007 and 2013—Robert Millet, professor emeritus of BYU Religious Education, proposed several criteria for determining official positions and doctrines of the Church. His criteria identified authoritative voices that transmit authoritative truths. Doctrine or "official positions" are found in (1) the four standard works and official declarations or proclamations, (2) general conference or other official gatherings by general Church leaders, (3) general handbooks or approved curriculum of the Church, and (4) the teachings of the Church *today*. He also posited that doctrine is time tested—perpetuated over time by leaders of the Church.[3] Ironically, what was an attempt to help bring clarity to the problem seemed to raise more questions than it answered. LDS philosopher Loyd Ericson pointed out that there was "no justification" for why Millett thought this "particular set of criteria should be used over any other."[4] The complicated nature of the subject is demonstrated by the fact that Millet responded to Ericson in the same journal,[5] and Ericson subsequently offered a rejoinder to Millet's response.[6] One glaring takeaway is that they could not even agree—and understandably so—on what the most authoritative voices and settings for Latter-day Saints are.

Similarly, in 2016 three BYU Religious Education professors published a piece wherein they propose potential sources of Latter-day Saint authority. These are (1) scripture—and better yet, repeated occurrences within scripture, (2) the united voice of the current brethren, (3) current—and

3. Robert L. Millet, "What Is Our Doctrine?," *The Religious Educator: Perspectives on the Restored Gospel* 4, no. 3 (2003), 15–33; Robert L. Millet, "What Do We Really Believe? Identifying Doctrinal Parameters within Mormonism," in *Discourses in Mormon Theology: Philosophical and Theological Possibilities*, ed. James M. McLachlan and Loyd Ericson (Salt Lake City: Greg Kofford Books, 2007), 265–81; Robert Millet, "What is Our Doctrine?" in *Common Ground, Different Opinions: Latter-day Saints and Contemporary Issues*, ed. Justin White and James Faulconer (Salt Lake City: Greg Kofford Books, 2013), 13–33.

4. Loyd Ericson, "The Challenges of Defining Mormon Doctrine," *Element: The Journal of the Society for Mormon Philosophy and Theology* 3, no. 1–2 (Spring & Fall 2007): 71.

5. Robert L. Millet, "Defining Doctrine: A Response to Loyd Ericson," *Element: The Journal of the Society for Mormon Philosophy and Theology* 5, no. 1 (Spring 2009): 1–7.

6. Loyd Ericson, "Is it Mormon Doctrine that Mormon Doctrine is True: A Rejoinder," *Element* 5, no. 1 (Spring 2009), 21–26.

continuously taught—teachings of General Authorities and general officers acting in their official capacity, and (4) recent Church publications or statements.[7]

Michael Goodman, a BYU Religious Education professor, offered his own three-point criteria for doctrine: (1) true doctrine is eternal and unchanging, (2) true doctrine is taught by the united voice of the brethren, and (3) true doctrine is salvific (i.e., essential for salvation).[8] Goodman's approach echoed a statement from the Church's newsroom that warned that "some doctrines are more important than others and might be considered core doctrines."[9]

Again, a year later, another Religious Education professor, this time Scott Woodward at BYU–Idaho, published a mechanism for his students to utilize while assessing proposed truths. He suggested that if the following are in place, then our confidence level might increase if a certain teaching is true: (1) Does the teaching accord with the repeated teachings of the scriptures? (2) Is the teaching consistently or unitedly proclaimed by the apostles? (3) Is the teaching confirmed by the Holy Spirit?[10] In Woodward's model, *the* authoritative voice for Latter-day Saints is not any one of these voices; it is rather a combination of them.

These are only a sampling of the many publications, blogs, and podcast episodes that grapple with this question. If the answers to "What is the primary authoritative voice for Latter-day Saints?" or "What is the Church's official position on this or that?" were so obvious, then so many people would not be both asking and attempting to answer these questions. But why is the issue of authority so confusing for many Latter-day Saints? I provide four brief examples below that further illustrate the

7. Anthony Sweat, Michael H. MacKay, and Gerrit J. Dirkmaat, "Doctrine: Models to Evaluate Types and Sources of Latter-day Saint Teachings," *Religious Educator* 17, no. 3 (2016): 101–25.

8. Michael Goodman, "What is LDS Doctrine?" LDS Perspectives Podcast, Episode 27, March 15, 2017, https://ldsperspectives.com/2017/03/15/lds-doctrine-michael-goodman/.

9. LDS Newsroom, "Approaching Mormon Doctrine," May 4, 2007, https://newsroom.churchofjesuschrist.org/article/approaching-mormon-doctrine; Elder D. Todd Christofferson, "The Doctrine of Christ," General Conference, April 2012; President Dallin H. Oaks, "Trust in the Lord," General Conference, October 2019.

10. Scott Woodward, "A Primer on Latter-day Saint Doctrine," *Scott Woodward.org*, April 19, 2020, http://www.scottwoodward.org/new/a-primer-on-latter-day-saint-doctrine/.

complexity. These are as follows: the authority of prophets, the Word of Wisdom, the nature of God, and race.

Authority of Prophets

In other faith traditions, the sacred texts are the primary authority. Some traditions, like Judaism, make room for secondary authorities (e.g., legal experts) to help make sense of laws contained within the sacred texts. Latter-day Saints add a layer of authority; not only are there sacred texts, but there are also modern-day prophets. Central to the question of official authoritative positions is the primacy of *living* prophets in Latter-day Saint thought.

A sentiment is often expressed that living prophets are more authoritative than dead prophets, even more than those dead prophets whose writings are preserved in scripture. This idea has been posited in various settings, including, for example, in 1897 when Wilford Woodruff relayed a story about Brigham Young, who said, "When compared with the living oracles those books [referring to the scripture] are nothing to me. . . . I would rather have the living oracles than all the writing in the books."[11] President Ezra Taft Benson echoed this notion in a 1980 Brigham Young University address: "Beware of those who would pit the dead prophets against the living prophets, for the living prophets *always* take precedence."[12] Likewise, in 1916, Elder Orson F. Whitney said the following, which was quoted six decades later by Elder Loren C. Dunn in his April 1976 general conference talk:

> The Latter-day Saints do not do things because they happen to be printed in a book [i.e., Scripture]. They do not do things because God told the Jews to do them [i.e., the Bible]; nor do they do or leave undone anything because of the instructions that Christ gave to the Nephites [i.e., the Book of Mormon]. Whatever is done by this Church is because God, speaking from heaven in our day, has commanded this Church to do it. *No book presides over this Church, and no book lies at its foundation.*[13]

---

11. *Report of the Semi-Annual Conference of the Church of Jesus Christ of Latter-day Saints*, October 1897 (Salt Lake City: The Church of Jesus Christ of Latter-day Saints, semiannual), 22 (hererafter cited as *Conference Report*).

12. Ezra Taft Benson, *The Fourteen Fundamentals in Following the Prophet*, BYU address, February 26, 1980, https://speeches.byu.edu/talks/ezra-taft-benson/fourteen-fundamentals-following-prophet/; emphasis added.

13. Orson F. Whitney, *Conference Report*, October 1916, 55; quoted in Loren C. Dunn, "A Living Prophet," *Ensign*, May 1976; emphasis added.

These statements seem clear enough—living prophets trump scripture. Full stop. Thus, one must look first to living prophets to find "official positions." If living prophets do not speak on a particular issue, only then should one look to the teachings of dead Latter-day Saint prophets and canonized scripture.

Along these lines, some have taught that Latter-day Saints must *always* follow the prophets. Consider President Benson's statement in the same 1980 speech: "If there is ever a conflict between earthly knowledge and the words of the prophet, you stand with the prophet and you'll be blessed and time vindicate you."[14] Elder Marion G. Romney more provocatively stated: "[Heber J. Grant] put his arm over my shoulder and said: 'My boy, you always keep your eye on the President of the Church and if he ever tells you to do anything, and it is wrong, and you do it, the Lord will bless you for it.'"[15] Elder David A. Bednar, speaking in a 2005 BYU devotional, stressed that Latter-day Saints must "promptly and quietly obey the counsel of the prophet in *all things* and at *all times*."[16] And in a more recent general conference address in 2014, Sister Carol McConkie declared, "Following the prophet is *always* right."[17]

At this point, my students and others should not be confused. Given what we read, we should assume that "official positions" and "truth" are posited by ordained prophets through revelation, or in scripture, as long as they do not contradict modern prophets. Moreover, Latter-day Saints are expected to always default to follow prophets' teachings. So why the confusion?

Well, first, many of these types of statements are rarely qualified, thus leading to confusion. Lifelong members of the Church have been taught repeatedly since childhood to "follow the prophets." While the aptly named children's hymn "Follow the Prophet" contains the word "prophet" sixty-eight times and "follow the prophet" fifty-nine times, the primary message exemplified by the song is rarely offered with clarification of what it actually means to follow the prophet. I have read on social media the following two comments: "If the prophet told me to wear purple socks to

---

14. Benson, *Fourteen Fundamentals*.

15. *Conference Report*, October 1960, 78.

16. Elder David Bednar, "Quick to Observe," Brigham Young University devotional, May 6, 2005; emphasis added.

17. Carol McConkie, "Live According to the Words of the Prophets," General Conference, October 2014; emphasis added.

Church, I would do it"; "If the prophet told me to kill someone, I would do it, no questions asked."

Are proponents of the paradigm of "always follow the prophet" referring to matters exclusively related to institutional functions and priesthood ordinances? Certainly, Elder Bednar's and Sister McConkie's comments extend beyond these. What about social, political, historical, familial, and financial matters? What about prophets who engage in scriptural interpretation? Must those interpretations be accepted without question as "official" interpretations? Are Latter-day Saints only required to follow prophets when they are transmitting a direct revelation from God, while all other statements are general thoughts that do not purport to be instruction from heaven? I myself have wrestled with these questions for two decades as I have tried to figure out where I fit into the grand scheme as a Latter-day Saint truth-seeker.

Despite the claim that living prophets take precedence over scripture and that Latter-day Saints must always follow the prophets, a counter-narrative has also been posited. For example, Elder B. H. Roberts understood that "the *only* sources of absolute appeal for our doctrine"—what is ultimately binding on Latter-day Saints—are the standard works (Bible, Book of Mormon, Doctrine and Covenants, and Pearl of Great Price).[18] President Harold B. Lee and Elder Joseph Fielding Smith both explained that if any member of the Church, even a prophet, teaches anything that contradicts what is in scripture, then Latter-day Saints are "not bound to accept it as truth." In fact, Joseph Fielding Smith was so bold to teach that if a prophet "writes something which is out of harmony with the revelations [referring to those contained in books of scripture], then every member of the Church *is duty bound to reject it*."[19] In a letter to a scholar, McConkie agreed that prophets have contradicted themselves and each other on multiple occasions, and used Brigham Young as an example: "Which Brigham Young shall we believe and the answer is: we will take the

18. Brigham H. Roberts, sermon, Salt Lake Tabernacle, July 10, 1921, printed in *Deseret News* 4, no. 7 (July 23, 1921); emphasis added.

19. Harold B. Lee, *The First Area General Conference for Germany, Austria, Holland, Italy, Switzerland, France, Belgium, and Spain of the Church of Jesus Christ of Latter-day Saints, held in Munich Germany, August 24–26, 1973, with Reports and Discourses*, Family and Church History Department, The Church of Jesus Christ of Latter-day Saints, Salt Lake City, 69; Joseph Fielding Smith, *Doctrines of Salvation*, ed. Bruce R. McConkie, 3 vols. (Salt Lake City: Bookcraft, 1954–56), 3:203–204; emphasis added.

one whose statements accord with what God has revealed in the standard works." In the same letter, he wrote, "Wise gospel students do not build their philosophies of life on quotations of individuals, even though those quotations come from presidents of the Church. Wise people anchor their doctrine on the standard works. . . . We do *not solve our problems by getting a statement from* the president of the Church."[20] McConkie expressed this same position in his classic *Mormon Doctrine*: "[P]rophets . . . do not rank with the standard works."[21]

Current Church leaders have recently reaffirmed this stance in a 2007 statement, repeated by Elder D. Todd Christofferson in the April 2012 general conference, and repeated again by President Dallin H. Oaks in the October 2019 general conference: "Not every statement made by a Church leader, past or present, necessarily constitutes doctrine. A single statement made by a single leader on a single occasion often represents a personal, though well-considered, opinion, but is not meant to be officially binding for the whole Church." The quote further explains that doctrine is found in "the four standard works of Scripture" and "official declarations and proclamations."[22] Note that this statement does not claim that everything in scripture and official declarations or proclamations are binding doctrine, but that binding doctrine is found *within* these sources; the same can be argued about the teachings of prophets.

The Word of Wisdom

Over eighty times between 1908 and 2002, Latter-day Saints were counseled not to consume caffeine. This counsel is found in Church-produced magazines, Church news, general conference reports, and publications of

20. Bruce R. McConkie, Letter to Eugene England, February 19, 1981. Retrieved from the Eugene England Foundation at http://www.eugeneengland .org/wp-content/uploads/2012/07/BRM-to-EE-Feb-80-Combined.pdf; accessed January 12, 2021; emphasis added.

21. Bruce R. McConkie, *Mormon Doctrine*, 2nd ed. (Salt Lake City: Bookcraft, 1966), 111.

22. LDS Newsroom, "Approaching Mormon Doctrine," May 4, 2007, https:// newsroom.churchofjesuschrist.org/article/approaching-mormon-doctrine; Elder D. Todd Christofferson, "The Doctrine of Christ," General Conference, April 2012; President Dallin H. Oaks, "Trust in the Lord," General Conference, October 2019.

prophets.[23] Yet, caffeinated drinks are now offered at Church-owned facilities like Brigham Young University. Were these statements about caffeine "official," given that the platform was repeated counsel, across time, in various publications, and in general conference? As we have seen, some within the Church maintain that modern prophets trump scripture. The Word of Wisdom was originally canonized in the 1830s as just that, a piece of wisdom for the "temporal salvation of all saints" and "not by commandment or constraint" (D&C 89:2). Thus, it was not a problem for Joseph Smith to purchase and drink beer from Frederick Moesser's store one month before his death or for Joseph Smith and his associates to drink wine in Carthage Jail in 1844.[24] In fact, the Word of Wisdom itself permits the consumption of "mild barley drink" (i.e., beer). However, Church members generally do not drink (or even sip) wine or beer today, and they no longer see the Word of Wisdom as temporal wisdom; instead, it is viewed now as a commandment from God, given statements from Presidents Brigham Young and Heber J. Grant.[25] In this case, Church members side with current leaders over canonized scripture.

Intriguing, however, is that despite prophets counseling members over eighty times in the last hundred years to avoid caffeine, Brigham Young University started serving caffeine in 2017.[26] Some pointed to the Church's statement on its Newsroom as a rationale for members to drink caffeine:[27] "The Church revelation spelling out health practices (Doctrine and Covenants 89) does not mention the use of caffeine."[28] This appeal to the canonized revelation is made while the revelation itself permits beer and

23. "Caffeine," in *Sermons and Speeches*, on *Gospelink*, Digital Library by Deseret Book.

24. Steven Harper, "Did Joseph Smith Obey the Word of Wisdom?" September 26, 2019, https://stevencraigharper.com/did-joseph-smith-obey-the-word-of-wisdom/.

25. "The Word of Wisdom," https://www.churchofjesuschrist.org/manual/doctrine-and-covenants-student-manual/section-89-the-word-of-wisdom.

26. Sean Rossman, Sept 21, 2017, "BYU Students Can Now Get Caffeinated Soda on Campus," https://www.usatoday.com/story/news/nation-now/2017/09/21/byu-students-can-now-get-caffeinated-soda-campus/690013001/.

27. Danielle B. Wagner, "Caffeine: What the Prophets Have Actually Said," August 25, 2017, *LDSLiving*, https://www.ldsliving.com/What-the-Prophets-Have-Really-Said-About-Caffeine/s/86182.

28. "Mormonism in the News: Getting It Right," August 29, 2012, The Newsroom Blog, https://newsroom.churchofjesuschrist.org/article/mormonism-news--getting-it-right-august-29.

prohibits frequent consumption of meat—neither of which are promoted today. In the case of caffeine, Church members side with the original revelation over numerous prophets who lived *after* that time. So which is it? Do we following modern prophets or scripture? The answer is not always clear.

The Nature of God

The classic debate between Brigham Young and Orson Pratt is another example of why the issue of "official" is sometimes confusing in the Latter-day Saint tradition. Brigham Young and Orson Pratt engaged in a decades-long debate about the nature of God. All of Orson Pratt's peers sided with Brigham Young.[29] In 1873, Brigham Young claimed that his position on the nature of God was "revealed to [him]."[30] After Brigham Young died, all the apostles moved away from his doctrine, and they sided with Orson Pratt's position. In 1897, Joseph F. Smith, who served as a counselor to Brigham Young, denounced Young's doctrine:

> President Young no doubt expressed his personal opinion or views upon the subject. What he said was not given as a revelation or commandment from the Lord. The Doctrine was never submitted to the Councils of the Priesthood, nor to the Church for approval or ratification, and was never formally or otherwise accepted by the Church. It is therefore in no sense binding upon the Church.[31]

Spencer W. Kimball also rejected Brigham's "false doctrine,"[32] as did Bruce R. McConkie.[33]

---

29. David John Buerger, "The Adam-God Doctrine," *Dialogue: A Journal of Mormon Thought*, vol. 15 (Spring 1982): 14–58; Gary Bergera, *Conflict in the Quorum: Orson Pratt, Brigham Young, Joseph Smith* (Salt Lake City: Signature Books, 2002).

30. Sermon delivered on June 8, 1873, and printed in the Deseret Weekly News, June 18, 1873.

31. Joseph F. Smith, Letter to the Honorable A. Saxey, Joseph F. Smith Papers, 1854–1918, 1896 September 4–1898 April 1; Church History Library.

32. "We warn you against the dissemination of doctrines which are not according to the Scriptures and which are alleged to have been taught by some of the General Authorities of past generations. Such, for instance, is [Brigham Young's] theory. We denounce that theory and hope that everyone will be cautioned against this and other kinds of false doctrine." Spencer W. Kimball, "Our Own Liahona," *Ensign*, November 1976, 77.

33. Bruce R. McConkie, "The Seven Deadly Heresies," *Brigham Young University*, June 1, 1980.

In short, the entire First Presidency and Quorum of the Twelve, except for Orson Pratt, agreed that Brigham's doctrine was revelatory. However, several Church leaders later rejected this teaching, and most Latter-day Saints today would agree with Orson Pratt's position.

The Race Doctrine

President Harold B. Lee taught that some people were "unfaithful or not valiant" in the pre-earth life, and so they were "permitted to take mortal bodies although under penalty of racial or physical or nationlistic limitations."[34] Elder Melvin J. Ballard taught that people who were not faithful in the preexistence were born to "Chinese mothers" and "Negro mothers," whereas faithful spirits were born to "*beautiful* white Latter-day Saint mothers."[35] Consequent to these beliefs was the teaching that interracial "mixing of seed" is forbidden. President Brigham Young advocated for the death penalty for any white man "who mixes his blood with the seed of Cain" (i.e., people of African descent),[36] and Elder J. Reuben Clark referred to interracial marriage as a "wicked virus."[37] In 1947, the First Presidency under George Albert Smith explained that not only has "the Lord forbidden" interacial marriage, but also that "social intercourse between the Whites and the Negroes should certainly not be encouraged."[38] Note that the 2013 statement, currently on the Church's website as of

---

34. Harold B. Lee, *Decisions for Successful Living* (Salt Lake City: Deseret, 1973), 165.

35. Melvin J. Ballard, "Three Degrees of Glory," delivered at the Ogden Tabernacle, in Bryant S. Hinkley, *Sermons and Missionary Services of Melvin J. Ballard* (Salt Lake City: Deseret, 1949), 247–48; emphasis added.

36. "If the white man who belongs to the chosen seed mixes his blood with the seed of Cain [i.e., African race], the penalty, under the law of God, is death on the spot. This will always be so." Brigham Young, March 8, 1863, *Journal of Discourses*, 26 vols. (London and Liverpool: LDS Booksellers Depot, 1854–86), 10:110.

37. "It is sought today in certain quarters to break down all race prejudice, and at the end of the road . . . is intermarriage. That is what it finally comes to. Now, you should hate nobody; you should give to every man and every woman, no matter what the color of his or her skin may be, full civil rights. You should treat them as brothers and sisters, but do not ever let that wicked virus get into your systems that brotherhood either permits or entitles you to mix races which are inconsistent." J. Reuben Clark, *Improvement Era* 49 (August 1946): 492.

38. Letter from the First Presidency (Smith, Clark, McKay), to Virgil H. Sponberg, May 5, 1947, in Bennion papers, as quoted in Lester Bush,

2021, rejects teachings on race by past prophets. In other words, current prophets are disavowing statements and proclamations of prior prophets:

> Today, the Church disavows the theories advanced in the past that black skin is a sign of divine disfavor or curse, or that it reflects unrighteous actions in a premortal life; that mixed-race marriages are a sin; or that blacks or people of any other race or ethnicity are inferior in any way to anyone else. Church leaders today unequivocally condemn all racism, past and present, in any form.[39]

We might also recall that following the 1978 revelation extending the priesthood and temple ordinances to all worthy adult members, Elder Bruce R. McConkie told the Saints to disregard previous statements of the Brethren regarding issues of race and priesthood: "Forget everything that I have said, or what President Brigham Young or President George Q. Cannon or whomsoever has said in days past. . . . We spoke with a limited understanding and without the light and knowledge."[40] Would not the same rationale apply in the case of prophets opining on ten thousand other unrevealed matters, regardless of whether they ended up being correct or mistaken on those opinions? Were these teachings "official positions" of the Church (i.e., revealed truth) fifty years ago but not now? Do eternal doctrines with salvific implications change that drastically and that quickly, thus giving Latter-day Saints doctrinal whiplash?

These types of paradoxes often lead to confusion among the Saints. When should Latter-day Saints follow the prophets' teachings, guidance, and interpretations? In their conference sermons, regional talks, regional training sessions, social media posts, fireside Q&As with youth and young adults, Church magazine articles, brief remarks at community events, remarks at historic building ribbon-cutting dedications, press conference answers, comments in Church-produced videos and documentaries, and published books? Given the aforementioned paradoxical schools of thought, the answer is unclear.

These are questions that I myself have grappled with, and I have heard my students ask them as well. The simple answer is, no, Latter-day Saints

"Mormonism's Negro Doctrine: An Historical Overview," *Dialogue: A Journal of Mormon Thought* 8, no. 1 (Spring 1973): 11–68.

39. "Race and the Priesthood," *Gospel Topics Essays*, The Church of Jesus Christ of Latter-day Saints, December 2013, https://www.churchofjesuschrist.org/study/manual/gospel-topics-essays/race-and-the-priesthood.

40. Bruce R. McConkie, "All Are Alike Unto God," CES Religious Educators Symposium, August 18, 1978, https://speeches.byu.edu/talks/bruce-r-mcconkie/alike-unto-god/, accessed on October 18, 2019.

do not believe in the infallibility of their leaders. As Elder Uchtdorf articulated in the 2013 general conference, "There have been times when members or leaders in the Church have simply made mistakes. There may have been things said or done that were not in harmony with our values, principles, or doctrine."[41]

So how can one find an "official position" on a given question? Or, how can one at least find out *if* the Church even has an "official position"? If there is no "official position" on a given issue, then what method do we employ to seek truth on the matter, or to establish an "official position" for ourselves? The Jewish community has grappled with the same problem for over two thousand years. Judaism is a legal religion. Jews are expected to perform many tasks, and they are prohibited from performing many other practices. Jews have authoritative sources that answer some questions but do not sufficiently answer others. How, then, do they solve this problem? Let us explore this question using Haas's essay as our reference point.

A Jewish Approach to "Official Positions"

Peter Haas explained the conceptualization of authority among the rabbis by walking his reader through Jewish history and demonstrating that many Jews, starting with the rabbis, defaulted to "the mode of public debate and discussion" as the primary process for establishing truth. He concluded his essay by articulating that the rational, dialectical mode—as opposed to emotion, miracle, and appeal to authority—"is the mode of Jewish discourse that has become baked-in, that is, become part of the very DNA of Judaism,"

> Despite all vicissitudes of history and changes in cultural surroundings, the open debate and discussion of what constitutes Judaism and its norms have proven to be both sustainable and productive. It is in this mode, maybe, that we as humans can most closely echo the voice of the Divine in our religious communities. (p. 51)

Remember from Haas's essay that Rabbi Eliezer appealed to miracles to prove the primacy of his claim when challenged. However, each time Eliezer relied on a spiritual witness to prove his own case, his peers said, "No proof can be brought from [this miracle]." After the third miracle, Rabbi Joshua said, "When scholars are engaged in a legal dispute, why do

---

41. Dieter F. Uchtdorf, "Come, Join with Us," General Conference, October 2013, https://www.churchofjesuschrist.org/study/general-conference/2013/10/come-join-with-us/.

you [heavenly witness] interfere?" He then said, "[The authoritative voice] is not in Heaven." The rabbis explained the meaning of this statement. Only reasoned argumentation can establish a particular claim. According to Haas,

> For [Jews], it is discussion and debate that are our vehicles for realizing Torah in community life, not this, that, or the other claim to intuitive or supernatural insight, no matter how apparently compelling. After all, anyone can claim to have had a revelation, but it is only through open discussion in the marketplace of ideas that communal consensus can achieve legitimacy. (p. 39–40)

The late Dr. Rabbi Byron Sherwin (philosopher and bioethicist) offered a Jewish perspective on the role of human beings in the process of identifying truth:

> For many Jewish ethicists and legalists, God has the initial word, but human beings have the last word. Though fallible by nature, their task is to apply divine wisdom—using human intelligence and intuition—to particular human situations. Objective divine revelation and subjective human speculation coalesce to produce guidelines for correct moral behavior. . . . Jewish tradition apparently found the human condition too precarious, human thought and emotion too unreliable, to leave the task of moral guidance to the vicissitudes of the human mind and heart alone. Jewish ethics grants us a vote but not a veto regarding moral principles that derive from revelation and tradition.[42]

God gives the foundation, the broad principles, and then allows humans to work out the particulars themselves. Given the limited nature of revelation and of divine-human interaction in Judaism, Dr. Jacob Neusner, a foremost scholar in Jewish studies, took seriously the role of the dialectic and scholarship. He made famous among Jewish studies scholars the line "What we cannot show, we do not know."[43] In other words, if a person cannot support a doctrine, legal claim ("legal" because Judaism is a system of law), or position with evidence, careful reason, and responsible scholarship, then they cannot claim to know the absolute truth on the matter.

When a Jew has a question about Jewish law, they consult someone, often a rabbi, who is deeply knowledgeable in Jewish beliefs and practices. The rabbi has rabbinical training, which entails an in-depth knowledge of the Tanakh (what Christians call the Old Testament), the Hebrew language, Jewish law, the writings of rabbinic sages, and the expositions of medieval

---

42. Byron L. Sherwin, *In Partnership with God* (Syracuse: Syracuse University Press, 1990), 51.

43. Jacob Neusner, *Rabbinic Literature and the New Testament: What We Cannot Show, We Do Not Know* (Eugene, OR: Wipf and Stock, 2004).

and modern scholars. These knowledgeable figures in the Jewish community would provide an intellectual and reasoned answer based on a combination of the founding texts of Judaism, subsequent debates of the rabbis, and current scientific knowledge. All of these voices, combined, serve as *the authoritative voice* for the Jewish people.

Here I will use one example to illustrate the dialectical approach in Judaism for establishing an official, or legal, position. An often-debated issue in Judaism is the role of women as communal leaders. On occasion, the conversation centers on whether a woman can serve as an authoritative judge to hear and adjudicate matters of law and practice. In the Hebrew Bible, the prophetess Deborah is called a *shaftah*—a judge or lawgiver—who served in that capacity for the entire Israelite people (Judg. 4:4–5). This seems authoritative enough—women can serve as judges. However, the rabbinic sages of late antiquity asked if, on the basis of Deborah's example, women in general can indeed serve as judges. Was Deborah an exception in this one case? One group of rabbis prohibited women from serving as judges for various reasons, while in another rabbinic source the issue is not raised at all, thus leaving the question open to further inquiry and debate.[44]

In the medieval and early modern periods, we find arguments both permitting and prohibiting women to serve as judges. Those who argued for permission cite the case of Deborah, and those who argued for prohibition cite the opinions of some of the rabbinic sages.[45] Some medieval commentators suggested that Deborah was an exception to the rule because she was a prophet—an extreme circumstance. The twelfth-century sage Maimonides understood from another biblical passage that positions of sovereignty are reserved for a "king," which is followed by explicit injunctions for male leaders (Deut. 17:14–20).[46] The implication for Maimonides is that leadership—including priests and judges—is reserved for males. In his ruling, Maimonides privileged the book of Deuteronomy over the book of Judges. For many Jews, Deuteronomy is more authoritative than the books of the prophets, because it is one of the five books of the Torah, the Law. Maimonides is universally recognized as the preeminent Jewish

---

44. Jerusalem Talmud, Sanhedrin 3:8, 21c; Yoma 6:1, 43b.

45. Aliza Bazak, "Women Serving as Judges: An Analysis of the Sources of the Law and Their Examination in Light of the History of Legal Interpretation Regarding Judgeship and Authority," in *To Be a Jewish Woman: Proceedings of the Third Biennial Conference 'A Woman and Her Judaism'* [Heb.], ed. Tova Cohen and Aliza Lavie (Jerusalem, 2005), 77–122.

46. Maimonides, *Hilkhot Melakhim*, 1:5

authority in matters of exegesis and halakhah (Jewish law). However, even he was not spared criticism. Later commentators challenged Maimonides; they questioned whether he had done justice to the "official" rulings in the Hebrew Scriptures, or if he had imposed his bias onto the biblical text.

The debate has continued today. Chana Henkin, founder and Dean of Nishmat, the Jeanie Schottenstein Center for Advanced Torah Study for Women in Jerusalem, wrote that women serving as judges "is *non-controversial*. Nowhere . . . is there an opinion [in the Torah] that [Jewish Law] prohibits in principle the issuing of a halakhic [i.e., legal] ruling by a woman."[47] She further argued that if an exception to the rule permitted Deborah to be a leader and judge, for whatever reason, could not the same argument be made today? Could not another exception be made that would permit a woman to be a judge? Henkin also quoted the authoritative wording of the Talmud to support her position. While the Talmud warns against an unqualified person being permitted to issue rulings, it also warns of the dangers of withholding a qualified person from issuing rulings. What if a woman was highly qualified to comment on Jewish law? Would she not be an ideal judge? What does gender have to do with anything?[48] According to this argument, how does a person acquire authority? The answer is *adequate knowledge on the subject*.

We could go on with examples of how rabbis and other Jews have conceptualized authority. Large volumes have dealt with this topic; however, Haas's essay and my short treatment in the few previous pages suffice for our purpose. In short, this particular "Jewish approach" is that (1) subjective miracles, spiritual feelings, or heavenly witnesses—although inspiring to experience—cannot be used to support a claim or to establish an authoritative position; (2) divine revelations, as at Mt. Sinai, often lacked specificity and leave room for interpretation—God generally provides broad parameters and only occasionally gives specifics; (3) God expects humans to participate in the process of seeking truth by wrestling with the particulars, which requires debate, deliberation, discussion, trial and error, and reliance on reasoned, human methods; (4) if we can't show it, we don't know it—meaning that on unrevealed matters, evidence must be provided to support a position; and (5) consequent to all of these points is that those steeped in Judaism and trained to employ methods of critical

---

47. Chanah Henkin, "Women and the Issuing of Halakhic Rulings," in *Jewish Legal Writings by Women*, ed. Micah D. Halpern and Chana Safrai (Jerusalem: Urim Publications, 1998), 284; emphasis in the original.

48. For the full argument, see Henkin, 278–87.

thinking (e.g., some rabbis, scholars, and other thinkers) are entrusted with playing a major role in formulating "official" Jewish legal matters and interpretation of scripture. Let me add that the situation within the community, as I have described above, broadly characterizes the Jewish people, although admittedly there have been and continue to be a diversity of thought.

A Latter-day Saint Dialectic Approach

I mentioned above that some traditions, like Judaism, make room for secondary authorities (scholars and legal experts) to help make sense of laws contained within the sacred texts. I mentioned that Latter-day Saints add a layer of authority (viz. prophets); but what about scholars and various other kinds of authorities (therapists, scientists, philosophers, and health professionals)? What role do they play for Latter-day Saints? Moreover, does a precedent exist within the Latter-day Saint tradition for employing a dialectical approach similar to what occurs in Jewish tradition? I have asked myself these questions for two decades. The answer I have reached is, yes, the various experts do play a role, and there is a precedent within our tradition for employing a dialectical approach. But in what realm and capacity is the dialectical approach appropriate? Many of my students and others are not confident in answering this question.

Elder Bruce R. McConkie interpreted the flood story as a scientific fact, and even criticized the "so-called geological" experts who concluded that a worldwide flood occurred over "ages of time" when in reality, "[it] occurred in a matter of a few short weeks," as suggested in scripture (at least according to McConkie's reading).[49] Elder John A. Widtsoe, a trained scientist, sided with current geological scholarship on the Flood over the biblical account: "It is doubtful whether the water in the sky and all the oceans would suffice to cover the earth so completely. . . . The scriptures must be read intelligently."[50] For McConkie, scripture is the superior authority over scientific theories, but for Widtsoe, current scientific scholarship was the superior authority in this case. Widtsoe's colleague in the Quorum of the Twelve, Elder James Talmage, agreed that Latter-day Saints must not necessarily privilege scripture over scientific scholarship: "We cannot sweep aside

---

49. Bruce R. McConkie, *Mormon Doctrine,* 2nd ed. (Salt Lake City: Bookcraft, 1966), 289.

50. John A. Widtsoe, *Evidences and Reconciliation: Aids to Faith in a Modern Day,* Vol. 1 (Salt Lake City: Bookcraft, 1943), 109–12.

all the accumulated knowledge in geology, archeology, or any other branch of science simply because our interpretation of some isolated passage of scripture may seem to be opposed thereto."[51] They are directly validating the contribution of science and critical thinking in the enterprise of establishing both truth and "official positions," even if those "official positions" are not institutional but personal positions.

I get a sense from my students and others that Latter-day Saints have been conditioned into an overreliance on prophets concerning every aspect of life, not just within the bounds of revelation, institutional policy, and administration of priesthood ordinances. Yes, Latter-day Saints believe that prophets—as stewards of priesthood ordinances and Church institution—hold certain keys to function in those capacities, but somehow many Latter-day Saints have extrapolated that narrowly defined role of prophets to all aspects of life. Many Latter-day Saints seem to think that Church leaders possess a vast knowledge of Church history and scripture that regular pew members do not. Perhaps many Latter-day Saints believe that God performs a revelatory data dump in their brains in the hours and days following their call to the apostleship.

About this, McConkie explained, "Though general authorities are authorities in the sense of having power to administer church affairs, they may or may not be authorities in the sense of doctrinal knowledge . . . or the receipt of the promptings of the Spirit." He further explained that simply being called into the apostleship "adds little knowledge or power of discernment to an individual."[52] Elder Boyd K. Packer echoed this sentiment when he said that unless a Church leader (in this case, bishops, stake high council members, stake presidents, and regional representatives) "knew the fundamental principles of the gospel before his call, he will scarcely have time to learn them along the way."[53] This also applies to prophets. In other words, the fifteen prophets fall on a spectrum similar to the general Church population in terms of their doctrinal understanding, ability to interpret scripture, and Church history knowledge. Some prophets might have a vast knowledgebase in these areas, while others, a very meager one. Thus, Latter-day Saints must not assume that apostles

---

51. Talmage, Letter to F. C. Williamson, April 22, 1933, Talmage Papers, 88, in L. Tom Perry Special Collections, Brigham Young University.

52. Bruce R. McConkie, "General Authority," *Mormon Doctrine* (Salt Lake City: Deseret Book, 1966), 309.

53. Boyd K. Packer, "Principles," *Ensign*, March 1985.

are all walking encyclopedias on all things doctrine, scripture, social issues, and history.

Joseph Smith was concerned that Latter-day Saints were depending too much on "the prophet" and, therefore, had become "darkened in their minds." He quoted a passage in Ezekiel to illustrate his point: "If the prophet be deceived when he hath spoken a thing . . . the punishment of the prophet shall be even as the punishment of him that seeketh unto him" (Ezek. 14:9–10).[54] This caution against relying too much on a prophet seems to stand against the aforementioned teaching by President Benson and others that Church members must always follow the prophet, even if the prophet is wrong. In fact, according to Joseph Smith, those who err because they followed the incorrect teachings of a Church leader will be punished as much as the prophet who led them. Similarly, Brigham Young lamented that Latter-day Saints were not judiciously considering leaders' teachings but were instead accepting them without question, and that they had adopted the counterproductive practice of mindlessly following the prophets: "I am fearful they settle down in a state of blind self-security, trusting their eternal destiny in the hands of their leaders with a reckless confidence."[55]

Near the end of the nineteenth century, Elder Charles W. Penrose distinguished between binding revelations and non-binding teachings: "President Wilford Woodruff is a man of wisdom and experience, and we respect him, but we do not believe his personal views or utterances are revelations from God."[56] In that same era, Elder George Q. Cannon, a counselor in three first presidencies, said, "The people who have embraced this Gospel have had to think for themselves. It is no light matter to become a 'Mormon.'"[57] On another occasion, Cannon was much more direct:

> Do not, brethren, put your trust in man though he be a Bishop, an Apostle, or a President; if you do, they will fail you at some time or place . . . but if we lean on God, He never will fail us. When men and women *depend on God alone and trust in Him alone*, their faith will not be shaken if the highest in

54. "Nauvoo Relief Society Minute Book," 51, The Joseph Smith Papers, accessed March 8, 2021, https://www.josephsmithpapers.org/paper-summary/nauvoo-relief-society-minute-book/48.

55. Brigham Young, "Eternal Punishment—'Mormonism' &c," January 12, 1862, *Journal of Discourses*, 9:150.

56. "The Doctrine of Revelation," *Millennial Star* 54, no. 12 (March 21, 1892): 191.

57. July 24, 1881, *Journal of Discourses*, 22:366.

the Church should step aside. . . . Perhaps it is His own design that faults and weaknesses *should appear in high places* in order that His Saints may learn to trust in Him and not in any man or woman.[58]

In the 1940s, a message was published in the Church's *Improvement Era* magazine that advocated for a complete and unquestioning reliance on Church leaders: "When our leaders speak, the thinking has been done." However, the president of the Church at the time, George Albert Smith, explicitly rejected this idea in a letter to the editor: "Even to imply that members of the Church are not to do their own thinking is grossly to misrepresent the true ideal of the Church."[59] Despite President Smith's rejection, the "thinking has been done" mentality seems to be the dominant view among Church members today. As noted earlier, President Joseph Fielding Smith empowered each member in the 1950s to accept judiciously the directives of prophets as long as they are congruous with scripture, and if they are not, then "every member of the Church is duty-bound to reject it."[60] The always-colorful Elder J. Golden Kimball expressed a similar principle in general conference:

> Some people fancy that because we have the Presidency and Apostles of the Church that they will do the thinking for us. There are men and women so mentally lazy that they hardly think for themselves. To think calls for effort, which makes some men tired and wearies their souls. No man or woman can remain in this Church on borrowed light.[61]

Many Latter-day Saints downplay the individual-authority paradigm by rushing to Doctrine and Covenants 1:38: "My word shall not pass away, but shall all be fulfilled, whether by mine own voice or by the voice of my servants, it is the same." This passage is often interpreted to mean that whatever the prophets say, especially from the pulpit, is the same as if God said it. The passage, however, does not make this claim. It clearly states that God's word will be fulfilled—his prophecies will be fulfilled—regardless of whether God himself spoke the prophecies or revealed them to prophets who then spoke them. Furthermore, "servants" is not referring

---

58. "Knowledge of and Dependence on God," *Millennial Star* 53, no. 42 (October 19, 1891): 658–59, quoted in *Gospel Truth: Discourses and Writings of President George Q. Cannon* (Salt Lake City: Deseret, 1974), 1:319; emphasis added.

59. President George Albert Smith, Letter to Dr. J. Raymond Cope, December 7, 1945, cited in "A 1945 Perspective," *Dialogue: A Journal of Mormon Thought* 19, no. 1 (Spring 1986): 38.

60. Joseph Fielding Smith, *Doctrines of Salvation*, 3:203–204.

61. J. Golden Kimball, *Conference Report*, April 1904, 97.

exclusively to prophets. The title of "servant" is found 380 times in the Doctrine and Covenants, and many of them are connected with figures who were not apostles or prophets (like missionaries and others who worked to build the Church).

Likewise, Latter-day Saints frequently appeal to President Ezra Taft Benson's 1980 BYU devotional address, "Fourteen Fundamentals in Following the Prophet." Among his fourteen points were: "The living prophet is more vital to us than the standard works"; "The prophet will never lead the Church astray"; "The prophet is not required to have any particular earthly training or diplomas to speak on *any subject* or act on any matter at any time"; and "The prophet may well advise on civic matters."[62] Benson expanded, it seems, the role of prophets far beyond what previous prophets had done, claiming that they can speak authoritatively on any subject at any time, including politics, and they are not required to inform their listeners that they are, indeed, speaking for God. For Benson, the current President's positions were both absolute and infallible, trumping both prior prophets and scripture. This talk was instantly popular with many Latter-day Saints. According to Benson's biographer, within two weeks of his speech, over six hundred requests for copies had come to Benson's office.[63] His talk has been repeated many times since then, including twice in the 2010 general conference, wherein two members of the Seventy repeated all of Elder Benson's fourteen points.[64]

This talk, however, stirred controversy, even in the national media.[65] Not only have several of Benson's points been challenged by other apostles, the Church's president at the time, Spencer W. Kimball, was agitated by the speech. Kimball's son and biographer wrote, "Spencer felt concern about the talk, wanting to protect the church against being misunderstood as espousing . . . unthinking 'follow the leader' mentality."[66] Following his speech, the First Presidency called Benson to stand before

---

62. Ezra Taft Benson, "Fourteen Fundamentals," February 26, 1980.

63. Sheri Dew, *Ezra Taft Benson: A Biography* (Salt Lake City: Deseret Book, 1987), 469.

64. Claudio R. M. Costa, "Obedience to the Prophets," General Conference, October 2010; Kevin R. Duncan, "Our Very Survival," General Conference, October 2010.

65. "What Mormons Believe," *Newsweek* 96 (September 1, 1980): 71; "Thus Saith Ezra Benson," *Newsweek* 98 (October 19, 1981): 109.

66. See Edward Kimball, *Lengthen Your Stride: The Presidency of Spencer W. Kimball: Working Draft* (Salt Lake City: Benchmark Books, 2009), chapter 16,

all general authorities on two occasions to explain, justify, and apologize for his statements; some "were dissatisfied with his response."[67] The day after his devotional speech at BYU, the First Presidency's spokesperson, Don LeFevre, commented to the press that it is "simply not true" that the President's "word is law on all issues."[68]

The notion that prophets are not necessarily the end-all-be-all in identifying and establishing "official positions" on a host of unrevealed matters is combined with some examples of prophets and scholars working *together* in the pursuit of truth, similar to the Jewish experience. In 2010, Church leaders sent a general authority Seventy and a historian to speak to the group of Swedish Saints who were struggling in their faith convictions. They spent several hours discussing doctrine, scripture, and Church history; the historian did most of the talking.[69] In 2012, Elder Boyd K. Packer directed a group to write scholarly essays on difficult gospel topics that were driving people out of the Church. These eleven essays were written by scholars between 2013 and 2015 that the apostles later approved to be included on the Church's website.[70] Elder Quinton L. Cook invited two scholars to join him in a 2018 young adult Q&A broadcast. Throughout the broadcast, Cook deferred to the scholars to answer historical questions. Cook's role was to offer a general apostolic testimony of the Church and its major doctrines.[71] It was not assumed that the apostle in this setting knew all the answers.

As we saw above, this parallels the practice, almost two thousand years old, within Judaism. However, adopting such an approach is not

---

page 13, in CD ROM included with Edward Kimball, *Lengthen Your Stride: The Presidency of Spencer W. Kimball* (Salt Lake City: Deseret Book, 2005).

67. See Kimball, *Lengthen Your Stride,* chapter 16, page 13; Dew, *Ezra Taft Benson,* 469; Woodward, "What Mormons Believe," 71; D. Michael Quinn, *The Mormon Hierarchy: Extensions of Power* (Salt Lake City: Signature Books, 1997), 111, 449fn, 353.

68. Kimball, *Lengthen Your Stride,* chapter 16, page 13. For more details and sources about the aftermath of Benson's address, see Matthew L. Harris, *Watchman on the Tower: Ezra Taft Benson and the Making of the Mormon Right* (Salt Lake City: University of Utah Press, 2020), 102–3, footnotes 105–12 on page 186.

69. Matthew L. Harris and Newell G. Bringhurst, *The LDS Gospel Topics Series: A Scholarly Engagement* (Salt Lake City: Signature Books, 2020), 1–2.

70. For the essays, see https://www.churchofjesuschrist.org/study/manual/gospel-topics-essays; for the backstory, see Harris and Bringhurst, *Gospel Topics,* 2–19.

71. Worldwide Devotional for Young Adults: A Face to Face with Elder Cook, Sept. 9, 2018, https://www.youtube.com/watch?v=kpLN6AomRQY.

without massive challenges. A few years ago, I heard a tenured BYU professor (speaking to a group of about two hundred, many of whom were students) say, "In other religions, the scholars lead the way and the clergy follow, but in our religion we have prophets who lead—scholars only contribute in little ways." It is no wonder that Church members, certainly our youth and young adults, are often confused about authority and identifying truth. This professor was conflating two very different endeavors: (1) Church administration and revealed knowledge, and (2) the enterprise of scholarship. Those sustained as prophets are expected to lead the way in Church administrative affairs (including priesthood ordinances); scholars lead the way in scholarship. Elders D. Todd Christofferson and M. Russell Ballard have addressed this very issue. Christofferson explained in 2012:

> In some faith traditions, theologians claim equal teaching authority with the ecclesiastical hierarchy, and doctrinal matters may become a contest of opinions between them. . . . Others place primary emphasis on the reasoning of post-apostolic theologians or on biblical hermeneutics and exegesis. We value scholarship that enhances understanding, but in the Church today, just as anciently, establishing the doctrine of Christ or correcting doctrinal deviations is a matter of divine revelation to those the Lord endows with apostolic authority.[72]

Notice Christofferson's clarification: prophets are the primary authority on doctrinal matters that have been solved by "divine revelation" (we might also add institutional policy and administration of priesthood ordinances). In my reading of it, prophets are not the primary authority on matters that fall outside this realm. In 2017, Elder Ballard seemed to want to correct the often-conflated roles of prophets and scholars when he emphasized the importance of seeking out appropriate authorities given the specific context:

> I am a general authority, but *that doesn't make me an authority in general.* My calling and life's experiences allow me to respond to certain types of questions. There are other types of questions that require an expert in the specific subject matter. This is exactly what I do when I need an answer to such questions. *I seek others including those with degrees and expertise in such fields. I worry sometimes that members expect too much from Church leaders* and teachers, expecting them to be experts in subjects well beyond their duties

---

72. D. Todd Christofferson, "The Doctrine of Christ," General Conference, April 2012, https://www.churchofjesuschrist.org/study/general-conference/2012/04/the-doctrine-of-christ.

and responsibilities. . . . Our [i.e., apostles'] primary duty is to build up the church, teach the doctrine of Christ, and help those in need of our help.[73]

Some might think Ballard would seek out "experts" only on matters unrelated to religion and scriptural interpretation; after all, haven't many Latter-day Saints been conditioned to think that prophets *are* the experts on religion and scriptural interpretation? This is what I and all of my companions taught on the mission: we need prophets to interpret scripture for us so that we can know the truth. According to our narrative, the reason why thousands of religions exist, many of which are based on the Bible, is because we didn't have prophets interpreting scripture for us, but now we do as of 1830. Note, however, that in a 2015 address, Ballard explicitly mentioned scripture as one area in which he seeks out "trained scholars" for clarification:

> When I have a question that I cannot answer, I turn to those who can help me. The Church is blessed with trained scholars and those who have devoted a lifetime of study, who have come to know our history and the scriptures. These thoughtful men and women provide context and background so we can better understand our sacred past and our current practices.[74]

I am not sure that a Church leader could be clearer on the limitations and boundaries of the role of prophets; yet it seems that a significant portion of Latter-day Saints too often default to asking the prophets, "What's the Church's official position on this?" even if the issue has not been solved by revelation and has nothing to do with institutional administrative policy or priesthood ordinances.

So what would this dialectical approach to establishing an authoritative position look like in a Latter-day Saint context? Let's examine a few topics the way Jews have fruitfully debated the case of Deborah.

---

73. Elder M. Russell Ballard, "Questions and Answers," BYU Devotional, November 14, 2017, https://speeches.byu.edu/talks/m-russell-ballard/questions -and-answers/; emphasis added.

74. Elder M. Russell Ballard, "To the Saints in the Utah South Area," September 13, 2015, https://www.lds.org/prophets-and-apostles/unto-all- the-world/to-the-saints-in-the-utah-south-area?; Elder Ballard made similar comments in his 2016 CES fireside, "The Opportunities and Responsibilities of CES Teachers in the 21st Century," on February 26, 2016, in the Salt Lake Tabernacle, https://www.churchofjesuschrist.org/broadcasts/article/evening-with -a-general-authority/2016/02/the-opportunities-and-responsibilities-of-ces- teachers-in-the-21st-century.

The first issue is whether Isaiah 7:14 refers to Jesus. Latter-day Saint scholars have debated this issue quite aggressively. Joseph Spencer (BYU Religious Education professor), in his 2016 book on Isaiah in the Book of Mormon, posited that Isaiah does not directly refer to Jesus, but rather to a child born to a "young woman" living at the time of Isaiah. For Spencer, the direct historical context does not allow for Jesus to be part of the equation in this particular prophecy, although he does allow for the possibility that this passage might act as a type for Jesus.[75] In 2020, Donald Parry (BYU professor of Hebrew in the Department of Asian and Near Eastern Languages) challenged Spencer's conclusion. Parry did not provide counterevidence within the context of Isaiah 7; he instead appealed to the Gospel of Matthew, which states that Isaiah 7:14 does refer to Jesus (Matt. 1:21–23).[76] Spencer's preemptive response to such an argument was, "It's entirely possible that [the author of Matthew] read the passage messianically," not that Isaiah 7 was necessarily messianic.[77] After quoting Matthew, Parry cited, as evidence to support his claim, four Latter-day Saint prophets who used Isaiah 7 to describe Jesus—not that they were authoritatively declaring that Isaiah 7 referred to Jesus.[78] Parry then made a case that one must know Biblical Hebrew at an advanced level in order to adequately interpret Isaiah,[79] which Spencer does not. This was an intriguing retort given that Parry did not actually appeal to Hebrew linguistic and textual evidence to make the case specifically for Jesus in Isaiah 7, but he appealed to the author of Matthew and four Latter-day Saint apostles. Note that none of these four apostles know biblical Hebrew, and none of them claimed that they were transmitting a divinely revealed interpretation.

In a very Jewish fashion, Joshua Sears (BYU Religious Education professor) entered the debate by writing a response to Parry's review.[80] He listed the arguments of both Spencer and Parry, and claimed that Parry

---

75. Joseph M. Spencer, *The Vision of All: Twenty-Five Lectures on Isaiah in Nephi's Record* (Salt Lake City: Greg Kofford Books, 2016), 209–210.

76. Donald W. Parry, "An Approach to Isaiah Studies," *Interpreter: A Journal of Latter-day Saint Faith and Scholarship* 34 (2020): 245–64 (esp. 250).

77. Spencer actually wrote this about Nephi, but the same logic could be applied to the author of Matthew, which Spencer himself acknowledged. Spencer, *The Vision of All*, 2010.

78. Parry, "An Approach to Isaiah Studies," 251–52.

79. Parry, 258–63.

80. Joshua M. Sears, "An Other Approach to Isaiah Studies," *Interpreter: A Journal of Latter-day Saint Faith and Scholarship* 37 (2020), 1–20.

misrepresented Spencer. According to Parry, Spencer in no way sees Jesus in Isaiah. Sears pointed out that Spencer does allow for the possibility of a dual meaning, one of which refers to Jesus. Sears also mentioned that Parry did not allow for a dual meaning of Isaiah 7 in his review of Spencer, but that elsewhere, Parry did argue that Isaiah 7 can be interpreted for an eighth-century BCE audience, but that this was a secondary meaning, the primary meaning being a reference to Jesus.[81] Since Parry used quotes from apostles in his argument, Sears used the same method to challenge Parry. He cited Elder Dallin H. Oaks, among others, who wrote, "The book of Isaiah contains numerous prophecies that seem to have multiple fulfillments. One seems to involve the people of Isaiah's day or the circumstances of the next generation. Another meaning, often symbolic, seems to refer to events in the meridian of time [i.e., Jesus's day]."[82] Here, Oaks seems to acknowledge that the more practical reading is that Isaiah 7 directly refers to events in Isaiah's own day, and only "symbolically" refers to Jesus's time—the implication being that the second reading is more hidden and spiritual, rather than direct and practical. Thus, one could leave Jesus completely out of Isaiah 7 and remain intellectually honest.

This discussion of Isaiah 7:14 illustrates that there is no "official interpretation" by the Church that solves this issue. Several prophets have discussed this verse, but one cannot simply appeal to one of their sermons to settle the debate. There are different opinions and nuances that must be considered, and the dialectical process of scholars and others can be a productive way to reach an authoritative position, while acknowledging that this position might shift as more evidence and considerations enter the equation.

A second example is Jesus's place of burial. When I take tour groups to Israel, we always visit the Garden Tomb. When I explain that scholars conclude that this could not be the site of Jesus's burial, sometimes a tourist asks, "But didn't a few prophets say that this site is where Jesus was buried?" Well, yes, some of them did make this claim: Harold B. Lee: "We felt it was definitely the place";[83] Gordon B. Hinckley: "We felt that we

---

81. Sears, 10.

82. Dallin H. Oaks, "Scripture Reading and Revelation," *Ensign* 25, no. 1, January 1995, 8.

83. Harold B. Lee, "Qualities of Leadership," address to the Latter-day Saints Student Association (LDSSA) Convention, August 1970. As cited in David B. Galbraith, D. Kelly Ogden, and Andrew C. Skinner, *Jerusalem: The Eternal City* (Salt Lake City: Deseret Book, 1996), 506.

were standing where the risen Lord had talked with Mary";[84] Spencer W. Kimball: "I feel quite sure that this is the place where His body was laid."[85]

I have often grappled with this issue as a scholar. Should I simply agree with these prophets without conducting my own research, as so many others do? What if the evidence shows otherwise? Am I bound to accept these statements as absolute revelatory fact? How have Latter-day Saints traditionally reacted to and utilized these statements from apostles? They have often used them to settle a non-revelatory, academic debate. For example, on one LDS discussion board in 2018, a debate ensued about the authenticity of the Holy Sepulcher location. After a long back and forth, with many links to biblical archaeologists, one participant wrote, "I find no good evidence to support any belief that The Church of the Holy Sepulchre is the site of Jesus's burial. Perhaps you [addressing his interlocutor] just believe that Constantine was more inspired than God's prophets? You do know that a LDS Church President felt the garden tomb was a likely spot for His burial, right?"[86]

Similarly, a Latter-day Saint scholar in 2005 reviewed the evidence for each supposed site of Jesus's tomb. After providing the evidence against the Garden Tomb location, the author negated the evidence by appealing to statements from Church leaders: "It must be noted, however, that latter-day prophets who have visited sites in the Holy Land have voiced some strong and impressive feelings about . . . the Garden Tomb."[87] Another scholar in 2003, while discussing Jesus's death, provided the evidence for and against each burial site. After reviewing the scholarly evidence against the Garden Tomb location, the author similarly negated the evidence by appealing to an apostle's statement: "These objections, and others, have persuaded the majority of scholars to reject the Garden Tomb as a candidate for the actual execution and burial site of Jesus. Latter-day Saints will, however, recall President Harold B. Lee's response to and comment

84. *Church News*, December 16, 1972, "Holy Land Tour Thrills, President Lee, Elder Hinckley," 12.

85. *Church News,* November 3, 1979, section 5.

86. Mormon Dialogue and Discussion Board, September 6, 2018, https://wayback.archive-it.org/3613/20191018093916/http:/www.mormondialogue.org/topic/70994-the-cross-and-religious-symbols/page/5/.

87. Andrew Skinner, *The Garden Tomb* (Salt Lake City: Deseret Book, 2005), 24–25.

on the Garden Tomb after a visit to Jerusalem." The author then provides the quote from the leader.[88]

Rather than settling this academic debate by defaulting to a few impressions from prophets, I suggest that we consider employing a dialectical approach using all methods of critical inquiry before drawing conclusions. Based on the aforementioned statements from Church leaders about the limitations of their own prophetic role, we might ask a few questions: Are these prophets experts in biblical archaeology? Did they claim to receive an unmistakable revelation from God on the location of Jesus's burial? Would these prophets have likely adjusted their conclusions based on new and scholarly information? Remember that Elder Talmage cautioned to not "sweep aside all the accumulated knowledge in geology, archeology, or any other branch of science simply because our interpretation . . . may seem to be opposed thereto."[89] In this case, archaeologists have determined through their method of science quite convincingly that the Garden Tomb was not a newly cut, first-century style tomb where "no man had been laid" (Matt. 27:60; John 19:41).

The Garden Tomb looks nothing like the other first-century tombs in the Land of Israel, nor do any of the tombs in the immediate area. Its structure and features closely resemble tombs in the eighth century BCE (seven hundred years before Jesus!). The first person to popularize this location was a British traveler Charles Gordon in 1883. No early Christian tradition places Jesus's burial in this area, which is significant because they tended to be highly conscious about preserving locations associated with Jesus. One BYU professor and biblical archaeologist, Jeffery Chadwick, who has been conducting archaeological surveys in the Bible lands for four decades, has concluded that the data does not support the Garden Tomb as being a viable candidate for a first-century tomb where Jesus would have been buried.[90]

These two brief examples illustrate how a dialectic approach can be utilized in the Latter-day Saint tradition on matters that fall outside of

---

88. Cecilia M. Peek, "The Burial," in Thomas Wayment and Richard Neitzel Holzapfel, *From the Last Supper through the Resurrection* (Salt Lake City: Deseret Book, 2003), 338–78 (quote from 376).

89. Talmage, Letter to F. C. Williamson, April 22, 1933, Talmage Papers, 88, in L. Tom Perry Special Collections, Brigham Young University.

90. See a brief treatment in Jerome Murphy-O'Conner and Barry Cunliffe, *The Holy Land: Oxford Archaeological Guides* (Oxford: Oxford University Press, 1998), 141; Jeffery R. Chadwick, "Revisiting Golgotha and the Garden Tomb," *Religious Educator* 4, no. 1 (2003): 13–48.

Church policy and administration of priesthood ordinances. Like the rabbis and scholars who debated the case of Deborah using various and sundry types of evidence, Latter-day Saints can do the same. These topics should be debated because they have not been settled unmistakably by revelation. Well-trained and knowledgeable individuals, then, have a role to play in establishing "official positions," even if the "official position" is that there is no "official position" and, therefore, the debate must continue. Joseph Smith taught that in July 1843, "One of the grand fundamental principles of Mormonism is to receive truth. Let it come from whence it may."[91] Brigham Young similarly maintained that being a Latter-day Saint means that "if you can find a truth in heaven, earth, or hell, it belongs to our doctrine. We believe it; it is ours; we claim it."[92] The implication, at least for me, is that Latter-day Saints look to various sources for truth, whether it be prophets, popes, pastors, philosophers, therapists, scientists, health professionals, or various other thinkers and experts. President Oaks provided his thoughts on this issue, some of which echo the Jewish experience: "I only teach the general rules. Whether an exception applies to you is your responsibility. You must work that out individually."[93]

As presented near the beginning of this essay, several of my colleagues concluded that identifying "doctrine," "truth," or "official teachings" must involve the following criteria (although many of them fail to state whether the entire criteria must be applied simultaneously or if only one criterion would suffice in a given case):

- Is repeatedly affirmed in the standard works (i.e., canonized scripture)
- Is found in *recent* official declarations or proclamations
- Is repeatedly taught in *recent* general conferences or in other official gatherings by general Church leaders
- Is found in *recent* general handbooks or approved curriculum of the Church

---

91. Nauvoo address, 9 July 1843, "Journal, December 1842–June 1844; Book 2, 10 March 1843–14 July 1843," p. [302], The Joseph Smith Papers, accessed March 15, 2021, https://www.josephsmithpapers.org/paper-summary/journal-december-1842-june-1844-book-2-10-march-1843-14-july-1843/310.

92. Journal of Discourses 13:335.

93. Dallin H. Oaks, "Dating versus Hanging Out," May 1, 2005, young adult fireside, https://www.churchofjesuschrist.org/study/ensign/2006/06/dating-versus-hanging-out.

- Is taught by the repeated or united voice of the brethren
- Is time tested—perpetuated over time by leaders of the Church
- Is eternal and unchanging
- Is salvific (i.e., essential for salvation)
- Is confirmed by the Holy Spirit

I wish not to misrepresent my colleagues, so I must emphasize that not every proposed criteria mentioned near the beginning of this essay includes all of these points. I simply lumped all of my colleagues' criteria together because there was significant overlap between them and because it allows for a broad view as I discuss them in general terms.

In my assessment, statements from prophets that fall within this list are "official positions" for what Latter-day Saints generally believe and emphasize *today*. However, the sets of criteria from my colleagues appear to be insufficient for ensuring that one can confidently identify authoritative statements for what is ultimate and timeless social, theological, or historical truths—as opposed to the biases and philosophies of humans. We will not deal with the first criterion (*repeatedly affirmed in scripture*) here. But let's examine the few subsequent points: true doctrine is found in recent declarations, proclamations, handbooks, and general conferences (or official gatherings by general Church leaders).

First, Latter-day Saints would need to be able to define "recent," "declarations," and "official gatherings." Even if an average, church-going Latter-day Saint could adequately define these terms, why would they need to privilege what is "recent"? Birth control was once forbidden (or strongly discouraged) but not now. Was it once doctrine (i.e., "recently" taught in those generations) but no longer? People of African descent were thought to be cursed and not valiant in the preexistence by leaders in prior generations; this has now been explicitly rejected by Church leaders. Cannot something be true even if it was taught in only one generation? And vice-versa, cannot something be false if it was taught in multiple generations? What if something is taught by the "united voice of the brethren" but then later disavowed by a different set of "united voices" (such as with teachings on race or Brigham's understanding of the nature of God that was supported by every apostle except one, which was later rejected by every apostle from Joseph F. Smith to the present)? We could go on, but the point is made. Each criterion on my colleagues' list is insufficient by itself; therefore, no one criterion by itself can be applied to determine whether a particular claim is either true or an "official position," a point on which my colleagues would probably agree.

If all the previous criteria of my colleagues are insufficient, in my opinion, then what do I utilize in answering a question about truth or the Church's official position on X or Y? It depends on the type of question I am dealing with. If I want to know what "the Church" emphasizes today, regardless of whether it is a divine truth, then I would apply one (or all) of the sets of criteria proposed by my colleagues. Those are the best sources (i.e., recent manuals, conference talks, and handbooks) for determining what is emphasized currently among Latter-day Saints. If I am dealing with questions about administrative policy or priesthood ordinances, then I would also consult the sources mentioned in my colleagues' criteria. The prophets and other general Church leaders are, indeed, stewards and administrators of the institution, its priesthood, and its ordinances.

The more confusing questions, however, are theological, social, historical, and scriptural in nature. Other than the primary, most important doctrines, my students are asking questions like: Can we watch R-rated movies? Should we pay tithing on gross, net, or surplus income? Should women stay at home or can they pursue graduate education and a career? Is birth control prohibited? Is interracial marriage discouraged? Is the earth six thousand years old or millions of years old (a question that has implications for what Latter-day Saint parents teach their children about the age of the earth and evolution given their curriculum in public schools)? These types of questions, and thousands more, have been answered in different ways (including contradictory ones) by Church leaders.

Thus, I suggest to my students and others that when I wonder if a particular piece of information is true or wonder what "the Church's official position" is—whether it be theological, historical, sociological, psychological, political, archaeological, anthropological, geographical, geological, biological, astronomical, or any other "ical"—then I employ two criteria. First, I ask myself, has this issue been answered and solved by revelation, or is this issue relevant to administration of the priesthood or institutional policy? Second, if the answer is "no," and I want to formulate an "official position" for myself, then I employ a dialectical approach. I use my brain. I debate and search.

Nowhere in my colleagues' criteria above do we find anything about the utilization of science, scholarship, and rational thinking when discerning whether a piece of information is true, or might be an "official position" of the Church. Most of my colleagues favor a framework of using a combination of scripture, prophets' teachings, and confirmation from the

Holy Spirit. However, I am proposing that we include a fourth factor: the dialectical approach. We do as Elder Ballard counseled: we consult experts who have authority (via their training), and then we search, concentrate, read, study, consult more experts, reread, question, debate, and think.[94] And that is the point!

Consulting prophets on non-revelatory matters, or on issues that fall outside of institutional policies and functions, is like asking a lawyer for medical advice or a medical professional for legal advice. Yes, someone might argue that my criterion of using scholarship, science, and reason to discover truth or establish personal "official positions" is also flawed. After all, how many scholars and scientists have "gotten it wrong"? My response is that, indeed, scholars, doctors, and other experts are *often* wrong, but prophets have also gotten things wrong, especially when they weren't "acting as prophets." Thus, we should not pit prophets against experts in contests for who is right or wrong. Everyone is fallible. However, while flawed, the intellectual approaches—the critical methods of scholarship, the peer review process, the debates—are best positioned to get us closer to truth than biased and flawed human thinking, personal feelings, social customs, traditions of the fathers, faith-promoting rumors, and unsubstantiated claims. All branches of science and scholarship are better at helping us identify what we know and don't know about a particular subject than are handbooks, hymnbooks, declarations, unrevealed teachings in ecclesiastical sermons, or official pamphlets. If a particular topic has not been settled unmistakably by revelation, then we are left with critical thinking.

In my understanding, it seems that several prophets are stressing that members must know *when* to follow the prophets and *when* to take their statements as truth or "official positions." And what seems to be the answer? To *always* follow the prophets *only when* they are acting as prophets. Joseph Smith counseled as much: "I . . . visited with a brother and sister . . . who thought that 'a prophet is always a prophet'; but I told them that a prophet was a prophet only when he was acting as such."[95] In January 2018, in his first press conference as the new President of the Church, Russell M. Nelson made this bold declaration: "Every member needs to

---

94. Elder Russell Ballard, "Questions and Answers," BYU Devotional, November 14, 2017, https://speeches.byu.edu/talks/m-russell-ballard/questions -and-answers/; emphasis added.

95. "History, 1838–1856, volume D-1 [1 August 1842–1 July 1843]," p. 1464, The Joseph Smith Papers, https://www.josephsmithpapers.org/paper-summary/ history-1838-1856-volume-d-1-1-august-1842-1-july-1843/107.

know the difference between what is doctrine and what is human. . . . Give your leaders a little leeway to make mistakes as you hope your leaders will give you a little leeway to profit by your errors."[96]

In sum, I have tried to take what I perceive as a general phenomenon among Jews, which is that the authoritative voice for seeking or identifying truth is a dialectical approach, not solely an appeal to ecclesiastical leaders. I utilized Haas's paper as a guide and attempted to argue that Latter-day Saints also have a precedent in our tradition for appealing to a dialectical approach to answer unrevealed doctrinal, theological, and historical questions, as opposed to appealing to leaders simply because they are leaders.

Furthermore, I have done my best at allowing my position to be shaped by how the prophets have talked about the limitations of their own authority. As a scholar of religion and a man of faith who has wrestled with the question of authority for two decades, who has students who frequently raise concerns about this issue, and who is raising five children of his own, I am simply attempting to propose a criteria for my students that will help them to know *when* to follow prophets versus when to employ a dialectical approach to establish their own "official positions."

Some might wonder how Latter-day Saints might learn from Judaism on this issue since Jews don't currently have a priesthood hierarchy with a president–prophet at its head. My response is that I am *only* comparing the non-revelatory aspects of our faith tradition with the non-revelatory aspects of Judaism. Both religions have scriptural texts that are believed to be revelatory. Both religions have statements of dead prophets that are quoted and consulted in order to answer questions of religious expectations. Both religions wrestle with questions that have unrevealed answers.

I stress that my position must not be taken to the extreme. I wish not to convey that Latter-day Saints must always be radical skeptics and reject every suggestion by bishops or prophets unless they provide a written revelation. But perhaps we should be a bit more sophisticated in our thinking about why we are doing what we are doing. If the answer is, "Because that's what we're told to do," then we are not following the prophets, because many of them have specifically warned that such an approach is inappropriate. It is ironic, then, that a hyper-literal interpretation of "following the prophets" itself isn't following the prophets.

---

96. "First Presidency News Conference," The Church of Jesus Christ of Latter-day Saints, January 16, 2018, accessed on May 25, 2020, https://www.youtube.com/watch?v=C8Cd3vcWYnc. The following link includes a time stamp for the exact quote, https://www.youtube.com/watch?v=C8Cd3vcWYnc&t=2373s.

Approaching God:
A Jewish Approach to Prayer[1]

Peter Knobel

The power of Jewish prayer is derived from the liturgy that is found in the daily and festival prayer book called the *siddur*. The prayers have an order and a structure that locates the individual within the more than four thousand years of Jewish history. The experience of prayer defies straightforward description. It is best understood through engaging in prayer. For Jews, the words of the *siddur* are indispensable, but genuine prayer depends on the worshipper's attitude and frame of mind, the skill of the prayer leader, and the strength of the praying community.[2]

A central issue for Jews is how to make required texts that are repeated thrice daily into genuine prayer.[3] While there is great emphasis on communal worship in Judaism, private spontaneous prayer is not only appropriate but encouraged. Jews frequently use the prayers from the *siddur* when they feel a need to pray. Also, within the required prayers there are places for the worshipper to insert his or her own petitions.

Following the destruction of the Temple in Jerusalem in 70 CE, prayer replaced sacrifice as the dominant mode of worship in Judaism.[4] The synagogue and the home are the main venues for worship, although a Jew can

1. Lawrence A. Hoffman, *The Way into Jewish Prayer* (Woodstock, VT: Jewish Lights, 2000) is an excellent, not overly technical introduction to Jewish prayer. He has also edited a multivolume commentary on the prayer book called *My People's Prayer Book*, also published by Jewish Lights. This multi-layered commentary provides insights into the history and meaning of the prayers.

2. Peter S. Knobel and Daniel S. Schechter, "What Congregants Want in Worship Perceptions from a CCAR Study," *CCAR Journal: A Reform Jewish Quarterly* 53:3 (Winter 2006): 35–48. While the study was limited to worshipers in Reform Congregations, it is clear that many of the same issues are experienced by worshippers in other denominations.

3. See the discussion under section *Keva* and *Kavanah*.

4. Torah study worship and deeds of loving kindness were also considered forms of worship; see *Pirkei Avot* 1:2. The word worship (*avodah*) in Hebrew originally referred to the Temple Service. After the destruction of the Temple, it

pray anywhere. The rabbis in the Mishnah and the Talmud created the basic rubrics of Jewish prayer[5] that eventually become codified in the *siddur*.[6] The *siddur* continued to develop mostly through additions until the modern period, when Reform Judaism emerged in the eighteenth century with its hallmark of prayer book reform. Today, Judaism is divided into four streams or denominations: Orthodox, Conservative, Reform, and Reconstructionist.[7] The *siddurim* (plural of *siddur*) of each group contain the same basic rubrics. However, each denominational *siddur* reflects the theology of the denomination and attempts to make prayers meaningful with commentaries, instructions on practice, translations, transliteration, and new texts. This is especially true of the Reform and Reconstructionist *siddurim*.[8] When Jews pray, they use the *siddur*. It may be a denominational prayer book or one created by the congregation to which they belong, but Jewish prayer is dependent largely on the *siddur*. For this reason and others, Judaism is a text-based religion.

As Rabbi Richard Sarason, professor of liturgy at the Hebrew Union College Jewish Institute of Religion, points out:

> Judaism's most basic textbook, it is often remarked, is neither the Bible nor the Talmud. It is rather the siddur, the Jewish prayer book, with which all traditionally practicing Jews interact at least three times every day. As the script for liturgical performance, the prayer book gives expression to the most fundamental Jewish communal aspirations, needs, beliefs, and values. By voicing its words and ritually enacting them in a communal liturgical space,

---

was understood as prayer. "Joshua ben Levi said, 'Prayer (meaning the Amidah) replaced sacrifice.'" *Babylonian Talmud Berakhot* 32b.

5. The main discussions are found in the Tractate *Berachot* in both the Mishnah and the Talmud.

6. Ismar Elbogen, *Jewish Liturgy: A Comprehensive History*, trans. Raymond P. Scheindlin (Philadelphia: Jewish Publication Society, 1993) is the classic work. On more recent research, see Ruth Langer, *Jewish Liturgy A Guide to Research* (Lanham, MD: Rowman Littlefield, 2015).

7. Within each of the streams, there are subgroups. For example, among the Orthodox there are Hasidim, Modern Orthodox, and Open Orthodox. They each use the same *siddur* with some variations. Each of the other streams has its own *siddur*, but within each group there are some congregations or subgroups that have created their own.

8. This will be explored later in the chapter.

each individual Jew ideally becomes energized to live out Jewish values in daily life: this is how worship, at its best, "works."[9]

Rabbi Lawrence Hoffman, the preeminent authority on liturgy and prayer in the Reform movement, offers a similar evaluation of the importance of prayer and liturgy:

> Prayer is a delivery system for committing us to the great ideas that make life worth living, because ideas that are ritually construed empower us to do what we would otherwise never have the courage to do. Prayer moves us to see our lives more clearly against the backdrop of eternity, concentrating our attention on verities that we would otherwise forget. It imparts Judaism's canon of great concepts and moves us to live our lives by them.[10]

Prayer is a *mitzvah* (commandment) in Judaism.[11] There are prescribed times and prescribed words. The required prayers may be recited privately, but there are some prayers that can only be recited in the presence of a *minyan* (a quorum of ten adults over thirteen years of age).[12] Thus, there is a strong emphasis on communal prayer in Judaism.

The proliferation of texts and practices presents a unique challenge to the discussion of prayer in Judaism. This chapter begins with an analysis of the structure and some content of the *siddur* used by Jews for daily, Sabbath, and festival worship. This is not meant to be a comprehensive analysis of the *siddur* but to point out features of the service relevant to the discussion of the meaning of prayer. The chapter examines some key units of the daily services.[13] Following the discussion of the *siddur*, the chapter focuses on how the texts are utilized in public worship and in private prayer, including the role of Hebrew, music, and nonverbal prayer language. It concludes with a selection of quotations on the theology and philosophy of prayer by some contemporary Jewish thinkers.

---

9. Rabbi Richard Sarason, "Worship and the Prayer Book," in *A Life of Meaning: Embracing Reform Judaism's Sacred Path*, ed. Rabbi Dana Evan Kaplan (New York: CCAR Press, 2018), 335.

10. Hoffman, *The Way into Jewish Prayer*, 104.

11. This means it is obligatory. Many Jews accept the obligation for daily prayer. However, for a large number of Jews, prayer is more episodic than regular. However, when Jews pray, they use the *siddur*.

12. In Orthodox congregations, only men are counted in the quorum necessary for public worship.

13. The chapter focuses mainly on the weekday morning service that is most complete.

Blessings

One of the main forms of prayer in Judaism is the *beracha* (blessing).[14] It is a prayer that begins or ends with the following formula: *"Baruch ata Adonai"*—"Blessed are You Lord."[15] This is often followed by the words *"Eloheinu Melech haolam"*—"Our God Sovereign of the Universe." The formula is then followed by a statement of the subject of the blessing. According to tradition, Jews are required to recite one hundred blessings per day.[16] Blessings are described by Rabbi Hoffman (mentioned previously) as "mini-theological essays." In addition to the blessings recited as part of the daily liturgy, there are blessings for the performance of *mitzvot* (commandments) as well as everyday activities.[17]

These occasional blessings help transform *ordinary* activities or occasions into *sacred* activities or occasions. The requirement to recite a blessing incites our sense of wonder. For example, before eating bread or wine, a Jew recites a blessing over the bread or wine.[18] The blessing of the wine is "Blessed are You, *Adonai*, Our God, Sovereign of the Universe, who creates the fruit of the vine." The blessing over the bread is "Blessed are You, *Adonai*, Our God, who brings for bread from the earth." It is an opportunity not only to express gratitude for the food that one is about to eat, but also to be aware of the obligation to address the problem of hunger. After the meal,

---

14. Often called "benedictions."

15. Adonai is a circumlocution for the Tetragrammaton, or the four letter *(YHVY)* in the proper name of God that was only pronounced by the High Priest during Temple times on Yom Kippur (the Day of Atonement). The most common translation of the word *Adonai* is "Lord." Because of the masculine character of the word "Lord" in some prayer books, it is left untranslated, and *Adonai* appears in the English translation. Sometimes it is translated "The Eternal," or simply "God."

16. "It was taught in a baraita R. Meir used to say: A person is obligated to say one hundred blessing a day." *Menachot 43b.*

17. For a list of the different blessings for various food and drink as well as for occasions and commandments, see Rabbi Nosson Scherman and Rabbi Meir Zlotowitz, eds., *The Expanded Art Scroll Siddur the Wasserman Edition* (Brooklyn: Mesorah Publications, 2010), 182–231.

18. Note that blessings are said "over" bread and wine. The wine and the bread are not consecrated. They remain ordinary bread and wine. T. Ber. 35ab writes that eating without saying a blessing is like stealing. Since God is the owner of everything, saying the blessing is how the Jew seeks permission to make use of what properly belongs to God.

there is a long blessing thanking God for the food. When Jews see a rain-bow, they recite, "Blessed are you, *Adonai*, who remembers the covenant." It is an allusion to God's promise to Noah to never destroy the world again by means of a flood (Gen. 9:12–17), but it also brings the person to a real-ization that humans have the power to destroy the world with weapons of mass destruction and pollution. It says in effect that humans are obligated to protect the planet from their own destructive powers. Therefore, blessings are not only a means of appreciation but also an impetus to action.

For example, before lighting candles to initiate the Sabbath and Holy Days, one recites a blessing because lighting these candles is a *mitzvah*. One says, "Blessed are You, *Adonai*, Our God Sovereign of the Universe, who sanctifies us by commandments and commands us to kindle the lights of the Sabbath." Sabbaths and Holy Days are concluded with bless-ings of separation (*Havdalah*). These set the boundary between ordinary and sacred time.

While many of the prayers in the *siddur* are blessings, there are also Psalms, readings of scripture, and other sacred texts, as well as liturgical poems known as *piyyutim*, which are part of the daily worship ritual.

The *Siddur*

The word *siddur* derives from the Hebrew root *sdr*, which means "order." The prescribed order of the service in the morning is (1) *Birchot Hashachar* (morning blessings), which begins with daily blessings and in-cludes the study of sacred texts; and (2) *P'sukei D'zimrah* (verses of song), a selection of songs, psalms, and biblical passages. These two opening sec-tions serve as preparation for the main rubrics that follow: (3) The *Shema* and its blessings (*Qriat HaShema*), which are a declaration of faith; (4) The *Amidah* (the Standing Prayer), also known as the *Sh'mone Esrei* (the Eighteen Blessings) or the *t'filah* (the prayer), which consists of prayers of praise, petition, and thanksgiving; (5) On Mondays, Thursdays, Sabbaths, and Holy Days, a communal reading of the Torah (*Seder Kriat HaTorah*); (6) Concluding prayers, which include *Aleinu*, a description of the Jewish idea of God and hope for future redemption, and a final *Kaddish* (an Aramaic prayer of praise) now associated with mourning.

Birchot Hashachar

Prayer requires preparation. Therefore, the *siddur* begins with a series of prayers and blessings associated with one's daily activities—from waking up to preparing oneself for the day. Upon awaking, one thanks God for restoring their life:[19] "I offer thanks to you, living and enduring Sovereign, for restoring my soul to me in compassion. You are faithful beyond measure." Each new day is a gift of God and begins with an expression of gratitude for being granted another day. This prayer is now also incorporated in the *siddur*. The following blessings were originally recited at home, and they too have been incorporated into the daily synagogue ritual:

> As you hear the crow of a rooster, say, "Blessed are You who gave the mind [or "the rooster"—Hebrew uses the same word for mind and for rooster] understanding to discern day from night." As you open your eyes, say, "Blessed are You who gives sight to the blind." As you sit up straight, say, "Blessed are You who releases those who are bound." As you get dressed, say, "Blessed are You who clothes the naked." As you stand up, say "Blessed are You who straightens those who are bent over." As your feet touch the floor, say, "Blessed are You who spreads the earth upon the waters." As you begin walking, say, "Blessed are You who stabilizes a person's steps." As you put your shoes on, say "Blessed are You who has given me all I need." As you fasten your belt, say "Blessed are You who girds Israel with might." As you cover your head, say, "Blessed are You who crowns Israel with splendor."[20]

These blessings describe the series of steps we take from waking to dressing to starting our day. They also affirm that our daily task is to imitate God. As God opens the eyes of the blind or clothes the naked, we should strive to be like God and should work for the betterment of the human condition.

Jewish anthropology emphasizes our dual nature. We are both physical and spiritual beings; therefore, there is a blessing for the body and a blessing for the soul:

> Blessed are You, Lord our God, Sovereign of the world, who with wisdom has fashioned the human, creating within him openings and closures, channels and cavities. It is well known to You that were one opening to close down or one closure to open up, one could not exist in Your presence a single moment. Blessed are You, Lord, healer of all flesh, who sustains our bodies in wondrous ways.[21]

---

19. Rabbinic anthropology conceive of sleep as a kind of death with the soul hovering over the body, and each morning body and soul are rejoined. It is a mini resurrection of the dead.

20. Ber 60a.

21. "The Talmud . . . provides a blessing also for handwashing, and even for leaving the bathroom successfully. It is not just in theory that the body is valued. Our urinary tract and intestinal system, for instance, are as much engaged in doing God's work as is our brain. Hospital patients and the chronically ill quickly discover

We are embodied individuals. Both the body and the soul are sacred. Embodiment is the experience of every human being. It is what makes each of us unique. Physical pleasure is considered a gift from God. To neglect these pleasures is considered sinful. Sex is for more than procreation; it is also for pleasure and well-being. With marriage being considered the proper context for sexual relations, our physical appetites, when exercised appropriately, are considered gifts from God. Thus, asceticism is largely rejected in Judaism.

Judaism teaches the importance of caring for our bodies because God owns them and lends them to us while we are alive. The body serves as the instrument that allows us to serve God. For examples, our hands can lift up the fallen, and our feet can propel us to rescue someone in danger. As Rabbi Reuven Kimelman, professor of Near Eastern and Judaic Studies at Brandeis, points out:

> The regular recitation of this blessing spurs awareness of ourselves as bodies. It instructs us to experience our body as a marvelous assembly of divine wonders. The intricate assembly of portable plumbing manifests an ingenious design attributable only to the great Designer. The recitation of the blessing after urination and defecation makes us aware of the delicate balance between well-being and illness as a function of a well-operating body. Precisely at the moment of the body's vulnerability we become aware of its vitality and viability. Each moment of life, it asserts, depends upon the co-ordination of the contraction and the dilation of the ducts and tubes of our multifaceted channel system. So fragile is it that, were but one to clog up or be perforated, the system would shut down. All the more surprising is how rarely it breaks down. The thesis of the blessing is that the marvelous workings of the body evidence a body fashioned by the wisdom of God.[22]

Sleep is considered like temporary death. Each morning we are revived—resurrected. This blessing (see below) underscores that the soul was in mint condition when we received it from God and thus should be returned as received. Any marks or blemishes on it are ours.[23] We begin life in a state of purity free from sin. Sin is not a state of being, but the acts

how much they depend on the vast network of ducts, tubes, and internal organs that healthy people take for granted. Judaism insists on daily prayers to draw our attention even to those in a positive way." Hoffman, *The Way into Jewish Prayer*, 118.

22. Reuven Kimelman, "The Rabbinic Theology of the Physical: Blessing Body and Soul, Resurrection Covenant and Election," in *Cambridge History of Judaism The Late Roman Rabbinic Period Vol IV*, ed. Steven T. Katz (Cambridge: Cambridge University Press, 2006), 594.

23. Judaism rejects the concept of original sin.

we perform that are contrary to the will of God as described in the Torah and our other sacred texts. Each day is a challenge and an opportunity to do what God wants us to do:

> My God, the soul You gave me is pure. You created, You formed it, You breathed it into me; You keep body and soul intact. And You will in the future take it from me and restore it to me in the hereafter. So long as the soul is within me I thank you, Lord my God, God of my ancestors, Master of all creation, Lord of all souls. Blessed are You Who restores souls to lifeless exhausted bodies.[24]

The combination of body and soul makes us who we are. This blessing, like the opening blessing upon awaking, understands each day as a mini resurrection of the dead and expresses the ultimate hope that when redemption finally comes, we will return in a recognizable form.[25]

This section includes a blessing for the study of Torah. Torah study is a *mitzvah* and considered by the Rabbis to be among the most important *mitzvot*. Therefore, it is included as part of the daily ritual. Torah is understood broadly to include biblical as well as rabbinic texts. The texts vary among the denominational *siddurim*. In the Reform *siddur Mishkan T'filah*, the following passage adopted from *Mishnah Peah* 1:1 (earliest of rabbinic texts, dating to the second century CE) speaks of a Jew's daily obligations:

---

24. Hoffman, *The Way into Jewish Prayer*, 115–16: "Classical Judaism understood the soul as something approaching the divine. The idiom used here is that God breathes the soul into us when we are born. Indeed, the Hebrew word for soul is neshamah, which also means 'breath.' We are born with it, and the moment it departs, we are no longer alive. To express their idea of there being something vibrantly 'more' to human existence, the Rabbis extended the fact of human breathing into a broader concept, imagining that God had breathed some of the divine essence into us at birth. That essence is 'exhaled' from us eventually, but while it is there, it is a reminder of the life-affirming and ever invigorating godliness that enlivens us." At death, the soul departs, but eventually God will return the soul to the body. Although, not all Jews accept the concept of resurrection. It is a clear and idealized understanding of the afterlife because we can only conceive of ourselves as ourselves if we are embodied.

25. In the Pittsburgh Platform of Reform Judaism of 1885, resurrection of the dead was rejected. However, in the latest *Siddur* of the Reform Movement *Mishkan T'fila*, the metaphor of resurrection of the dead has been restored as an option in the second blessing of the Amidah. For a full discussion of resurrection of the dead in Judaism, see Neil Gilman, *The Death of Death* (Woodstock, VT: Jewish Lights, 1997). He argues for the importance of resurrection of the dead as being a crucial metaphor to understanding Jewish anthropology.

These are things that are limitless, of which a person enjoys the fruit of this world, all the principle remains in the world to come. They are: honoring one's father and mother, engaging in deeds of compassion, arriving early for study morning and evening, dealing graciously with guests, visiting the sick, providing for the wedding couple, accompanying the dead for burial, being devoted in prayer, and making peace among people. But the study of Torah encompasses them all.[26]

In summary, *Birchot Hashachar* is preparation for prayer, but in reality it also serves to prepare the Jew for the day ahead by expressing appreciation for our physical and spiritual nature, reinforcing values, and inspiring righteous action.

Pesukei D'Zimrah

This section consists of opening blessings, psalms, and biblical passages that praise God, express gratitude, and celebrate the Exodus from Egypt. They are chanted and sung, creating an elevated mood leading to the *Shema* and its Blessing.

The Shema *and Its Blessings*

In Hebrew, this section is called *Seder Kriat Shema* (the order of the recitation of the *Shema*). In a strict sense, this section is not a prayer but a statement of faith. As Lawrence Hoffman describes it: "It is a conversation largely about God. It is essentially the Jewish creed."[27] The body of the *Shema* consists of three paragraphs drawn from Deuteronomy and Numbers. It begins with a call to worship that indicates the beginning of the statutory prayers and that the upcoming rubric is a public recitation of Torah. The leader of the service calls out in Hebrew, "Praise *Adonai,* to whom praise is due forever," and the congregation responds, "Praised be *Adonai,* to whom praise is due forever and ever." It is one of the most dramatic moments in the service. At that moment, the worshippers come together as a praying congregation.

The Call to Worship also appears at the beginning of the blessings that precede the reading of the Torah in the Torah service. The use of the Call to Worship at the beginning of the *Shema* makes it clear that this section

---

26. Elyse Frishman, ed., *Mishkhan T'filah A Reform Siddur* (New York City: CCAR Press, 2007), 44. In the Reform movement, it has been set to music and functions as an inspiration to actions of loving kindness and social justice.

27. Hoffman, *The Way into Jewish Prayer*, 22.

functions as a public reading of the Torah. Since the whole of the Torah cannot be read every day, this section serves as a substitute. There are two blessings before the reading of the *Shema*, and one blessing following the *Shema*. The first blessing describes God as the Creator of the universe, the second blessing describes God's love for Israel as the revealer of Torah, and the blessing that follows the scriptural passages describes God as the redeemer of Israel. In the evening service, an additional blessing asks God's protection during the night.

The *Shema* and its blessings are the Jewish proclamation of monotheism: God is one; God created the world; God revealed the Torah to Israel; God redeemed Israel in the past and will redeem Israel in the future. All Jewish theologies must address creation, revelation, and redemption. This section derives its name from the first word of the opening line, *Shema* ("hear"). These words, "*Shema Yisrael Adonai Eloheinu Adonai echad*"— "Hear, O Israel *Adonai* is our God, *Adonai* is one" (Deut. 6:4)—are key to understanding Judaism. The *Shema* is the first prayer that Jews learn as children. It is a proclamation of Jewish faith. It is so important that it has been described as the watchword of our faith. Jews recite it in the morning on arising and in the evening as they go to sleep as part of the morning and evening service and as the last words they say before they die.

In the morning, the blessing before the *Shema* focuses on the creation of light. In the evening, it focuses on the coming of the night. The second blessing focuses on God's love for Israel through the gift of Torah. The blessing following the recitation of the *Shema* recalls the Exodus from Egypt, specifically citing words from Exodus 15, the Song of the Sea, which according to the Torah was recited by the Israelites after they safely navigated the Red Sea. In the evening, a second blessing is added after the *Shema*, which asks God to guard and protect us during the night and to awake us the next morning. This makes sense psychologically because nighttime is a scary time. We hope for a safe restful night; we awaken refreshed in the morning.

The *Shema* consists of three passages from the Torah: Deuteronomy 6:4–8 is designated as accepting the yoke of the kingdom; in it, the Jew affirms God's sovereignty. Deuteronomy 11:13–21 is designated as accepting the yoke of the commandments; in it, the Jew affirms the obligation to obey God's will. Numbers 15:37–41 describes the commandment to put fringes or tassels on the corner of our garments as a reminder of the commandments. The three passages read:

Hear, O Israel! The LORD is our God, the LORD is one. You shall love the LORD your God with all your heart and with all your soul and with all your might. Take to heart these instructions with which I charge you this day. Impress them upon your children. Recite them when you stay at home and when you are away, when you lie down and when you get up. Bind them as a sign on your hand and let them serve as a symbol on your forehead,[28] inscribe them on the doorposts of your house and on your gates. (Deut. 6:4–8)[29]

Therefore impress these My words upon your every heart: bind them as a sign on your hand and let them serve as a symbol on your forehead, and teach them to your children—reciting them when you stay at home and when you are away, when you lie down and when you get up; and inscribe them on the doorposts of your house and on your gates—to the end that you and your children may endure, in the land that the LORD swore to your fathers to assign to them, as long as there is a heaven over the earth. (Deut. 11:13–21)[30]

The LORD said to Moses as follows: Speak to the Israelite people and instruct them to make for themselves fringes on the corners of their garments throughout the ages; let them attach a cord of blue to the fringe at each corner. That shall be your fringe; look at it and recall all the commandments of the LORD and observe them, so that you do not follow your heart and eyes in your lustful urge. Thus you shall be reminded to observe all My commandments and to be holy to your God. I the LORD am your God, who

---

28. This is understood as the commandment of *Tefillin* phylacteries, which are small black boxes with leather straps containing the words of the *Shema* owritten on a piece of parchment according to the same rules as the writing of a Torah scroll. One is placed on the forehead and the other bound around the arm. See the section on The Nonverbal Language of Prayer, where the phylacteries and the fringes are discussed further.

29. The words of the *Shema* are inscribed by a scribe on a piece parchment placed in a small case (mezuzah) that is attached to the entry way in every Jewish home, and many people place the *mezuzah* at every door in the house except the bathroom door. It is the custom when entering the home to touch the mezuzah as sign of reverence. The home is a sacred place. In Hebrew, it is called a *mikdash meat* (the Temple writ small). The *mezuzah* identifies the home as being a Jewish home.

30. The text suggests that the fate of the Jewish people is bound up in its obedience to God. Whether one takes this literally or not, it tells us that our actions have consequences. This paragraph is omitted in Reform prayer books because of the theological difficulty of identifying reward and punishment with the events of nature. Since this paragraph deals with nature as an instrument for reward and punishment, some have interpreted it as a metaphor for the destruction that comes from polluting the environment.

brought you out of the land of Egypt to be your God: I, the LORD your
God. (Num. 15:37–41)[31]

Amidah

The word *Amidah* means "standing." Thus, this prayer is recited standing. It has other names as well: *Hat'filah* (the Prayer) or the *Shemone Esrei*
(the Eighteen Blessings). It is the main rubric of the worship service and
begins with three blessings of praise, continues with blessings of petition,
and concludes with three blessing of thanksgiving. On the Sabbath and
Holy Days, the blessings of petition are eliminated, and a blessing for the
Sabbath or the Holy Day is inserted.

Within the *Amidah*, there are specific opportunities for personal petition. The first blessing is known as the *Avot* (Patriarchs) because it addresses God as the God of Abraham, the God of Isaac, and the God of
Jacob. In many non-Orthodox prayer books, the names of the matriarchs
are inserted after "the God of Isaac"; it continues, "the God of Sarah, the
God of Rebecca, the God of Leah, and the God of Rachel." The wording
"the *God of* Abraham, the *God of* Isaac, and *God of* Jacob, the *God of* Sarah,
the *God of* Rebecca, the *God of* Rachel, the *God of* Leah" conveys the notion that each Patriarch and Matriarch experience God in his or her own
way and by implication so does each individual worshipper. The function
of this blessing then is to introduce the worshipper to God as a descendent
of the Patriarchs and Matriarchs to create a sense of familiarity.

The next blessing, known as *Gevurah*, describes God's power and concludes with a recognition that God's ultimate power is the power over
death—namely, that God can resurrect the dead. This is an acknowledgment that the worshipper believes that God has power to grant his or her
petitions. The blessing after that is known as the *Kedushah*, which proclaims God's holiness. The text imagines that God is served by a heavenly
angelic choir whose function is to proclaim God's holiness (Isa. 6:3, Ezek.
3:23). The community then is understood to be imitating the angels. This
is the pinnacle of praise. The effect of introducing one's self to God, acknowledging God's power, and appreciating God's holiness enables the

---

31. The attaching of special fringes or tassels is interpreted as the commandment
of wearing a *Tallit*, a special fringed garment used for prayer and worn by Orthodox
Jewish men as a special undershirt. Looking at the fringe has the didactic purpose
of reminding the Jew of the *mitzvot* and his or her obligation to obey them. See
more about this in the section the Non-Verbal Language of Prayer.

worshiper and congregation to feel psychologically prepared to offer their petitions.[32]

The stage is now set for the community to offer its petitions[33] for knowledge, repentance, forgiveness, redemption, healing, a good year, ingathering of the exiles, rebuilding Jerusalem, restoring the Davidic dynasty, and hearing petitions. After the petitions, the community offers three concluding blessings of thanksgiving. The first is a prayer for the acceptance of prayer, the second is a prayer for acknowledgment of God's blessings, and the last is a prayer for peace.

This brief description does not do full justice to the prayer or to the creative material that some *siddurim* add. However, it should be understood as a powerful statement of the community's needs and its hopes and dreams. It offers the individual worshipper the opportunity to stand in solidarity with the community. It allows the worshipper to feel the strength and support of the community as they express personal needs. One is praying both for individual needs and for community needs. In traditional congregations, the *Amidah* is first recited silently and then repeated by the service leader. In other streams, it may be recited partially in silence and partially orally with or without repetition. During the blessings for healing, one thinks about and prays for those of their relatives and friends who are in need of healing. In the blessing, hearing petitions add one's own specific needs to those of the community.[34]

---

32. Petitionary prayer is problematic for many people, especially when one believes that one's petitions have not been answered or have been rejected. Some of the issue around petitionary prayer will be addressed in the concluding section of the chapter. The power of the petitions does not lie directly in whether the petitions are granted but in having been able to express them as part of a community, which gives support to the individual and community and perhaps to better deal with the vicissitudes of life. The question of whether prayer affects God is an important theological question. However, prayer can have a powerful effect on the individual and the community.

33. Some of the petitions are modified by the different streams to conform to their own theologies.

34. Peter Knobel, "Reflections on Prayer," in *A Life of Meaning*, ed. Dana Evan Kaplan (New York: CCAR Press), 331. "For many years I ran five miles every morning. Now that running is out of the question, I walk that same distance instead. This alone time has become, for me, a vehicle for engaging in extended prayer. Most important to me is a part of the Amidah: Sh'ma Koleinu, 'God, hear our voice.' Traditionally when this prayer is recited, one pauses to add one's personal petitions. When I recite this prayer during my morning exercise, I often

The Torah Reading[35]

Torah is read on Sabbaths, holidays, Mondays, and Thursdays. It is both *Talmud Torah* (Torah study) and a reenactment of the theophany at Mt. Sinai.[36] Rabbi Arthur Green, professor of religion at Hebrew College in Boston, describes the ideal meaning of the Torah service:

> For Jews, the cardinal religious experience is *matan Torah* (the giving of the Torah). The central part of our self-understanding is that Sinai-revelation is *always* happening. Every generation of Jews ever to be born or converted was there at Sinai. *Ma' amad Harsinai* (standing at Mount Sinai) means standing there with your heart open, knowing what you have to learn, knowing what you have to do. . . . Rudolph Otto writes about Sinai as the *mysterium tremendum*, the great trembling before God. . . . [T]he experience of receiving the Torah is the experience of two great religious emotions for us *ahavah veyir' ah* love and awe—together. The awe doesn't diminish the love, and the love is filled with awe.[37]

When the Torah is taken from the Ark, the congregation rises and the Torah is carried in procession through the congregation. The congregants reach out to touch the scroll with the fringes of their *Tallit* (prayer shawl) or their *siddur.* Excitement fills the room. The Torah is taken to the *bima* (the raised reading stand) and undressed. Members of the community are called up to recite a blessing over the reading or to chant the Torah portion. It is a great honor to receive an *Aliyah* (to be called up to recite the blessing over the reading), as chanting the Torah portion or reading

---

engage in an extended conversation with God. I address God in an intimate and personal way. It is like having a conversation with a trusted friend or advisor who listens but does not speak. These conversations have helped me through many a personal crisis and aided me in clarifying my thinking and goals. At the end, although I have no explicit response, I feel that that there is a 'listening ear,' and I can discern with greater clarity the path that I must take."

35. Jeffery A. Summit, *Singing God's Words: The Performance of Biblical Chant in Contemporary Judaism* (Oxford University Press, 2016), 59–61. Professor Summit provides a comprehensive description of the service, which captures the drama of the recreation in the contemporary synagogue of the moment when Moses reveals the Torah to Israel. To hear the Torah chanted, go to www.oup.com/us/singinggodswords.

36. Ruth Langer, "From Study of Scripture to a Reenactment of Sinai: The Emergence of the Synagogue Torah Service," *Worship* 72:1 (1998): 43–67.

37. Summit, *Singing God's Words*, 62.

from the Torah is a special role that requires preparation and skill.[38] When the Torah reading is completed, the congregation rises, the scroll is lifted, and the text is shown to the congregation, which chants in Hebrew, "This is the Torah which Moses placed before the Children of Israel upon the command of Adonai through Moses." At this moment, the congregation acknowledges that it is transported back to Mt. Sinai. The Torah Service also includes prayers for the community, for the government, for the state of Israel, for healing, and for having been spared from tragedy, disaster, or illness. There are additional prayers to celebrate important life cycle moments like the birth of a child, an upcoming marriage, and a child reaching the age of maturity (i.e., Bar and Bat Mitzvah). On Sabbath and Holy Days, there is an additional biblical reading from the Prophets called the *haphtarah*, following which the Torah is ceremonially returned to the Ark.

The power of the service is both emotional and intellectual. The rabbi or a learned member of the community will offer a lesson from the Torah reading. The words and the drama combine to invite the presence of the Divine into the congregation. Since revelation in Judaism is verbal and has been recorded in the Torah, the Torah has become the visual presence of God in the community.

Concluding Prayers

Among the most important prayers in the concluding prayer is the *Kaddish* (Sanctification). It is in Aramaic, not in Hebrew, and while it has a long and important history, this concluding *kaddish* has become associated with mourning. "It is a doxology (that is a prayer that praises God) and does not even mention death, nonetheless it somehow possesses the ability to connect one generation to the next as the mourner's expression of grief *par excellence*."[39] People who are remembering a deceased parent, sibling, child, or spouse rise and recite this prayer. Since the *Shoah* (the Holocaust), it is the practice in Reform Congregations to invite the entire congregation to rise in memory of those who have no one to recite *Kaddish* for them. "Primarily, the power of the *Kaddish* derives from its language. That too is a kind of a paradox, in that the *Kaddish* ultimately

---

38. *Singing God's Words* is an extended analysis of the role that chanting the Torah has in the contemporary synagogue across denominational boundaries.

39. Peter Knobel, "The Mourner's Kaddish: An Enduring Inspiration and Challenge," in *Kaddish*, ed. David Birnbaum and Martin Cohen (New York: New Maxtrix Publishing, 2016), 183.

expresses the concept that God is beyond verbal description. Indeed, its core idea is precisely that language is inadequate for providing a vocabulary that adequately conveys the praise of God in a manner befitting the grandeur and magnificence of the Deity."[40] It is the rhythmic repetition of words chanted, sung, or recited, rather than their explicit definitions, that creates the powerful effect worshippers all seem to find in the *Kaddish*.

The third paragraph of the *Kaddish* is a series of words, all meaning "praised," one added to the other each in the same grammatical form. In effect, the author of the prayer took out a thesaurus and looked up all the synonyms for "praise." When the words are read, they create meaning beyond the meaning of the words: "Blessed, praised, honored, exalted, extolled, glorified, adored, and lauded be the name of the Holy Blessed One, beyond all earthly words and songs of blessing, praise, and comfort. To which we say Amen."[41]

Private vs. Communal Prayer

Participation in communal worship has prayer as its goal, bringing the experience of the divine presence to the community. Since prayer is a *mitzvah* and has regular set times, it provides regular ongoing opportunities to engage in prayer, forcing the worshipper to recite the liturgy even when the worshipper is not in the mood to pray in the hope that the words will inspire real prayer. However, the recitation of the liturgy has other purposes as well. It connects one to the community and reaffirms the community's values. There is also a social component to public worship—having other people with whom to spend time and enjoy company.

One of the purposes of prayer as well as the study of scripture is to promote righteous actions. Thus, the sermon or the *dvar Torah* (Torah lesson) on the Sabbath or holidays is an important learning. Either a rabbi or a member of the community offers an interpretation of the week's Torah reading or delivers a message meant to inspire the congregation to some specific action.

Private prayer is important and can have powerful effects. The following is a description of my own experience as a congregational rabbi functioning as a pastor:

---

40. Knobel, 183.

41. To hear the whole *kaddish* read, see https://www.youtube.com/watch?v=luk85AVuHCg.

A simple act of prayer can truly surprise us. Twice in my rabbinate I have entered the hospital room of a comatose patient, taken hold of the person's hand to recite the Sh'ma, and the person awoke. In one case the person completed the words of the Sh'ma with me. These occurrences seemed miraculous and were remarkably powerful. Prayer can be equally powerful even when the hoped-for event does not occur. I remember being in the hospital completing my rounds of visiting congregants when I ran into a person whose husband was in a coma in the intensive care unit. I offered to go into the ICU with her and pray for him. The man died. But my presence and prayers led to a connection that allowed me to help a family through a difficult moment and to comfort them through the funeral and mourning process. I am never sure why things work out the way they do, and I remain agnostic about God's role, but I do know that prayer is a very significant part of my life.[42]

Keva *and* Kavanah[43]

Essential to understanding prayer in Judaism is the relationship between *keva* (the fixed text) and *kavanah* (intention). While *kavanah* is usually translated as "intention," its true meaning is to perform the liturgy with meaning so that the recitation of the words (*keva*) becomes an experience of prayer.[44] There is no question that spontaneous prayer, which is evoked by personal experience, is meaningful and seeks to reach the Divine. With a fixed text, it is easy to recite the words by rote as if they were meaningless syllables. Thus, cultivating *kavanah* can be challenging.

How does one develop the proper frame of mind? How can one avoid rote recitation when the words are so familiar that one can recite them without even looking at the text? The rabbis of the Talmud were aware of the difficulty of developing the proper frame of mind to recite the *Amidah*. The fixing of its Eighteen Blessings is attributed to the rabbinic sage, Rabban Gamaliel:

> Rabban Gamaliel says, "Each day one should pray the eighteen benedictions." Rabbi Joshua says, "A summary version of the eighteen is sufficient." Rabbi Akiva says, "If one is fluent in prayer, one should say all eighteen, but if not, the summary version suffices." Rabbi Eliezer says, "If you make your prayer a fixed task, your supplications are invalid."[45]

---

42. Knobel, "Reflections," 332.

43. See Hoffman, *The Way into Jewish Prayer*, 33–35.

44. "Prayer is an experience of profound connection to something beyond ourselves." Knobel, "Reflections," 329.

45. *Mishna Berakhot* 4:3, 4:4.

While constructing the *Amidah*, the Rabbis began by designating the number and theme. Once these were fixed, they discussed how they should be recited: (1) as a whole as designated, (2) only in summary, or (3) creatively.

Possible conflicts between *keva* and *kavanah* have existed from the very beginning, as illustrated by these quotes:

> One should not stand to recite the Prayer unless one is in a serious frame of mind. The pious men of old would pause for an hour and then pray so that they might direct their hearts toward God. One who is praying, even if a king extends a greeting, even if a snake is coiled to strike at his heel he should not interrupt his prayer.[46]

> Rabbi Shimon says be careful in reciting the *Shema* and the *Amidah*. When you pray do not make your prayer fixed, pray for mercy and supplication before God.[47]

The rabbis of Talmud were aware of the problem. Their goal was to perform the prayer with meaning and intensity. They understood that one needs to be in proper frame of mind and that this requires preparation. They also understood that prayer could be rote recitation of words and that a fixed liturgy needed spontaneity. For Jews, this is a special challenge since prayer is a *mitzvah*. However, many contemporary Jews do not participate regularly, and thus having a fixed text is both a benefit and a challenge. It is a benefit because there are words to help them pray. It is a challenge because it is difficult to recite the words in a manner that touches them deeply.

The *siddur* is the primary source for Jewish prayer. It is the accumulation of our experience and history; it is our way of speaking to and about God, but it remains merely text on the page if we do not open our hearts and our lives to its meaning. To learn to pray with *kavanah*, one needs to study and learn the liturgy. While prayer is a basic human need, praying using liturgy is an acquired skill. And like all sacred texts, liturgy often requires commentary. Rabbis today, as in the past, add meditations and explanations that bring new meaning to ancient words. They seek to open the spiritual message of the liturgy. For example, it is necessary to find techniques for creating an atmosphere that is conducive to prayer. Immediately before the *Amidah*, the *siddur* quotes Psalm 51:17: *"Adonai s'fatai tiftach ufi yagid t'hilatecha"*—"Adonai, open up my lips that my

---

46. *Mishna Berakhot* 5:1.
47. *Mishna Avot* 2:13.

mouth may declare your praise." This is a prayer that the words of our mouths become expressions of our hearts.

A contemporary Reform rabbi, Sheldon Zimmerman, uses this Psalm verse to create a meditation to help the worshiper pray the liturgy:

A Prayer for Prayer.

My God
My soul's companion
My heart's precious friend
I turn to You.
I need to close out the noise
To rise above the noise
The noise that interrupts—
The noise that separates—
The noise that isolates.
I need to hear You again.
In the silence of my innermost being,
In the fragments of my yearned-for wholeness,
I hear whispers of Your presence—
Echoes of the past when You were with me
When I felt Your nearness
When together we walked—
When You held me close, embraced me in Your
love, laughed with me in my joy.
I yearn to hear You again.
In your oneness, I find healing.
In the promise of Your love, I am soothed.
In Your wholeness, I too can become whole again.
Please listen to my call—
help me find the words
help me find the strength within
help me shape my mouth, my voice, my heart
so that I can direct my spirit and find You in prayer
In words only my heart can speak
In songs only my soul can sing
Lifting my eyes and heart to You.
Adonai S'fatai Tiftach—open my lips, precious God,
so that I can speak with You again.[48]

---

48. Rabbi Sheldon Zimmerman, "A Prayer for Prayer," in *Healing of Soul, Healing of Body: Spiritual Leaders Unfold the Strength and Solace of Psalms*, ed. Rabbi Simkha Y. Weintraub (Woodstock, VT: Jewish Lights Publishing, 1994), 102.

Similarly, Rabbi Jonathan Magonet, a Reform rabbi from the United Kingdom, composed the following reading to reflect on the issue of *Keva* and *Kavanah*:

> Liturgy defines the community that prays
> Prayer is the offer of each individual
> Liturgy affirms the values of the Community
> Prayer sets those values on our lips and in our hearts
> Liturgy unites those who share a tradition
> Prayer connects us to all who pray
> Liturgy offers a language for our prayer
> Liturgy places us with in history
> Prayer opens us to the future
>
> Liturgy provides a place in which to pray
> Prayer tests the truth of what we play
> Liturgy brings God into the world
> Prayer helps make room for God in our lives.[49]

The new Reform *siddur* created a unique format with the Hebrew text of the prayer on the right side of the page accompanied by a transliteration of the Hebrew to facilitate the participation of those who do not know or have difficulty with the Hebrew, a faithful translation of the Hebrew, and a source commentary on the bottom of the page. On the facing left hand page are alternative prayers on the same theme as the prayer on the right side of the page and a spiritual commentary at the bottom of the page.

Role of Hebrew

A significant goal of Jewish education is Hebrew literacy. While this goal includes the ability to read and understand all of the important sacred texts, it is especially important for participation in synagogue services because Hebrew prayers are a significant part of the service.[50] Since many worshippers have only a rudimentary knowledge of Hebrew, most contemporary *siddurim* provide translations of the prayers, and in many cases provide transliteration of the Hebrew so that even a person unfamiliar with the Hebrew letters can follow the Hebrew prayers and join in con-

---

49. Quoted in Samuel Barth, "Keva–Kavanah (Liturgy–Prayer)," The Jewish Theological Seminary, December 31, 2012, https://www.jtsa.edu/keva-kavanah-liturgy-prayer.

50. In Orthodox and many Conservative congregations, the service is entirely in Hebrew.

gregational responses or singing. The continued use of Hebrew provides Jewish prayer with a sense of authenticity and unity as a person realizes that Jews all over the world have recited these same words for millennia. It also allows Jews to attend Jewish worship anywhere in the world and to find passages that are familiar, carrying meaning even if one is not able to translate them word for word.[51]

Because of all this, Hebrew is essential to Jewish prayer. The prayer book opens right to left rather than left to right as an English book, emphasizing that the *siddur* is basically a Hebrew book and that the Hebrew prayers have a special place in the Jewish understanding of worship. Prayer in Hebrew can be difficult both for those who know the language and those who do not know the language. The words and concepts can be theologically problematic if taken literally, especially for those who have difficulty with many of the biblical and rabbinic descriptions of God as King, Father, and Almighty. Hebrew for those who do not know the language can seem like the recitation of nonsense syllables and be very off-putting. However, the regular worshipper often becomes sufficiently familiar with the Hebrew text and is able to recite it without even looking at the prayer book and at the same time infuse the words with their own personal meaning. This type of divided consciousness is very important for understanding the *kavanah.*

Role of Music

Chant and music are integral to Jewish worship. Chant encourages congregational participation, with the service leader, or the Hazan (cantor), bringing an aesthetic dimension to the worship service. The way in which prayers are sung or chanted highlights meaning and significance of the content. To aid in this, there are special styles of chanting called *nusach.* These differ on weekdays, Shabbat, and holidays and help the worshiper enter into the unique character of the occasion.

One of the most moving and solemn moments in the whole liturgical year comes at the beginning of Yom Kippur (the Day of Atonement), when *Kol Nidrei,* an Aramaic formula for the forgiveness of vows, is chant-

---

51. Recently, I had twenty-six members of my former congregation on a trip to Germany. On Friday night, we went to a synagogue for services; the synagogue used the Conservative prayer book *Siddur Sim Shalom.* Even though the services in the German synagogue were different than the services at our home congregation, the group was able to participate fully. If the service had been mostly in German rather than Hebrew, we would not have been able to participate.

ed to a very old melody. Jews flock to the synagogue in large numbers on the evening of Yom Kippur (popularly called *kol nidrei* eve). The words themselves are a prosaic legalistic formula, the content of which has been controversial for centuries, but the melody sets the tone for the entire day. Legend has it that Jews who were forcibly converted to Christianity in Spain after 1492 sung this melody in secret to disavow their conversion. The melody sends a message of repentance and forgiveness that transcends the written text, causing one to feel the power of the moment and be struck by a connection to the transcendent.

On Rosh Hashanah (the Jewish New Year), the sounding of the *shofar* (the ram's horn), which is surrounded with important pieces of liturgy, ushers in the New Year celebrating God as king, judge, and redeemer. The primary *mitzvah* of Rosh Hashanah is to hearken to the sound of the *shofar*. It is one of the major reasons so many Jews attend a synagogue in large numbers on Rosh Hashanah, as it ushers in a time of personal and communal renewal and acts as a spiritual wake-up call.

Many of the most familiar hymns of today's synagogue service are sung to melodies that were drawn from the cultures where Jews lived, and this practice continues today. In addition, there is a growing trend among the non-Orthodox streams to provide new musical settings to the standard texts and to utilize themes or words from those prayers to create new prayers. For example, the late American singer-songwriter Debbie Friedman adapted the words of the *Mishebeirach for healing*[52] into an English-Hebrew prayer, which is at the same time personal and communal. It is easy to learn, and its melody is emotionally compelling. Prior to this prayer, the names of those for whom the congregation is praying are read, and then the leader will often invite participants to add names. The leader will often include the names of people who have been the victims of violence or natural disaster and include more generally those nameless ones whose lives are broken and in need of healing. It often brings people to tears as they think about those who are in need of healing:

> *Mi sheberakh avoteinu*
> *M'kor habrakhah l'imoteinu*
> May the source of strength who blessed the ones before us,
> Help us find the courage to make our lives a blessing
> And let us say: Amen

---

52. *Mi shebeirach* (The one who blessed) is the generic name of a series of prayers recited after the reading of the Torah. One such prayer is for the healing of the sick.

Mi sheberakh imoteinu
M'kor habrakhah l'avoteinu

Bless those in need of healing with *refuah sh'leimah*
The renewal of body, the renewal of spirit
And let us say: Amen[53]

While the current trend is toward greater congregational participation, engaged listening to solo or choral music continues to be an important part of Jewish worship. Although instrumentation is not used in Orthodox synagogues, it is common in Reform congregations, where the guitar has largely replaced the organ, and many Reform and Reconstructionist synagogues have bands that accompany the worship. This is also becoming increasingly true in Conservative synagogues as they attempt to revitalize the worship experience for those who do not identify with the more traditional style of chanting. For synagogues that do incorporate music into their sermons, it enlivens the words, and individual voices blend to become a single congregational voice.[54]

Non-Verbal Language of Prayer

Prayer is more than just reciting words; there is a non-verbal language of prayer. It consists of wearing special clothing and engaging in particular actions or gestures that symbolize status and intent and focus the attention of the worshiper on the meaning of the words. The gestures also mimic interactions among human beings. For example, the central prayer, the *Amidah*, is literally the standing prayer.[55] During the week, the *Amidah* is primarily a prayer of petition. One stands and takes three steps forward before beginning the prayer, symbolically entering God's presence. At the beginning and the end of the first blessing, the *Avot*, one bends the knees and bows from the waist at the word *Baruch* ("blessed") as a sign of greeting and of respect and stands straight at the word *Adonai*.

The *Kedushah*, the third blessing in the *Amidah* prayer, proclaims God's holiness. It is derived from passages in Isaiah and Ezekiel and evokes an image of a celestial chorus praising God. Based on the angels calling out to one another in the prayer, the tradition is to bow to the left and

---

53. MT 371. To understand the power of this prayer, listen to Debbie Friedman sing it. https://www.youtube.com/watch?v=pHKo3CjuzpY.

54. Knobel and Schechter, "What Congregants Want," 41–42.

55. For a full account of the gestures and their meaning, see Uri Ehrlich, *The Nonverbal Language of Prayer* (Tubingen: Mohr Siebeck, 2004).

to the right as in imitation of the angels. In the line that proclaims God's holiness, the word "holy" is repeated three times. On each mention, participants raise up on their toes, symbolically reaching for holiness.

In the concluding section of the service, a prayer called the *Aleinu* is recited. After praising God as the Sovereign of the Universe, a line reads, "Therefore we bend the knees, bow and give thanks before you the King of Kings, the Holy One Blessed Be He." At the word "knees," participants bend their knees, at the word "bow" participants bow at the waist, and at the words "before the king" participants stand straight. The importance of these gestures as contributing to the meaning of prayer cannot be underestimated.

Among Orthodox males, the *kipa* (skull cap or yarmulka) as well as *tallit qatan* (special fringed undershirt) are part of their ordinary dress. For the morning prayer service, they don a large prayer shawl called a *tallit* that has four specially tied corner fringes called *tzitzit*. In the biblical verses containing the *shema,* God commands the Israelites to put fringes *on the four corners of their garments.*[56] They also put on phylacteries called *tefillin* as part of their daily prayer regimen that are in response to the biblical injunction that one should "bind these words up on their arm and place them as frontlets between their eyes."[57] During the recitation of the *Shema,* one covers the eyes in concentration. When the prayer speaks about the ingathering of the exiles from the four corners of the earth, one gathers together the four fringes of their *tallit,* symbolizing the ingathering of the exiles.

The vast majority of non-Orthodox males and now an increasing number of females are choosing to wear both a *kipah* and a *tallit* for worship. Women among the non-Orthodox streams are also choosing to wear *tefillin.* They do so as part of the preparation for prayer and a vehicle for increasing *kavanah,* just as dressing up for any special occasion promotes proper attitudes and behavior.

Some Thoughts on the Theology and Philosophy of Prayer

This section briefly presents perspectives of some contemporary Jewish thinkers on prayer. Each of them makes clear that although Jews use a fixed text, prayer itself transforms the words on the page to a relationship with God. Lawrence Hoffman (mentioned previously) described prayer as follows:

---

56. The commandment to put fringes is derived from Numbers 15:38.
57. The command for the phylacteries is derived from Deuteronomy 6:8.

Jewish prayer is an act of personal piety. It is a response to my life of faith and an affirmation of my membership first in the Jewish People and more broadly in the human community as a whole. It is a manifestation of my certainty that this Jewish People to whom I belong matters in history, and that I matter, too, because I enjoy a covenant with this God of history—however I may picture, describe, or define the God in whom I trust.[58]

Perhaps the most influential Modern Orthodox thinker is the late Joseph B. Soloveitchik, who explained that prayer is the medium through which a person can relate to God. This relationship is dialogical. He analogizes it to prophecy:

The foundation of prayer is not the conviction of its effectiveness but belief that through it we approach God intimately and the miraculous community embracing finite man and his Creator is born. The basic function of prayer is not its practical consequences but the metaphysical formation of a fellowship consisting of God and man.[59]

Petitional prayer arises from a profound sense of one's need and desire for God's help, inspired by one's sense of absolute dependence or one's pain at the feeling of God's absence. In contrast, prayers of praise and thanksgiving do not bring about contact with the Divine, but are the responses to contact with Him. The institutionalization of prayer by the Rabbis was an attempt to educate people in their own existential reality—sometimes it is only through prayer that we can come to the realization that we must pray. Meaningful prayer must be just that. It must reflect my own concerns and needs and my own sense of dependence on God. It is not a *means* of influencing God, but the expression of my desire to do so; I beseech God to address my concerns, to help me with my problems, to relieve my pain and distress.[60]

Abraham Joshua Heschel, one of the most prominent Jewish thinkers of the twentieth century, writes:

Unless, therefore, God is at least as real as my own self; unless I am sure that God has at least as much life as I do, how could I pray? . . . What marks the act of prayer is the decision to enter and face the presence of God. To pray means to expose oneself to Him, to His judgment. . . . Great is the power of prayer. For to worship is to expand the presence of God in the world. God is transcendent, but our worship makes Him immanent.[61] To pray is to

58. Hoffman, *The Way into Jewish Prayer,* 17.
59. Joseph B. Soloveitchik, *Worship of the Heart: Essays on Jewish Prayer* (New York: Ktav Publishing House, 2004), 35.
60. Soloveitchik, 28.
61. Abraham Joshua Heschel, "The Spirit of Jewish Prayer," *Moral Grandeur and Spiritual Audacity: Essays* (New York: Farrar, Straus and Giroux, 1996), 109

take notice of the wonder, to regain a sense of the mystery that animates all beings, the divine margin in all attainments. Prayer is our humble answer to the inconceivable surprise of living.[62]

Mordecai Kaplan, the founder of the Reconstructionist Movement and a religious naturalist, writes:

As the power that makes for world order and personal salvation, God is not a person but a Process. Nevertheless, our experience of that Process is entirely personal. . . . Critics of the conception of God as Process object to it on the ground that it reduces prayer to a form of talking to oneself. In a sense that is true, but we must understand in what sense it is true. All thinking—and prayer is a form of thought—is essentially a dialogue between our purely individual egocentric self and our self as representing a process that goes on beyond us. . . . When we wish to establish contact with the Process that makes for human salvation, we can do so only through an appeal to the higher self that represents the working of the Process within us. From that higher self, which is identical with our conscience, the moral censor of our acts, and which represents God as operative in our life, we seek the answer to prayer.[63]

Rabbi Harold Kushner, a disciple of Mordecai Kaplan, writes:

Prayer is not a matter of coming to God with our wish list and pleading with Him to give us what we ask for. Prayer is first and foremost the experience of being in the presence of God. Whether or not we have our requests granted, whether or not we get anything to take home as a result of the encounter, we are changed by having come into the presence of God. A person who has spent an hour or two in the presence of God will be a different person for some time afterward.[64]

For me, a Yale-trained Reform rabbi, prayer is

[An] experience of profound connection to something beyond ourselves. During the worship service, there are often moments when I feel deeply connected to an entity greater than myself. God? The Source of Being? The Shechinah? The Soul of the universe? The Rock of Israel? Divine Friend? Sacred Partner? I cannot really name what I mean, but I feel connected. At these moments I am not rationally examining my theology, but experiencing something important and meaningful that speaks to the deepest aspects of my being. Prayer is an experience inspired by words addressed to God, but it is more than just the words. This connectedness does not occur all of the

62. Abraham Joshua Heschel, *Man's Quest for God* (New York: Charles Scribner's Sons, 1954), 5.

63. Mordecai Kaplan, *Questions Jews Ask* (New York: Reconstructionist Press, 1956), 105–6.

64. Harold Kushner, *Who Needs God* (New York: Summit Books, 1998), 148.

time or even as frequently as I would like, but it can occur amid community in a worship service or even when I'm alone. When it happens, it feels real and it feels important—both as a moment in my spiritual life and related to my membership in the Jewish community and the Jewish people.[65]

The efficacy of petitionary prayer is a matter of great theological discussion. I have found that two quotations that appear in the Reform *siddur,* *Mishkan T'filah,* have helped me to understand the spiritual value of petitionary prayer without truly solving the theological dilemmas. The first is from Rabbi Ferdinand Isserman: "Pray as if everything depended on God. Act as if everything depended on you" (Mishkhan T'filah, page 165). And the second is from Abraham Joshua Heschel: "Prayer invites God's Presence to suffuse our spirits, God's will to prevail in our lives. Prayer may not bring water to parched fields, nor mend a broken bridge, nor rebuild a ruined city. But prayer can water an arid soul, mend a broken heart, rebuild a weakened will (Mishkhan T'filah, page 165)."[66]

These brief citations provide a taste of the myriad complex discussions about prayer in the contemporary period. The literature on prayer is vast, and this chapter cannot do it full justice. The challenges to praying with a fixed text are many, but a fixed text provides the opportunity to have regular prayer experience. Familiar words facilitate prayer, communal solidarity, identity, and righteous action. The three elements of the Jewish approach to prayer are liturgy, worship, and prayer. There is liturgy, which consists of the words meant to be uttered. There is worship, which is the way in which the words are performed in community. There is prayer, which connects the worshipper to God through the vehicle of liturgical worship. This does not always happen, but when it does it provides a strong incentive to keep trying.

---

65. Knobel, "Reflections on Prayer," 330.
66. Knobel, 332–33.

Approaching God:
Jewish and Latter-day Saint
Prayer and Worship[1]

Loren D. Marks and David C. Dollahite

Dedicatory Note: *The authors respectfully dedicate this chapter to the great-souled mensch, Rabbi Peter Knobel, who passed away during our final preparations of this chapter.*

We are grateful to Trevan Hatch and Leonard Greenspoon for constructing a volume that can serve as a bridge between Judaism and The Church of Jesus Christ of Latter-day Saints. In this chapter, we draw heavily from the late Rabbi Peter Knobel's chapter, "Approaching God: A Jewish Approach to Prayer," which is filled with insights regarding how a diverse people with more than four thousand years of history participate in personal and communal prayer. We encourage readers of Knobel's chapter to attend to his footnotes, as he provides much of interest there. We strive to follow his example by rewarding the diligent reader with some stimulating footnotes as well.

With both Jewish and LDS audiences in mind, we write hoping that learning more about one another's approaches to prayer and worship will increase understanding and mutual appreciation between members of the oldest Abrahamic faith and members of a relatively new one. In our response, we highlight ideas from six main themes in Knobel's chapter: (1) the lasting legacy of Jewish prayer, (2) prayer as worship and vital work (*avodah*), (3) communal and private prayer, (4) dcripture study worship as a companion to prayer, (5) Jewish prayer and LDS temple worship, and (6)

---

1. We gratefully acknowledge careful reading and constructive feedback on earlier drafts of this chapter from Jamie Ryan, Heather Howell Kelley, Ashley LeBaron, Alan Hawkins, Randy Bluth, Kristina Gibby, Nathan Leonhardt, Michael Harris, Jill Marks, Kyle Walker, Linda Hoffman Kimball, Christian Kimball, Jeff Hill, Brady Eisert, Michael Goodman, Mary Dollahite, Rachel Lambourne, Katy Dollahite, Jonathan Dollahite, and Luke Dollahite.

tikkun olam—repairing the world. Before we address these connections, we briefly discuss our own religious backgrounds, and then gender and prayer.

Where Are We Coming From?

For readers who might wish to know where we are coming from as we write about Jewish and LDS approaches to prayer and worship, we share a bit about ourselves. We are both active Latter-day Saints who teach and conduct research on religion and family life at Brigham Young University,[2] an institution sponsored by The Church of Jesus Christ of Latter-day Saints. Loren was raised in the Church, and Dave, raised Episcopalian, converted to the LDS faith when he was nineteen years old.[3] We both served full-time missions for the Church. Each of us married our wife in an LDS temple and raised our children in the faith. Further, prayer and worship (the foci of this chapter) are integral in our personal and family lives.

What we write does not necessarily reflect official positions of the Church. Our understandings of and perspectives about the Jewish and LDS faiths are our own.[4] Certainly, other Latter-day Saints might emphasize different connections, while some with different perspectives from ours might well take issue with how we characterize the Church and its members. Further, we are scholars of contemporary family life and not historians; thus, while our focus will be on current practice, we recognize that some might wish for greater depth of discussion about the history of changes related to gender and public prayer, blessings of healing, and

---

2. As scholars, we have published more than one hundred scholarly articles and two books about religion and family life and are co-directors of the American Families of Faith project at BYU. Most of these studies have included Jewish families (along with Christian and Muslim families).

3. Dave's lifelong interest in and love for Judaism and the Jewish people began with the fact that he has a Jewish godmother. Over the years, he has attended a great many Jewish services in several states. Dave currently teaches a class called Family in World Religions that includes extensive coverage of Jewish family life.

4. To help our Jewish readers have a better sense for our approach to religion, it might help to make a comparison with branches of Judaism (i.e., Ultra-Orthodox, Modern Orthodox, Conservative, Reform, Reconstructionist). Although it does not, if the LDS faith did have something like the different branches found in Judaism, in many ways our approach to our faith would be consistent with the way many Modern Orthodox Jews approach theirs. That is, fully embracing the core beliefs and practices of the faith while also engaging in contemporary culture and scholarship in ways we believe are consonant with our faith.

temple practice. Much of interest must go unsaid; we strive to focus on what we see as central.

Gender and Prayer for Jews and Latter-day Saints

There are a number of interesting similarities among and differences between the ways that prayer is gendered among the Jewish and Latter-day Saint religions. While there is a history of gendered religious worship (including prayer) in both the Jewish and LDS contexts,[5] here we deal only with current practice by briefly mentioning some similarities and differences.

Jewish Prayer and Gender

In Orthodox Judaism, men are obligated to perform public prayer three times a day. Women are generally exempted from time-bound obligations, including prayer, but are expected to pray at least once a day. An Orthodox *minyan* (quorum of ten for daily public prayers) consists only of adult males (thirteen years and older). Among Orthodox Jews, only married men wear the prayer shawl (*tallit*) for prayer and only *bar mitvah* (boys thirteen years and older) and men wear the phylacteries (*tefillin*) for morning prayers. In Orthodox synagogues, a partition (*mechitza*) separates men and women during prayer. Reform and Conservative Judaism have eliminated most gender distinctions in prayer and other religious actions and obligations. For example, in Orthodox Judaism, fathers bless each of their children each *Shabbat* (Sabbath), while in Reform and Conservative Judaism the blessing may be given by mothers or fathers.[6]

Latter-day Saint Prayer and Gender

In The Church of Jesus Christ of Latter-day Saints, women and men are both expected to offer daily personal prayers, and both are invited to

---

5. Our own sense is that LDS practice is somewhat analogous to the Modern Orthodox branch of Judaism in that there have been a number of changes in LDS practices intended to include more participation of women in religious observance and faith community leadership while preserving the idea that males, by virtue of being ordained to the priesthood, continue to have certain distinctive religious responsibilities and opportunities.

6. Heather H. Kelley et al., "*Shalom Bayit*—Peace of the Home: Ritual and Tradition in American Jewish Families," *Marriage and Family Review* 54 (2018): 706–18.

offer prayers in LDS gatherings and services. Church teachings exhort daily personal, couple, and family prayer, and these are the contexts where the vast majority of prayers are offered. Typically, couple- and family-spoken prayers are offered on a rotating basis (family members take turns) from both genders and by persons of various ages. Thus, most prayers offered in LDS homes and meetings are offered by women and men, with children and youth frequently praying as well. In the LDS faith, two written (liturgical) prayers (sacrament and baptismal prayers) are offered only by males holding the Aaronic Priesthood, and temple dedicatory prayers are offered only by men holding the Melchizedek Priesthood. Some non-written prayers are offered only by men in the priesthood, such as blessings of children; priesthood blessings of healing, comfort, and counsel; dedication of buildings, homes, and graves; and some temple prayers. It is also LDS tradition that the father calls on family members to pray during family meals and gatherings.

We now turn to the first of six central themes rooted heavily in Rabbi Knobel's work.

Theme One: The Lasting Legacy of Jewish Prayer

We greatly admire the incredibly long legacy of Jewish prayer. In the second sentence of his chapter, Rabbi Knobel explains that "prayers have an order and a structure that locates the individual within the more than four thousand years of Jewish history" (p. 87).[7] Consider the staggering scope outlined here for a moment: more than four millennia! During this time, countless empires and regimes have risen, fallen, and faded into oblivion, including those of ancient Egypt, Babylon,[8] and Rome—as well as Hitler's Third Reich. Many of these regimes conquered, slaughtered, enslaved, imprisoned, and oppressed the Jewish people[9]—but most

---

7. See Chaim Potok, *Wanderings: History of the Jews* (New York: Random House, 1980), 3, where he asks: "How is it that after . . . four thousand years of tense, fructifying, and often violent cultural confrontations—with ancient paganism, with Greece and Rome, with Christianity and Islam, and, for the past two hundred years, with modern secularism—how is it that after all this, Jews still exist and are still—as I am here—attempting to understand and interpret their history?"

8. For an in-depth description of Babylon's prophesied fall, even while Israel was in captivity, see Jeremiah 51:29–64, including "As Babylon hath caused the slain of Israel to fall, so at Babylon shall fall the slain of all the earth" and "Thus shall Babylon sink . . ." (v. 49, 64).

9. An important point for members of The Church of Jesus Christ of Latter-day Saints to understand is that the Jewish people are descended from all of the Twelve

of those regimes eventually exited off the world stage of power while a small remnant of Jews,[10] with their sacred prayers and patterns of worship, have indeed remained—as many of the Israelite prophets, including Isaiah, Jeremiah, Ezekiel, and Micah, foretold.[11] The permanence of Jewish prayer, Jewish tradition, and the Jews as a people[12] across myriad contexts is an enigma almost without parallel. In the Jewish tradition of rabbis citing one another, Knobel references Rabbi Lawrence Hoffman:

> Prayer is a delivery system for committing us to the great ideas that make life worth living, because ideas that are ritually construed empower us to do what we would otherwise never have the courage to do. Prayer moves us to see our lives more clearly against the backdrop of eternity, concentrating our attention on verities that we would otherwise forget. It imparts Judaism's canon of great concepts and moves us to live our lives by them. (p. 89)[13]

We live in a twenty-first century culture where much is temporary. Knobel's point that Jewish prayers have an order housed within more than four millennia of Jewish history demands our attention and respect in an increasingly ephemeral and disposable world. Prayer has been a hallmark of Jewish permanence. But why has Jewish prayer had the staying power

---

Tribes of Israel. As it says in the "Who Is a Jew" section of the *Judaism 101* website, "the word 'Jew' now refers to all of the physical and spiritual descendants of Jacob/ Israel." Many mistakenly think that the Jews only descend from Jacob/Israel's son Judah. In fact, the people known as Jews descend from the people who lived in Judea, the land of inheritance for members of the tribes of Judah, Benjamin, and Levi. But because Jerusalem was the capital city and the city which housed the holy temple, people from all other tribes came to live in Jerusalem. In the same way that any great city or capital city has a diverse population, Jerusalem and Judea had people from all over the kingdom of Israel. Thus, when the Ten Tribes were carried away captive by the Assyrians in the eighth century BCE, there were people of those ten tribes (the other ten sons of Jacob/Israel) who were not carried away but who lived in Jerusalem and whose descendants are known as Jews.

10. The word "remnant" is used at least eighty-five times in the King James Version of the Old Testament or Hebrew Bible. See, for example, Ezekiel 14:22: "Yet [in spite of the destruction, there] shall be left a remnant that shall be brought forth, both sons and daughters."

11. We will resist the temptation to overview the remarkable (e.g., Nobel prize-winning) and disproportionate influence this resilient remnant have had on the past and contemporary world.

12. Bloom, *The American Religion.*

13. Lawrence A. Hoffman, *The Way into Jewish Prayer* (Woodstock, VT: Jewish Lights Publishing, 2000), 104.

to outlast the political and religious regimes that have sought to squelch both the Jewish people and their prayers?[14] A portion of the answer to these questions regarding permanence involves the focus of Jewish prayer on the permanent or eternal.

In a shifting world where the notion of eternal truth is often scoffed at, Jewish prayer (referring to concepts invoked by Knobel) involves great ideas bigger than the individual, a context and backdrop of eternity more expansive than the fleeting present, and a focus on verities that deserve the worshipper's concentrated attention. Prayer in its purer form, then, is not merely something we say—it is a transformative process that conveys ideas to us, empowers us, helps us see life clearly, and focuses us on what truly matters. These explanations of prayer fill us with holy envy[15] and move us to live our lives through the permanent power of prayer.

Theme Two: Prayer as Worship and Vital Work

We deeply respect the Jewish view that prayer is not merely something said but something lived. This has strong parallels in the LDS Restoration. Many Latter-day Saints are familiar with, and may accept as an article of faith, the phrase, "Pray as if everything depended on God. Act as if everything depended on you."[16] Church leaders (both LDS and Catholic) have expressed similar sentiments, but, as Rabbi Knobel outlines, the above call for combining faith and action in prayer also hails from Jewish tradition and appears on page 165 in the *Mishkhan T'filah,* the Reform Siddur (prayer book).

Indeed, prayer as a blending of words, action, and living is conveyed throughout Knobel's chapter, including the statement that "it was taught . . . [that a] person is obligated to say one hundred blessings a day (*Menachot* 43b)" (p. 90n16). In other words, one hundred prayers a day amounts to an ongoing dialogue with Deity, a weaving of sacred word and intentional action from the rising from bed in the morning until the day's end. For some, this pattern will call to mind one of several LDS scriptural

---

14. See Daniel 6 for a prototypical example where praying to the Hebrew God was punishable by death.

15. Holy envy involves a deep admiration and honoring of beautiful elements in faith traditions outside of our own.

16. This phrase has been variously attributed to St. Augustine and St. Ignatius and has been used in past LDS Church instructional manuals.

passages urging the reader to "pray always."[17] Yet, as Knobel reminds us, praying morning and night—or even one hundred times a day—is not the core issue. Intent, attitude, quality, and sincerity are the weightier matters. Knobel writes that "one of the purposes of prayer as well as the study of scripture is to promote righteous actions" (p. 102). He further states, "The experience of prayer defies straightforward description. It is best understood through engaging in prayer. . . . [G]enuine prayer depends on the worshipper's attitude and frame of mind" (p. 87).

Knobel later indicates that "the question of whether prayer affects God is an important theological question." Without offering a response, Knobel then notes that whether or not God is affected, "prayer can have a powerful effect on the individual" (p. 99n32).

This is yet another idea that blends well with central chords of the LDS Restoration, if not necessarily actual practice among the Saints.[18] An LDS text states, "Prayer is the act by which the will of the Father and the will of the child are brought into correspondence with each other. The object of prayer is not to change the will of God."[19] If prayer is (1) the aligning of the supplicant's will with God's will but (2) God's will does not change, this seems to imply that (3) true prayer involves the "act" of the worshipper moving her or his will to align with God's. Indeed, prayer of this quality can have the powerful effect on the individual that Knobel describes. Praying in such a way, not only with our lips but with a willingness to bend body and soul into harmony with the will of our Creator, frames a successive LDS statement that reads, "Blessings require some work or effort on our part before we can obtain them. Prayer is a form of work and is an appointed means for obtaining the highest of all blessings."[20]

Where does this notion of prayer as "work" originate? We turn to a key Hebrew word and concept that Knobel introduces in one of the first footnotes of his chapter. He explains, "The word worship (*avodah*) in Hebrew originally referred to the Temple Service. After the destruction of the Temple, it was understood as prayer" (p. 87n5). By way of extension,

---

17. These include six in the Book of Mormo and thirteen in the Doctrine and Covenants.

18. Our sense is that most active (observant) Latter-day Saints do tend to believe that God will listen to and answer their prayers. Thus, many likely do strive to exert their faith in a way that would lead God to answer their prayers, even though they understand that they should say, "Thy will, not mine, be done" (Luke 22:42).

19. *LDS Bible Dictionary*, 752–53.

20. *LDS Bible Dictionary*, 753.

we note that in Hebrew the word *avodah* means both work and worship. *Avodah* expresses the combined, conscious intent that goes into every action. The focal point is that any outward performance, including prayer, requires a sacred inner content in order to make the act itself sacred. *Avodah* is a conceptual gem—the combining of worship and work into one. True prayer in Judaism is both. It is the words and the actions; it is the lips that speak truth and the feet that tread the true path.

Theme Three: Communal and Private Prayer

We deeply respect Judaism's powerful guidance for both communal and personal prayer that can connect people to God and to others in their community.

Communal Prayer

Rabbi Knobel explains that central goals of communal worship are unified prayer and inviting the divine presence to the community. This is a lofty aim that meets with no small resistance. He explains, with a voice of experience, "Prayer is a *mitzvah* [commandment] and it has regular set times, [and] it provides regular ongoing opportunities to engage in prayer . . . even when the worshipper is not in the mood to pray." During times when there is a lack of desire to pray, there is the "hope that the words will inspire real prayer" (p. 102). Knobel also notes the rabbinical teaching that "sometimes it is only through prayer that we can come to the realization that we must pray" (p. 111). This notion is mirrored in Brigham Young's teaching that "it matters not whether you or I feel like praying, when the time comes to pray, pray. If we do not feel like it, we . . . pray till we do."[21]

Great teachers and leaders often have a vision for their people, but they also tend to have a keen awareness of the barriers that prevent their people in their current state from achieving that vision. One such barrier in many LDS congregations is the use of phones and electronic tablets for games, texting, and other non-sacred use during church meetings. An Orthodox Jewish scholar similarly commented, "Our devices are so addictive that some Orthodox young people are having a hard time turning off

---

21. John A. Widtsoe, ed., *Discourses of Brigham Young* (Salt Lake City: Deseret Book, 2009), 44.

their phones on Shabbat, to the concern of their elders."[22] It seems that the Saints share this dilemma with their Jewish friends—as well as the prescribed cure. For those who are distracted or do not feel like praying, Knobel suggests that Jewish communal prayers offer the invitation to pray until we catch the divine presence and feel the desire to connect with the Creator (instead of with the Wi-Fi).

Let us delve a little deeper. While most communal prayer extends the invitation to pray to everyone, including the distracted and reluctant, there are deeply sacred types of communal prayer in Judaism that are not necessarily for those in reluctant states of mind. One such prayer is the *Amidah*.[23] *Amidah* means "standing," and this prayer is indeed recited while standing. The standing prayer must not be perfunctory.[24] It is deep, sacred, and symbolic. Indeed (from *Mishna Avot* 2:13), "one should not stand to recite the [*Amidah*] Prayer unless one is in a serious frame of mind" (p. 104). This is also the case with certain "standing" prayers in LDS temple worship. The shared principle is that the mind and heart must be right so that the God's influence or spirit will be fully welcomed, not restrained.

Personal Prayer

Along with the power of communal prayer, personal prayer is also important. As Knobel states,

> Following the destruction of the Temple in Jerusalem in 70 CE, prayer re-placed sacrifice as the dominant mode of worship in Judaism. The synagogue and the home are the main venues for worship, although a Jew can pray anywhere. (p. 87–88)

In Knobel's footnotes, he offers readers a window to his own personal world of worship and conversation with God:

> For many years I ran five miles every morning. Now that running is out of the question, I walk that same distance instead. This alone time has become, for me, a vehicle for engaging in extended prayer. . . . [D]uring my morning exer-

---

22. Marks, Hatch, and Dollahite, "Sacred Practices and Family Processes in a Jewish Context," 451.

23. The final prayer in the *Amidah* begins, "My God, keep my tongue from evil and my lips from speaking deceitfully," which is similar to words spoken in blessings in LDS temples.

24. Further, Knobel writes, "There are some prayers that can only be recited in the presence of a *minyan* (a quorum of ten adults over thirteen years of age)" (p. 89).

cise, I often engage in an extended conversation with God. I address God in an intimate and personal way. It is like having a conversation with a trusted friend or advisor who listens but does not speak. These conversations have helped me through many a personal crisis and aided me in clarifying my thinking and goals. At the end, although I have no explicit response, I feel that there is a "listening ear," and I can discern with greater clarity the path that I must take. (p. 99n44)

However, Knobel also confesses, "I am never sure why things work out the way they do, and I remain agnostic about God's role, but I do know that prayer is a very significant part of my life" (p. 103). For us, this transparent, authentic, personal testimonial, blending both faith and questions, was one of the pinnacles of Knobel's chapter. His reflection captures the essence of the archetypal Jewish struggle around questions regarding the existence (or non-existence) of God and if and how God might engage with human beings and human actions such as prayer.

Working and worshipping (*avodah*), connecting, extending conversations with God, and seeking help through personal crisis are all notable purposes and blessings of personal prayer referenced by Knobel. An additional intent is that of expressing praise and gratitude, whether in personal or communal prayer. On the act of praise, Knobel restates that the *Amidah* (the Standing Prayer) includes prayers of praise and thanksgiving.

While the *Amidah* is communal, many private prayers of thanks are also urged throughout each day in Judaism. Knobel explains that "upon awaking, one thanks God for restoring their life" (p. 92). He further relates that Rabbinic tradition "conceive[s] of sleep as a kind of death with the soul hovering over the body, and each morning body and soul are rejoined. It is a mini resurrection of the dead" (p. 92n19). As thanks for this resurrection and revitalization, "each new day is a gift of God and begins with an expression of gratitude for being granted another day" (p. 92).

In like manner, the Book of Mormon prophet Alma similarly exhorts, "[W]hen thou risest in the morning, let thy heart be full of thanks unto God; and if ye do these things, ye shall be lifted up at the last day" (Alma 37:37). Indeed, Jewish teachings that one should begin, end, and permeate each day with expressions of gratitude are further paralleled in LDS scripture with the command, "Thou shalt thank the Lord thy God in all things" (D&C 59:7).

Theme Four: Scripture Study Worship as a Companion to Prayer

We deeply respect the way that Judaism connects the study of sacred texts with prayer. As important as daily prayer (communal and private) may be in Judaism, prayer does not stand alone. Knobel explains that "Torah study is a *mitzvah* and considered by the Rabbis to be among the most important *mitzvot* (commandments). Therefore, it is included as part of the daily ritual" (p. 94). Indeed, the phrasing that Knobel uses is "Torah study worship," not "reading of Torah." This is an important distinction for those of us who have too often engaged in mere reading instead of study worship.

Citing a passage (*M. Peah* 1:1) from the *Mishkan T'filah*, Knobel emphasizes both a Jew's daily obligations and the powerful breadth of sacred text:

> These are things that are limitless . . . honoring one's father and mother, engaging in deeds of compassion, arriving early for study morning and evening, dealing graciously with guests, visiting the sick, providing for the wedding couple, accompanying the dead for burial, being devoted in prayer, and making peace among people. But the study of Torah encompasses them all. (p. 95)

In stating the *Shema*, the line between Torah and prayer (if one existed at all) is removed. Although "in a strict sense, [the *Shema*] is not a prayer but a statement of faith" (p. 95), it is central to Judaism. Inclusive of three passages (Deut. 6:4–8; 11:13–21; Num. 15:37–41), the "*Shema* describes the commandment to put fringes or tassels on the corner of [Jewish] garments as a reminder of the commandments" (p. 96–97):

> Impress these My words upon your every heart: bind them as a sign on your hand and let them serve as a symbol on your forehead, and teach them to your children—reciting them when you stay at home and when you are away, when you lie down and when you get up; and inscribe them on the doorposts of your house and on your gates—to the end that you and your children may endure, in the land that the LORD swore to your fathers to assign to them, as long as there is a heaven over the earth.

The focus on the divine words and the charge to "teach them to your children," as well as the emphasis on home, house, and children, will be familiar to LDS readers. The words of the sacred text are to be studied, to be recited, to be inscribed, to become part of life from morning until night. All this is to be done "to the end that you and your children may endure." Compare those central Jewish ideas with these LDS verses:

> I [God] have given unto you another law and commandment. Wherefore teach it unto your children, that all men, everywhere, must repent, or they can in nowise inherit the kingdom of God, for no unclean thing can dwell there, or dwell in his presence. . . . Therefore I give unto you a commandment, to teach these things freely unto your children. (Moses 6:56–58)

And again, inasmuch as parents have children in Zion . . . that teach them not to understand the doctrine of . . . the living God . . . the sin be upon the heads of the parents. . . . And they shall also teach their children to pray, and to walk uprightly before the Lord. And the inhabitants of Zion shall also observe the Sabbath day to keep it holy. (D&C 68:25, 28, 29)

Clearly, in both Abrahamic traditions, sacred scripture is not only revered but also includes the charge of teaching due respect for the commandments to one's own children. In spite of the strong similarities, there are aspects of Jewish worship vis-à-vis sacred text that are unique and striking. Knobel describes that in a synagogue setting,

When the Torah is taken from the Ark the congregation rises and the Torah is carried in procession through the congregation. The congregants reach out to touch the scroll with the fringes of their *Tallit* (prayer shawl) or their *siddur*. Excitement fills the room. The Torah is taken to the *bima* (the raised reading stand) and undressed. Members of the community are called up to recite a blessing over the reading or to chant the Torah portion. It is a great honor to receive an *Aliyah* (to be called up to recite the blessing over the reading). (p. 100)

Knobel writes, "Orthodox males . . . don a large prayer shawl called a *tallit* that has four specially tied corner fringes called *tzitzit*" (p. 110).[25] As we have attended Shabbat services in various synagogues, we have been moved to see many worshippers kiss their *tzitzit* and then touch the Torah scroll with reverence. The accompanying Torah study, Knobel explains, is a symbolic "reenactment of the theophany at Mt. Sinai" (p. 100).[26] Knobel cites Rabbi Arthur Green, who teaches,

The central part of our self-understanding is that Sinai-revelation is *always* happening. Every generation of Jews ever to be born or converted was there at Sinai. *Ma'amad Harsinai* (standing at Mount Sinai) means standing there with your heart open, knowing what you have to learn, knowing what you have to do. (p. 100)

Knobel continues:

When the Torah reading is completed, the congregation rises, the scroll is lifted, and the text is shown to the congregation. . . . At this moment the congregation acknowledges that it is transported back to Mt. Sinai. (p. 101)

---

25. The commandment to add fringes is derived from Numbers 15:38.

26. Ruth Langer, "From Study of Scripture to a Reenactment of Sinai: The Emergence of the Synagogue Torah Service," *Worship* 72 (1998): 43–67.

This vivid image calls to mind for us the words of LDS educator Karl G. Maeser, who observed, "There is a Mt. Sinai for every child of God, if only he can be inspired to climb it."[27]

Theme Five: Jewish Prayer and Temple Worship

We deeply respect the precision present in Jewish prayer, in part because of the many ways that Jewish sacred clothing, gestures, words, and intent are consonant with various elements of temple worship—meaning worship in the ancient Jewish Temple and in contemporary LDS temples.[28] In this section, we reference insights shared by Rabbi Knobel regarding Jewish prayers and blessings (some of which are echoes of practices in the Second Jewish Temple in Jerusalem) and connect them with contemporary LDS temple worship. We also mention a few additional practices regarding Jewish prayer and blessings discussed by Rabbi Alfred Kolatch in his encyclopedic work, *Inside Judaism.*

As Knobel makes clear, Orthodox Jewish prayer is quite liturgical. On the other hand, LDS prayer and worship is liturgical in certain situations (i.e., in temples), but, for the most part, it is more extemporaneous. There is no LDS prayer book used in chapels, temples, or homes, and the vast majority of prayers offered by the Saints are of the more spontaneous variety.[29]

---

27. Ernest Wilkinson, "The Calling of BYU," in *Educating Zion*, ed. John Welch (Provo, UT: BYU, 2014), 36.

28. There is not space here to discuss in detail the connections between practices from the first Jewish Temple (Solomon's) and the second Jewish Temple (Herod's Temple) and practices in LDS temples. While there are some similarities (e.g., wearing of sacred clothing, focus on rituals performed by priesthood, washings, focus on atonement, vicarious atoning work, and a veil between sacred places and more sacred places), there are also a number of important differences. Rather, our approach compares contemporary Jewish practices (some of which has some basis in practice from the ancient temples) and the practices in contemporary LDS temples. LDS scholar Ann N. Madsen provides an insightful comparison of Solomon's temple with the Salt Lake Temple here: "Solomon's Temple Compared to the Salt Lake Temple," in *An Eye of Faith: Essays in Honor of Richard O. Cowan*, ed. Kenneth L. Alford and Richard E. Bennett (Provo, UT: Religious Studies Center, 2015), 69–89.

29. Even so, there is some structure and form to the more extemporaneous prayers that typically begin with the person saying, "Our Heavenly Father" or "Our Father in Heaven," and almost always closing with the person saying, "In the name of Jesus Christ, Amen." But most personal and communal prayers typically are spoken (or thought) "from the heart" of the person praying. It is

LDS Temple Dedicatory Prayers

One particular type of written LDS prayer is the dedicatory prayers for LDS temples. The pattern for dedicatory prayers for temples was set by Joseph Smith, the founding prophet and first president of the Church, in his dedicatory prayer for the first LDS temple dedicated in 1836 in Kirtland, Ohio (see D&C 109). Since that time, the president of the Church (believed to be a prophet, seer, and revelator), under inspiration from God, writes out a dedicatory prayer for each new temple being dedicated.[30] This prayer is then read at all sessions of the dedication.

Temple dedicatory prayers conclude with the Hosanna Shout (Hosanna means "God Save Us"). A description from the *Encyclopedia of Mormonism* explains:

> The Hosanna Shout is whole-souled, given to the full limit of one's strength. The congregation stands and in unison shouts the words "Hosanna, Hosanna, Hosanna to God and the Lamb. Amen, Amen, and Amen," repeating them three times. This is usually accompanied by the rhythmic waving of white handkerchiefs with uplifted hands. The epithet "Lamb" relates to the condescension and Atonement of Jesus Christ.
>
> The Hosanna Shout memorializes the pre-earthly Council in Heaven, as "when . . . all the sons of God shouted for joy" (Job 38:7). It also recalls the hosannas and the waving of palm branches accorded the Messiah as he entered Jerusalem. And hosannas welcomed him as he appeared to the Nephites. President Lorenzo Snow taught that this shout will herald the Messiah when he comes in the glory of the Father.[31]

The LDS Hosanna Shout is fascinatingly similar to a sacred Jewish practice called *kapparot* (atonements), which is performed by Ultra-Orthodox Jews on the day before *Yom Kippur* (the Day of Atonement), when females wave a white hen over their heads three times and males wave a white rooster over their heads three times. In his book *Inside Judaism*, Rabbi Alfred Kolatch describes *kapporot* as follows:

> As the bird is waved overhead, the following words are pronounced: "This is my substitute, my vicarious offering, my atonement. This cock/hen shall meet

---

expected that both personal and communal prayer would typically involve first some expressions of gratitude to God and then some requests. The words that are spoken or thought do not typically involve reciting or reading prayers.

30. As of April 2019, there are 201 temples around the word that have either been dedicated (162), are under construction (12), or are announced (27).

31. Lael J. Woodbury, "Hossana Shout," in *Encyclopedia of Mormonism*, 4 vols. (New York: Macmillan Publishing Company, 1991), 2:659.

death, but I shall enjoy a long, pleasant life of peace." . . . The primary reason for using a cock or hen in the ceremony was that after the destruction of the Temple no animal used in the sacrificial Temple rites could serve as a symbol of atonement in Jewish life. . . . The custom of *kapparot*, which is not mentioned in the Talmud, seems to have begun among the Jews of Babylonia.[32]

The Hosanna Shout also resonates with Knobel's discussion of the *Kedushah* blessing that proclaims God's holiness. The sacred text surrounding this blessing explains that God "is served by a heavenly angelic choir whose function is to proclaim God's holiness. The community then is understood to be imitating the angels. This is the pinnacle of praise" (p. 98). Similarly, the dedicatory prayer of the Kirtland Temple reads, "Help us by the power of thy Spirit, that we may mingle our voices with those bright, shining seraphs around thy throne, with acclamations of praise, singing Hosanna to God" (D&C 109:79).[33] The hymn sung at all subsequent temple dedications, "The Spirit of God Like a Fire Is Burning," includes the refrain "We'll sing and we'll shout with the armies of heaven. Hosanna, Hosanna, to God and the Lamb." This is another example of communal LDS prayer that exhibits striking commonalities with communal Jewish prayer.

Vicarious Prayers in Judaism

A central reason Latter-day Saints build temples is to accomplish vicarious work for deceased ancestors and to do essential ordinances for them that they can no longer perform themselves. This idea intersects with a fascinating aspect of Jewish prayer that allows vicarious prayers for those who cannot offer prayer for themselves. It is part of Jewish law (*halakah*) that one who does not know how to pray may fulfill his or her obligation to pray by vicarious means. In their book on Jewish prayer, Rabbi Ethan Tucker and Rabbi Micha'el Rosenberg quote from the *Shulhan Arukh* (OH 124:1), one of the most revered sources of teaching on Jewish law, and indicate that following communal prayers, the prayer leader

> repeats the prayer, so that if there is someone who does not know how to pray, he may have intention to what the leader is saying, and discharge [his obliga-

32. Alfred. J. Kolatch, *Inside Judaism: The Concepts, Customs, and Celebrations of the Jewish People* (Middle Village, NY: Jonathan David, 2006), 285.

33. Another related LDS scripture indicates that the Lord considers "the song of the righteous [to be] a prayer unto me, and it shall be answered with a blessing upon their heads" (D&C 25:12).

tion] through it. . . . The *Mishnah* establishes the principle that only one who is obligated (in a *mitzvah*) may fulfill another person's obligation towards it.[34]

Sacred Garments and Robes

While the authentic sincerity of the heart, mind, and soul are vital to prayer, Knobel reminds us that for some forms of communal prayer, "special clothing" is worn and "particular actions or gestures" are also employed. He states:

> Prayer . . . consists of wearing special clothing and engaging in particular actions or gestures that symbolize status and intent and focus the attention of the worshiper on the meaning of the words. . . . The central prayer, the *Amidah*, is literally the standing prayer. (p. 109)

Many LDS readers will feel a sacred kinship and connection with this symbol-laden prayer offered while wearing sacred clothing and recited communally while standing.

Knobel explains, "As you cover your head, say, 'Blessed are You who crowns Israel with splendor'" (p. 92). This crowns of splendor concept hails from several references in Exodus and Leviticus to the priestly garments and robes of Aaron, including the cap called a mitre. As explained in Exodus, the mitre is not so much a hat as a preliminary to a crown—it is, in fact, a crown holder. Moses is told in Exodus 29:4–6:

> And Aaron and his sons thou shalt bring unto the door of the tabernacle of the congregation, and shalt wash them with water. And thou shalt take the garments, and put upon Aaron the coat, and the robe of the ephod, and the ephod, and the breastplate, and gird him with the curious girdle of the ephod: And thou shalt put the mitre upon his head, and put the holy crown upon the mitre.

The sacred clothing that many Jews wear for prayer includes the prayer shawl (*tallit gadol*) and the smaller white undergarment worn by Orthodox Jewish men (*tallit katan*). Both of these include four fringes (*tzitzit*) that serve to remind those who wear them about their covenant to observe the commandments of God.

Latter-day Saints also wear sacred clothing that remind them of their covenants. These include temple garments[35] that, like the Jewish *tallit*

---

34. Ethan Tucker and Michael Rosenberg, *Gender Equality and Prayer in Jewish Law* (Brooklyn, NY: KTAV, 2017), 18.

35. A video that explains the meaning and use of these items of sacred clothing has been prepared by the Church of Jesus Christ. See "Temple Garments,"

katan, are worn every day under regular clothing and also include four marks that remind the wearer of their covenants to honor the laws and commandments of the Lord. Sacred clothing also includes temple robes worn by LDS women and men during certain ceremonies in the holy temple.[36] In short, Jews and Saints both have articles of sacred clothing that assist them in their worship and "remembering." Part of the temple robes are head-coverings worn by both women and men. Thus, prayers in LDS temples are similar to Orthodox Jewish prayers in that women and men pray with their heads covered.[37]

Kiddush Blessing as Echo of Ancient Jewish Temple Practice

The Jewish *Kiddush,* or blessing over the wine, is a central practice for observant Jews on *Shabbat* (Sabbath) and a number of holy days. In his volume, *Inside Judaism*, Rabbi Alfred Kolatch states:

> It is traditional to fill to overflowing the cup of wine over which Kiddush is recited. This is often explained as an expression of hope that life's goodness and bounty will be as abundant as the wine that is being blessed, but a more basic reason is related to the sacrificial system that was operative in temple times. When burnt- and peace-offerings were made, an entire container of wine was poured onto the altar. After the temple was destroyed and wine was used in connection with home rituals, a custom developed of filling the cup of wine to its very brim. When reciting the Kiddush, many traditional Jews pick up the wine goblet, which has been filled to capacity, and cup it in both hands. They then remove their left hand and hold the goblet with only their right hand approximately three inches (one *tefach*) above the table. Some people nestle the bottom of the cup in their right palms and grasp it with five fingers to be in compliance with the verse in the book of Psalms (145:16): "Thou openest Thine hands and satisfiest every living thing with favor."[38]

LDS temple practices also include specified physical actions with ritual meaning. The specifics are not discussed, but the patterns echo Jewish practice as well as practices in a number of other older religious traditions

---

Newsroom, https://www.mormonnewsroom.org/article/temple-garments.

36. "Sacred Temple Clothing," *The Church of Jesus Christ of Latter-day Saints,* https://www.lds.org/media-library/video/2014-01-1460-sacred-temple-clothing.

37. LDS temple robes are white, like the white prayer shawls and the white robe called a *kittel* that is worn by many Orthodox Jewish males at their weddings, during various holy days, and in which they are buried. Similarly, a Latter-day Saint who has received his or her endowment is buried in temple clothing.

38. Kolatch, *Inside Judaism*, 295–56.

worldwide.[39] Jews and Latter-day Saints both hold sacred the 23rd Psalm ("The Lord is My Shepherd") and the acknowledgement that, like the ancient Psalmist, "thou anointest my head with oil; my cup runneth over." Many Jews and Saints similarly cling to the personal hope that "goodness and mercy shall follow me all the days of my life: and I will dwell in the house of the Lord forever" (Psalm 23:5, 6).

Sacred Washings in Jewish and LDS Practice

Ritual washings are an important part of Orthodox and Hasidic Jewish observance, including, in some cases, before prayer.[40] Knobel repeatedly emphasizes that prayer is much more than reciting words and further notes that there is a non-verbal language of prayer. This non-verbal language is at least twofold in that it involves, first, actions before the prayer (in order to be clean) and, second, symbolic actions during the prayer. According to Latter-day Saint scholar Donald W. Parry,

> To ensure religious purity, Mosaic law required that designated individuals receive a ritual washing, sometimes in preparation for entering the temple (Ex. 30:17–21; Lev. 14:7–8; 15:5–27). The washings and anointings of the biblical period have a parallel today in The Church of Jesus Christ of Latter-day Saints. . . . Many symbolic meanings of washings and anointings are traceable in the scriptures. Ritual washings (Heb. 9:10; D&C 124:37) symbolize the cleansing of the soul from sins and iniquities. They signify the washing-away of the pollutions of the Lord's people (Isa. 4:4). Psalm 51:2 expresses the human longing and divine promise: "Wash me thoroughly from mine iniquity, and cleanse me from my sin" (cf. Ps. 73:13; Isa. 1:16). . . . The anointing of a person or object with sacred ointment represents sanctification (Lev. 8:10–12) and consecration (Ex. 28:41), so that both become "most holy" (Ex. 30:29) unto the Lord.[41]

---

39. Many Latter-day Saints will find it meaningful that a sacred practice of Orthodox Jews involves cupping their hands while speaking sacred words that are an echo of practices in the Second Jewish Temple.

40. This includes washing of hands upon waking, before eating bread, and before prayer, as well as full immersion in a mikvah for various purposes. See Menachem Posner, "Washing Hands Before Praying and Studying," *Chabad.org*, accessed May 19, 2021, https://www.chabad.org/library/article_cdo/aid/655978/jewish/Washing-Hands-Before-Praying-and-Studying.htm.

41. Donald W. Parry, "Washing and Anointings," in *Encyclopedia of Mormonism*, 4 vols. (New York: Macmillan Publishing Company, 1991), 4:1551.

Both women and men serve in LDS temples performing and administering in these sacred washings and anointings.[42]

In his chapter, Knobel shares a Jewish blessing. We include here only excerpts, noting the explicit form of gratitude:

> As you hear the crow of a rooster, say, "Blessed are You who gave the mind understanding to discern day from night." As you open your eyes, say, "Blessed are You who gives sight to the blind." . . . As you stand up, say "Blessed are You who straightens those who are bent over." . . . As you put your shoes on, say "Blessed are You who has given me all I need." As you fasten your belt, say "Blessed are You who girds Israel with might." (p. 92)

Knobel continues by citing Rabbi Lawrence Hoffman, who explains that the Talmud provides a blessing for a person's "urinary tract and intestinal system, for [they] are as much engaged in doing God's work as is our brain" (p. 92n21). Knobel further explains, "Jewish anthropology emphasizes our dual nature. We are both physical and spiritual beings; therefore there is a blessing for the body and a blessing for the soul" (p. 92). A careful reading of these Jewish blessings indicates a blessing of the mind to understand and discern, eyes that see with clarity, a spine with strength to stand up straight and not be bent over, and feet that take stable steps. The rabbis further teach about the girding of the loins, vitals, and bowels as humans fulfill their mission on the earth. These blessings will hold familiar echoes for many LDS readers.

In his chapter, Knobel notes multiple blessings that reference both body and soul. One of these concludes, "So long as the soul is within me I thank you, Lord my God, God of my ancestors, Master of all creation, Lord of all souls. Blessed are You Who restores souls to lifeless exhausted bodies" (p. 94). A second related Jewish blessing concludes, "Blessed are You, Lord, healer of all flesh, who sustains our bodies in wondrous ways" (p. 92). These blessings will call to mind much for Saints, including these LDS texts that also reference blessings of body, spirit, and soul:

> And all saints who remember to . . . [walk] in obedience to the commandments, shall receive health in their navel and marrow to their bones; And shall find wisdom and great treasures of knowledge, even hidden treasures; And shall run and not be weary, and shall walk and not faint. And I, the

42. "Women are set apart to administer the ordinances to women, and men are set apart to administer the ordinances to men." Allen Claire Rozsa, "Temple Ordinances," in *Encyclopedia of Mormonism*, 4 vols. (New York: Macmillan, 1991), 4:1444.

Lord, give unto them a promise, that the destroying angel shall pass by them, as the children of Israel, and not slay them. Amen. (D&C 89:18–21)

For whoso is faithful unto the obtaining these two priesthoods of which I have spoken, and the magnifying their calling, are sanctified by the Spirit unto the renewing of their bodies. They become the sons of Moses and of Aaron and the seed of Abraham . . . and the elect of God. (D&C 84:33–34)

The Jewish and LDS foci are strikingly similar.[43]

Prayer Circles

Prayer circles in temples are one type of Latter-day Saint prayer that has important connections with Jewish prayer and worship. According to LDS scholar George S. Tate,

The prayer circle is a part of Latter-day Saint temple worship, usually associated with the endowment ceremony. Participants, an equal number of men and women dressed in temple clothing, surround an altar in a circle formation to participate unitedly in prayer. . . . The formation of the prayer circle suggests wholeness and eternity, and the participants, having affirmed that they bear no negative feelings toward other members of the circle (cf. Matt. 5:23–24), evoke communal harmony in collective prayer—a harmony underscored by the linked formation, uniformity of dress, and the unison repetition of the words of the leader. The prayer has no set text, but is, among other things, an occasion for seeking the Lord's blessing upon those with particular needs whose names have been submitted for collective entreaty.[44]

Like the Jewish *minyan* (a quorum of ten adults that is required for some Jewish prayers), the LDS prayer circle recognizes the power of numbers that may be present in communal prayers spoken by a group of persons united in sincere faith. Like Jewish prayer in a *minyan*, an LDS prayer circle

---

43. There are also fascinating connections with the anointings done in the Orthodox Christian faith as part of the sacrament of chrismation that immediately follows baptism, when various parts of the newly baptized person's body are anointed with chrism (holy oil). "The body is anointed as follows: the nostrils: (For sweet fragrance); the ears: (To hear the words of faith); the mouth: (My mouth shall speak wisdom); the chest: (For healing of soul and body); the feet: (to walk in your footsteps, O Lord); the hands: (Your hands have made me and fashioned me, O Lord); the back: (Whosoever wishes to come after me, Let him deny himself and carry their Cross and follow me.)." John Shimchick, "Orthodox Baptism," *American Serb History 101,* 2002, https://babamim.com/orthodox_baptism.

44. George S. Tate, "Prayer Circle," in *Encyclopedia of Mormonism,* 4 vols. (New York: Macmillan Publishing Company, 1991), 3:1120.

is conducted while wearing sacred clothing. Like the Jewish *Amidah*, the prayer circle involves a group of people standing and praying in unison.[45]

We now address a further similarity. *Hoshana Rabbah* is a sacred Jewish ceremony on the last day of *Sukkot* (Festival of Booths), which is considered the last of the Days of Judgment that began on *Rosh Hashana* (New Year). *Hoshana Rabbah* means Great Supplication and involves worshippers making seven circuits of the inside of the synagogue, reminiscent of the practices in the Second Temple. A brief discussion of those sacred prayers offers,

> [A]s recorded in the *Mishnah*: "It was customary to make one procession around the [temple] altar on each day of Sukkot, and seven on the seventh day" [*Sukkah 4:5*]. The priests carried the palm branches or willows in their hands. The entire ceremony is to demonstrate rejoicing and gratitude for a blessed and fruitful year. Moreover, it serves to tear down the iron wall that separates us from our Father in Heaven, as the wall of Jericho was encompassed "and the wall fell down flat" (Joshua 6). Furthermore, the seven circuits correspond to the seven words in the verse *Erhatz benikayon kappay, va'asovevah et mizbahakha Hashem*—"I wash my hands in purity and circle around Your altar, O Lord" (Psalms 26:6).[46]

Worshippers surrounding an altar while pouring out supplications is also an apt description of LDS prayer circles held in holy temples. This prayer is offered just before those present go from a room representing this earth to a room representing heaven (the Celestial Room).[47]

---

45. The LDS temple prayer circle consists of equal numbers of men and women who in unison repeat the words of the leader (always a male holder of the priesthood). In the temple endowment room, women and men sit in separate sections. Thus, a Jewish married couple attending an Orthodox service at a synagogue and an LDS married couple attending an endowment session at a temple would have a similar experience in the sense that they would arrive together, enter the building, sit in separate sections during worship, and then reunite after worship concluded.

46. Cantor Macy Nulman, "Hoshana: Beseeching God," *My Jewish Learning*, https://www.myjewishlearning.com/article/hoshana-beseeching-god/.

47. At the occasion of the dedication of the Rome Italy Temple (the Church's 162th dedicated temple), the Church collaborated with journalists from the Vatican to make a film about the temple that shows various rooms inside. See "Two Apostles Lead a Virtual Tour of the Rome Italy Temple," *Newsroom*, March 7, 2019, https://www.mormonnewsroom.org/article/virtual-tour-rome-italy-temple.

Prayers at the Western Wall and in Latter-day Saint Temples

Another aspect of LDS prayer in the holy temple that is similar to Jewish prayer is the LDS temple prayer roll. Many Jews who go to the Western Wall in Jerusalem to pray believe that prayers offered there have special power. People often write out prayers on a white piece of paper and place it in a crack between the stones of the wall. In a practice that has some interesting similarities, Saints who attend the temple may submit the names of those for whom they would like a special prayer said during the prayer circle that provides "an occasion for seeking the Lord's blessing upon those with particular needs whose names have been submitted for collective entreaty."[48] They do so by writing the names of people they wish prayed for on a piece of white paper that is slipped into a box that is later placed on an altar of the temple during prayer circles. Most active (observant) Saints believe that placing someone's name on the prayer rolls of the temple has special meaning and that the prayers spoken around the altars of the temple have special power.[49]

The Priestly Benediction

Jewish men who are descendants of Aaron from the patrilineal line are considered priests (*Kohanim*).[50] In the ancient Jewish Temple, multiple times a day the priests would mount a platform and stand before the people of Israel and recite the Priestly Blessing or Priestly Benediction. The priestly blessing is described in the Hebrew Bible:

> And the LORD spoke to Moses: Speak unto Aaron and his sons: Thus shall you bless the people of Israel. Say to them: The LORD bless you and keep you! The LORD deal kindly and graciously with you!; The LORD bestow His favor upon you and grant you peace! Thus they shall link My name with the people of Israel, and I will bless them. (Num. 6:23–27, JPS)

From the time the Jewish Temple was destroyed in 70 CE, the Priestly Blessing or Priestly Benediction has been pronounced on certain Jewish

---

48. Ludlow, *Encyclopedia of Mormonism*, 1120.

49. Names of persons of any faith can be placed on an LDS temple's prayer roll. Further, persons of any faith can call an LDS temple and have the name of a loved one placed on the prayer roll for that particular temple.

50. LDS scripture recognizes this priesthood. In the Doctrine and Covenants, it states, "And the Lord confirmed a priesthood also upon Aaron and his seed, throughout all their generations, which priesthood also continueth and abideth forever with the priesthood which is after the holiest order of God" (D&C 84:18).

holidays (in Israel it is spoken every day at various places). In Orthodox synagogues, *Kohanim* pronounce the Priestly Blessing in Hebrew over the congregation in a certain way. In *Inside Judaism*, Rabbi Kolatch explains:

> While pronouncing the Priestly Benediction, the Priest assumes a posture known as *nesi'at kapa'yim* ("raising of the hands"). He stretches both arms and hands forward, extending the fingers straight ahead and separating the little finger and ring finger of each hand from the other fingers, forming a V shape. The thumb of each hand is separated from the index finger so that the formation of each hand looks like the Hebrew letter *shin*, the first letter of *Shaddai*, the name of God. . . .
>
> In a later period, outstretched hands became symbolic of the priesthood. It is common to find this representation engraved on tombstones of members of the priestly family. . . . Traditionally, the hands of the Priests are washed by Levites before they mount the pulpit . . . [and] the Kohen covers his face and hands with his tallit so that no physical blemish can be seen. . . .
>
> Today, rabbis who are not Kohanim often pronounce the Priestly Benediction upon a bar or bat mitzvah, upon a couple under the marriage canopy, and also as the concluding benediction at a religious service.[51]

In this sacred blessing, a direct descendent of Aaron, a Jewish priest, receives a ritual washing, removes his shoes, stands with a prayer shawl, raises his arms with his hands[52] in a specific way, and speaks sacred words.[53] The second author of the present chapter attended a service at

---

51. Alfred. J. Kolatch, *Inside Judaism: The Concepts, Customs, and Celebrations of the Jewish People* (Middle Village, NY: Jonathan David Publishers, 2006), 407–8.

52. Leonard Nimoy, a Jewish actor who played a Vulcan named Spock in the *Star Trek* TV and film series, employed the "Vulcan hand salute" in which he held his right hand in the way that *Kohanim* hold their hands while offering the Priestly Benediction. While holding his hand thus, Nimoy had Spock say, "Live long and prosper" which was Nimoy's summary of the essence of the text of the Priestly Benediction. Indeed, the global popularity of the *Star Trek* franchise has led to the surprising fact that a sacred Jewish religious ritual that has been continuously practiced for three thousand years has become a widely recognized part of popular culture. See Matt Phillips, "The history behind Leonard Nimony's Vulcan salute," *Quartz*, February 27, 2015, https://qz.com/352855/the-secret-history-behind-leonard-nimoys-spock-salute/.

53. In her discussion of the morning prayers (*Shacharit*) on *Yom Kippur* (Day of Atonement), the holiest day of the Jewish year, Blu Greenberg states, "One of the special features of *Shacharit* is the *Avinu Malkenu* prayer, Our Father, Our King. The first *Avinu Malkenu* is a confession. We clap our right hand over our left breast as a sign of remorse and guilt and say, 'Our Father, We have sinned before You.'" *How to Run a Traditional Jewish Household* (New York: Simon &

an Orthodox Jewish synagogue[54] when the Priestly Benediction was con-
ferred. He experienced a sense of spiritual power very similar to when he
has been present in a congregation when an LDS Apostle gives an "apostolic blessing" to a congregation.

Theme Six: *Tikkun Olam*—Repairing the World

Another feature of Jewish prayer captured by Rabbi Knobel is the accompanying reminder that "our daily task is to imitate God. As God opens
the eyes of the blind or clothes the naked, we should strive to be like God
and should work for the betterment of the human condition" (p. 92). This
beautiful and lofty ideal that "we should strive to be like God" by laboring,
committing our resources, and serving our fellow humans who are part of
God's kingdom is closely tied to the Jewish concept of *tikkun olam*. The
phrase *tikkun olam* is featured in the Jewish congregational prayer called
the *Aleinu. Tikkun olam*, as interpreted in Orthodox Judaism, references
abandoning all forms of idolatry and—by extension—giving all adora-
tion and attention to the one true God. While *tikkun olam* has somewhat
varied meanings across the branches of Judaism,[55] the central theme is
to repair the world. In the words of the twentieth-century Jewish writer
Chaim Potok, "For some mysterious reason, God's world was imperfect.
Man's task was to help God perfect it."[56]

Many Jewish blessings begin with the phrase, "Blessed are You, Lord
our God, King of the universe" (*Baruch atah Adonai, Eloheinu melech
ha'olam*), indicating that God is king over all. Saints also believe that God
is the King of the universe, and the sacred objectives of helping God build
His kingdom and working together to heal the world are beautiful and
familiar to the Saints. The official Church website explains, "The law of
consecration is a divine principle whereby men and women voluntarily
dedicate their time, talents, and material wealth to the establishment and

---

Schuster, 1983), 325. Sacred prayers using specific gestures as signs of devotion
to God are familiar to Latter-day Saints who have worshipped and prayed in LDS
temples.

54. The Chabad House at the University of Massachusetts-Amherst.

55. For a rabbinical discussion, see Lauren Geller, "What is the Real Meaning
of Tikkum Olam?" *Jewish Journal*, October 8, 2017, https://jewishjournal.com/
culture/religion/225990/real-meaning-tikkun-olam/.

56. Potok, *Wanderings*, 1.

building up of God's kingdom."[57] The LDS concept of consecration is strikingly similar to Judaism's sacred charge of *tikkun olam.*

Indeed, the Jews and the Saints share the hope of establishing a repaired and healed world—a true Zion. Although visions of exactly what that world should look like vary, we also share the view that this ideal is best reached both by striving to *imitate God* and by giving what we have to those who need it most. The rabbis place authentic prayer at the center of this hope—and dualistically, *tikkun olam* is also at the center of the *Aleinu* prayer.

Our Hopes for Our Readers

Many of our LDS friends who were kind enough to read a previous version of our chapter mentioned the power of Rabbi Knobel's words in inviting them to greater devotion in their lives of prayer and worship. More than one said that LDS prayers (their own and those they hear) are far too often casual, meager, perfunctory, shallow, and otherwise not consistent with the praise due God. Many were reportedly moved by Knobel's "confession" that he perseveres in prayer despite not being certain of God's responsiveness to his prayers. We hope that our readers—including our fellow Saints—who are wrestling with doubts about the responsiveness or even existence of God, the truthfulness of the Church, or other spiritual and religious doubts will follow Knobel's example of persevering and continually engaging in authentic prayer.

In connection with this volume's aim to carefully consider "the learning of the Jews" (1 Ne. 1:2) and invite all to learn from our Jewish friends, we have noted highlights including (1) the lasting legacy of Jewish prayer, (2) Jewish prayer as worship and vital work (*avodah*), (3) the sacred roles of communal and private prayer in Judaism, (4) deep, intentional scripture study worship as a companion to prayer, (5) Jewish prayer and LDS temple worship, and (6) the overarching Jewish aim of *tikkun olam*—repairing the world. Additionally, other aspects of Judaism have inspired sufficient holy envy in us that we have addressed these features in both our academic research and our writings to public and LDS audiences. Among several, we mention the following eight "take home" messages related to prayer, worship, and observance from our own studies of Jewish families:

---

57. "Consecrate, Law of Consecration," The Church of Jesus Christ of Latter-day Saints, accessed May 19, 2021, https://www.churchofjesuschrist.org/study/scriptures/gs/consecrate-law-of-consecration.

1. Religious observance, rituals, and traditions can help facilitate successful marriage and parent-child relationships. These religious expressions reportedly provide time for "bonding" and can help "relax [the] tensions" of everyday life. (The Jewish *Shabbat* or Sabbath celebration is exemplary in this respect, prompting us to call it the "family ritual *par excellence.*") [58]

2. Orthodox Jews take a one-day break from electronic devices to focus solely on faith and family without distraction. (How might doing likewise enrich our own church and family worship, our level of sacred focus, and our depth of relationships?)

3. Observant Jews do not discuss "the cares of the world," including money, business, or related concerns, to help make the Sabbath an "island of sacred time" and a respite from the "wrestle with the world." This allows time, energy, and focus to discuss heavenly, eternal, and spiritual things that bring deeper delight.

4. Jewish families often "share the Sabbath" by inviting guests. One way for Latter-day Saint families to make the Sabbath a delight is by inviting others into their homes.

5. Jewish women usher in Shabbat on Friday just before sundown by lighting two candles. As part of this, a Jewish wife solemnly prays for the Jewish temple to be rebuilt and prays for family members. To end the Sabbath, Jewish men pray the *Havdalah*, which includes praying for the spirit of the Sabbath to linger throughout the week.

6. Like our Jewish brothers and sisters, we can learn that the Sabbath is an ideal time to bless our children—literally and figuratively— and to celebrate our shared walk of faith.

7. Our Jewish friends celebrate both the creation of the earth and the redemption from slavery on the Sabbath. (Latter-day Saints can rejoice in the Lord and celebrate our redemption from death and sin on the Sabbath.)

8. Jewish families intentionally celebrate the sacred and familial joy of life. Across many generations and many cultures, the ancestors of

---

58. Loren D. Marks, Trevan G. Hatch, and David C. Dollahite, "Sacred Practices and Family Processes in a Jewish Context: Shabbat as the Weekly Family Ritual *Par Excellence,*" *Family Process* 57 (2017): 448–61.

our Jewish friends have been persecuted and killed. Tragically, anti-Semitism is increasing across the earth, and Jewish lives remain under various kinds of threats. Despite or because of this, our Jewish friends frequently say, with gusto, the Hebrew phrase *l'chaim!* (To life!). They take extra care on the Sabbath day to celebrate life—particularly a life devoted to worshipping God and binding couples and families together in and through that worship.[59]

Indeed, there is much we can learn from our Jewish sisters and brothers—and from their sacred tradition. We are again grateful to Rabbi Knobel for inviting us onto his sacred ground and inspiring us to strive to ascend spiritual mountains through prayer, study, and worship offered with *avodah* and real intent.

We hope that Jewish readers of our chapter gain some meaningful insights about how their LDS friends worship. For readers who are neither Jewish nor LDS, we hope you find many deep connections between Jewish and LDS approaches to prayer and worship to be of some intellectual interest and, perhaps, find yourself moved as you strive to make prayer and worship a more meaningful part of your life.

Jewish Kabbalistic teachings about an original divine unity that was shattered lead to Jewish emphasis on repairing the world (*tikkun olam*). A core LDS teaching is that, before birth, human beings lived with God (Heavenly Father and Heavenly Mother) as spirit children and heaven involves a return to live with Heavenly Parents. Thus, both Jewish and LDS prayer ultimately is about re-approaching God.

---

59. These are borrowed and adapted from: David C. Dollahite and Loren D. Marks, "Making the Sabbath a delight: Seven lessons from strong Jewish families," *Meridian Magazine* (February 20, 2018); and Heather H. Kelley, Ashley B. LeBaron, David C. Dollahite, and Loren D. Marks, "What We Can Learn From Ritual and Tradition in American Jewish Families," *Meridian Magazine* (September 23, 2019).

Women and Judaism in the Contemporary World: Tradition in Tension

Ellen Lasser LeVee

Religious Tensions in the Contemporary World

It is taken for granted that women and religious traditions are in tension. On the one hand, there are feminists who condemn religious traditions for being patriarchal and therefore oppressive to women. On the other hand, there are religion's denunciation of western materialism with its egalitarian perspective and hollow appeal to women. This essay offers a more nuanced perspective. Rather than religion being inherently oppressive, this essay observes that oppressiveness becomes a concern with modernity. Rather than materialism's egalitarian seductions, this essay suggests sources of egalitarianism within religion. While the tensions between women and religious traditions are real in the contemporary world, these tensions are more a product of the tensions between religion and the contemporary world than between women and religion.

In particular, this essay considers women and Judaism. Judaism constitutes a unique religious world with its own history and complex inner dynamics. Certain of its features, such as its ethnic character, its basis in a system of law (halakha), and its covenant with God that includes concern for society's vulnerable, are distinctly social. In combination with each other, they have informed Jews' individual spiritual lives. However, with western materialism comes secularity, where spirituality is primarily a private choice. The individualistic nature assigned to religion contradicts Jewish experience, undermining Jewish existence in the contemporary world. How is the social nature of Judaism sustained when spirituality is an individual matter? Jewish history has provided limited experience with this unprecedented situation.

Within this context, Jewish women, who have always been an inextricable part of Jewish life, have questioned their place in Judaism. Some have felt like outsiders.[1] Women's traditional spiritual expressions, fitting a life of social consequence, appear inadequate when individual spirituality, epitomized by men's roles, predominates. With spirituality a matter of choice, Jewish women choose how to live their Judaism along a range of options. Some women are perfectly content with the roles assigned to them by Jewish tradition, but others reject those roles or look to what has previously been assigned to men. Secular individualism and egalitarianism have become indissolubly linked.

This essay breaks that link. While the tensions Jewish women experience are expressed through egalitarian concerns, the argument here is that it is not egalitarianism but rather the contemporary world's individualistic social structure that poses conflicts for Jewish life. Judaism provides homes for all the varying options mentioned above. Liberal varieties of Judaism, accepting individualism, adapt to contemporary social mores to fully incorporate egalitarianism; the most traditional varieties of Judaism, maintaining Judaism's communal structure, preserve Jewish tradition while hardening opposition to contemporary mores that involve egalitarianism. And then there are varieties that try to mediate between the extremes, preserving Judaism's traditions with its communal structure while adopting more egalitarian gender roles. Among these three general options, the highly preserving mode, seeming to represent authentic Judaism, appears oppressive to the eyes of those fully adapting to the contemporary world, who anachronistically project it back in time. However, the position that mediates between adapting and preserving is where the social represented by tradition meets secular individualism. Here is where women are more likely to experience a sense of the oppressiveness of their tradition in the contemporary era as they grapple with issues of equality.[2]

Thus, this essay explores the confrontation between Judaism and contemporary society. The next section looks briefly at Jewish women in history to gain perspective on the relationship between them and their tradition, suggesting the relative absence of an experience of oppression,

---

1. See, for example, Rachel Adler, "The Jew Who Wasn't There: Halakhah and the Jewish Woman," 12–18, and Cynthia Ozick, "Notes toward Finding the Right Question," 120–51, in *On Being a Jewish Feminist: A Reader*, ed. Susannah Heschel (New York: Schocken Books, 1983).

2. "Starting a Conversation: A Pioneering Survey of Those Who have Left the Orthodox Community," *Nishma Research*, June 19, 2016, 7, http://nishmaresearch. com/assets/pdf/Report_Survey_of_Those_Who_Left_Orthodoxy_Nishma_ Research_June_2016.pdf.

while also introducing a resource for egalitarianism in the concern for the vulnerable that is part of Jewish tradition. The third section considers various changes in Jewish tradition as a result of the impact of the contemporary world on Judaism, distinguishing different approaches to the confrontation between the contemporary world and Jewish tradition and introducing another resource for gender equality in the role that halakha plays in sustaining relationships in Jewish life. The fourth section discusses the implications of the different approaches for how Jewish women have responded to these changes, for the most part overcoming experiences of oppression. Indeed, perceptions of oppression felt by Jewish women are most likely to occur among those women who experience the intersection of tradition and the contemporary world. The chapter concludes with a discussion of the egalitarian sources within Judaism. With Jewish tradition holding within it resources for women's religious and social equality, western materialism's individualism poses a far greater challenge. With this, the source of tensions between women and Judaism is better explained by the collision between Jewish tradition and the contemporary world rather than by being grounded within Judaism.

Jewish Women Historically

The contemporary world has brought change to Jewish life, but the seeds of the current tensions between Jewish women and their tradition lie in the past. Here, three issues are particularly relevant. One is surely the general subordination of women to men throughout Jewish history. I consider subordination to be a structural social feature, not necessarily synonymous with oppression.[3] To be sure, women are vulnerable to oppression because of subordination, but subordination, in and of itself, need not be oppressive, particularly in societies where gendered capabilities are both appreciated for their contributions to the social world and where care for the other marks personal relationships. A second issue is the other side of this subordination of women, Judaism's heritage of concern for society's vulnerable. Judaism has a history of protecting the dignity of those who are poor and weak. This protection extended to women. Finally, a third decisive contribution to the present predicament of women's dissatisfaction with traditional Judaism is the responsiveness of Jewish culture to the

---

3. See Carol Gilligan, *In a Different Voice* (Cambridge: Harvard University Press, 1993), where a distinction between hierarchy and a network of relations is developed, especially in Chapter 2, "Images of Relationship," 24–63.

larger surrounding culture. At the same time that Jews preserved tradition, they also adapted that tradition to the social conditions of the time.[4]

Throughout Jewish history, these issues have intertwined with each other. The subordination of women was not just characteristic of Jewish societies, but throughout world history, women were subordinate to men, certainly in the social worlds inhabited by Jews. Jewish law did not break with those worlds but worked within their parameters. In turn, there were efforts to ameliorate the difficulties women encountered. While some of these efforts reflected the mores of the surrounding society, some were products of Jewish halakha. The picture that emerges is that of respect for women's moral and spiritual capacities while recognizing the social limitations that had been placed upon women.

This respect for women's moral and spiritual capacities is in fact grounded in the Hebrew Bible. Although men and women have different social positions, their character is essentially the same.[5] Nowhere does the Bible "depict women as sex objects, or weak, or reticent."[6] They are neither "considered inferior, less wise, less moral, or in need of keepers."[7] Even Eve is not blamed for original sin, a concept foreign to Judaism. Rather, in the Bible, she is "the mother of all life" (Gen. 3:20). Jewish tradition holds both Adam and Eve responsible for disobedience to God, and the consequences of that sin, its punishments, result in the social realities found throughout the ancient Near East.[8]

---

4. Gershom Scholem, "Revelation and Tradition as Religious Categories in Judaism," in *The Messianic Idea in Judaism* (New York: Schocken Books, 1974), 282–303.

5. Tikvah Frymer-Kensky, "The Ideology of Gender in the Bible and the Ancient Near East," in *Studies in Bible and Feminist Criticism* (Philadelphia: The Jewish Publication Society, 2006), 185–94. Also Tikvah Frymer-Kensky, "Gender and Its Image: Women in the Bible," in *In the Wake of the Goddesses: Women, Culture and the Biblical Transformation of Pagan Myth* (New York: Fawcett Columbine, 1993), 118–43.

6. Tikvah Frymer-Kensky, "Women Jews," in *Studies in Bible and Feminist Criticism* (Philadelphia: The Jewish Publication Society, 2006), 412.

7. Frymer-Kensky, 412.

8. There are sources that do blame Eve for the sin of eating from the Tree of Knowledge of Good and Evil, but there is no single monolithic view of women as evil. See Daniel Boyarin, "Different Eves," in *Carnal Israel* (Berkeley, CA: University of California Press, 1995), 77–106. Also Chava Weissler, "Prayers in Yiddish and the Religious World of Ashkenazic Women," in *Jewish Women in Historical Perspective*, ed. Judith Baskin (Detroit: Wayne State University Press, 1998), 169–92.

With this in mind, the subordination of women in the ancient Near East can be seen not only as the influence of the surrounding societies, but also as a response to women's physical vulnerability, especially when pregnant and raising young children. Ironically, women's subordination ameliorated some disadvantages of women's physical weaknesses in ancient society. Their vulnerability was protected by male property ownership, explaining why husbands, though not wives, could have more than one spouse. With more women married, more women were protected. To be sure, this also subjected women to the prerogatives of their husbands, but laws of ritual purity put some restrictions on the most intimate of those prerogatives.[9] In fact, subordination functioned in a variety of ways depending on the individuals involved. While women's lives were not easy and men exercised considerable power over them, marriage was the greatest assurance of a flourishing life for women, and oppressiveness was not necessarily characteristic of biblical women's experience.

Indeed, women's oppression appears to indicate the disintegration of society. The book of Judges is the example par excellence. Although the book of Judges was codified in the rabbinic era, it reflects a range of possibilities for biblical women. The range is ordered not chronologically but rather according to the moral deterioration of society, and the greater the societal deterioration, the more women suffered. Deborah as a judge in Israel appears in the early pages of the book (Judg. 4:4–5), while the story of the abuse of the Levite's concubine ends the book (Judg. 19–21).

The biblical world was a harsh place for everyone. Yet, it was infused with the religious, giving life meaning. Ordered hierarchically, it established that those with wealth and power protected and respected those who were vulnerable, though as the prophets relate, that did not always, or even usually, happen. Based on an agrarian life, the home was the economic center. Within this context, the Hebrew Bible presents women leading full lives, governing their households, and staying religiously active through prayer, prophecy, cult, and charitable acts.[10]

The world changed dramatically in the Second Temple period. The Jews were conquered, and national sovereignty was ended, first with the Persians, then the Greeks, and finally the Romans. A time of religious

---

9. Anthropology views laws of purity as they function to protect the weak. See Mary Douglas, *Purity and Danger* (London, UK: Routledge Press, 1992), Chapter 9, 140ff., in particular p. 142.

10. Carol Meyers, *Discovering Eve: Ancient Israelite Women in Context* (New York: Oxford Press, 1988).

ferment, it produced the beginnings of both Christianity and Judaism. The rabbis came from a sect called the Pharisees, which translated biblical religion into the form known as Rabbinic Judaism. The rabbis saw themselves as continuing biblical tradition through halakha, but they emphasized prayer and study rather than the Temple Service. Jewish life for them became based in learning and application of halakha.

Life in the Jewish world reflected the changes of this period. Women remained socially subordinate while still held in respect. With Palestine conquered and property destroyed, the impoverishment of the population called for ways to facilitate marriage. Thus, the ketubah, a marriage contract, developed that allowed men to marry without first providing an expensive dowry to the father. The ketubah specified that the wife, at the dissolution of the marriage, whether by the husband's death or by divorce, was to receive money rather than her father before the marriage could be consummated. The ketubah, in fact, also curtailed a husband's impulse to initiate a divorce for trivial reasons (only husbands had the right to initiate divorces) and specified rights and protections for the women within marriage.[11] The ketubah was an instrument for ameliorating some of the period's most oppressive consequences. Moreover, as women could at this period also supplement family incomes, they could thereby gain social status.

In the distinctly religious world, practices eventually accommodated a world without a Temple as the central cultic institution. While men populated the houses of worship to pray and study as substitutes for the cult, the home was also a center for religious activity. With prayer, obligations for cooking and eating, maintaining the laws of marital purity, and arranging for the Sabbath and holiday celebrations, it mirrored cultic activities. These, along with charity and general management of the household, gave women's lives meaning, albeit very distinct from men's, but consistent with what was found in surrounding societies.

The medieval world brought more changes but also a consolidation of tradition. Two distinct communities developed.[12] Jews spread throughout Europe and the Middle East. The Christianity of Europe nurtured one trajectory of Jewish life and the Islam of the Middle East facilitated another,

---

11. Judith Hauptman, *Rereading the Rabbis: A Woman's Voice* (Boulder, CO: Westview Press, 1998), 60–76, Chapter 3. The rest of the book makes a similar argument with respect to other aspects of women's lives.

12. There was also a distinct community in Spain where Islam and Christianity met and vied for power. The Inquisition and expulsion eventually destroyed this community as Jews fled to Europe and the Middle East.

continuing the interactions between Jewish tradition and the larger society. The pietism and scholasticism of Christianity fostered Jewish pietism and the classic commentaries of the Middle Ages. The codes and scholars of Islam reinforced such developments among the Jews in Islamic lands.[13]

In this period Jewish communities were subject to expulsions, migrations, and even massacres. Women's social subordination to men was hardly significant against the backdrop of such suffering. Indeed, religious life flourished, and women's personhood was protected in ways that sometimes exceeded the larger society's norms.[14] Women's religious lives generally reflected the larger societies in which they lived, mirroring the distinctions between Christian or Muslim societies. So, Jewish tradition was maintained at the same time as it adapted to changes in societal conditions, all the while also ameliorating some of the tradition's oppressive features for women.

The modern period again revolutionized Jewish life. During this period, Western Europe eventually invited Jews to participate in the European social world, and Jews eagerly took up the invitation. In central Europe, Jews were legally allowed to participate in society but were not socially welcomed. Here the denominations—Reform, Conservative, and Orthodox Judaisms—have their roots, reflecting the sectarianism of their societies. In eastern Europe, where Jews experienced murderous pogroms, they were not allowed into society, but with the currents from the west and the ethnic attachments found in their societies, some Jews left their religion to identify ethnically as Jews. Other Jews turned to Hasidism, a popular mystical form of Jewish practice emphasizing prayer and good deeds rather than study. With such variety, most Jews strictly maintained tradition. Yet, some gave it up altogether, and others chose options in between. Migrations to America and the smaller flow of Jews to Palestine began two new centers of Jewish life that were less traditional. In the Islamic world, where its scholars rejected modernization, Jews for the most part conformed to the larger society. While becoming middlemen between the European colonists and the Arab population, most Jews maintained their traditions.

Despite these changes and the wide variation in Jewish identification, the subordination of women continued. Indeed, it was systematized

---

13. Talya Fishman, *Becoming the People of the Talmud* (Philadelphia: University of Pennsylvania Press, 2011).

14. See Rachel Biale, *Women and Jewish Law: The Essential Texts, Their History, and Their Relevance for Today* (New York: Schocken Books, 1984). This is particularly true of issues pertaining to divorce (81–83) and wife-beating (93–96).

through the codes that became dominant in Jewish life during this period. Jewish traditions were to be carefully preserved, and the amelioration of women's vulnerabilities were thereby limited. To be sure, women's subordination was not unique to the Jewish community but existed throughout the world. However, as modernity spread in the west, as life became progressively easier, and as women became increasingly able to support themselves, the differences between men's and women's religious expressions became more problematic. With Western values of liberty and equality informing aspirations, and the concern with preserving Jewish tradition trumping the amelioration of women's vulnerabilities, the tensions between Jewish women and their tradition began to emerge.

Judaism in the Contemporary World

In the above historical account, not only was women's subordination apparent, but so was the institution of various ways to ameliorate that social subordination. The two distinct dynamics within Judaism, one preserving tradition despite the various social worlds it encountered and the other adaptive, responding to changing societal circumstances, were also both operating. As changes were made, Jewish tradition's continuing concern for society's weaker members addressed women's vulnerability. In the confrontation with secularity, both preserving and adapting dynamics have continued to operate, but generally they have informed different options in that confrontation. Thus, fragmentation has increased in the contemporary world, and different historical, sociological, and ideological influences support different fragments. Historically, a dramatic geographical and demographic shift occurred. Sociologically, the historical shifts put various structural pressures on Jewish tradition, magnifying divisions between options. In turn, Jewish tradition made multiple ideological adjustments.

With World War II, almost one-third of the world's Jewish population was destroyed, mostly in Central and Eastern Europe. This destruction hit some of the most traditional Jewish communities in the world at that time. American Jewry became the largest community of Jews. Then, with the establishment of the State of Israel, the Jews in Muslim countries were forced to flee their homes, decimating the Jewish communities there. Most went to Israel, constituting half of that country's Jewish population. Israel became the second-largest community of Jews in the world, only recently surpassing the United States in Jewish population. These two centers together account for over 80 percent of world Jewry.[15]

While traditional European Orthodox communities were annihilated in World War II, the last sixty years has seen a resurgence of Orthodoxy. Its high fertility and strong retention rates as well as policies in both the United States and Israel have contributed to its growth. America's separation of church and state, alongside its openness, has led both to increased assimilation of America's liberal Jews and also to the increasing presence of Orthodox Jews in American Jewish communal life. In Israel, the hegemony of Orthodoxy in Israel's religious affairs has played a decisive role in facilitating the growth of that community there. However, also important has been the Orthodox grounding in the major work of codes, the *Shulchan Arukh*, compiled in the sixteenth century, which characterizes both communities of Orthodoxy. The disruptions to tradition from destruction and migration in the twentieth century called forth the clarity of response afforded by codes,[16] a response supported by sociological processes and ideological positions.

Turning first to sociological processes, it is useful to consider certain structural forms that influence religious expression. These structural forms are shaped by two dimensions, one concerned with defining the boundaries of a social world (group) and another concerned with the relationships within that world (grid).[17] The possibilities for these structural forms include a strong group and grid, a weak group and grid, a strong group with a weak grid, and a weak group with a strong grid. Contemporary Judaism includes all of these possibilities, as in the accompanying table.

The four categories of this table represent ideal types. In actuality, there is a range where different categories blend into each other. Groupness among Jews, concerned with boundaries between groups, is reflected in how strongly Jews may identify with being Jewish. Clearly a range exists, from those who identify strongly to those for whom it

---

15. Sergio DellaPergola, "2018 World Jewish Populations," *Berman Jewish Databank & American Jewish Yearbook*, accessed October 30, 2019, https://www.jewishdatabank.org/content/upload/bjdb/2018-World_Jewish_Population_(AJYB,_DellaPergola)_DB_Final.pdf.

16. Haym Soloveitchik, "Rupture and Reconstruction: The Transformation of Contemporary Orthodoxy," *Tradition* 28, no.4 (Summer 1994): 320–76.

17. The following is based on the work of Mary Douglas, *Natural Symbols: Explorations in Cosmology* (New York, Pantheon Books, 1982). Her book is more general and does not discuss Jewish structures.

Grid/Group	High Group	Low Group
High Grid	**Preserving Tradition** Haredi *[Douglas's Hierarchy]*	**Mediating Preserving & Adapting** Modern Orthodox *[Douglas's Isolates]*
Low Grid	**Adapting Tradition** Some secularists, especially Israelis Strongly identified Liberal Jews *[Douglas's Enclave]*	Assimilating Jews *[Douglas's Individualists]*

matters very little. Among those most strongly identified, the boundary between Jew and non-Jew is clear. As that identity grows weaker, the more amorphous that boundary becomes. Different from this is grid. For Jews, grid, concerned with relationships within a group, is traditionally defined by halakha—that is, Jewish law. Of course, halakha helps to also maintain group boundaries, but a Jew need not observe halakha to maintain boundaries, as becomes apparent with liberal and secular Judaisms. Rather, the more observant a Jew is of halakha, the stronger the grid of relationships between Jews. In traditional anthropological literature, hierarchy managed relationships between people. For Jews, halakha replaces the grid of hierarchy. This is notable. Rather than inequality being the glue for relationships within a society, concern for others within the group holds the society together.[18] This has implications for women's status, providing support for an egalitarian approach to woman. Separate from this, it can be observed that where such concern is less prominent, the grid of relationships between Jews correspondingly weakens. Again, a range exists.

General identities of Jews, distinguished by looking at each of the categories as ideal types, produces four discernible groups of Jews. A Jew who strongly identifies as a Jew and is also observant would belong to the high group, high grid category. These are the most strictly observant of Orthodox Jews, often called haredi, and they can be identified as putting emphasis on preserving tradition. So difficult is this preservation in contemporary society that Orthodox Judaism has responded with efforts to strengthen both group and grid. This is where the codes become prominent. 'Going by the book' reinforces both group and grid. In fact, the grid is made even more rigid, with halakha being interpreted in the most

18. See Gilligan, *Different Voice*, 24–63.

stringent ways and the addition of practices that protect the observance of established halakha. In part, this nurtures religious feeling, but it is also a way to avoid a slippery slope toward assimilation represented by less observant Jews. Regarding boundaries, various degrees of distance between society and the Jewish group are maintained, although even among the haredi, this separation is imperfect.[19] A notable concern with who is in and who is out also serves to fortify groupness. These patterns are as true for Israel as they are for American Orthodoxy.

It is also possible for a Jew to strongly identify as a Jew and not be particularly observant (high group, low grid). This group is concerned with adaptation, where identifying as Jewish is important but tradition is also adapted to contemporary mores. This is where highly active liberal Jews who practice very little halakha find themselves, as well as some secular Jews, particularly secular Israelis. The freedom these groups have to choose what halakha to practice undermines its authority, weakening grid. Indeed, the emphasis on groupness may be seen as a form of adaptation, where the grid of halakha is viewed as unjustifiable and onerous, and is therefore replaced by groups that have more salience in the contemporary world. In America this means that a Jewish community often forms around a synagogue, hence the liberal Judaisms. In Israel, national identity itself is an adaptation to contemporary social norms.

Without a strong grid, groupness is undermined. This is exacerbated in the contemporary world by individualism, where no form of group may seem justifiable. In turn, when group itself is weak, grid is further undermined, for only relationships defined by individuals, making their own freely chosen decisions, are important. Individualism is thus linked to being cosmopolitan with an openness to others that acknowledges the equality of all people. This is low grid and low group. Religion, in general, has a very limited role, making secularity prominent. Many of the most assimilated Jews are found here. It is not surprising that among these Jews there is a high intermarriage rate—that is, marriage between Jews and non-Jews. The most liberal forms of Judaism have found ways to include these intermarried Jews, blurring the line that distinguishes the two categories and providing an example of the range that exists between categories.[20]

---

19. Matthew Williams, "To Educate a Jew: Outreach, Assimilation, and the Reformation of American Orthodox Judaism," (PhD diss., Stanford University, June 2021).

20. It is possible to consider the liberal Judaisms as belonging to Douglas's Individualist category because of their openness to others. Enclaves (the adapting

The fourth category is the most anomalous. Grid is high, although group is relatively low. The most prominent example of this are those who practice halakha (high grid) but are also open to the world outside of the groupness of Jewishness. While the boundaries of the group still have strength, particularly because of a strong grid reinforcing relationships within the group, they are nonetheless weakened by such openness. Here are found those who mediate between preserving Jewish tradition through their observance of halakha and adapting Jewish tradition to contemporary mores within the bounds of that halakha. This possibility involves the greatest tensions between western secularity and Jewish tradition because both are a part of the lives of these Jews.

Each of these structural possibilities have ideological positions which serve to reinforce each option. In liberal communities, the centrality of reason has undermined religion. The Holocaust strengthened questions about God's existence, and halakha, already seen as old-fashioned, lost further authority because it was thought to be developed by men rather than given by God. Yet, neither secular Jews nor the liberal movements totally reject Jewish tradition; postmodernity allows for what is personally meaningful, so tradition is shaped to fit the contemporary social world. The adaptive dynamic found within Jewish tradition fits with this perspective. Zionism is one example, and the innovations in Jewish practice of the liberal movements provide another. Such innovations have not always or even necessarily followed established halakha; rather, they conform to current social standards, with changes to and the creation of rituals or liturgy while omitting long-standing halakhic practice. Still, many changes are based in classic Jewish sources, and these movements see themselves as self-consciously continuing Jewish tradition. Included in this endeavor is concern for the vulnerable, which has encouraged an egalitarian response to women's issues. However, the chief component is the centrality of personal autonomy. Individual Jews pick and choose how to live their Jewishness, whether secular Israeli or liberal Jews.

---

category) are defined by Douglas as concerned with boundaries, which liberal Judaisms, except perhaps Conservative Judaism, are not. However, because of their distinctive Jewish identities and structure as organizations, liberal Judaisms act in many ways like enclaves. This may be part of the range of these categories or it may be something peculiar to Judaism. Because of their self-conscious Jewish identity and their adapting propensities, which distinguish them from the other categories, I chose to put liberal Judaisms in this distinct category.

Orthodoxy, too, has its ideological validation. Under the centrality of reason, it turns to one of the great medieval rabbis, Moses Maimonides, a highly acclaimed scholar and philosopher. His thirteen principles of Jewish faith have become a part of the daily Orthodox liturgy. Among these are the immutability of halakha. This ideology of immutability reinforces the importance of the codes, like the *Shulchan Arukh,* at the same time as the influence of the *Shulchan Arukh* reinforces the immutability of halakha. Here the dynamic of tradition is strong, and anything suggestive of innovation is suspect, if not altogether avoided. The egalitarian ethic of the contemporary world is considered to be one such innovation. Thus, Orthodoxy preserves group and grid, making it holy, justifying a status quo.

Ironically, as much as this ideology is used to maintain the distinctiveness of Jewish life, it is a response grounded in the Western philosophical tradition, where truth is immutable and God is absolute. With modernity's development, although God became an irrational idea, the authority of truth is still dominant. Halakha becomes representative of God, as absolute and unchanging truth, giving halakha a kind of Western sanction. Of course, Orthodoxy maintains its belief in God, and with God as Giver of truth in the form of halakha, Orthodoxy combines both western and Jewish ideological traditions. In other words, Orthodoxy, as well as liberal forms of Judaism, assimilated Western ideas that reinforced its agenda.

However, as compelling as this narrative seems, it has not been the only way halakha has been viewed.[21] Evidence of a different approach was apparent above in Judaism's ability to respond to different historical circumstances. There, focus was on how to fulfill the covenant with God within the varying social worlds that Jews inhabited. Halakha was not absolute but responded to those varying social worlds. Rather than one true way, those worlds influenced the relationship to God, shaping halakhic practices in accord with dominant religious currents. This explains how Judaism could transition from Temple worship to prayer and Talmudic study, and how Jewish tradition could respond differently to Christian and Muslim environments. It involves a human partnership with God through the effort to mediate between God's command and its application within human society. In this model, the halakhic expert is focused not only on preserving the halakha, but also on adapting it so as to effectively

---

21. Gershom Scholem, "Revelation and Tradition as Religious Categories in Judaism," in *The Messianic Idea in Judaism and Other Essays on Jewish Spirituality* (New York: Schocken Books, 1971), 282–303, discusses the creativity of Jewish tradition.

nurture a moral relationship between Jews and a spiritual relationship between human and Divine given an ever-changing social world.[22]

This ideology is most at home in the mediating category of strong grid and weak group, where Jewish tradition meets the contemporary world. However, it is a difficult position to maintain in contemporary society. Jewish communal ties have been weakened by secular individuality, and legal precedence has acquired an authority that restricts halakhic options. It is more prominent in Israel because of the structural factors shaping the Orthodox rabbinate there,[23] and because of the added "groupness" of Israel. This added groupness can provide stronger support for maintaining the difficult balance between preserving and adapting Jewish tradition.

Thus, historical trends, structural changes, and varying ideological currents work together to establish the different fragments of Jewish life. While in the past the Jewish social world could sustain its groupness, both through external pressures and through its halakha, at the same time it had some flexibility in moderating the grid of halakha to take into account Jewish experience within the parameters of particular social worlds. In the contemporary world, that has changed. External pressures count for less in maintaining Jewish groupness, and the authority of halakha has weakened. This has contributed to the prominence of liberal and secular forms of Judaism, which, with their strong group and weak grid, have accepted the contemporary world. In emphasizing the adaptive aspects of Jewish tradition, they have taken on the contours of contemporary life while maintaining some aspects of Jewish tradition to a lesser or greater degree. The most stringently Orthodox Judaism's response, with its strong grid and strong group, has emphasized the preserving dynamic of Jewish tradition, for the most part, rejecting the contemporary world. It has avoided as much as possible the influence of contemporary society, strengthening its grid of halakha and ideologically securing its separation from the world outside its community. The effort to mediate between adapting and preserving tradition resides in the category of relatively weak group, strong

---

22. A good example of this position is Benjamin Lau, "The Challenge of Halakhic Innovation," *Meorot*, September 2010, http://www.yctorah.org/wp-content/uploads/2016/03/the-challenge-of-halakhic-innovation-rav-benny-lau.pdf.

23. Tamar Ross, "Orthodox Israeli Feminists Meet Our American Cousins," in *Tablet*, March 7, 2017, http://www.tabletmag.com/jewish-arts-and-culture/books/226723/orthodox-feminism-blu-greenberg. See also accompanying text to footnote 32 below.

grid, where Jewish tradition and contemporary mores are mostly likely to meet and create tensions.

Jewish Women in the Contemporary World

These developments have had enormous implications for Jewish women in the contemporary world. Four distinct categories of women emerge. Three of these reflect three of the four structural divisions developed above. The most individualist division will not be dealt with here. Rather, the fourth category exemplifies what may happen when two different categories of grid and group confront each other. Thus, the four distinct types of women that emerge are (1) haredi women with a strong group and strong grid; (2) Jewish women in America who belong to liberal Judaisms with a strong group and weak grid; (3) the collision between these two categories as they arise in Israel when a secular woman wants a divorce and must attain it through the Orthodox establishment; and (4) modern Orthodox women who participate in the strong grid of observance of halakha, but whose group identity is weakened by their openness to the contemporary social world. These women mediate between Jewish tradition and the contemporary world. Where the first two categories have reduced tensions between the secular world and Jewish tradition by choosing one or the other, the last two categories must confront the intersection of Jewish tradition with the contemporary world.

Jewish women in America who belong to liberal Judaisms (with a strong group and weak grid) are a type familiar to most Americans. While tradition is lived as a private matter of personal choice, there is for most Jews one central communal religious institution: the synagogue. In liberal communities, it reflects the egalitarian values of the larger society. Traditionally, to convene public prayer, there had to be a quorum of ten men. Men and women did not sit together; a partition separated them with women usually relegated to the margins. Women did not lead the congregation in prayer or read from the Torah.[24] All that has changed. In most liberal synagogues, women are now counted in the quorum (if counting even occurs), there is mixed seating, and women fully participate on behalf of the congregation. In the 1970s, women were first admitted to the rabbinate, beginning with the Reform movement. In 1985, the first

---

24. The first five books of the Bible can be found as a single scroll. This scroll, called a Torah, is read in its entirety as part of synagogue services over the course of one year, or in some synagogues, three years.

Conservative woman rabbi was ordained. Women have full equality with men in all aspects of religious life. For the Reform, tradition was no barrier. For Conservative Jewry, the law was negotiated to allow for women's participation, requiring that women's obligations be indistinguishable from men's. With personal choice determining religious practices in the home and changes in synagogue tradition mirroring the equality found in much of American society, tensions between women and Judaism are virtually nonexistent.

The social world of haredi women (with their strong grid and group) looks quite different, but again tensions between Jewish women and their tradition are generally negligible. Jewish life does not center around the synagogue. The grid of halakha itself constitutes Jewish life, and the home is a central part of that grid. There, women's roles are crucial. In fact, in many haredi communities, women do not attend synagogue regularly, most praying in the privacy of their own homes. While the exigencies of childcare explain this phenomenon and these families do tend to be large, non-attendance at synagogue extends beyond the child-rearing age.[25] In this context, changes in the synagogue are unnecessary.

The home is run according to the *Shulchan Arukh*. Where once a Jewish woman learned her halakhic home practices from her mother, who learned them from her mother, going back in unending generations, Jewish home practices are now taught in school as halakha. However, while women are more educated in Jewish law and lore than ever before, not only does going by the book offer less flexibility in actual practice, it may also subtly undermine women's authority in the home.[26] Still, concern for observing halakha is paramount, so generally rather than being seen as subordinate to men, it is seen as obedience to God. Much depends on individual interactions between men and women as to whether this life is experienced as oppressive.

In addition to household management, haredi women often need to add to family income. This may be due to a husband's poor secular education, something not always valued, or to the emphasis put on men's increased Jewish learning. Thus, alongside the demands of raising a family—to be sure, often shared by the husband in these communities—are

---

25. Orthodox Jewish women identify as less religious than men. See "The Gender Gap in Religion around the World," PEW Research Center, March 22, 2016, http://www.pewforum.org/2016/03/22/religion-is-equally-or-more-important-to-women-than-men-in-most-countries.
26. Soloveitchik, "Rupture and Reconstruction." See in particular footnote 18.

the pains and satisfactions of such work. With the importance of deeds of kindness that support communal cohesion, a woman's life is full, bringing religious validation and often personal gratification. Indeed, with the larger society affirming women's work outside the home and Judaism valuing both the work outside and inside the home, the personal meaningfulness of this demanding schedule is reinforced. On the whole, when the system works as it is ideally supposed to, tensions between women and their tradition are minimal.

However, most systems do not always work in ideal ways. Breakdowns in this system are most likely to occur when the actual does not match the ideal. Perhaps a man, woman, or child does not conform to community expectations, or perhaps a poor relationship exists between a husband and wife. These are occasions when the rigidity of going by the book may, although not necessarily will, cause tension. The sheer effort to maintain the ideal can create difficulties. However, in particular, Jewish laws of divorce favor men and can make it difficult for women to get divorced. Women cannot initiate divorce. Without a religious divorce, women cannot remarry. If they were to do so, the children from any subsequent union would be *mamzerim* (bastards) and forbidden to marry Jews. This is so intolerable that most women will often remain without husbands rather than subject any future children to the status of *mamzerim*. Some husbands have used this to blackmail their wives for money or child custody, or just for spite. Unfortunately, the haredi community has no systematic solution. This issue creates the most tension experienced by Jewish Orthodox women within their tradition, although the haredi do have a lower divorce rate than the general population.[27]

Turning to the next group of women, when secular Israelis (who often belong to the high group, low grid category) confront the Israeli Orthodox establishment (with its high group and high grid), this issue becomes even more problematic. In Israel, tradition bumps up against the contemporary world more frequently. This intersection need not be particular to women, and it is sometimes merely inconvenient rather than oppressive, but it is

27. "In National Survey OU Finds that Orthodox Jewish Marriages are Stronger Than in Society as a Whole," *Orthodox Union*, January 13, 2010, https://www.ou.org/news/in_national_survey_ou_finds_that_orthodox_jewish_marriages_are_stronger_tha/; and Daniel Schonbuch, "New York – Responding to the Rising Divorce Rate in the Orthodox Community," *Vos Iz Neias?*, September 3, 2013, http://www.vosizneias.com/140424/2013/09/03/responding-to-the-rising-divorce-rate-in-the-orthodox-community/.

a source of tension. Going to synagogue does not define Jewish identity in Israel, and synagogues are not a focus of concern.[28] Yet, while either extremes of Judaism in America do not generally experience tensions, in Israel tradition may be experienced as oppressive when the contemporary world collides with it. For women, one form comes with concerns for modesty, where they have been harassed for not dressing in a prescribed fashion.[29] At its worst, women can experience themselves primarily as sexual objects rather than as human beings, something that is more likely to happen to women who are outside of a particular haredi community. More generalized is Orthodox Judaism's control over family law, which puts women at a distinct disadvantage in acrimonious divorces.

This issue has been so great a problem that the fourth group of women (those in the strong grid, weak group category) have worked to confront it. The Conservative movement, whose members fall along a range from the adapting mode to the mediating mode, has responded to the halakhic difficulties by adding a clause to the Jewish prenuptial agreement (ketubah).[30] The modern Orthodox have encouraged the signing of an additional prenuptial agreement. Rather than changing tradition, Orthodoxy has preferred to supplement tradition.[31] While on the whole a successful means of circumventing problems, it is more prominent in America than Israel, though still not universal even in America.

In turning to this last category of women, tensions between Jewish tradition and the contemporary world are also very apparent. Here, Jewish tradition's responsiveness to the larger social context comes in the form of attempting to mitigate the tensions between the two social worlds. In these communities, besides the tension mentioned above regarding divorce, two spheres central to Jewish religious life—the intellectual and the spiritual—are particularly the occasion for tension. There are some differ-

28. The one major exception is Women of the Wall, where there is virulent disagreement about women's practices at the Jewish holy site in Jerusalem known as the Western Wall. However, even here it is mostly a battle between women who come from the diaspora and the Israeli Orthodox establishment.

29. Allison Kaplan Sommer, "Shameful in Beit Shemesh," *The Forward*, April 1, 2014, http://forward.com/sisterhood/195618/shameful-in-beit-shemesh/.

30. Rivka C. Berman, "The Ketubah, Standard Text: A Conservative Perspective," *Jewish Celebrations*, February 16, 2017, http://www.jewishcelebrations.com/Wedding/Conservative/KetubahText.htm.

31. "Signing the Prenup," *The Prenup*, accessed October 30, 2019, https://theprenup.org/the-prenup-forms/.

ences between the United States and Israel, although frequent interactions between the two communities diminish variation. In the United States, Orthodox rabbis tend to have prestige that the Israeli rabbinic bureaucracy does not enjoy. This gives the American Orthodox rabbi more authority than the established Orthodox bureaucracy in Israel—except with respect to marriage and divorce, where the bureaucracy has hegemony. This has resulted in more varied Orthodox options in Israel.[32] In addition, and in part because of this, there has been greater availability of higher levels of Jewish education for women in Israel, building a cadre of educated Jewish women that the United States is only beginning to provide.

Because of the centrality of study in Judaism, women's learning has had a prominent place in modern Orthodox women's concerns. In the more liberal Orthodox communities, women study the same subjects that at one time were reserved for men only, in particular study of the Talmud.[33] In Israel, men and women may study together; however, in the United States Orthodox men and women usually study separately, preserving Orthodox distinctiveness from liberal denominations. Still, so important is this learning that even in America, these women are often taught by teachers recognized as masters of Talmud within the community.

As of now, there are limitations on what women can do with this learning. Valued in and of itself, learning has allowed women to become teachers. Opportunities to advise are also possible. Some women have become specialists in laws pertaining to intimacy between husband and wife, responding to women who have questions in this area. Other women have become specialists in Jewish family law, and they work with women who are going through divorces to protect their interests.[34] However, for all the knowledge they acquire, the possibility of a woman becoming a rabbi is particularly controversial.

Tied to a specific concept, *serara*, women are forbidden communal authority. In the contemporary world, there is a wide range in applying this that has allowed women to take on some authoritative communal roles; however, it is one of the major reasons for refusing to allow women

32. Ross, "Orthodox Israeli Feminists."

33. Rochelle Furstenberg, "The Flourishing of Higher Jewish Learning for Women," *Jerusalem Center for Public Affairs, Jerusalem Letter*, May 1, 2000, http://www.jcpa.org/jl/jl429.htm.

34. Furstenberg.

to become rabbis.[35] Here the preserving model has strongly influenced the mediating model, for women's subordination is seen not as sociological but as an absolute. This is apparent when considering its halakhic background. To be sure, it is grounded in a biblical verse (Deut. 17:15), but it rests on an interpretation introduced by Maimonides, the preeminent medieval rabbi and philosopher mentioned earlier. Regarding women's ordination, *serara* is not used in authoritative literature before Maimonides, nor is it viewed as normative in the *Shulchan Arukh*, composed about three hundred years later.[36] Ultimately, custom itself has justified women's subordination. Only one institution in the United States trains women for rabbinic roles in the Orthodox community, and it has been condemned by even the more moderate Orthodox leadership. In Israel, women have learned privately with rabbis, and there is currently one institution that grants rabbinic ordination to women.[37]

Positions after ordination also vary between countries. The abundance of rabbis in Israel and civil service status lead both men and women into teaching. Few men, and even fewer women, have the opportunity to serve as community rabbis. In America, female rabbis have found positions with congregations, revealing a level of acceptance within the wider American Orthodox community, despite condemnation by the leadership. That Orthodox communities are open to these women highlight their integration into contemporary culture, differing from the condemning leadership, who not only follow their teachers but also are concerned with the esteem of their colleagues. In addition, in the more moderate Orthodox communities, the role of rabbis' wives, who now have their own careers and no longer participate in communal life the way they once did, has changed. The acceptance of women as rabbinic leaders is not just about

---

35. Rabbi Daniel Feldman et al., *Orthodox Union*, "Statement on Female Clergy," February 1, 2017, https://www.ou.org/assets/Responses-of-Rabbinic-Panel.pdf. See also Michael J. Broyde and Shlomo M. Brody, "Orthodox Women Rabbis? Tentative Thoughts that Distinguish Between the Timely and the Timeless," *Hakirah,* http://www.hakirah.org/Vol%2011%20Broyde.pdf.

36. Nathaneiel Helfgot, "Women Communal Leadership and Modern Orthodoxy," *Tradition's Blog Text and Texture,* February 18, 2010, http://text.rcarabbis.org/women-communal-leadership-and-modern-orthodoxy-by-nathaniel-helfgot/.

37. Yeshivat Maharat in New York and Har'el Beit Midrash in Israel. Rabbi Daniel Landes also grants ordination to women.

opportunities for women; it also provides for the needs of a community committed to tradition and embedded within the contemporary world.

In turning to particularly spiritual issues, a range of synagogue practices is apparent. Here the tensions between tradition and the contemporary world are so great that even the most right-wing Conservative synagogues conform to egalitarian values. Modern Orthodox women struggle with a number of ways to mitigate the tensions. The most liberal, arguably halakhic but certainly not traditional, has been the development of partnership prayer groups. These groups started in Israel and are slowly spreading throughout the world. These prayer groups maintain the physical division between men and women in the prayer space, but the division is architecturally more open. Rather than women being relegated to the margins, a partition between the sexes runs down the middle. This partition may be lower than in haredi synagogues or less opaque.

Usually ten women and ten men must be present to begin services, and more controversially, women may participate in the service at those points that are not halakhically defined as prayer. Also, most of these prayer groups call women up for the Torah reading and even allow women to read from the Torah. The effort is to give women as much opportunity to participate in the prayer service as the halakha might be interpreted to allow.[38] The interpretation is a very liberal one and subject not just to controversy but also to prohibition by the modern Orthodox leadership in America.

Equally discouraged, but nonetheless on the Orthodox scene, are all-women prayer groups. These are groups of women who come together for formal prayer on various occasions, perhaps on a Sabbath once a month or on holidays. Although these women pray together as prescribed for individuals, a woman leads the prayers. Their services include reading from a Torah. While it is conceded that these groups fall within halakhic bounds, they lack precedence and have been prohibited by the modern Orthodox establishment for that reason. Still, they persist quite widely in America and in some places in Israel.[39] Both partnership and women's prayer groups reflect collisions between the contemporary world's egalitarian values and Jewish tradition, and through their innovations, the attempt is made to accommodate both.

---

38. "Partnership Minyan," last modified October 26, 2019, in *Wikipedia* is an excellent starting point for information on this effort.

39. "Women's Tefillah Groups," Jewish Orthodox Feminist Alliance, accessed October 30, 2019, https://www.jofa.org/women-s-tefillah-groups.

There have also been less radical options that have made their way into the moderate Orthodox settings, achieving a normative status. They involve more inclusive spaces and additional ceremonies for girls. Prayer spaces have been configured as described for partnership minyans, with the division between men and women in the middle and less obstructionist partitions between the sexes. Non-traditional ways to mark occasions special to women include celebrating the birth of a daughter and a girl's coming-of-age ceremony, known as Bat Mitzvah.[40] While these occasions are a response to the egalitarian pressures of the larger society, they also reflect the desire to celebrate girls' lives in ways consonant with halakha. Notably, women in these communities often attend synagogue more regularly than was observed of women in haredi communities. In other words, more liberal Orthodox communities, with women more a part of the contemporary world, tend to be more responsive to ways in which halakha and contemporary mores can combine.

Evident from this examination is that Jewish communities continue to respond to their environments, and the greatest tensions appear where the traditional Jewish world encounters the contemporary one, or vice versa. On the one hand, a relatively isolated haredi community has less need for addressing egalitarian issues because the whole structure of their social world serves the women there, for the most part, in meaningful ways. On the other hand, the more open a community is to the larger world, the more necessary it is to respond to the changes that such openness entails. For liberal Jews in America, changes have been so dramatic that their communities are essentially indistinguishable from the larger society except for their Jewish content. This may lead to problems of assimilation, but it certainly mitigates tensions between women and Judaism. For secular Jews in Israel, Judaism defines the culture, but secular materialism is equally pervasive, and both are a matter of choice, again mitigating tensions.

However, tensions arise in Israel when secular confronts haredi and when modern Orthodox women, whether in America or Israel, desire to participate in the quintessentially religious spheres once solely the domain of men. In fact, the haredi influences the more moderate Orthodox establishment, putting pressures on the women in modern Orthodoxy who look to the mediating model of Jewish tradition. Thus, while the mediat-

---

40. No doubt the increased wealth of Jewish communities as well as the older age at which girls get married in the contemporary world has contributed to the increasing prominence of Bat Mitzvah ceremonies, for presumably in earlier times the wedding ceremony took the place of a Bat Mitzvah.

ing model provides for advanced learning and varying options in women's prayer, allowing a contemporary form of spiritual pleasure and growth otherwise closed to women, the innovative nature of some of these options has made them suspect.[41] Thus, the women who find themselves at the intersection of Jewish tradition and the contemporary world experience the greatest tensions.[42] So saying, it is not so much Jewish tradition that oppresses women but rather the tensions between Jewish tradition and the contemporary world that are experienced by Jewish women as oppressive.

Tradition in Tension

Although a relatively small minority of women experience tension between their Jewish practice and the contemporary social world, this minority is significant because it highlights the source of the tensions: not within Jewish tradition, but between Jewish tradition and the contemporary world. The primary source of tension appears to be concerned with the issue of equality. Throughout Jewish history, women have been subordinate to men. That has now become a problem.

The adapting model follows contemporary mores. It rejects women's subordination along with any forms of distinction between men and women. The preserving model rejects contemporary mores. Through its ideology of the halakha as absolute and immutable, the latter sees the subordination of women to men as divinely ordained. To be sure, women may relatively freely express their choices in the secular world (via career); however, in the religious world, their roles are proscribed. These models do not usually experience tension between Jewish tradition and the contemporary world. However, the mediating model sees women's subordination as a product of the social world rather than as an absolute. Women's vulnerabilities, once protected through their subordinate status in the social structure, are now in many ways currently addressed through medicine, technology, social mores, and legal auspices. Consequently, these women

---

41. There is a range with Open Orthodoxy as most adaptive. Still within modern Orthodoxy there is a strand that accepts change except where women's issues are concerned, for these issues represent a particular challenge that undermines tradition. See Adam S. Fertzinger, "Feminism and Heresy: the Construction of a Jewish Metanarrative," *Journal of the American Academy of Religion* 77, no. 3 (2009): 494–546. The influence of western thought as described above reinforces immutability for all Jewish Orthodoxy.

42. *Nishma Research*, "Starting a Conversation."

must negotiate between the halakha that is sacred in Jewish tradition and the contemporary world's value of equality. Their subordinate status is not only unnecessary but problematic.

Yet, the mediating model is not simply negotiating between tradition and the contemporary world; it is also negotiating between foundational aspects of Jewish tradition. One of these foundational aspects is Judaism's tradition of both preserving and adapting tradition to current times. To negotiate between Jewish tradition and the contemporary world is part of the heritage of Jewish tradition, as was apparent in the historical section. However, also foundational to Jewish tradition is Judaism's concern for the vulnerable. This concern, involving acts of kindness, has been considered in Jewish tradition to be one of the three pillars upon which the whole world exists.[43] This significance is crucial, for it, in fact, informs Judaism's social nature.

Judaism's social nature is unquestionable. Certainly the ethnic character of Jewishness supports this. Traditionally, halakha shaped that social world. In doing so it created that world through the regulation of relationships—between human and Divine and between humans. Concern for the vulnerable allows for the dignity of both participants in human relationships. Such dignity gives the relationship integrity, making it moral. So halakha, as it shapes a social world, works to assure a morality dependent on an equality of moral worth where every individual is perceived as made in God's image.[44]

This is in striking contrast to hierarchy. Recall that above the grid of social relationships in Judaism was based on halakha rather than hierarchy. Whereas hierarchy addresses social order, halakha is concerned with moral relationships. Hierarchy distorts relationships. Rather than the coequal dignity of each participant in a relationship, power must be taken into consideration. That halakha forms the grid in the Jewish world indicates the centrality of moral relationship. This centrality is what informs the social world of Judaism and what gives the social its importance.[45]

---

43. *Pirke Avot*, 1:2.

44. For a good introduction to this topic see the Wikipedia entry for *Kavod HaBriyot* (dignity of human beings), https://en.wikipedia.org/wiki/Kavod_HaBriyot.

45. It is interesting to note the emphasis in the great twentieth-century Jewish thinkers on relationships. See Franz Rosenzweig, *The Star of Redemption* (Notre Dame: University of Notre Dame Press, 1985); Martin Buber, *I and Thou* (New York: Charles Scribner's Sons, 1958). For a good sample of Emmanuel Levinas'

Here, then, raises the greatest point of tension with contemporary society: not equality but individualism. Individuals are certainly important in Jewish tradition. Without each individual's dignity, the integrity of a relationship is compromised. However, Jewish tradition's respect for the individual is not an individualism that is independent of community. Jewish religious life was never confined to individual expressions of spirituality. While halakha defines the relationship between Jew and God, it also defines relationships between Jews, between Jews and non-Jews, and even between Jews and the natural world. It is profoundly relational. This is the basis of Judaism's social nature that runs so counter to western secularity's privatization of religion.

This, then, is why the contemporary world is so problematic for Judaism. As individualism influences liberal forms of Judaism, their adaptations to the contemporary world make use of that which is inimical to Judaism, paving the way for greater individualism and assimilation into the contemporary world. More Orthodox forms of Judaism work hard to protect themselves from the structural forces of an individualistic social structure, so they fortify their boundaries and strengthen their grid. This inflexibility solidifies the subordination of women, but such inequality is a consequence. It is not the primary cause of the tensions some Jewish women may experience, nor is it the primary cause of the conflict between Jewish tradition and the contemporary society.

In fact, gender equality is not simply a product of secular individualism, it is also a response to Judaism's own deepest spiritual heritage. Consequently, with little historical evidence of Judaism's oppression, with those currently preserving tradition generally not experiencing oppression, and with resources for the equality of the genders to be found within Jewish tradition, the premise that Judaism is oppressive to women is highly questionable. Rather, the tensions that Jewish women experience are a result of the conflict between Judaism as a social entity and the individualism dominant in the contemporary world. Individualism and equality must not be conflated. With that distinction comes a nuance that may better address the tensions that Jewish women do experience with their tradition.

---

thinking, see *Is it Righteous to Be?: Interviews with Emmanuel Levinas*, ed. Jill Robbins (Stanford: Stanford University Press, 2001).

4B

Modern Mormon Women in a Patriarchal Church

Camille Fronk Olson

Modern religions, whose doctrinal roots stretch back into antiquity, naturally encounter tensions as they merge or collide with evolving societal changes. Tensions may be especially felt in religious practices involving women and families due to significant changes in opportunities, expectations, and involvement of women in the public sphere. In her article on the subject, Ellen Lasser LeVee identifies those streams of Judaism that are particularly vulnerable to such tensions and suggests resolution may be found by applying a historical perspective.

Some women in The Church of Jesus Christ of Latter-day Saints report similar tensions between their religious loyalties and their desire to fully engage in the contemporary world. Therefore, seeking resolution for Latter-day Saint women's feelings of conflict by reviewing historical context may prove meaningful.

LeVee's historical approach is intriguing for analyzing this parallel dynamic in Mormonism for a second reason. Because men hold all positions of hierarchical priesthood leadership within The Church of Jesus Christ, women are frequently perceived as inherently oppressed in their faith. In Judaism, however, according to LeVee, religious patriarchy is *not* the source of this tension but rather rigid interpretations of Jewish law based on traditionalism and customs of the past. The same may apply to Mormonism. An all-male leadership hierarchy is an easy scapegoat for women feeling marginalized. Perhaps the greater cause of these feelings of oppression is the tendency among leaders and members alike to misinterpret doctrine in order to retain traditionalism.

A third and final reason for considering the historical perspective is that it can be helpful in describing changes within the Latter-day Saint community according to LeVee's grid-group paradigm. In the early days of Mormonism, when converts to the faith immigrated to close-knit communities in and around the Utah Territory, the cultural boundaries were made strong through both a highly defined belief system and isolation, creating a strong group and strong grid dynamic. As Church membership has increased in numbers and presence around the world, the group has weakened. The grid is typically not as strong in areas where Latter-day Saint communities are sparse and individuality more noticeable, but it is made stronger through a prominent and united hierarchy that clearly defines role structures. Contemporary liberal social movements, such as changes in marriage laws in many countries, have considerably weakened the grid as formerly defined role structures are brought into question among traditionalists and progressives in the Church.

Clarification of Differences

For women of Judaism, a variety of faith interpretations is available to accommodate personal philosophies. For members of The Church of Jesus Christ, there are no comparable options for choosing a reformed, conservative, orthodox, or nondenominational congregation to fit one's personal philosophy of Mormonism. Whether their personal philosophies be more traditional, more liberal, or anywhere in between, Latter-day Saint (LDS) women are expected to meet together, serve together, and form a loving ward family with those members who live in the same geographical area. Their congregations are made up of people who they did not particularly choose. Furthermore, at the head of the worldwide Church, a seasoned group of fifteen men serve as the highest authority, define doctrine, and declare policy for all affiliated men and women.

The Historical Role Model for Latter-Day Saint Women

No woman is more prominently portrayed as a role model for practicing Latter-day Saint women than Mother Eve. She is highlighted in each of the standard works of LDS scripture and in their sacred temple worship. Church doctrine is strikingly different from other Christian interpretations of the Fall that blame Eve for all of mortal life's difficulties. It also differs from Jewish interpretations that assign punishments to both Eve *and* Adam for their fateful decision. For LDS members, God did not punish our first parents. Their choice activated His plan. He sent them to a fallen world where they could learn by faith, from making mistakes, and through sincere repentance granted by a suffering Savior. Latter-day Saints actually *praise* Eve for her choice made in the Garden of Eden. Foundational scripture teaches that by choosing the Fall, Eve and Adam enabled God's plan to proceed for all His children.

In 1830 (the year that the Church was organized), Joseph Smith received a clearer translation of the Genesis story, which is published in the book of Moses within the Pearl of Great Price. In this latter-day account, Adam and Eve were grateful for the Fall because they learned how it would benefit "all the families of the earth." Adam prophesied, saying: "Blessed be the name of God, for because of my transgression my eyes are opened, and in this life I shall have joy, and again in the flesh I shall see God" (Moses 5:10). In response, Eve "was glad, saying: Were it not for our transgression we never should have had seed, and never should have known good and evil, and the joy of our redemption, and the eternal life which God giveth unto all the obedient" (v. 11).

After being driven from the garden, our first parents are described as laboring together, parenting together, calling on the name of the Lord together, receiving commandments from God together, sacrificing offerings from their flocks together, and "[making] all things known unto their sons and their daughters" together (5:1–5, 12). They functioned together as a partnership in which each of them was blessed and beloved of God while navigating trials and temptations in a fallen world.

The Book of Mormon was published earlier that same year. This book of scripture, translated by Joseph Smith, contains a doctrinal explanation for the necessity of the Fall in God's plan for the salvation of His children. The ancient prophet Lehi taught that—

> [I]f Adam [and Eve] had not transgressed he would not have fallen, but he would have remained in the garden of Eden. And all things which were created must have remained in the same state in which they were after they were created; and they must have remained forever, and had no end. And they would have had no children; wherefore they would have remained in a state of innocence, having no joy, for they knew no misery; doing no good, for they knew no sin. But behold, all things have been done in the wisdom of him who knoweth all things. Adam fell that men might be; and men are, that they might have joy. (2 Ne. 2:22–25)

Finally, in 1918, Joseph F. Smith, sixth president of the Church, saw in vision the Savior's visit to righteous spirits of the dead. Among the "vast congregation" of "mighty and great" spirits who received the Lord's blessing and commission, President Smith saw "Father Adam . . . and our glorious Mother Eve, with many of her faithful daughters who had lived through the ages and worshiped the true and living God" (D&C 138:38–39). There is no hint in these passages of inferiority in Eve or women in general. Members of the current First Presidency of the Church have reinforced this interpretation of Eve as doctrine. As one member of the Quorum of Twelve Apostles, Russell M. Nelson, now the president of the Church, explained:

> We and all mankind are forever blessed because of Eve's great courage and wisdom. By partaking of the forbidden fruit first, she did what needed to be done. Adam was wise enough to do likewise. Accordingly, we could speak of the fall of Adam in terms of a mortal creation, because "Adam fell that men might be" (2 Ne. 2:25). Other blessings came to us through the Fall. It activated two closely coupled additional gifts from God, nearly as precious as life itself—agency and accountability. We became "free to choose liberty and eternal life . . . or to choose captivity and death" (2 Ne. 2:27).[1]

In the same general conference of the Church, another member of the Quorum of Twelve, who is now the first counselor in the First Presidency, Dallin H. Oaks, also praised Eve's choice in Eden:

> It was Eve who first transgressed the limits of Eden in order to initiate the conditions of mortality. . . . Adam showed his wisdom by doing the same. And thus Eve and "Adam fell that men might be" (vs. 25). Some Christians condemn Eve for her act, concluding that she and her daughters are some-how flawed by it. Not the Latter-day Saints! Informed by revelation, we celebrate Eve's act and honor her wisdom and courage in the great episode called the Fall. . . . Modern revelation shows that our first parents understood the necessity of the Fall.[2]

The tenets of Mormonism portray woman as praiseworthy, essential to God's plan, and equal in importance to man. One cannot deduce from these teachings that she needs supervision by men because of any innate or assumed inferiority.

Influence from a Fallen World

Despite a strong declaration of women's equal worth and importance in Mormon doctrine, many LDS women have felt marginalized, ignored, or even oppressed by their local priesthood leaders or male family members.[3] Misunderstanding, misuse, and even abuse of positions of authority are further evidence of a fallen world. Joseph Smith warned of humankind's

---

1. Russell M. Nelson, "Constancy Amid Change," General Conference, October 1993.

2. Dallin H. Oaks, "The Great Plan of Happiness," General Conference, October 1993.

3. See Neylan McBaine, *Women at Church: Magnifying LDS Women's Local Impact* (Salt Lake City: Greg Kofford Books, 2014).

tendency to abuse their perceived authority in direct contradiction to God's laws. The Prophet wrote to members of the Church: "We have learned by sad experience that it is the nature and disposition of *almost all men*, as soon as they get a little authority, as they suppose, they will *immediately begin to exercise unrighteous dominion*" (D&C 121:39; emphasis added). Given our fallen natures, there will inevitably be some unrighteous dominion, even from leaders who are struggling towards truly selfless service.

Furthermore, Joseph Smith warned that when men use their positions of power "to cover [their] sins, or to gratify [their] pride, or to exercise control or dominion or compulsion upon the souls of the children of men, *in any degree of unrighteousness*, behold, the heavens withdraw themselves; the Spirit of the Lord is grieved; and when it is withdrawn, Amen to the priesthood or the authority of that man" (D&C 121:37; emphasis added). According to LDS doctrine, God will not support those who misuse His power to subjugate, ignore, or marginalize women.

Clearly, it is the widespread culture of our modern world that condones infidelity in marriage, pornography, the objectification of women, and premarital sex. LDS teachings and doctrine have never done so. Therefore, negative stereotypes of the value of women in the Church are arguably influenced and perpetuated by traditional practices and perceptions from secular society.

In her analysis of Jewish women, LeVee observed, "Much depends on individual interactions between men and women as to whether this life is experienced as oppressive" (p. 158). Likewise for LDS women. If fathers, husbands, and sons respect the intelligence and perspectives of women and promote equal authority of mothers and fathers in the home, and if bishops, stake presidents, and mission presidents value women's insights and suggestions, Latter-day Saint women are less likely to feel oppressed in their faith.

Practices and Changes in Women's Stewardships in Latter-day Saint History

To appreciate religious principles that underscore policies in the Church requires an understanding of the historical context in which policies and practices were initiated for a particular time. It means developing skills to separate cultural baggage from divine decrees that are timeless. For Latter-day Saints to develop such skills, they must retain in mind God's overarching purpose—"to bring to pass the immortality and eternal life" of

His sons and daughters (see Moses 1:39). His laws and commandments are then given to His children to facilitate and inspire that purpose.

Spiritual maturity in the Church requires women and men to discern between foundational doctrine and mutable policies that are initiated in response to specific needs at a given time. For example, strengthening families has remained paramount in LDS doctrine, with duties of mothers and fathers exceeding all other responsibilities. To support that doctrine, Church authorities have given women different counsel at various times pertaining to family planning, education, careers, and efforts to improve society outside the home depending on current societal issues and philosophies. Their counsel responds to a world that is changing in order to protect children and the sanctity of the home in those particular conditions. Counsel and practices have become more elastic in recent years to accommodate various cultures in the world and expanding women's roles and leadership opportunities. The immediate response is a weakened group and weakened grid. Time will tell whether adjustments to these changes will in turn create a stronger group and grid.

Historically, plural marriage is often cited as a form of oppressing women in early periods of the Church. From the perspective of many polygamous wives of the era, however, polygamy granted women increased independence and opportunities for education and leadership.[4] During these years, women participated in healing blessings, prayed and spoke in general meetings, and supported their families in every way while their husbands were far from home preaching the Restored Gospel. LDS women achieved the right to vote in 1870 when Utah was still a territory and made suffrage a condition of acceptance for statehood in 1896. In a stunning example of their influence on the larger society, without counsel, directives, or any involvement whatsoever from male hierarchy, LDS women galvanized in multiple mass "indignation" meetings throughout the territory to protest federal legislation that would deny US citizenship to anyone practicing polygamy.[5]

After the Manifesto ended Church-sanctioned plural marriage, Utah received statehood, and women gained suffrage, Mormon families and

---

4. Laurel Thatcher Ulrich, *A House Full of Females* (New York City: Vintage Books, 2017).

5. Jill Mulvay Derr et al., ed., *The First Fifty Years of Relief Society: Key Documents in Latter-day Saint Women's History* (Salt Lake City: The Church Historian's Press, 2016), 242–45, 305–37; Neylan McBaine, *Pioneering the Vote* (Salt Lake City: Shadow Mountain, 2020).

gender roles largely echoed those in the nation at large. In the following de-cades, punctuated by world wars and economic depression, women tended to stay close to home, away from public discourse, unless they were needed in industry to back war efforts or to support their fatherless families.

The mid-twentieth century saw dramatic growth in the Church, es-pecially internationally, and new societal expectations for women. LDS women asked different questions in response to changes in families and opportunities for women, questions such as: "How could single sisters feel accepted in a marriage-minded church? Should mothers of young children work outside the home? Was abortion always wrong? Or birth control? Should women join the military forces? How could a traditional Relief Society address the needs of all its diverse sisters? And what about the Equal Rights Amendment?"[6]

In her twenty-ninth year as Relief Society General President, Belle Smith Spafford acknowledged the dynamic times in which she led all the women in the Church. She explained:

> [T]remendous changes . . . have taken place in the social, economic, indus-trial, and educational life of most countries in the world since Relief Society was founded. And I don't think any change in the world has been more sig-nificant than the change in the status of women. At the time Relief Society was founded, a woman's world was her home, her family, and perhaps a little community service. Today a woman's world is as broad as the universe. There's scarcely an area of human endeavor that a woman cannot enter if she has the will and preparation to do so. Yet, in the midst of all this change, the organizational structure of the Relief Society, the basic purposes for which it was established, *have remained constant, and the Church programs that have implemented these purposes have been adaptable to the needs of women in each succeeding era.*[7]

Multiple new programs and policies were initiated by the Church to address the unprecedented growth in the female labor force and needs of an expanding and diverse international church in a dramatically changing world.[8] While holding firm to the doctrine of families, leaders introduced

---

6. Jill Mulvay Derr, Janeth Russell Cannon, and Maureen Ursenback Beecher, *Women of Covenant: The Story of Relief Society* (Deseret Book: Salt Lake City, 1992), 348.

7. Belle Smith Spafford, "Reaching Every Facet of a Woman's Life: A Conversation with Belle S. Spafford, Relief Society General President," *Ensign,* June 1974; emphasis added.

8. Derr, Cannon, and Beecher, *Women of Covenant,* 349–52.

policies that reduced and simplified programs that would be prohibitive in the international Church and unnecessarily time-consuming in areas where membership was plentiful. Relief Society leaders followed the "reduce and simplify" directives in redefining their purpose while giving greater support for young mothers to safeguard their children. It was during this era that Church publications and curriculum were placed under the umbrella of a new general correlation department rather than under the purview of separate auxiliaries or departments. This meant that the women's Relief Society no longer owned their own magazine, cooperative store, and hospital. They no longer maintained industries to support their choices for social causes and fund-raising organizations to finance their society.[9]

Certainly, many women felt a tremendous loss in autonomy when these changes occurred. Inevitably, there were false assumptions about women's weakness to govern, to manage, and to discern needs. The new policies, however, invited greater unity, cooperation, and communication between men and women in the Church to assist in God's purpose to save souls. Policies in place today are still addressing the need to forge this cooperation by assigning fewer specific programs and granting more encouragement to act as inspired by the Spirit. Clarifying and more inclusive language for women in the temple and participation of women as authorized witnesses for priesthood ordinances have infused further confidence in women's needed contributions. It is a huge work in process.

Evidences of Accommodation

With a historical perspective, LeVee allows for adaptation of religious law to accommodate spiritual growth in the modern world, which thereby reduces tension between loyalty to faith and active contribution to the public sphere. By contrast, she contends that the haredi model (strict adherence to Jewish Law and custom while rejecting everything in secular society) often exacerbates tension by reinforcing traditionalism and a return to the past, when women were vulnerable and wholly dependent on men. For members of the Church of Jesus Christ, something akin to the haredi model occurs when we emphasize the perceived immutability of traditionalism regardless of its absence in official Church discourse. What happens if one inadvertently confuses Church counsel on a particular social issue, given for a particular situation in a particular time, with founda-

---

9. Derr, *Women of Covenant*, 304–46; Helen Claire Sievers, "What Women in the Church Have Lost in My Lifetime," *Exponent II* 33, no. 3 (Winter 2014): 18–22.

tional doctrine? Continued misunderstanding gradually shapes a limiting and incomplete definition of women's stewardship in the Church.

Church leaders have often cautioned against confusing temporary programs and counsel for foundational doctrine. For example, Virginia H. Pearce, former counselor in the Young Women General Presidency, stressed the need to consider the historical context in which counsel was given. She wrote, "When we can see the historical problem being addressed, we can separate the application from the doctrine-based principle. Only then can we make the leap to apply the principle to our modern lives, enriched but unencumbered by historical circumstances."[10]

Elder Boyd K. Packer of the Quorum of the Twelve explained the importance of discerning the difference between doctrine and policy when he taught,

> Procedures, programs, the administrative policies, even some patterns of organization are subject to change. The First Presidency are quite free, indeed quite obliged, to alter them from time to time. But the *principles,* the *doctrines, never* change. If we overemphasize programs and procedures that can change, and will change, and must change, and do not understand the fundamental principles of the gospel, which *never* change, we can be misled.[11]

General priesthood leaders in the Church of Jesus Christ have authority to explain doctrine and adapt policy to accommodate changes in society when such changes support God's plan for His children. Multiple accommodations and corrections to traditional practices are currently in place. These new policies are increasing opportunities for women's personal spiritual maturity, and strengthening their efforts to further the Lord's work in the family and larger community. They do not create doctrine but rather work to clarify doctrine by suggesting applications for a modern world. The following represent recent accommodating policies and practices:

- Women speak and pray in general conference

- The male-only priesthood session of general conference being replaced with one that includes all members twelve years of age and older

---

10. Virginia Pearce, "Angels and Epiphanies," *The Beginning of Better Days: Divine Instruction to Women from the Prophet Joseph Smith* (Salt Lake City: Deseret Book, 2012), 7.

11. Boyd K. Packer, *Mine Errand From the Lord* (Salt Lake City: Deseret Book, 2008), 310.

- Women participate in Church councils at ward, stake, and general levels

- Young Women may officiate in temple baptisteries

- Women are encouraged to pursue an education in their chosen fields of study

- The minimum age for women to serve full-time missions was reduced to nineteen years old

- More women are speaking to and teaching audiences made up of men as well as women

- Women with children may be employed as full-time seminary teachers

- General leaders make reference to our Heavenly Mother and Heavenly Parents

Official discourses by the highest authorities in the Church today also reflect efforts to clarify doctrine and dispel outdated traditions pertaining to women in the Church. General Authorities speak inclusively and encouragingly to women to engage their efforts in the Lord's work beyond home and family, yet without decreasing the eternal importance of family, including the need for dedicated mothers and fathers. For example, building on past teachings from Boyd K. Packer, one of the Quorum of the Twelve, President Russell M. Nelson made a "plea" to the women of the Church to use their gifts to build the kingdom in a variety of ways. He explained:

> President Packer declared, "We need women who are organized and women who can organize. We need women with executive ability who can plan and direct and administer; women who can teach, women who can speak out. . . . We need women with the gift of discernment who can view the trends in the world and detect those that, however popular, are shallow or dangerous."[12]
>
> Today, let me add that we need women who know how to make important things happen by their faith and who are courageous defenders of morality and families in a sin-sick world. We need women who are devoted to shepherding God's children along the covenant path toward exaltation; women who know how to receive personal revelation, who understand the power and peace of the temple endowment; women who know how to call upon the powers of heaven to protect and strengthen children and families; women who teach fearlessly.[13]

---

12. Boyd K. Packer, "The Relief Society," General Conference, October 1978.

13. Russell M. Nelson, "A Plea to My Sisters," General Conference, October 2015.

The timeless doctrine of family is restated. Added counsel reflects accommodations to a changing world where women's voices, skills, and perspectives are needed and welcomed.

Women's increased participation in all aspects of secular society today has understandably elicited questions about women's presumed lack of authority in The Church of Jesus Christ of Latter-day Saints. Elder Dallin H. Oaks therefore clarified the Church's doctrine on women and priesthood authority:

> We are not accustomed to speaking of women having the authority of the priesthood in their Church callings, but what other authority can it be? When a woman—young or old—is set apart to preach the gospel as a full-time missionary, she is given priesthood authority to perform a priesthood function. The same is true when a woman is set apart to function as an officer or teacher in a Church organization under the direction of one who holds the keys of the priesthood. Whoever functions in an office or calling received from one who holds priesthood keys exercises priesthood authority in performing her or his assigned duties.[14]

His clarification challenges us men and women to rethink the manner in which we use terms like "priesthood" and "authority." It also reminds us that power and authority in the Church are not evidence of increased stature and glory of the individual, but are the means to receive the Lord's grace in order to minister to others.

Conclusion

There will always be those who conclude that Latter-day Saint women are inescapably oppressed because theirs is a patriarchal religion. Many modern Mormon women will no doubt continue to encounter attitudes of condescension within the Church. These attitudes, however, do not grow out of LDS doctrine and current teachings from the patriarchal leadership. In a growing Church with a lay clergy who receive virtually no previous training and a membership that expects near perfection from their leaders, there will almost assuredly continue to exist unrighteous dominion, resistance to change, hurt feelings, and desires to be accepted by a fallen world. A historical perspective requires a review of conditions at the time Church policies and applications were initiated. Individuals and families must discern the intentions of policies, and seek the Spirit as they interpret Church

---

14. Dallin H. Oaks, "The Keys and Authority of the Priesthood," General Conference, April 2014.

direction in their lives. Considering LDS doctrine, scripture, and current teachings, it is clear that women's perspectives, contributions, and abilities are essential elements of God's plan. Women are invited and needed to build his kingdom today, perhaps more than ever before.

Notwithstanding clarifications that are available by considering the historical context of religious teachings in the Church, LDS women will likely always feel tension between their faith and the world. They will continue to interact with imperfect leaders who make mistakes as they learn to become true shepherds in daunting assignments. Tension will persist due to an even greater threat to resolution: the values of the world are in stark and dynamic opposition to the values of Mormonism. God's plan for eternal families is incomprehensible to the world. Sacrifice and service without remuneration or political cachet is foreign to the socially ambitious.

The challenge for LDS women may therefore be to determine whose approval they most desire. What value does doctrine have in their lives? What is their chief motivation? Are they willing to research policies and practices of the past to understand the environment in which they were given? Are they able to hear the language of scripture without tainting the message with the voice of a secular world? Are they strong enough to resist taking offense when no offense was intended? Can they forgive and pray for those called to shepherd them? The answers are rarely easy. But then, why should we expect "easy"? The Lord intends to establish a faithful people who will follow His timeless laws and rise above the ever-changing values of a secular world. At a time of dramatic changes that increasingly promote women's participation and voice in the Church, the possibility of creating a stronger grid in Mormonism amid an increasingly secular world is perhaps more possible than ever.

Faith as Memory:
Theologies of the Jewish Holidays

Byron L. Sherwin

Losing one's memory means losing one's mind.[1] To remember is to re-mind. Bereft of certain remembrances, one becomes dismembered from the divine, from one's own self, from one's past, from one's faith-community.[2]

For Judaism, faith is memory; recall of the past is a call to faith in the present. As Abraham Heschel has written:

> When we want to understand ourselves, to find out what is most precious in our lives, we search our memory. . . . That only is valuable in our experience which is worth remembering. Remembrance is the touchstone of all actions. Memory is a source of faith. To have faith is to remember. Jewish faith is a recollection of that which happened to Israel in the past. . . . Recollection is a holy act: we sanctify the present by remembering the past.[3]

No command to believe is stated in Hebrew scripture. Rather, memory of events, of experience, is prescribed. The transmission of the faith-tradition from generation to generation is vested in the conveyance through memory of experienced events. For example, a verse in Deuteronomy (4:9) reads:

> Take heed to yourself diligently, lest you forget the things your eyes saw, and lest they depart from your heart all the days of your life, make them known to your children and your children's children.

The prophets of Israel did not formulate creedal propositions. Rather, they offered memories of moments illuminated by the divine presence.

---

1. The essay, Byron L. Sherwin, "Faith as Memory: Theologies of the Jewish Holidays," was originally published in *Commitment and Commemoration: Jews, Christians, Muslims in Dialogue,* ed. Andre LaCocque (Chicago: Exploration Press, 1994), 95–110; it is reprinted here with permission of Exploration Press.

2. According to hasidic theology, each Jew is *"aiver ha-Shekhinah,"* that a "limb of God," a "divine member." This is similar to the Christian Body as the Church being the Corpus Christi, the Body of Christ. Dismemberment means separation from the divine. For Judaism, remembrance is an entrée to rememberment.

3. Abraham Joshua Heschel, *Man is Not Alone* (Philadelphia: Jewish Publication Society, 1951), 162–63.

They did not enjoin the people to define God (Isa. 43:10); they were not a committee of definers of God.

In his classic work *Kuzari,* the medieval poet and philosopher Judah Halevi observed that the Ten Commandments do not begin with a creedal proposition, but with a memory of an experienced event: "I am the Lord your God who brought you out of the land of Egypt, out of the house of bondage" (Ex. 20:1). For Halevi, faith is rooted in the memory of events. Tradition's task is to transmit experience as memory.[4] Memory makes the past present and the future possible. The foundation for faith in the present is forged by the perpetuation of certain memories of the past. As Deuteronomy (32:7) tells us: "Remember the days of old, consider the years of ages past; Ask your father, he will inform you, Your elders, they will tell you."

Observance of many Jewish feasts and fasts offers a prime example of the nexus between faith and memory. Already in the biblical period, the process of transforming the nature-festivals of Mesopotamia into com-memorations of remembered events in Israel's history had begun.[5] For example, the festival of "*Aviv*" (Spring) was transformed into Passover, a festival commemorating the Exodus from Egypt (see Ex. 13; Deut. 16:3).

By the first century, it seems that the nature-festivals of Mesopotamia's polytheistic and pagan cult had been reformed to comply with the mono-theistic and demythologized features of Israelite faith. Nature-festivals were celebrated as harvest festivals, with recognition of divine grace through sacrifice and celebration at the Temple in Jerusalem as a major motif. Commemoration of historical events was present, but not yet dom-inant. However, after the destruction of the (Second) Temple, the motif of memory and commemoration prevailed. Once severed from their land and from the Temple cult, the Jews focused upon the historical features of the festivals. Indeed, in the diaspora, even the Land and the Temple cult entered the orbit of the people's cherished memories.[6]

---

4. Judah Halevi, *Kuzari,* trans. Hartwig Hirschfield (New York: Schocken, 1964), 1:21–26, 46–47.

5. See, for example, Helmer Ringgten, *Israelite Religion* (Philadelphia: Fortress Press, 1966), 51.

6. I deliberately have chosen not to discuss the celebration of the festivals in biblical times, such as those connected with the Temple cult and of those that may have predated the Temple cult. Nor have I chosen to discuss the various intriguing theories regarding biblical "enthronement" or "reenactment" rituals, many of which have been put forth by the Swedish School of modem biblical scholarship.

Rabbinic Judaism transformed Israelite faith into a historical religion. The memories of Israel's past were firmly embossed upon the festivals that comprised the Jewish liturgical year.[7] As the preeminent Jewish historian of our century, the late Salo W. Baron, put it:

> It is well known, for instance, that the ancient Israelite festivals were taken over from the earlier cultures of Canaan and Babylonia. But in each case ancient Judaism changed the fundamental meaning of the festival first by adding to it, then by substituting for its natural and historical interpretation.[8]

Similarly, as Heschel observed:

> To Israel the unique events of historic time were spiritually more significant than the repetitive processes in the cycle of nature, even though physical sustenance depended upon the latter. While the deities of other peoples were associated with places or things, the God of Israel was the God of events: the Redeemer from slavery, the Revealer of the Torah, manifesting himself in the events of history rather than in things or places.[9]

Remembrances of the formative events in Israel's biblical past—the Exodus from Egypt and the revelation at Sinai—became prominent features

---

The reason for this choice is not that these issues lack significance, but because, in my view, they lack a certain relevance to a theological exposition of the Jewish holydays. Though it has often been said, it is nonetheless necessary to state again that Judaism is not equivalent to Hebrew scripture. Rather, Judaism is how Jewish tradition interpreted Hebrew scripture. Consequently, the focus of my attention is on the meaning of the Jewish holydays within the context of classical Jewish religious interpretation, primarily during the talmudic and medieval periods.

7. On the festivals in rabbinic literature, see, for example, George Foot Moore, *Judaism* (Cambridge: Harvard University Press, 1927), 1:40–69.

8. Salo W. Baron, *A Social and Religious History of the Jews* (New York: Columbia University Press, 1952), 1:5. For a more popular view, see, for example, Hayyim Schauss, *The Jewish Festivals* (New York: Union of American Hebrew Congregations, 1938), 43–44.

9. Abraham Joshua Heschel, *The Sabbath* (New York: World, 1963), 63. Compare this discussion to Eliade's paradigm of the "archaic man" who refuses "to accept himself as a historical being, his refusal to grant value to memory and hence to the unusual event." See Mircea Eliade, *Cosmos and History* (New York: Harper, 1959), 85. On the "God of the Jewish people ... who carelessly intervenes in history, who reveals his will through events," see p. 104. See also Eliade, *The Sacred and the Profane* (New York: Harper, 1961), 110. "For Judaism, time has a beginning and will have an end. The idea of cyclical time is left behind." See also Mondford Harris, "History, Memory, Action," *Conservative Judaism* 26:4 (Summer 1972): 58–63.

of holyday observance. For example, the summer harvest festival, *Shavout* or Pentecost, designated by scripture as the "feast of ingathering" the wheat harvest and the summer fruits (Ex. 34:22; Num. 28:26), became identified by the rabbis as the anniversary of the revelation of the Torah at Sinai.[10] The Jewish liturgy identifies this festival as "the time of the giving of the Torah."

The association of the Feast of Booths (Lev. 23:34) with the fall harvest was overshadowed by its identification with the booths in which the Israelites dwelt during their sojourn in the wilderness after the liberation from Egypt (Lev. 23:41–43). Though both the agricultural and the historical origins of this festival are stated by scripture, the historical meaning subsequently became dominant. The "booth" was now more closely identified with historical memory of the desert experience, and less strongly identified with the booths in which the field-workers would dwell during the harvest. Here, too, nature gave way to history.

On Passover, the memory of the Exodus became the central motif. The Sabbath, the day of rest, is also associated with the Exodus. Slaves have no Sabbath. According to a verse in Deuteronomy (5:15), one should observe the Sabbath as a means of remembering Egyptian slavery and the liberation from bondage. While the Sabbath is also a commemoration of creation, the link with the memory of freedom from slavery provided an experiential referent that reference to creation could not offer—in other words, Israel participated in the Exodus, but only God witnessed the creation of the world. The Jewish liturgy for the Sabbath preserves referents both to the Exodus and to Creation.[11]

Holydays such as *Purim*, the Feast of Lots, *Hanukah*, and *Tisha B'Av* had clear historical references from the outset of their celebration. Purim refers to the events narrated in the biblical story of Esther. Hanukah refers to the liberation from oppression by Syrian Hellenists. *Tisha B'Av* is linked to the destruction of the Temple in Jerusalem as well as to other tragedies in Jewish history.[12] Even the apparently ahistorical occasion of

---

10. See *Pesahim* 68b; *Exodus Rabbah* 31:16. In the *Guide of the Perplexed* (3:43), Maimonides succinctly states, "The Pentecost is the day of the giving of the Torah." See Louis Finkelstein, *The Pharisees* (Philadelphia: Jewish Publication Society, 1966), 115–18.

11. See the *kiddush* (blessing over wine) for the Sabbath.

12. See *Tannit* 26b, 29a. Traditions also relate *Tisha B'Av* to events such as Moses's shattering the Ten Commandments, the destruction of the fortress at Betar, and the expulsion of the Jews from Spain in 1492 (specifically August 2, 1492, which corresponded that year with *Tisha B'Av*).

the Jewish New Year (*Rosh ha-Shanah*), denoted by scripture as a Day of Remembrance (Lev. 23:24) (though the object of remembrance is not stated), is described by the talmudic rabbis and later by the Liturgy either as the anniversary of the creation of the world or as the anniversary of the creation of the first human being.[13]

Reflection upon the role of remembrance in the Jewish liturgical years yields a variety of insights into the nature of Jewish faith. Because faith is articulated as memory, and because memory of the formative events of ancient Jewish history is identified with the Jewish holydays, it should not be surprising to find that central concepts of Jewish theological concern are associated with the religious festivals. Thus, the structure of Jewish theology is not systematic, but liturgical. As the nineteenth-century rabbi Samson Raphael Hirsch put it, the Jewish liturgy is Judaism's catechism. Celebration of the Jewish festivals conveys the Jewish theological agenda. For example, Passover relates to redemption, Pentecost to revelation, *Sukkot* (the Feast of Booths) to divine providence, Sabbath to creation, *Tisha B'Av* to theodicy.[14]

Theological concepts and concerns are not permitted to remain abstract propositions. Rather, they are communicated as specific memories through festivals of celebration and remembrance. For Judaism, theological concepts never atrophy into abstract creeds, because they are continuously being vocalized through deeds. The function of rituals associated with the various Jewish holydays is to internalize in the life of each member

---

13. On *Rosh ha-Shanah* as Adam's "birthday," see *Leviticus Rabbah* 29:1; as the birthday of the biblical patriarchs, see *Rosh ha-Shanah* 10b. The liturgy for *Rosh ha-Shanah* (*musaf-amidah*) states, "Today is the birthday of the world." This also seems to be based on *Rosh ha-Shanah* 10b.

14. Three Jewish thinkers who relate fundamental ideas of Jewish theology to the holydays are the fifteenth-century Spanish commentator Isaac Arma, the sixteenth-century kabbalist Judah Loew of Prague, and the early twentieth-century German philosopher Franz Rosenzweig. See Isaac Arama, *Akedat Yitzhak* (Pressburgh, 1849), Sermon No. 67, 99b. Arma relates six theological concepts to the festivals listed in Leviticus 23, as follows: Sabbath-creation, Passover-God's power, *Shavuot*-revelation, *Rosh ha-Shanah*-providence, *Yom Kippur*-repentance, *Sukkot*-immortality. See the discussion of Arama by Menahem Kellner, *Dogma in Medieval Jewish Thought* (New York: Oxford University Press, 1986), 159–61. On Judah Loew, see Byron L. Sherwin, *Mystical Theology and Social Dissent* (New York: Oxford University Press, 1982), 39–40. Rosenzweig relates the Sabbath and the "pilgrimage festivals" to creation, revelation, and redemption. See Franz Rosenzweig, *The Stgar of Redemption*, trans. William H. Hallo (New York Holt, Rinehart & Winston, 1970), 308–28.

of the people the memory of an event in the life of the people. Consider, for example, this citation from the *Passover Haggadah*:

> In each generation, each individual should consider himself or herself as if he or she was redeemed from Egypt, as it is said, "It is because of what God did for me when I went free from Egypt" (Ex. 13:8). For the Holy One redeemed not only our ancestors, but *us with them*, as it is said, "God took *us* out of there to bring us to the land promised to our ancestors" (Deut. 6:23). Therefore, we must . . . praise God who . . . took us from slavery to freedom.[15]

The liturgy for the *Seder*, the Passover meal, is called *Haggadah*, "telling." This relates to the biblical injunction to pass down memories of experience to one's children: "You shall tell your child on that day: It is because of what the Lord did for me when 1 went free from Egypt" (Ex. 13:8). History is remembered; it is retold; but it is not reenacted. Tradition is passed down by the telling within linear time. Reenactment, on the other hand, aims at obliterating time. The goal in Jewish ritual is to remember and not to reenact an event.[16] The uniqueness of the event can be recited, but it cannot be repeated. However, what can be reenacted is the *meaning* of the event. Indeed, for the tradition to continue, for the story to have perpetual and perpetuated meaning, it must be internalized.[17]

By the internalization of memory through ritual, we become our ancestors' contemporaries. Present and past converge at the moment of celebration and commemoration. Memory is the stimulus, and ritual and liturgy are the vehicle that bind past and present, ancestor and descendant, ancient experience and contemporary faith.

The expectation that commemoration of the Exodus would bring about a personal as well as a communal experience of liberation is expressed by the hasidic master, Nahum of Tchernoble. He suggests that two types of liberation are necessary for Passover observance to be considered complete. One type celebrates the liberation of Israel from Egypt. The second type is the liberation of each person from that particular thing that enslaves him

---

15. This text in the *Haggadah* is based on M. Pesahim 10:5, 6. See the insightful analysis by the Baruch M. Bokser, *The Origins of the Seder* (Berkeley: University of California Press, 1984), 86–87.

16. See the illuminating study by Monford Harris, "The Passover Seder: On Entering the Order of History," *Judaism* 25, no. 2 (Spring 1976): 167–74.

17. Certain Jews, such as Yemenites and Russian Caucasians, do "reenact" the Exodus as part of their Passover observance. However, this is an ethnic curiosity rather than a normative practice.

or her. Unless the individual liberates himself or herself from his or her own particular Egypt, the celebration of Passover is not complete.[18]

The Hebrew word for memory is "*zakhar*." But memory does not merely signify mental recall, but includes a call to action. The meaning of this term is not affirmation of dogmas but evocation of deeds. Liturgy and ritual serve as vehicles to prevent memory from deteriorating into an abstract reminiscence. Remembrance through observance of the festivals stifles the proclivity toward abstract theological speculation, toward intellectual voyeurism devoid of commitment. As Abraham Heschel put it, "An esthetic experience leaves behind the memory of a perception and enjoyment; a prophetic experience leaves behind the memory of commitment."[19]

In his analysis of the syntax of the word "*zakhar*"—"remembrance" in Hebrew scripture—the biblical scholar J. Pedersen observed that "*zakhar*" does not refer to an "objective memory image of some thing or event, but that this image is called forth in the soul and assists in determining its action. . . . Therefore *zakhar* may also mean to begin an action, to proceed to something, as when Elihu says, 'Proceed (*zekhor*) to magnify God's work which people sing of' (Job 36:24)."[20]

This understanding of "*zakhar*" as memory pregnant with action, with memory as a directional signal for the performance of particular deeds, is found in a variety of classical Jewish sources. For example, in the first hasidic book, the *Toledot Ya'akov Yoseif*, Jacob Joseph of Polnoye wrote:

> In every place in Scripture where one finds the commandment to remember, one is commanded to perform a specific deed whereby one links memory to action, as in the commandment of the fringes (see Num. 15:37–41) and those like it which are like a knot (on one's finger to remind one) not to forget (to do something).[21]

Memory is a call to action, to commemoration. However, the call is directed to those who share a memory of an event. For example, the command to commemorate the Exodus is addressed to those who experienced it. As the text in Exodus reads:

---

18. Menahem Nahum of Tchernoble, *Ma'or Einayim* (Jerusalem, 1966), "Tzav," 130–31.

19. Abraham Joshua Heschel, *God in Search of Man* (New York: Harper, 1955), 212.

20. Johannes Pedersen, *Israel: Its Life and Culture*, vol. 1 (London: Oxford University Press, 1926), 106–7.

21. Jacob Joseph of Polnoye, *Toedot Ya'akov Yoseif* (Jerusalem, 1967), "Mattot," 598. See also Zohar III, 93b.

This day shall be for you one of remembrance; you shall celebrate it as an institution for all time (Ex. 12:14). . . . Remember this day, on which you went free from Egypt, the house of bondage, how the Lord freed you from it with a mighty hand; no leavened bread shall be eaten (Ex. 13:3). . . . And you shall explain it to your son on that day: It is because of what the Lord did for me when I went free from Egypt (Ex. 13:8) (see also Deut. 16:1–8).

In this view, participation in the life of the faith-community is a prerequisite for commemorating events in the history of that faith-community. For example, the Passover liturgy tells of four sons. Of these, the wicked son asks:

"What does this ritual mean to you?" (Ex. 12:26), i.e., to you and not to him. Since he excludes himself from the community and denies God's role in the Exodus, you should confront him and say: "This is done because of what God did for me when I went out to Egypt" (Ex. 13:8). For me and not for him. Had he been there, he would not have been redeemed.

Rejection of the memories bequeathed to us is a form of spiritual self-disinheritance. One can only pity the person who fails to hear the melody of the memory. In this regard, commenting on the biblical description of revelation of the Torah at Sinai, the hasidic master Moses Hayyim Ephraim of Sedlykow told this tale:

A certain man played so exquisitely on a violin that anyone who heard his playing could not be restrained from dancing. The closer one was to the sound of the music, the stronger the urge to dance and the greater one's pleasure and joy from the music. Once a deaf person came around. He did not see the person playing the violin, and because he was deaf, he could not hear the music. All he saw were people dancing in joy and ecstasy. He muttered to himself, "They are mad. They are mad."[22]

Participation in the life of a faith-community means participation in its memories. It entails being able to discern the nuances of its medley of memories. To participate means to act, to observe, to celebrate. Memories are pregnant with action. Memories that do not stimulate action are stillborn. For Judaism, there is no faith without correlative deeds, without observance of ritual and law (*halakhah*).

The continuity of a faith-community depends upon its ability to perpetuate its memories. Memory is then simply the retelling of what we once knew, of what we once experienced. According to a midrash, the

---

22. Moses Hayyim Epharim of Sedlykow, *Degel Mahaneh Ephraim* (Jerusalem: Hadar, 1963), "Yitro," 111.

souls of all future generations of Jews stood at Sinai with the generation of the Exodus to receive the Torah. The hasidic master Elimelekh of Lizensk once said, "I not only remember the giving of the Torah at Sinai, I even remember who stood next to me then and there."[23] More recently, an Israeli newspaper told the story of two strangers who meet on a crowded bus in Tel Aviv. One says to the other, "Don't I know you from somewhere?" The other facetiously says, "Maybe we stood together at Sinai." The more friendly stranger holds out his hand and says, "You must be right. How have you been all of this time?"

Tradition is selective in terms of which memories of which events it seeks to emphasize and to perpetuate. Consequently, *heilsgeschichte* ("sacred history") and not *historische wissenschaft* ("scientific history") determines the contours of memories of past events and selects which memories are to play a role in the liturgical life of the faith-community. The works that constitute the sacred canon, rather than archaeological discoveries or the claims of extra-canonical works or the products of philological-historical method, decide how the past is to be understood by and transmitted to the future. Thus, while memory engenders faith, faith shapes memory. Faith forms memory by selecting the significant, by determining what is to be remembered and how it is to be remembered. Faith forms and transforms memory. Memory both stimulates and transmits faith.

The demilitarization of Jewish memory by rabbinic tradition may serve as an example of how faith shapes memory. For instance, there are no Jewish festivals commemorating military victories. Joshua's defeat of the Canaanites, David's conquest of Jerusalem, and Samson's victory over the Philistines have no liturgical referents.

What about Hanukah? Is Hanukah not rooted in the memory of the military victories of the Maccabees? Do not the Books of the Maccabees and Josephus recount these military victories and relate them to Hanukah? They do. However, this is not the story tradition sought to remember.

The story of the military victory of the Maccabees is not preserved in Jewish canonical literature. The books of the Maccabees are outside the canon. They are apocryphal, or non-canonical. The talmudic discussions of Hanukkah focus on the miracle of the single cruse of oil in the desecrated Temple that lasted eight days rather than one day.[24] Hanukah became a festival of lights, not of fights. The liturgy recalls those who remained faithful to the Torah in times of oppression rather than the military ex-

---

23. *Sefer Ohel Elimelekh* (Jerusalem, 1968), para. 63, 8b.
24. See *Shabbat* 21b.

ploits of the Maccabees. Indeed, God—and not the Maccabees—is described as the one who vanquishes the enemy.[25] The liturgy focuses on the miracle not on the military, on divine providence and not on successful military strategies. Indeed, classical Jewish religious literature stresses the ideological rather than the military conflict in its discussion of Hanukah.[26] The emphasis is on the battle of ideologies—Judaism vs. Hellenism, totalitarianism vs. liberty, and not on the battle of armies.

While memory is a dominant theme in the celebration of the Jewish festivals, expectation also plays a role. In linking memory to expectation, past and future converge in the present. For example, the ram's horn (*shofar*) blown on the Jewish New Year is as much a reminder of the blasts characteristic of the expected messianic redemption as they are the recalled revelation at Sinai. The redemption from Egypt is the precedent upon which faith in the final messianic redemption is predicated. Here one encounters a polarity between memory and expectation, between remembrance of historical events and hopes for a time that brings history to its eschatological conclusion.[27] For example, the Sabbath is a commemoration both of the beginning and of the end. It is both a remembrance of creation and a "foretaste of the World to Come."[28] Or, as Martin Buber said, "He who does not himself remember that God led him out of Egypt, he who does not himself await the Messiah, is no longer a true Jew."[29]

---

25. This is also true of Passover. Some have explained the absence of mention of Moses in the Passover Haggadah as being related to the tradition's stress upon God's exclusive role in redemption, to the exclusion of human efforts or human agents. For example, the Passover Haggadah states, "God took us out of Egypt not by an angel, not by a seraf, not by a messenger; rather the Holy One Himself." A similar sentiment regarding the redemption of the people celebrated on Purim and Hanukah is found in the *al-ha-Nisim* prayers recited on those festivals.

26. See the discussion of the meaning of Hanukah offered by Judah Loew of Prague in his *Ner Mitzvah* (B'nai Brak, Israel: Yahadut, 1962).

27. See the discussion in *Rosh ha-Shanah* 11a of when the final redemption will come and how it will occur in the same month as the liberation from Egypt. In the Sefardic *musaf-Kedushah*, reference is made of God saying, "I will redeem you in the end as in the beginning." According to Saadya Gaon, a rational reason for expecting God's final redemption is because of the precedent set by the redemption from Egypt; see his *Emunot ve-Deot* (*Beliefs and Opinions*), 8:1.

28. See *Berakhot* 57b.

29. Quoted in Will Herberg, ed., *The Writings of Martin Buber* (New York: World, 1961), 31.

While memory of past events serves as a call to action, so does the evocation of other types of remembrance. For example, the biblical injunction of remembrance regarding the New Year has no specific historical referent. A verse in Leviticus (23:24) reads: "In the seventh month, on the first day of the month, you shall observe a complete rest, a sacred occasion commemorated with loud blasts." While, as was noted, some rabbinic and liturgical texts relate the New Year to the creation of the world or to the creation of the first human being, and while others relate the "loud blasts" to the revelation at Sinai, still other sources posit an ahistorical referent for memory. For instance, some texts relate remembrance to the demand that the individual remember his or her sins, his or her covenantal commitment, and seek reconciliation with the divine through repentance. The blast of the ram's horn may be compared to an alarm clock, awakening the awareness of the need for self-scrutiny and self-improvement. Other texts, particularly liturgical ones, interpret the biblical call to remembrance as a call to God to recall the steadfast faith of one's ancestors and to apply their merit to the penitent's deficit of good deeds. One asks God to remember him or her with grace and forgiveness when determining one's fate on the basis of an evaluation of one's deeds.[30]

The Hebrew word *"zakhar"* means not only "memory" but also "male." This observation was utilized by the medieval Jewish mystics to provide the celebration of the Jewish holydays with an additional level of meaning. For the kabbalists, the main purpose of human action is not anthropocentric but theocentric. They developed ideas found in earlier rabbinic texts that considered human actions as opportunities for rectifying and repairing the shattered cosmos, and more particularly the Godhead itself. For the Jewish mystics, each act has the ability either to help further or fragment the divine, either to accelerate or retard the messianic advent. For the kabbalists, human action has theosophical-theurgic implications and effects.[31]

According to the Jewish mystics, there are "masculine" and "feminine" elements within the Godhead (i.e., the *Sefirot*). Human actions may affect the desired reunification and harmony of these elements, or they may bring about an undesirable disaffection and conflict between these ele-

---

30. On these themes, see the liturgy for *Rosh ha-Shanah* and *Yom Kippur*, such as in the "reader's repetition" of the *Amidah* prayer for *musaf*.

31. On the theosophical and theurgic motives as being dominant in Jewish mystical thought, see Moshe Idel, *Kabbalah: New Perspectives* (New Haven: Yale University Press, 1988).

ments. Observance of the laws and commandments stimulates harmony, while sin increases disharmony.

The medieval Jewish mystics both amplified the meaning of already existing rituals related to holyday observance and introduced new rituals for holyday observance. Many of these relate to the goal of inducing harmony between the "male" and "female" features of the divine personality. A paradigmatic example relates to Sabbath observance.[32]

In the version of the Ten Commandments found in Exodus (20:8), one is enjoined to "remember" the Sabbath day. Here we have the word "*zakhor*," which the kabbalists understood as a double entendre, referring both to remembrance and to maleness. In the Deuteronimic version of the Ten Commandments, the command is to "observe" or to "guard" (*shamor*) the Sabbath day (Deut. 5:12). The medieval kabbalistic text, *Sefer ha-Bahir*, observes:

> Why is it said: "Remember the Sabbath" and "Observe the Sabbath"? "Remember" ("*zakhor*") refers to the male ("*zakhor*") and "observe" refers to the female.[33]

According to the kabbalists, the goal of Sabbath observance is to bring about the reunification of the male and female aspects of the divine.[34] In kabbalistic literature, one encounters similar views regarding the meaning of observance of the other Jewish holydays.[35] The *zivvuga kaddisha*—"sacred coupling" (in the parlance of the Zohar)—has certain similarities with hierogamy or *hieros gamos* known in other religious traditions.[36] However, one can detect a different focus in kabbalistic texts. While many other traditions portray the "sacred marriage" as an imitation of the divine coupling, the kabbalists perceive humanly performed sacred deeds as stimulating the divine coupling. For the kabbalists, human activ-

---

32. On the Sabbath in Jewish mysticism, see the thorough study by Elliot Ginsbur, *The Sabbath in Classical Kabbalah* (Albany: SUNY, 1989).

33. Reuven Margaliot, ed., *Sefer Ha-Bahir* (Jerusalem: Mosad ha-Rov Kook, 1951), 79. See also Zohar 1, 48b.

34. See the discussion in Tishbi's classic work *Mishnat ha-Zohar*, now available in English translation: Isaiah Tishbi, *The Wisdom of the Zohar*, trans. David Goldstein (London: Oxford University Press, 1989), 1223–28. Also see Ginsbur, *Sabbath*, 69–74, 101–22.

35. See Tishbi, *Wisdom*, 1238–1259 and sources noted there. Note, Gershom Scholem, *On the Kabbalah and Its Symbolism* (New York: Schocken, 1965), 137–46.

36. See Mircea Eliade, *The Myth of the Eternal Return* (Princeton: Princeton University Press, 1965), 23–27.

ity—particularly sexual activity—is theurgic and not imitative. The goal
of the kabbalist is not to mimic but to transform the divine. By effecting a reunion of the male and female elements of the divine through the
performance of sacred deeds related to holyday observance, the individual
celebrant stimulates the influx of divine blessing into the world.

By adding this layer of meaning upon the observance of the Jewish
holydays, the kabbalists provided a rubric of meaning that might be applied even to those holydays unrelated either by history or interpretation
to memories of past events. One example is the celebration of the New
Moon, a festival related not to history but to nature, to a cyclical event
rather than to linear time. The moon is related by the kabbalists to the
Shekhinah—the feminine aspect of the divine. The goal is to liberate
Moon/*Shekhinah* from exile, and to restore her to her original fullness.
The liberation of the moon from her cosmic exile would then be reflected
in the end of Israel's terrestrial exile, which is identified with the advent
of messianic redemption.[37] Thus, while the medieval kabbalists shifted
the focus of holyday observance from the anthropocentric to the theocentric, from memory to theurgy, they did not abandon the focus on history.
Indeed, a central goal of the kabbalists was to encourage through observance the acceleration of history towards its eventual messianic climax.

Before concluding this discussion of the Jewish holydays, reference
should be made to a number of contemporary trends of understanding
and observing the Jewish holydays.

Each generation of Jews has perceived a contemporary meaning in the
paradigms of the past embodied in the holydays. Indeed, the continuity
of tradition has largely been assured by the ability of each generation to
perceive its contemporary situation in the mirror of tradition. As Rabbi
Abraham Isaac Kuk put it, "The Torah is like a mirror. Like a mirror, the
Torah always stays the same, but each generation sees its own reflection, a
different reflection, in the same mirror."

Throughout the generations, in many different lands, the Passover
paradigm of captivity and freedom, or the Hanukah paradigm of religious
oppression and subsequent liberation, was perceived in terms of past as
prologue, memory of the past as contemporary experience. With specific
reference to today, it is not coincidental that the massive efforts currently
being expended by American Jewry on the emigration of Jews from the
former Soviet Union is called "Operation Exodus."

---

37. See Scholem, *On the Kabbalah and Its Symbolism*, 151–52.

Each generation identified a contemporary figure with Haman—a demagogue desiring the annihilation of the Jewish people. Torquemada, Chemelnitzki, and Hitler were perceived as contemporary reincarnations of Haman, the perennial and archenemy of the Jews. The festival of Purim serves as an annual reminder that a Haman lurks waiting to attack in each generation. The constant hope is that as Haman was defeated, so will be his later incarnations. In January 1991, the new Haman was perceived to be Sadam Hussein. That the Gulf War ended at the time of Purim was seen by many Jews as a contemporary version of the biblical tale. According to midrash, "Rabbi Nathan said: Haman came to serve as a reminder for all generations, as it is said, 'These days of Purim should not fail from among the Jews, nor the memory of them perish from their descendants' (Esther 9:28)."[38]

The two formative events for contemporary Jewry are the Holocaust and the establishment of the State of Israel. Response to these events by world Jewry has led to a number of significant changes in the celebration of the Jewish liturgical year. One example is the initiation of new Jewish holydays, such as *Yom ha-Atzma'ut* (Israel Independence Day), *Yom ha-Shoah* (Holocaust Memorial Day), and, primarily in Israel, *Yom Yerushalayim* (Jerusalem Day), celebrating the reunification of Jerusalem during the 1967 war.[39]

That new Jewish holydays have been established for the first time in hundreds of years demonstrates the profound significance afforded the events they commemorate. That these holydays have received the endorsement and encouragement of much of the Orthodox rabbinate, a group largely ideologically resistant to change and innovation, is significant. Nonetheless, a number of problematic issues with regard to these new holydays merit mention.

One such issue is the introduction into the Jewish liturgical year of celebrations of military victories as such. While David's conquest of Jerusalem did not lead to the establishment of a commemorative festival, the 1967 reunification of Jerusalem did. This is but one indication of how the demilitarization of the Jewish liturgical year imposed by rabbinic and medieval tradition is currently being uprooted and reversed.

---

38. Jacob Lauterbach, ed., *Mekhilta de Rabbi Yishmael* (Philadelphia: Jewish Publication Society, 1933), 2:159.

39. On *Yom ha-Atzma'ut*, see Shelomo Goren, *Torat ha-Moadim* (Tei Aviv: Zioni, 1964), 568–98. On *Yom Ha-Atzma'ut* and *Yom Yerushalayim*, see Charles S. Liebman and Elizer Don-yehiya, *Civil Religion in Israel* (Berkeley: University of California Press, 1983), 153–55.

This new approach to telling and remembering Jewish history, and to celebrating certain events that comprise it, has led to a retelling of past events, a revisioning of memory, a restructuring of the meaning of the Jewish liturgical year. As Liebman and Don-Yehiya have observed correctly in their insightful study *Civil Religion in Israel*, there must be an inevitable clash between traditional Jewish symbols and values and those of Israel's "civil religion": "The symbols and values, expressed in traditional forms, conflict with the needs and values of the modern state."[40]

One example of the transformation of the traditional focus of festival observance and meaning relates to Hanukah. Originally a "minor" holiday in the Jewish liturgical year, it has become in recent generations a major festival. In America, this seems to have occurred because Jews felt a need to have a counterpart to Christmas. In Israel, this seems to have occurred because Hanukah could be easily reinterpreted to conform with the dogmas of the civil religion of the State of Israel.

As was noted above, the talmudic rabbis and the medievals largely demilitarized Hanukkah. The war of the Hasmoneans was downplayed while the miracle of the oil and the rededication of the sanctuary were stressed. Indeed, Hanukkah means "rededication." The clashes on the battlefield were minimized; the clash of ideologies—Judaism vs. Hellenism—was emphasized. When the liturgy speaks about the Maccabean triumph, it assigns the victory to divine intervention rather than to military acumen. However, in the civil religion of Israel, the military victory becomes the central motif. A religious holiday is transformed into a primarily national holiday. The Maccabees and not God are awarded the victory. The rededication of the Sanctuary is all but forgotten. Not divine redemption but self-redemption through military skill is stressed. The Maccabees are presented not as fighters for religious freedom or for the preservation of Jewish religious life and thought, but as patriots, as guerillas rebelling against military occupation and national subjugation.[41] The past is viewed as a prologue: the IDF (Israel Defense Forces) are considered the Maccabees of our generation. The victory of the Maccabees over the Syrians becomes the precedent for the defeat of Syria in modern Israel's wars. The past is understood in terms compatible with the realpolitik of today's Middle East conflict.

---

40. Liebman and Don-Yehiya, 16. Also see their extensive discussion and analysis of the reinterpretation of the Jewish liturgical year according to the civil religion of Israel.

41. Liebman and Don-Yehiya, 52–53.

Even *Yom ha-Shoah* has been given a military focus. In Israel, the official name of this commemoration is *Yom ha-Shoah ve-ha-Gevurah*—the "Day of Holocaust and Heroism"—with increasing importance being afforded Jewish armed resistance during the Second World War with the Warsaw Ghetto uprising often perceived in Israel as the prelude to the formation of the IDF, as a paradigm rather than as an exception to Jewish responses to Nazism.[42] It is further significant that commemoration of the Holocaust was not subsumed under previously established Jewish holydays commemorating national disasters, such as the Ninth of Av (*Tisha B'Av*)—the day commemorating the destruction of the Temples and numerous other catastrophes. This may be grounded in the perception of the Holocaust as a unique, unparalleled, and incomparable event in Jewish experience. Nevertheless, the choice of 27 Nissan as the date for *Yom ha-Shoah* is curious since there is no significant referent for that date in the annals of the history of the Holocaust. While some associate that date with the Warsaw Ghetto uprising, the date of *Yom ha-Shoah* does not exactly coincide with any significant date related to the uprising. What is also noteworthy is that the Ninth of Av does in fact coincide with a significant date in Holocaust history—namely, the initiation of the use of the gas chambers at Treblinka (which, unlike Auschwitz, was almost exclusively involved with the mass murder of Jews to the exclusion of members of other national or religious groups).[43] In this regard, one may speculate that the relationship on the calendar between *Yom ha-Shoah* and *Yom ha-Atzma'ut* (the latter occurs a week after the former) articulates a major dogma of the current "civil religion" of Israel, and of the "civil religion" of American Jewry—namely, linking the Holocaust to the emergence of Israel, death to rebirth, murder to resurrection.[44] In a sense, the relation of

---

42. See Amos Elon, *The Israelis* (New York: Holt, Rinehart & Winston, 1971), 206; Liebman and Don-Yehiya, 151–53.

43. On the problematics of the date for *Yom ha-Shoah*, see Abraham P. Bloch, *The Biblical and Historical Background of the Jewish Holy Days* (New York: Ktav, 1978), 253–58. Bloch recommends *Lag Ba'Omer*, the traditional festival of rejoicing because of a respite from catastrophe, as a proper day for *Yom ha-Shoah*, as that coincides with the anniversary of Hitler's death. On Treblinka and *Tish B'Av*, see Nora Levin, *The Holocaust* (New York: Schocken, 1973), 319. In 1942, *Tisha B'Av* corresponded to July 23.

44. For an extensive presentation of the civil religion of American Jews, see Johnathan S. Woocher, *Sacred Survival: The Vibil Religion of American Jews* (Bloomington: Indiana University Press, 1986), 131–57.

Yom-ha-Shoah to *Yom ha-Atzma'ut* might be interpreted as a Jewish parallel to Good Friday and Easter.

In the United States, growing concern for ecological issues, and in Israel, the civil religion, have encouraged a shift of focus from history back to nature with regard to observance of certain Jewish holydays. For example, Zionist ideology's emphasis upon the rebuilding of the land of Israel through agricultural development predictably led to the return to the biblical or even the pre-biblical view of the holydays as being primarily nature-festivals. Particularly among the "secular" Israelis, this has brought about a desacralization, even a "repaganization," of the Jewish festivals.[45] Furthermore, as was already noted, the remilitarization and nationalization of the meaning of traditional Jewish holydays inevitably has led to their de-theologization.

In my view, the growing secularization of Judaism, evident in contemporary interpretations of the Jewish festivals, poses a profound threat to the continuity of Jewish faith. Theological concepts endemic to Jewish faith are being ignored or forgotten. Traditional memories are being cast into oblivion or recast beyond recognition. Religious festivals are being purged of their religious meaning. Nationalistic themes are replacing theological motives. It is therefore not surprising that a 1990 demographic study found that in the United States, 95 percent of those surveyed who identified as Jews did not see commitment to Judaism as the essential component of their Jewish identity.[46]

Jewish continuity is in danger, not because of antisemitism from without but because of a progressive amnesia from within the Jewish community. As Abraham Heschel put it, "We are like messengers who have forgotten the message." The late Nobel laureate for literature Isaac Bashevis

---

45. The "back to nature" theme in Zionist ideology is too complex for discussion here. The "return to the Bible" must be understood as a nationalistic trend and not a religious one. Indeed, it articulates a rejection of talmudic and medieval rabbinic authority, often identified by Zionist ideologists with the "abnormal" diasporic Jewish experience.

46. *Highlights of the Council of Jewish Federations 1990 National Jewish Population Study* (New York: Council of Jewish Federations, 1991), 28. "Further analysis shows that less than 5 percent of all respondents consider being Jewish solely in terms of being a member of a religious group, whereas 90 percent define being Jewish as being a member of a cultural or ethnic group."

Singer used to say that Jews suffer from many diseases, but amnesia is not one of them. However, I am afraid he was wrong.[47]

Unless Jews recapture and preserve their memories, they will do to themselves what massacres, pogroms, and the Holocaust were unable to accomplish to obliterate Judaism: to make of it a forgotten memory. Again, to quote Heschel:

> The tasks, begun by the patriarchs and prophets and continued by their descendants, are now entrusted to us. We are either the last Jews, or those who will hand over the entire past to generations to come. We either forfeit or enrich the legacy of the ages. . . . We of this generation are still holding the key [to the sanctuary hidden in the realm of spirit]. Unless we remember, unless we unlock it, the holiness of the ages will remain a secret of God.[48]

---

47. On the discontinuity of Jewish memory in the modern period, and the problems it poses, see the insightful work by Yosef Hayim Yerushalmi, *Zakhor: Jewish History and Jewish Memory* (Seattle: University of Washington Press, 1982). On page 93, Yersuhalmi writes, "Only in the modern era do we really find, for the first time, a Jewish historiography divorced from Jewish collective memory and, in crucial respects, thoroughly at odds with it."

48. Abraham Joshua Heschel, *The Earth is the Lord's* (New York: Schumann, 1951), 107.

Memory in Ritual Life

Ashley Brocious

Memory can be a way to make religious life and ritual come alive. Byron Sherwin writes in "Faith as Memory: Theologies of the Jewish Holidays" that in Judaism, festivals act as a way to create a concrete medium for memory: "Theological concepts and concerns are not permitted to remain abstract propositions," he writes. "Rather, they are communicated as specific memories through festivals of celebration and remembrance" (p. 185). Jewish festivals such as Sukkot and Passover look back at stories of the past in order to commemorate and make meaning of a collective Jewish memory. This use of memory in religious ritual is not unique to Judaism; it has an important place in most religions—and Mormonism in particular, where ritual is not simply understood as commemorative but as salvific. Like Judaism, Mormonism understands the act of recollection itself to be a tool. "If we pay close attention to the uses of the word *remember* in the holy scriptures," Elder Marlin K. Jensen noted in a 2007 General Conference address, "we will recognize that remembering in the way God intends is a fundamental and saving principle of the gospel."[1] Admonitions to remember, Jensen points out, "are frequently calls to action: to listen, to see, to do, to obey, to repent." As Jensen demonstrates, memory becomes an important tool in LDS conceptions of the gospel, one capable of launching the participant into greater realms of spiritual practice and communion.

Sherwin's idea that memory can protect against abstract theology in religion is one that has important resonance in Mormonism as well, which understands that memory, in fact, can be a kind of antithesis to stagnation. As we will see by the end of this paper, however, the act of recollection must be done carefully, so that an authenticity and multiplicity of meanings can flourish, as Sherwin demonstrates. Like Judaism, memory is something in Mormonism that must be cultivated in ways that

---

1. Marlin K. Jensen, "Remember and Perish Not," General Conference, April 2007.

allow it to be both relevant and expansive—a way to look back to the past in order to recall the meanings that have purpose for the present.

Recollection as Tool

For Sherwin, a faithful community is one that recalls the past and uses the memory for fortitude in the present moment. Recollection is a tool of faith, he claims: "The foundation for faith in the present is forged by the perpetuation of certain memories of the past" (p. 182). What he means by "faith" is an ability to perceive something that was true in the past and believe that it can remain true in the present. The story of the Exodus found in Passover, for example, is told as something that continues to live on: God rescued Israel, and He will continue to rescue Israel. "Memory makes the past present and the future possible," Sherwin states, pointing out that this is a movement across time upon which faith relies (p. 182). Faith is not simply a matter of recalling events but in believing that what they demonstrate is still available.

Mormonism also understands recollection as an important tool of faith. In LDS scripture, recollecting the past, in many cases, becomes a way to bolster strength and fortitude in the present. In one passage in the Book of Mormon about the Exodus, Alma recalls divine rescue from captivity in order to sustain his own faith as well as his son's in the belief that God will continue to rescue his children from captivity:

> He [God] has brought our fathers out of Egypt, and he has swallowed up the Egyptians in the Red Sea; and he led them by his power into the promised land; yea, and he has delivered them out of bondage and captivity from time to time. . . . I have always retained in remembrance their captivity; yea, and ye also ought to retain in remembrance, as I have done, their captivity. (Alma 36:29)

Recollection in this moment serves to catalyze a narrative from the past into a prototype of the current reality. Alma's words demonstrate that God continues to liberate from captivity, something from which he hopes his son can also draw strength. His injunction here to "retain in remembrance" recognizes a kind of slippery quality to memory. To forget, the passage shows, would be to lose sight of the power of divine deliverance, not just in the past but in the present moment as well.

In fact, forgetfulness is often a mark of human failing and weakness in LDS scripture. "How quick the children of men do forget the Lord their God," Alma declares (Alma 46:8). In one passage, a father pleads for his children to remember the statutes of the Lord as a way for them to maintain spiritual alertness: "My sons, I would that ye would remember; yea, I would that ye would hearken unto my words. O that ye would awake; awake from a deep sleep, yea, even from the sleep of hell" (2 Ne. 1:12). Forgetfulness in this description becomes a kind of sinful stupor. To remember is a way of awakening, like coming out of a metaphorical sleep, and turning from sin. It is a decisive turning point into action and progress. The contrast between the faithless and the faithful, interestingly enough, is often a matter of remembrance.

This contrast between the faithful and faithless and their ability to remember is a common theme in the stories of Lehi's sons. Nephi's efforts in trying to rouse his brothers' faith often demonstrates their "forgetfulness" of God and His commands. In one scene, Nephi recalls the Israelite Exodus in order to provoke his brothers' faith in God's power. Their fathers, Nephi claims, "were led forth by his [God's] matchless power into the land of promise" (1 Ne. 17:42) much like themselves, whose father was commanded "that he should depart into the wilderness" (v. 44) for a promised land. Drawing this parallel between themselves and the Israelite Exodus, Nephi demands why such a memory does not soften his brothers: "Why is it that ye can be so hard in your hearts?" (v. 46). His brothers, according to this description, are like the Israelites themselves, who "did harden their hearts from time to time, and they did revile against Moses" (v. 42). Invoking the story of the Exodus provides Nephi a framework for both comprehending his brothers' resistance as well as trying to compel them into a more faithful perspective of their wilderness wanderings. But this scene demonstrates that those who continually forget the past, like Nephi's brothers, stand in stark contrast to the ones who remember. For Nephi, past memory becomes a springboard from which to extract courage and faith. But his brothers continually "forget," a behavior that the Book of Mormon understands to be a kind of rebellious act. For those who are careless and sinful, recollection often eludes them.

Interestingly, this notion of memory can be turned on its head. Forgetting can be a way of letting sin go in LDS scripture. In repenting, memory can be wiped clean: "I could remember my pains no more; yea, I was harrowed up by the memory of my sins no more" (Alma 36:19). Interestingly, then, the pain of sin can be cleared from memory at the same time that remembrance itself can be a tool for greater faith and resilience. Remembrance can both awaken a sinner and propel repentance, which can wipe painful and harmful recollections away. This tension between remembrance and forgetting shows that at root memory can be a tool used in both directions: to forget and to remember. Theologically it is a tool of faith; it is also a tool of repentance functioning at times in op- positional ways. Nonetheless, the faith journey we've seen depicted in the Book of Mormon shows human moments of both faith and forgetfulness, where one must turn back again to the stories of the past for fortitude. At the same time, repenting and revising memory is also part of the journey. Remembering, then, becomes a continual process and effort.

For Sherwin, memory provides a well-spring of faith for the current generation to draw from. Fortitude from the past comes from the com- munity's efforts to bring remembrance into being in the present. "Bereft of certain remembrances," Sherwin writes, "one becomes dismembered from the divine, from one's own self, from one's past, from one's faith- community" (p. 181). The faith community, then, has responsibility to pass memories on. Quoting Exodus 13:8, Sherwin notes that there is biblical injunction to pass down memories: "You shall tell your child on that day: It is because of what the Lord did for me when I went free from Egypt" (p. 186). Jewish festivals provide a way to ritualize and commem- orate memory, to make the past present for the current generation. To remember is to understand one's place in time, he shows, as well as one's connection to the divine and one's community—without such memory, there is a loss.

Mormonism also understands this loss. As made apparent in LDS scripture, to remember is a matter of action and faith, a way to more deeply be attuned to the large scope of divine plan and one's place within it, while at the same time providing fortitude and strength. Faith is culti- vated through story and memory as a way to bring it out of stagnation, to be more than abstract theology. Resilience and faith, then, are seemingly among the results for those communities who cultivate a deep sense of religious memory.

Recollection as Renewal

Sherwin shows that Jewish festivals throughout the year (such as Sukkot, Passover, Purim, and Shavuot) recall events and experiences of the Jewish people, not simply as a historical exercise but as a *renewal* of Jewish memory and practice. He describes these festivals as a "nexus between faith and memory" (p. 182), a central point where past and present merge in a moment of ritual. These festivals work to bring time together—a renewal of the past for a renewal of the present.

Perhaps the most consistent and commonplace ritual of renewal that uses this kind of nexus of time is one Jews and Latter-day Saints have in common: the Sabbath. Sherwin notes the imperative statement found in the Ten Commandments to "remember" the Sabbath day (Ex. 20:8). It is to be a day of remembrance commemorating both divine rescue from Egypt (Deut. 5:12–15) and creation (Ex. 31:13–17). One is to stop on Sabbath and remember that God himself offers rest. Hence, in Judaism, Shabbat is a celebration. It uses memory not as a passive act but as an active one, where the day itself becomes its own entity outside of usual time. This day of remembrance and rest provides a weekly renewal. For both Jews and Latter-day Saints, the Sabbath provides a theological space in order to bring into being "specialized" time in which the participant can dwell, where memory itself is not located solely in past, present, or future, but has formed a nexus point that centers the participant's engagement and renewal. The participant ceases, puts time on hold, in order to recall the past and renew the present.

In this act of merging time, such rituals can also look forward into the future. Sherwin calls this a future "expectation," where the rite seemingly looks forward and backward at the same time. He describes it this way: "In linking memory to expectation, past and future converge in the present." He then offers the Sabbath as an example of "a commemoration both of the beginning and of the end. It is both a remembrance of creation and a 'foretaste of the World to Come'" (p. 190). These kinds of rituals seem to have one eye on the past and one eye to the future. The LDS sacrament, as one example, looks back to the event of the Atonement at the same time as it looks forward to a fulness of redemption. It uses memory as a way to merge time in the act of renewing commitment. During this ordinance, participants recall the event of the Atonement, using bread and water as a token of recollection, in order to renew their commitment to Christ. The Sacrament prayers explicitly reference this act as a moment of remembrance, performed to inspire a constancy in memory going forward: "that they may eat [bread] in remembrance of the body of thy Son . . . and [witness] that they [will] always remember him and keep his commandments" (D&C 20:77). Remembrance inspires action in the present and into the future.

This is true of other ordinances: baptism is a moment of looking back at the burial of the natural man as well as a looking forward to a rebirth and resurrection. The present converges in pulling together both the past and future to provide a larger theological framework in which the participant plays a part. The rite creates a space for the participant to have a place in the larger theological process—where each can renew an individual commitment and position in a larger cosmic undertaking.

As Sherwin shows, then, there are occasions where memory can have a fluidity—moving across past, present, and future as a way of allowing a participant to take time to recall, re-center, and find renewal. Time "stops" in a sense or becomes "specialized" during the ritual moment by creating a nexus point. The rite also gives the individual participant a place in a larger theological order, participating not simply in a communal recollection but in an individual one where the participant can be changed, renewed, and even propelled to action by the experience itself. For Jews and Latter-day Saints, the Sabbath provides this opportunity each week. Ritual and memory, then, in its most powerful function offers a participant a framework through which recollection aids engagement and internalization through its use of time itself.

Recollection as Internalization

Sherwin writes that the overall purpose of ritualized recollections is to *internalize* the meaning of the past event: "The function of rituals associated with the various Jewish holydays is to internalize in the life of each member of the people the memory of an event in the life of the people" (p. 186). But how is memory internalized? For Sherwin, internalization is a personalization. He cites the Passover Haggadah as a text that asks the festival participant to direct the Exodus story to themselves: "Each individual should consider himself or herself as if he or she was redeemed from Egypt" (p. 186). By internalizing the memory, one participates as if he or she were living the past experience. One feels as if one is a participant in the story itself. Sherwin writes,

> By the internalization of memory through ritual, we become our ancestors' contemporaries. Present and past converge at the moment of celebration and commemoration. Memory is the stimulus, and ritual and liturgy are the vehicle that bind past and present, ancestor and descendant, ancient experience and contemporary faith. (p. 186)

The story lives on, and is experienced again, by the participants of the current generation as if they were alongside their ancestors.

Sherwin is clear, however, that the past cannot necessarily be repeated. What can be generated from the past is a *meaning* that can be recalled into the present. He writes, "Tradition is passed down by the telling within linear time. Reenactment, on the other hand, aims at obliterating time.

The goal in Jewish ritual is to remember and not to reenact an event." The living component of a festival commemoration is what that event comes to signify. "What can be reenacted," Sherwin writes, "is the *meaning* of the event." The meaning lives on and creates the thread across time. "For the story to have perpetual and perpetuated meaning," he claims, "it must be internalized" (p. 186). Internalization, then, is making meaning through recollection, coming to a deeply felt understanding.

True internalization, in LDS understanding, would be going beyond the motions to deeply held belief. In taking the Sacrament, for example, we can, according to Elder Peter F. Meurs, take the moment as an "opportunity to more fully yield our hearts and souls to God."[2] It is through a process of internalization that one avoids superficial performances. However, Sherwin's definition of internalization brings an interesting spin to thinking about the LDS internalization process. For Sherwin, there is a collective memory in Judaism that is being invoked and shared between the generations. Something that was alive in the past is made alive in the present again, creating a line of continuum. But in LDS ritual and ordinances, the focus is not as much on continuum but on individual salvation. One engages in a ritual to be changed, made new, and propelled further along a route toward returning to God. But what if the very experience of recollection was essential to this internalization (and salvific) process? What if, in being made new (or, renewed) in an ordinance rite, one understood that it is the meaning itself that is the power behind the rite? What is recalled is not the event itself, but the *meaning* of the event—with the understanding that the meaning itself may also have a fluidity to it. To participate in baptism, for oneself or by proxy, may not have an entirely fixed meaning. It could feel and function differently on different occasions as what is recollected shifts and moves for individual participants, leaving the door open for a variety of spiritual experiences and meanings.

This brings forward a kind of liberating realm of possibilities for ritual—an unfixed number of meanings and experiences for participants to engage with. Sherwin notes that a reworking of meaning is the natural state of memory as it passes through the generations. He points out that the Jewish festivals originated in nature harvest celebrations. The summer harvest festival became Shavuot, the fall harvest became Sukkot, and the spring harvest became Passover. These festivals then become a kind of liturgical calendar that took on theological meanings: Shavuot recalls

---

2. Peter F. Meurs, "The Sacrament Can Help Us Become Holy," General Conference, October 2016.

revelation, Sukkot recalls deliverance, and Passover recalls redemption. He notes that in the post-Temple tradition, the rabbis were careful to keep Jewish festivals from becoming military celebrations. The medieval kabbalists then included their own mystical meanings. In the present day, in a world with the state of Israel, secular and nationalistic meanings have arisen. "Each generation of Jews has perceived a contemporary meaning in the paradigms of the past embodied in the holydays," he states. He goes further to quote Rabbi Abraham Isaac Kuk, who used an image of a mirror to describe each generation's engagement with the past: "The Torah is like a mirror. Like a mirror, the Torah always stays the same, but each generation sees its own reflection, a different reflection, in the same mirror." This process, for Sherwin, promotes tradition's continuity: "Indeed, the continuity of tradition has largely been assured by the ability of each generation to perceive its contemporary situation in the mirror of tradition" (p. 193). This "mirror" indicates that the past becomes alive again and again as each generation reengages with it, seeing something different in the reflection. This is a regenerative cycle, something ongoing that the generations must allow or at least acknowledge about their religious traditions.

But Sherwin is hesitant to claim that all retellings of the past are helpful. Some meanings are harmful, others lose sight of the larger story, and some are coerced into other ideologies. He writes of his fears that in this generation, "traditional memories are being cast into oblivion or recast beyond recognition" (p. 197). The past taboo against festivals for military victories have been disregarded to include Israeli victory celebrations in the Jewish world. New efforts to secularize, according to Sherwin, mean that "religious festivals are being purged of their religious meanings. Nationalistic themes are replacing theological motives" (p. 197). Sherwin is fearful of such changes and its effect on Judaism at large. The fear, for Sherwin at least, seems to be that when a generation overidentifies with a story, they may shape it to match current events in a way that violates its larger (and richer) array of meanings. Hanukah has reached a new height of popularity, he claims, because it has nationalistic use for Israel. "The past is understood in terms compatible with the realpolitik of today's Middle East conflict," he writes. The meaning has been shifted (badly, in his opinion) away from divine aid into military prowess. In this new version, "not divine redemption but self-redemption through military skill is stressed" (p. 195). The story has been co-opted to suit the purposes and agenda of the current generation rather than a more authentic search for meaning without a prescribed end.

It is a disconcerting problem because it seems that there is a thin line between a generation simply finding meaning relevant to their context, on the one hand, and coercing a forced meaning to fit their needs, on the other. It is hardly a Jewish problem, but one possible in any religious tradition. In Mormonism, the problem may be just as prevalent and just as damaging as it is to contemporary Judaism. Secularization is not a problem just for Jewish continuity but for religious continuity in general. When secularization hits ritual "meanings," it may co-opt the religious theological endeavor for the entire community. What, then, are authentic approaches to understanding ritual that keep it from being co-opted by outside ideologies (nationalistic, feminist, liberationist, etc.) for a particular end, while at the same time allowing for these generational concerns and interpretations to stay present? The answer, it seems, may be in the memory-keeping itself. In preserving the memory of the rite, recollecting it in a way that keeps a *fluidity* and *multiplicity* of meanings intact, one version of the story may be kept in check from dominating all the rest. The community itself must preserve memory in a way that the religious theology cannot be overrun by the secular. But the religious cannot be made too rigid, too unwieldy, that it becomes its own sort of dogma. Variety may be key, after all. Meaning itself must be made a tool, not a weapon.

Sherwin's fears of co-option, of stripping out religiosity, of restructuring meaning in harmful ways are real concerns for any religious community. Elaboration, in fact, may often be the beginning of losing sight of deeper ritual meaning. Elie Weisel writes of his horror at the extravagance of American bar mitzvahs: "Here, a bar mitzvah is a small wedding. I don't understand it. I know people who took out loans with the bank to be able to finance these. Some of these affairs were outrageous."[3] He sees the nonessential entertainment, gifts, and extravagance potentially distracting participants from the essential meaning of the rite. "All this should *mean* something," he states, noting that some meanings are more important than others:

> It should not simply mean that you get a lot of presents, or a lot of money, or a trip to Jerusalem. We need meaning now more than in my time. . . . This is not only a matter for celebration and bringing friends and being happy and dancing with the orchestra. It's an internal thing. You must feel something. How do you create such a feeling?[4]

---

3. Elie Wiesel, "I am not God's Policeman," in *Opening the Doors of Wonder: Reflections on Religious Rites of Passage,* ed. Arthur J. Magida (Los Angeles: University of California Press, 2006), 166.

4. Wiesel, 166.

It seems that cultivating a *feeling* of the rite's meaning, an internalization, can take it beyond festivity and into its deeper religious and theological purposes. If future generations are to reinfuse ritual and practices in a way that hearkens back to its theological roots and meanings for better relevancy in the modern day, it is perhaps materialism and externalities that will have to be stripped first for a deeper and simpler theological base. Letting it rest in that simplicity, rather than in bombarding or coercing it into a realm it doesn't belong, is perhaps the true struggle of ritual regeneration. Meaning can be internalized best when its roots extend beyond superficial performance into the heart of the tradition. Memory can be distilled to its most powerful, regenerative force—something that moves beyond abstraction into changing and renewing the participant through internationalization. As Sherwin has demonstrated, internationalization is ultimately the process of meaning making.

To conclude, it is clear that memory and ritual is something that has the potential to supply a religious person with a fortitude of faith, meaning, renewal, and purpose. In Judaism, festivals become the events of memory where the current generation can reach back to the stories of the past, grapple with its meaning, internalize it in ways that are renewing, and learn to carry the tradition forward as a gift to the next generation. Through festivals, they celebrate together, understanding that a communal event is an agent for a communal memory. The LDS tradition ritualizes in different ways than the Jewish tradition, but the purposes of invoking memory have large crossovers between the traditions. Mormonism also understands that memory-keeping can catalyze spirituality, propel into action, locate participants into a cosmic order, and provide meaning that can be internalized and renewing. One is *changed* by true memory-keeping. Abstract theology comes to life in the process of recollection and remembering. Theology is most powerful when it is not co-opted by outside forces or put into a dogmatic box, but rather when it can be inflected with the traditions' deepest interpretative potential. Ritual itself then can be a means for making such renewal and internalization possible. The key, as Sherwin points out, is remembering. Forgetfulness is a mark of disconnection from the faith-community and from the past. Those who truly engage are those who truly take time to remember.

Sacrality and Particularity:
Jews in an Early Modern Context

Dean Phillip Bell

In many parts of the Hebrew Bible the ancient Israelites are depicted as a chosen and special people to God. In Exodus 19:5–6, for example, God declares to Moses: "Now then, if you obey Me faithfully and keep My covenant, you shall be My treasured possession among all peoples. Indeed, all the earth is Mine, but you shall be to Me a kingdom of priests and a holy nation. These are the words that you shall speak to the children of Israel." The term for "treasured possession" is *segulah*, which carries a wide range of meanings from treasure to characteristic, quality, peculiarity or specificity, and body, as well as adaptation and conformity.

The connection between chosenness and obedience and conformity to God's covenant makes the Israelites valued and holy. Similarly, consider Deuteronomy 7:6–8:

> For you are a people consecrated [*qadosh*, holy] to the Lord your God: of all the people on earth the Lord your God chose you to be His treasured people [*am segulah*]. It is not because you are the most numerous of peoples that the Lord set His heart on you and chose you—indeed, you are the smallest of peoples; but it was because the Lord favored you [*mayahavat*] and kept the oath He made to your fathers that the Lord freed you from the house of bondage, from the power of Pharaoh king of Egypt.

The covenantal condition is maintained as an explanation for the selection of the Israelites, but here the Deuteronomist adds the historical condition of God removing the Israelites from bondage in Egypt, which provides a further dimension to the unique condition of the relationship. It is precisely the unique nature and the freeing of the Israelites that were featured, among other core issues, in medieval debates between Jews and Christians.[1]

---

1. Expanding this concept further, Deuteronomy 14:2 notes: "For you are a people consecrated to the Lord your God: the Lord your God chose you from among all other peoples on earth to be His treasured people." Or again, in Deuteronomy 26:18: "And the Lord has affirmed this day that you are, as He promised you, His treasured people who shall observe all His commandments, and that He will set

In these and other biblical passages, the Israelites are presented as a unique and special people, a sensibility that helped shape a good deal of rabbinic and Jewish discourse, development, and interaction with others. The Israelites are elevated above other nations and closely connected to (holy to or consecrated to) God, whose commandments they must fulfill. In a complex relationship, the Israelites' obligation to fulfill the commandments is seemingly both a prerequisite for and a result of this special status and connection.

The Early Modern period, roughly the sixteenth through the eighteenth centuries of the common era, provides a valuable context for understanding how this special status ascribed in the Bible played out in questions about both internal Jewish identity and interactions with non-Jews, particularly complicated issues in societies in which Jews were a tiny minority and in which Christian and Muslim theology had a quite nuanced relationship and historical experience with Judaism. Although the dialectic between particularism and universalism has been frequently challenged in recent scholarship, that tension is useful in understanding this set of issues in an Early Modern context. Equally valuable for our purposes are issues of acculturation and accommodation (perhaps more useful terms for the Early Modern period than "assimilation"). In what follows, I will provide a brief overview of the Early Modern period, with specific emphasis on Jewish experiences in Western, Christian Europe, before turning to a few key examples that allow for a fuller exploration of these and related issues.

An Early Modern Context

The Early Modern period, which has received particularly extensive attention over the past several decades, was both medieval and modern in some ways—traditional and innovative. As such, it provides an intriguing context in which to explore questions of particularity and universality, especially given the significant globalization that occurred during this period. As a period of religious reform across the globe, it also allows us to examine the notion of sacrality in greater detail as well.[2]

---

you, in fame and renown and glory, high above all the nations that He has made; and that you shall be, as He promised, a holy people to the Lord your God."

2. See, for example, Merry E. Wiesner-Hanks, *Religious Transformations in the Early Modern World: A Brief History with Documents* (New York, 2009); and Elaine M. Fisher, *Hindu Pluralism: Religion and the Public Sphere in Early Modern South India* (Berkeley, 2017).

Many historians have pointed to several key characteristics of Early Modernity: rapid and massive changes in human organization and interaction between humans and nature, growing globalization (through exploration, trade, and even the exchange of knowledge), the development of large and stable states (with centralized administrations and administrative structures), increasing populations, the intensification and diffusion of various technologies, and the almost simultaneous revival and reformation of numerous religions across the globe. Early Modern Jewish history has likewise been seen as a period of transition and balanced between internal concerns and external developments, particularly relevant given the diverse settings in which Jews found themselves in Western and Eastern Europe, across the Ottoman Empire, and in smaller populations in the Americas, Asia, and Africa. In what follows, I explore the notion of sacrality, particularism, and universalism in Early Modern Jewish discussions of community, religious polemics, and debate, before turning to a specific case study of Jewish response to the plague in early seventeenth-century Italy.

Notions of Sacrality:
Communal Organization and "Holy Community"

The primary Hebrew term used for "community" by Jews in the sixteenth century was *kehillah*. In its biblical and Talmudic context, this word had the rather general meaning of an assembly of people.[3] In the Babylonian Talmud, tractate *Rosh Hashanah*, and elsewhere, however, we read of the "holy community" (*kehillah kedosha*) of Jerusalem.[4] By the Middle Ages and Early Modern period it was fairly common for Jews to denote their communities as "holy."[5] But what was the purpose and implication of the use of this term? Medieval Ashkenazic communities, it has been argued, consciously

---

3. Exodus 12:6, for example, references "all the assembled congregations of the Israelites." (See also Numbers 14:5.) The sense of the term *kahal* (used in the early modern period to mean both the community as well as the governing community council) as an assembly of a mass of people is further confirmed throughout the Writings and Prophets. (See Joshua 8:35, for example.) Regarding talmudic notions, see, for example, Babylonian Talmud tractates Pesahim 64a or Kiddushin 41b.

4. 19b; or in Yoma 69a; see also Betzah 14b (holy community at Jerusalem) and 27a (holy congregation of Jerusalem); Tamid 27b (holy congregation in Jerusalem).

5. See Dean Phillip Bell, "Jewish Community in Central Europe in the Sixteenth Century," in *Defining Community in Early Modern Europe*, ed. Michael J. Halvorson and Karen E. Spierling (Aldershot, 2008), 143–62.

emulated the Talmudic sacred congregation of Jerusalem through their emphasis on prayer and Torah study.[6] According to one explanation, for Jews,

> the idea that Jewish communities were holy instilled their lives with a strong sense of value and mission. In addition, as a result of the Jewish encounter with medieval Christianity, the sanctity of the community, and its members, acquired added, perhaps, unexpected, dimensions of meaning.[7]

What is more, Ashkenazic Jews also viewed the community as the embodiment of a court, perhaps contributing to the perceived sense of sanctity.

Jews writing in Hebrew during the sixteenth century continued to describe their communities as "holy." In Padua, in northern Italy, for example, the members of the Jewish community referred to themselves as "people of the holy community."[8] The designation "holy community" apparently could also refer to individual congregations within the same city. In 1603, for example, one document referenced "the holy community Ashkenazi" and "the holy community Loazi,"[9] referring to the German and Italian Jewish communities in Padua respectively. The sixteenth-century German Jewish chronicler and statesman Josel of Rosheim similarly wrote,

> In the year 5294 (1533/34), there was dissension and strife [within] the holy community of Prague between the community and the Horowitz people and others, and, consequently, many feuding camps arose in other communities in Bohemia.[10]

Despite the strife within the community, Prague remained holy in his description, while the other settlements of Jews in Bohemia were simply denoted as "communities." At times, therefore, the term "holy" was used to indicate a large or important gathering of Jews. Not surprisingly, non-Jewish sources did not utilize the term "holy" when discussing Jewish communities. The Padua community was referred to as "our holy community"

---

6. Jeffrey R. Woolf, "'Qehillah Qedosha': Sacred Community in Medieval Ashkenazic Law and Culture," in *A Holy People: Jewish and Christian Perspectives on Religious and Communal Identity*, ed. Marcel Poorthuis and Joshua Schwartz (Leiden, 2006), 223.

7. Woolf, 219.

8. Daniel Carpi, ed., *Minutes Book of the Council of the Jewish Community of Padua, 1577–1603* (Jerusalem: Israel National Academy of Sciences and Humanities, 1973), 1:77.

9. Carpi, 2:5.

10. Joseph [Josel] of Rosheim, *The Historical Writings of Joseph of Rosheim: Leader of Jewry in Early Modern Germany*, ed. Chava Fraenkel-Goldschmidt, trans. Naomi Schendowich (Leiden: Brill, 2006), 326 [Hebrew, 298].

in one Hebrew document, but the terms were translated into Italian simply as *la nostra università* ("our university").[11]

For Jews, the notion of chosenness was a badge of communal and theological honor, as in medieval debates, such as between Moses ben Nahman (Nahmanides) and Pablo Christiani, or late medieval and Early Modern polemical literature. In *Sefer Nizzahon Vetus* (late thirteenth or fourteenth century), the Jewish author examines a range of biblical and New Testament passages in the context of debate and polemics with Christianity. In discussing Jeremiah 31:31–33,[12] the author notes that Christians argue that the passage refers to Jesus and to the replacement of things like circumcision with baptism and the transfer of the day of the Sabbath from Saturday to Sunday. But, the polemicist retorts, the New Testament itself notes that Jesus did not come to destroy but rather to fulfill the words of Moses. In this sense, then, Christians contradict their own holy writings when they assert that Jeremiah indicates that there is a new Torah and that Jesus abolished the entire Torah of Moses. The author also notes that the passage under examination references the House of Israel and the House of Judah, and not a Torah of Jesus.[13] Similarly, in glossing Isaiah 65:9 ("And I shall bring forth a seed out of Jacob"), the author reiterates that the biblical reference is to the Jews and not to Jesus, as interpreted, without any basis he maintains, by Christians.[14]

It was not only in theological debate that Early Modern Jews argued for precedence and special status. A number of Early Modern Jewish writers sought to secure the position of Jews in the rapid development of science by pointing to alleged Jewish advances in distant history. Indeed, in Renaissance Italy, Jews often presented Hebrew culture as superior to all other cultures. The famous Jewish exegete Isaac Abarvanel, for example, saw a biblical

---

11. Carpi, *Minutes*, 2:204.

12. "See, a time is coming—declares the Lord—when I will make a new covenant [berit hadasha] with the House of Israel and the House of Judah," and continuing in 31:32–33, "It will not be like the covenant I made with their fathers, when I took them out of the land of Egypt, a covenant which they broke, though I espoused them—declares the Lord. But such is the covenant I will make with the House of Israel after these days—declares the Lord: I will put My Teaching into their inmost being and inscribe it upon their hearts. Then I will be their God, and they shall be My people."

13. David Berger, trans., *The Jewish-Christian Debate in the High Middle Ages: A Critical Edition of the Nizzahon Vetus* (Philadelphia: Jews Publication Society of America, 1979), 89–90.

14. Berger, 118.

model for the Venetian republic. Johanan Alemanno (1433–c. 1504) found the model for the Florentine city-state in the Bible. Similarly, Messer Leon (c. 1470/72–c. 1526) argued that all of Ciceronian rhetorical figures could already be found in the Bible and further that the Bible contained still more not mentioned by classical authors. Indeed, Early Modern Jews often looked to biblical and rabbinic writings for evidence that Jews already knew particular fields of learning. Justified by these precedents, they then integrated these disciplines into Jewish discourse.

The discussion of holiness or chosenness could have another side, however, in Early Modern discourse. It could be taken up by Christians as a means to attack the Jews, even as Christian polemicists might concede the original special, or peculiar, nature of the Jews and their religion. For the sixteenth-century Christian reformer Martin Luther, for example, "Jew" was a categorical descriptive not a contemporary people per se, whom Luther would argue were in any event no longer true Jews. A key issue throughout much of Luther's writings about the Jews and Judaism focused on questions of lineage and descent. His concept of Jew was important to his larger theology precisely because of the true Jewish relationship to Christ. In Luther's concern with a return to the pure past, true Christianity bypassed the medieval church, the councils and the popes, and sought descent and lineage from Jesus himself. To that extent, Luther truly refashioned himself and the true remnant of Christians as Jews. This meant of course that there was no longer any room for Jews as Jews; Luther made that quite clear from his earliest to his last writings. The issue of descent, of assuming identity, and of abrogating completely (or I should say replacing) the concept of Jew was at the heart of Luther's position regarding the Jews.

The concept of descent and Luther's criticism of the Jews ran parallel. Already in his Romans commentary Luther was very concerned with the patriarch Abraham and the Jews' relationship to him. Commenting on Romans 4, Luther argued that Abraham was not justified by works "as the arrogant Jews and unbelievers think" but through faith; Abraham had faith before he had circumcision.[15] Again, in his writings of 1535 on Genesis, Luther noted the Jews' arrogance and boastfulness; the Jews, he argued, "gloried in their descent, that they were the sons of Abraham."[16] But, Luther concluded, the Jews were no longer the people of God:[17]

---

15. Martin Luther, *Luther's Works*, ed. Jaroslav Pelikan, 55 vols. (St. Louis, 1955–86), 25:3537.

16. Luther, 1:268.

17. Luther, 1:360.

Nowhere do they have a continuing abode; they are hated and despised by all men; they live most wretchedly in dirt and filth; they are not permitted to engage in the more honorable occupations—and who could enumerate all the hardships of the enemies of Christ?[18]

In his last major writings that mention the Jews, Luther's positions, or at least his primary concerns, had changed little. His "Treatise on the Last Words of David" focused upon questions of exegesis, the Trinity, and the Messiah, while criticizing the Jews and their "arrogant" notion of descent along the way. Luther early on praised King David for his modesty and not boasting of his circumcision or his descent;[19] he then later repudiated the Jews for precisely the opposite:

Now, if we are willing to believe the Jews, or Israel, it is far more reasonable to give those Jews, or Israel, credence, who have for approximately 1500 years to date governed the Church publicly in all the world, also have overcome devil, death, and sin, who have interpreted the writings of the prophets, and who have continuously worked miracles through their disciples. I repeat that it is far more meet that we believe such true and acknowledged Jews and Israelites than these false and unknown Jews or Israelites who have wrought no miracle these 1500 years, who have interpreted no writings of the prophets, who have perverted everything, who have done nothing in the open but underhandedly and clandestinely, like children of darkness, that is, of the devil, have practiced nothing but blasphemy, cursing, murder, and lies against the true Jews and Israel, that is, against the apostles and prophets. And they continue this daily and thus prove that they are not Israel or Abraham's children and in addition despoilers, robbers, and perverters of Holy Scripture. Therefore it behooves us to recover Scripture from them as from public thieves wherever grammar warrants this and harmonizes with the New Testament. The apostles furnish us with many precedents for this.[20]

Luther's 1538 "Against the Sabbatarians (Letter to a Good Friend)" also detailed the main issues already noted, particularly regarding the Messiah, Babylonian exile, and circumcision. Again, Luther concluded with a play on the concept of Jew:

So you must tell them that they themselves should take the initiative in keeping Moses' Law and becoming Jews. For they are no longer Jews, since they do not observe their Law. When they have done this, we shall promptly emulate them and also become Jews.[21]

---

18. Luther, 1:264; see also 1:263.
19. Luther, 15:271.
20. Luther, 15:344.
21. Luther, 47:79.

In his later and venomous anti-Jewish writings, including the infamous 1543 "On the Jews and Their Lies," Luther extended this discussion. This work is perhaps the most significant work on Jews and Judaism written by Luther, not only for its relation to his consistent theological positions, but also for its frequent appropriation since the sixteenth century. There are four major parts to this work. In the first part Luther spends a great deal of ink discussing questions of Jewish boasting regarding lineage, circumcision, and homeland. Part one echoes the bulk of Luther's previous writings about Jews, though here Luther was very pointedly not concerned with converting any Jews, an act that he by then assumed to be impossible.[22] Again, Luther went through the litany of accusations: Jews revile Christianity, and they boast of their nobility with "devilish arrogance." In a very apocalyptic vein, Luther noted that "Jews, Turks, papists, radicals abound everywhere," claiming to be the church and God's people.[23]

The notion of sacrality and of particularity guided a good deal of Early Modern discussion by and about Jews. This situation could be even more complicated given the forced conversions of Jews in parts of Europe or the hybrid identities formed by Jews in the midst of and after the expulsion from Spain at the end of the fifteenth century. In these and other cases, the very notion of Jewish could become quite complex,[24] signaling for some recent historians the very birth of modern and fragmented Jewish identity.[25] In order to better appreciate the balance of Early Modern Jewish experiences, which continued to see Jewish life and experiences in the context of religious constructs and which balanced internal concerns with interaction with the broader, non-Jewish world, let us turn to a brief case study that focuses on a Jewish discussion of response to the plague in seventeenth-century Italy.

---

22. Luther, 47:137.

23. For a similar discussion by the reformer Martin Bucer, and the response of the Landgrave Philip of Hesse and the Jewish political leader Josel of Rosheim, see Dean Phillip Bell, "Jewish Settlement, Politics, and the Reformation," in *Jews, Judaism and the Reformation in Sixteenth-Century Germany,* ed. Dean Phillip Bell and Stephen G. Burnett (Leiden: Brill, 2006): 421–50.

24. See Miriam Bodian, *Hebrews of the Portuguese Nation: Conversos and Community in Early Modern Amsterdam* (Bloomington: Indiana University Press, 1997).

25. See Yirmiyahu Yovel, *The Other Within: The Marranos: Split Identity and Emerging Modernity* (Princeton: Princeton University Press, 2009).

Engagement with the Non-Jewish World:
Between Particularity and Universalism

Firmly under Venetian rule for most of the period between 1405 and 1797, the city of Padua in northern Italy was acclaimed for its medical college. Many Jews had come to Padua to study at the university, which admitted eighty Jewish students between 1517 and 1619, and 149 between 1619 and 1721. Jews had first settled in remote parts of the town, but they eventually made their way to more central locations. In 1602, a ghetto was established for Jews in Padua. As with other such spaces, the ghetto in Padua was known for its narrow and cramped quarters and its frequent epidemics. The ghetto remained in operation until the French destroyed it in 1797.

The Great Plague epidemic of 1629–1631 resulted in the deaths of about 280,000 people throughout northern Italy and had a devastating effect on the Jews of Padua, where two-thirds of its members succumbed to the disease. While the plague did not initially affect the Jews when it reached Padua in the spring of 1630,[26] it fell on the inhabitants of the ghetto during the ten days of repentance between Rosh Hashana and Yom Kippur. By Rosh Hodesh Adar 5391 (February 3, 1631), 170 Jews had died. After that, there was a lull in deaths, but in the month of Sivan (June) the plague began anew across the city.[27] In Padua 19,000 (or 59%) of the 32,000 residents died.[28] The Padua Jewish population witnessed a proportionally significant decline. In 1585, there had been 280 Jews in Padua and 439 by 1603, out of a total population of 35,263.[29] In 1630–1631 there were 721 Jews, of whom 634 were afflicted by plague and 421 died.[30] According to Rabbi Abraham Catalano,

> And the plague stopped. And the number of dead in the plague was four
> hundred and twenty-one. Two hundred and thirteen recovered from the

---

26. This particular outbreak of plague in 1630–1631 claimed 46,000 of 140,000 residents in Venice. Similarly, there was a 61 percent mortality rate in Verona where 38,000 died.

27. Abraham Catalano, "A World Turned Upside Down," ed. Cecil Roth, *Kobetz al Yad* (1946): 67–101 [Hebrew], here at 67. The translations presented here draw from and, at times, expand that presented in Alan D. Crown, "The World Overturned: The Plague Diary of Abraham Catalano," *Midstream* 19, no. 2 (February 1973): 65–76.

28. George C. Kohn, *Encyclopedia of Plague and Pestilence: From Ancient Times to the Present* (New York: Facts on File, 2001), 201.

29. Catalano, "A World Turned Upside Down," 68.

30. Catalano, 68.

plague and seventy-five people were not affected by the plague, including me, the young writer, praised be to God. Twelve people ran away from the Ghetto before the plague started, none of whom died.[31]

The accounts by Catalano and others reveal that although there were some tensions, relations between Jews and Christians in the region were generally good during the crisis. Jews who fled from the city were able to find lodgings among non-Jews outside the city.[32] Jews in Padua also received support from other Jewish communities, especially from those in Venice and Ferrara.[33] Jewish accounts of responses to plague revealed both particularistic and universal concerns, underscoring the extent to which Jews were both separate from and part of broader society.

In response to the Early Modern plague, it was common for local and regional authorities to establish quarantine houses (lazarettos). These served many people during the great epidemic of 1630. In Bologna, one had over 500 and a second some 400 patients; at Florence there were more than 900 people in such a facility; in Verona over 4,000; and in Padua, by August 1631, some 2,000.[34] Various boards of health were also established in attempts both to prevent the plague and, when it did erupt, to treat the sick and bury the dead. Such boards could have rather broad powers, often hiring communal physicians and dictating access to the city and trade. On June 21, 1630, the Padua Health Board, for example, ordered all Friars to remain in their convents.[35] To keep people out of houses where plague was confirmed, infected houses were locked and bolted from the outside and in some cases guarded and marked with various signs, such as red crosses.[36] On May 18, 1631, alone, the Board ordered 137 houses closed, with 771 people confined (5.6 average per house).[37] By July 1631, the Padua Health Board employed 110 people to serve the 100,000 inhabitants of the city.[38]

The author of one particularly lengthy Hebrew account of the plague was Rabbi Abraham Catalano (d. 1642), mentioned above, who had studied

---

31. Catalano, 92–93.

32. Catalano, 69.

33. Catalano, 69.

34. Carlo M. Cippola, *Cristofano and the Plague: A Study in the History of Public Health* (Berkeley: University of California Press, 1973), 80.

35. Cippola, 40.

36. Cippola, 29–30.

37. Cippola, 158.

38. Cippola, 133.

Torah and medicine (he earned a medical degree).[39] He was not registered as the rabbi of the community, even though he taught Torah and sat on the *bet din* (court). In addition to his account of the plague, he also authored a small book on good behavior (*middot*). The Catalan family was not to be found among the Sephardic Jews from the land of Catalonia, but with the Ashkenazim who had already been in Padua in the sixteenth century before the Sephardim arrived. The Catalan synagogue followed Ashkenazic customs.[40] In 5370 (1609/1610), Abraham married Sarah bat Natan Yehuda Halperin from the small city of Cittadella, located near Padua. Sarah died during the plague, after twenty-one years of marriage. Their son Moshe Hayyim authored a liturgical poem (*piyyut*) appended to the account and read on Tisha b'Av.

The text of this account is quite long and covers a great deal of material. The author stressed the notion that God punishes with the plague, but he also discussed at great length the practical means to address the plague and the means by which one can save his family and community. He began by asserting that:

> I will speak and moan, I will complain from the bitterness of my spirit (I am Abraham Catalano), to inform the generations to come and the children who should be born of things as they happened. And I will faithfully make known to the generations three useful lessons from this story.
>
> The first lesson is to understand that this is God's way. Our God's wrath is kindled and there is no one who can save us from His hand. The living being will take it to heart to end transgression and limit sin lest the evil adheres to him and he dies for his sins.
>
> The second lesson is that the generations to come will know how to behave and properly prepare for a devastating plague in the world in their days as we did at this time. In this report I will describe not only everything that we did but also all that is appropriate to be done to be saved from the plague in general and after it dissipates.
>
> The third lesson is to save children naturally from pestilence that prowls in the darkness and to make known to them in this report how specifically a family should behave in order to survive.[41]

He moved on to record various rules and regulations from the Jewish community and from the local and territorial authorities. Catalano reviewed the timing of the outbreak and spread of the plague, and he described in detail the death of many individuals, including his own family members.

---

39. Catalano, "A World Turned Upside Down," 70.
40. Catalano, 69.
41. Catalano, 73.

The plague could surface internal communal concerns. The author, who served on the central board formed to respond to the plague, frequently noted the preparations that were made to provide money and food for the poor and the broader community, as well as medical attention provided for the sick and burial for the dead. As the plague progressed, participation in formal religious services decreased, even as confessions, lamentations, and supplications were added to the prayers. In many important ways, the Jewish community was a discrete entity within the city and region. Jews were responsible to govern and take care of the Jewish population, at times within a broader Jewish setting and at other times within the larger context of local and regional non-Jewish authorities. To that extent, the focus of Jewish actions had to be both inward and outward looking, as Jews negotiated to address local and particular conditions even as they were placed within the political and religious conditions of Paduan and Venetian authorities.

Not surprisingly, therefore, this text, like others, reveals a complex relationship between Jews and Christians. In the early stages of the plague in the city, the Jews in the ghetto appeared to be relatively unscathed. The author presented a variety of theories about how the plague penetrated into the Jewish quarter—for examples, via the family of the non-Jewish gatekeeper or the goods of a Jewish merchant from abroad. Later, when the plague spread disastrously to the ghetto, Christians were forbidden by the city and Venetian authorities from entering it. Throughout the ordeal, Jews negotiated with the non-Jewish authorities on a broad range of concerns, from disinfection of goods to expenses related to the lazaretto, the return of goods, and the reopening of the ghetto. Despite restrictions on travel, some Jews and others fled the plague for other cities, towns, and rural areas yet unaffected by the disease.

By the seventeenth century many city and regional authorities had well-developed procedures and staffing to address the threat or outbreak of plague. A variety of ordinances dictated measures to be taken and behavior expected of residents as well as visitors. The quarantine of people and goods and the disinfection of goods from contaminated houses were particularly common—and frequently the source of a great deal of conflict. With the cessation of the plague, the commissioner of health (provveditore) and the ministers summoned Catalano and directed him to select a place for the disinfection of the Jewish goods. If a location was not selected, Catalano reported, "then everything we have would be burnt, and no gentile would be allowed in our places until we had done so."[42]

---

42. Catalano, 94.

The tension in the text between generalized actions, typical in plague outbreaks, with distinctions between Jews and Christians is palpable throughout the text. These distinctions did not always signal hostility, for one senses in many parts of the text close living proximity of Jews and Christians and regular interactions, especially for business purposes. Even after selecting a place, which was costly to rent for these purposes, Catalano noted:

> Still, we needed the good will of the commissioner, and when the approval of the commissioner and ministers was requested they were not willing to listen because they said that this place was too far from the lazaretto and that we would spread the disease. They told us that we should build a place near our lazaretto or use the place Brentelle that we had rented. And we told them that whenever the plague had occurred in the past sixty years the Jews had disinfected their belongings in the village of Montà, which was far away from the lazaretto, and that the place Brentelle was too small and insufficient (for our needs).[43]

The officials required that Jews construct wooden houses for the disinfection process or pay them the cost for using the wooden houses that they had. The cost was immense and resulted in Jews growing angry and contesting this requirement. After some back and forth discussion, "The commissioner and the ministers forced us to send to the disinfection place all the belongings that were found in the ghetto, except those that had been signed and sealed by the health authorities."[44]

Catalano, his political sensibilities stirred, recorded the Jews' complaints and the ongoing negotiations. He wrote:

> We demanded to know why such requirements were made for us but not for the rest of the people of the city, who had to send only those items that were in the room of the sick person, or everything from the houses in which nobody resided. Why do they take our beds from underneath us and why can't we hold on to our clothes of white linen, as is customary in the entire world. We demanded that a copy of this decree be sent to Venice and we requested from the ministers there its cancellation. The commissioner heard our voice and said that each person could claim his bed and clothes of white linen, but that the rest should be sent outside the camp for disinfection. All this was achieved only after intervening and negotiating and after I went many times before the advocate and before the commissioner and the ministers, because there could not be found then an advocate for us, as they had all died or run away.[45]

---

43. Catalano, 94–95.
44. Catalano, 95.
45. Catalano, 95.

Here, as elsewhere, Catalano revealed a complex religious and political situation in which Jews perceived that they were being treated uniquely and unfairly. Underlying the negotiation was the complex political situation outside the Jewish community as well as the lack of leadership within the Jewish community, as many communal leaders had died or fled the plague.

With the commissioner intent on enforcing the decree and barring the entry of Gentiles into the ghetto until the disinfection had been completed, the Jewish community began the process of sending their possessions outside the ghetto. Here, as throughout the document and indeed throughout much of Early Modern Jewish history, the porous nature of the ghetto walls was evident. The ghetto was both a separation and a site of interaction.[46] Catalano also outlined the administrative steps that were taken to determine what possessions should be burned or taken for disinfection, and he described the roles of various people in that process, noting the large amount of time and money that this process involved.[47]

---

46. "When we saw that the commissioner intended to enforce the decree delaying the entry of the gentiles into the ghetto until after all of our belongings were sent for disinfection and the ghetto cleaned, we proceeded as fast as we could and we started sending all our belongings outside the Ghetto." Catalano, 95.

47. "On Rosh Hodesh Elul we started sending everything that had been sentenced to be burned—[made of] feather [and] hides, and all the moveable goods and the like, which had been handled by the dead or sick or that was in the room of the dead or the sick. We sent the gravediggers to the houses that had no inhabitants because their residents had died or were sent to the lazaretto. Reb Joseph Treves, who was sick but recovered, received wages in the amount of seven liras per day. The moveable goods that needed to be burned were selected on a house by house basis and they were piled up heap by heap, bundle by bundle, and tied together so that nobody would [be tempted to] behave foolishly with the goods. What was suitable for disinfection was placed in the corner and the house was cleaned well. When they were done the possessions that were to be burned were taken to the city walls by wagons and everything was burned there. Those things that needed to be burned from the remaining houses [were collected] and all the preparations were made before the wagons returned to the Ghetto in order not to delay the disinfection of the goods. The goods to be burned were placed in fifty wagons, four each day, two in the morning and two in the evening, because we did not want them to come in the heat of the day. All the items that were designated for burning in each and every house were written down in a book. Reb Isaac Israel Coronel the Sephardi and Reb Abraham Ferrarese, who were sick and recovered, marked all the goods in the first house with the letter "A" and in the second house the letter "B" and so on from house to house. The goods were taken on carts to the ship that we rented for twenty scudi. Reb Isaac Da Fano took the goods with him for one ducat per day, and with

While the situation within the ghetto was somewhat unique, the general issues that the Jewish community faced and the responses of the governing authorities were rather typical in the midst of Early Modern plague epidemics. The internal Jewish actions related to contaminated houses mirrored those of the broader population, drawing from the medical and scientific theories and best practices and policies of the day. Catalono wrote:

> After all the goods were sent for disinfection we cleaned all the contaminated houses of the holy community. I applied tar and sulphur and after plastering each and every room the windows were left open for several days. We signed a testimonial from our board to the commissioner that all of the contaminated goods had been taken from the ghetto and been fumigated properly and requested to bring into the ghetto the people from quarantine; however, they were not go out from their houses for eight days in order to see whether something would happen or not.[48]

Revealing both the tensions with some Christians (especially the authorities) and the importance of interactions with other Christians for business purposes, Catalano rued, "And still Christians were forbidden to enter into the ghetto and the ministers stood firm in their decision because they said that the days of the quarantine for the ghetto had not passed since the last death." The Jews, according to Catalano's narrative, "said to them, 'why do you decide to close the ghetto based on one case of death? If one person is sick close his house, not the whole ghetto.'" The non-Jewish commissioners remained firm in their resolution, fearing recurrence of the plague within the ghetto:

> They did not want to listen and they said that "if in a few days nothing happens in your courtyards, we will give you permission to open all the gates and the Christians may come and go." We were very afraid to bring the people who were in quarantine into the ghetto, lest the plague break out again and the ministers close the entire ghetto again. Despite our fears, all the unfortunates were returned to the ghetto, despite the fact that some of them were sick with high fevers. They returned to their homes on the fifth of Tishrei 5392 [1632].[49]

In other parts of the work, Catalano provided descriptions of the lazarettos as well as various medical treatments for the plague. People were allowed to return from the lazaretto upon a doctor's testimony of their good

---

him went thirty gentiles and one Jew, for three liras per day for each one of them, and the place was too small and insufficient, as said." Catalano, 95–96.

48. Catalano, 96.
49. Catalano, 96–97.

health.[50] The lazaretto itself was divided into two sections, one for those who had been sick and recovered and a second for those who were still sick.

Regarding medications, Catalano leveraged his medical training. He wrote, "If the doctor tells you to take these drugs—Elettuario, Conservi, Preservativi—and you would be protected from the plague, do not believe him, as this is not going to help you and not going to save you." Continuing on, Catalano asserted:

> I saw many who followed this course and died bitterly and many others who did not take any of them and were not infected, or were sick and recovered, and the plague did not distinguish between them. Many important doctors contracted plague and many were unaffected. I saw at that time that there were many who always placed a citron under the nose to filter the vapors leaving or temper impurities, which I thought was nonsense. Who knows if the smell from breathing the air resulting from those vapors stimulates good health. Although I was adorned with the crown of medicine and I know what the doctors say about Preservativi I did not look to record anything from the writings in their books. I only wrote what I remembered and thought would be useful for future generations.[51]

As he signaled at the start, Catalano ended with some practical advice:

> When a plague surrounds your house, do not rent your house and let it stand empty. If there is pestilence inside your house you must leave the house. If you do not own another house, rent a house to ameliorate your condition. And if you are poor and you cannot afford any on these, separate yourself in your house from the sick there or run away.
>
> Prepare enough food that will last for many days—grain, wine, oil and everything needed for you and your household, and also [from the smallest and most mundane things], from a thread to a shoe lace, so that you will not get close to where the plague is and you will be protected from all that is evil.
>
> If a plague strikes your town, take your precious belongings and seal them in the room with the health stamp; [take] only a change of clothes if you slip.[52]

Reiterating the political aspects of plague response and the need to address particular (individual and communal needs) in the midst of more universal conditions and challenges, he reminded the readers of his community

---

50. "The next day we received permission from the ministers also to bring [back] the people who resided in the lazaretto once [there was] a doctor's testimony regarding their health. The doctor Francesco Bianchini saw them and testified that they were healthy and that even if they had long-standing fevers there was no fear that they were seriously ill." Catalano, 97.

51. Catalano, 97–98.

52. Catalano, 98.

to remember to maintain and send a delegate to Venice before a plague erupts, "so that he can help you when you are in trouble and if a matter comes up against you before the ministers, which is not religious [in nature], whether [for example] to hand over the ghetto or a single person, this one can stand there in the breach."[53]

Conclusions

Early Modern Jews navigated a complex and increasingly changing world. They were rooted in a tradition that they understood to cast them as special and particular, holy. That status was used polemically in their religious and even communal self-identification, but it could also be challenged and used against them. The debate over sacrality was especially charged in the Early Modern period in the context of religious reformations and Confessionalization, and it mirrored the Jews' efforts to walk the line between religious tradition and change. But the notion of sacrality and particularity pointed to issues beyond religion. Communal organization and the way that Jews understood themselves were attacked throughout the later Middle Ages and into the Early Modern period, with expulsions and anti-Jewish sentiments and actions. Increasingly, hybridity asked Jews to hold different identities (sometimes changing religious identities, as in the case of conversos and apostates) that balanced internal Jewish needs and adherence to growing local, regional, and even national and imperial authorities. It both challenged how Jews saw the world and themselves, and it often served to reinforce their very representation of themselves, their histories, and traditions.

In response to natural disasters such as plague, Jews were simultaneously separate from the societies they inhabited through segregation and marginalization and yet also a part of those societies. As the discussion of plague in Padua revealed, Jews were conceptually and legally removed from their Christian neighbors even as they (and their Christian neighbors) had strong ties and sought to maintain or restore relations and interactions. While maintaining Jewish religious traditions and communal structures, Jews also drew from and imbibed a good deal of the broader culture in which they lived—in how they understood and responded to disasters scientifically and practically. Jews had experiences that could be unique and shared with other residents of cities and villages where they resided.

---

53. Catalano, 98.

Do such experiences provide insights for the relations between different groups in the Early Modern world or today? Even in a society that was changing rapidly and globalizing—leading to experiences with and attempts to understand various cultures and practices—particularity could (and can continue to) serve as a valuable way to maintain identity and connection to longer term traditions. Such particularity, especially in an age that tends to downplay or dissolve difference (some times in the very guise of appreciating diversity), may leave individuals and groups quite vulnerable to marginalization or stigmatization or worse. Although postmodern sensibilities theoretically bristle at the notion of objectivity and embrace difference and the variety of interpretations, the more fundamentalist side of the postmodern mentality can be rather dismissive of individuals or groups that set boundaries or make truth claims for themselves.

But as much recent research about vulnerability suggests, being vulnerable can lead to negative consequences but can also be constructive in that it allows for new ways of thinking, self-searching and identity construction, and forethought about and response to challenges.[54] On a similar note, we know that a related concept of vulnerability, resilience, may also be useful in a changeable and complex world. Not simply rebounding from challenges, but truly growing defines a nuanced resilience that is open and flexible even as it is rooted in tradition, rich social and communal networks, and powerful communication and narratives that shape and protect an individual or community.[55]

The ways that Early Modern Jews dealt with the question of how to be a special, unique, or peculiar people, especially while living in and engaging with a dominant, changing, and different (both religiously and, as we approach the end of the Early Modern period and enter Modernity, increasingly secular) surrounding culture may be valuable for faith communities today, which are attacked in many ways for their difference, insularity, or traditional foci. A good deal of scholarship on Early Modern Judaism and Jewish society over the past half century has discussed the notion of Jewish acculturation and accommodation (as opposed to assimilation), noting that Jews could be quite successful in absorbing aspects of surrounding society without fundamentally altering their own social

---

54. For an overview, see Dean Phillip Bell, "Vulnerability in Judaism: Anthropological and Divine Dimensions," in *Exploring Vulnerability*, ed. Heike springhart and Günter Thomas (Göttingen: Vandenhoeck and Ruprecht, 2017), 93–106.

55. Bell, 93–106.

structures and identities. Even internally, Early Modern Jewish community has frequently been cast as able to "neutralize" diversity and divergence and maintain a coherent sense of community (what the historian Jacob Katz noted as "the semi-neutralizing society," and which he argued engaged in a degree of "halakhic [legal] flexibility").[56]

The Early Modern Jewish experience provides some possible insights for balancing the notion of remaining unique (and even a "light unto the nations"), without compromising values or forsaking traditions, while also actively engaging in the world. Early Modern Jews were not always successful in this regard. They could be attacked for their particularism, and their sense of special status could be demeaned or even co-opted. Such sentiments might also, on the other hand, alter Jewish perceptions of and interactions with non-Jews. Increasingly, some Jews left Judaism or constructed hybrid religious identities (sometimes willingly and sometimes in response to conditions around them). Jews often suffered physical attacks and more often social and political marginalization.

Still, Judaism survived, albeit in changed forms and with more or less "success" in different contexts. As recent scholarship has pointed out, even the "immutable" could be changed for the sake of perceived or represented religious continuity or simple survival.[57] Ironically, the Jewish notion of sacrality and particularity has been the source of much of the attack on Judaism over the years. Yet it is also precisely what has helped Judaism to survive, and it has nourished Jewish social and communal sensibilities.

It has become something of a truism in the study of anti-Judaism and anti-Semitism that Jews are more persecuted the more they are integrated into society. The evidence from nineteenth-century Germany during debates over emancipation is striking in this regard. When Jews maintained their own identity, they were of course more easily identifiable and seen as different, but they were also easy to identify and thus less likely to be represented as infiltrating society for allegedly corrupt or corrosive purposes. Being particular leaves one visible and vulnerable, but that vulnerability is also a source of strength, and it can be leveraged to face the remarkable range of changing conditions and challenges that beset all people.

---

56. See, for example, Jacob Katz, *Exclusiveness and Tolerance: Studies in Jewish-Gentile Relations in Medieval and Modern Times* (New Jersey: Behrman House, 1983).

57. Marc B. Shapiro, *Changing the Immutable: How Orthodox Judaism Rewrites its History* (Oxford: Littman Library of Jewish Civilization, 2015).

Building Sacred Community:
A Response to Dean Phillip Bell

Andrew C. Reed

Religious communities establish boundaries in myriad ways, some explicitly framed, while others tend to build gradually, almost imperceptibly at first. Over time, religious groups create rules for who is inside and who is outside. Again, these rules take both formal and informal patterns. Dean Phillip Bell's article, "Sacrality and Particularity: Jews in an Early Modern Context," provides many useful insights into the nature of religious communities and their efforts to accommodate and acculturate among other religious and secular communities over time. Bell argues that within the Early Modern period, Jewish notions of chosenness and particularity, as a result of their covenantal condition (Isa. 49:8), occasionally placed them at odds with the majority Christian community in Europe.

Historically, the Israelites' understanding of religious adherence to law (*halakhah*) derived from "a prerequisite for and a result of this special status and connection" (p. 210). In the pursuit of divine investiture of blessing and protection, the Israelites established patterns and rituals that delineated differences from surrounding communities—both to mark them as separate and to provide opportunity to pursue their Godly charge. Deutero-Isaiah suggested this divine purpose during the post-Babylonian period:

> And now the Lord has resolved—
> He who formed me in the womb to be His servant—
> To bring back Jacob to Himself,
> That Israel may be restored to Him.
> And I have been honored in the sight of the Lord,
> My God has been my strength.
> For He has said:
> "It is too little that you should be My servant
> In that I raise up the tribes of Jacob
> And restore the survivors of Israel:
> I will also make you a light of nations,
> That My salvation may reach the ends of the earth."
> (Isa. 49:5–6)

The divine call for Israel to be "a light of nations" caused them to seek understanding in the possible ways that such a mandate might be accomplished. The myriad ways the topic of chosenness mapped onto the divine charge cannot be addressed here, but it is sufficient to nod toward the nineteenth century given the objective assigned to this chapter. It was during that very period (in 1853) that Samuel Holdheim, among the first reform rabbis, argued:

> It is the destiny of Judaism to pour the light of its thoughts, the fire of its sentiments, the fervor of its feelings upon all souls and hearts on earth. Then all these peoples and nations, each according to its soil and historic characteristics, will, by accepting our teachings, kindle their own lights, which will then shine independently and warm their souls. Judaism shall be the seed-bed of the nations filled with the blessing and promise, but not a fully grown matured tree with roots and trunk, crowned with branches and twigs, with blossoms and fruit—a tree which is merely to be transplanted into a foreign soil.[1]

In order to provide a critical response to the work of Bell from a Latter-day Saint perspective, picking up the story of the Early Modern period and transitioning into the "modern" era seems to the author the most responsible direction to move. Such a decision is based not on intellectual laziness nor on avoidance of the issue, but out of a desire to trace the implications of Jewish thinking in a critical period of Jewish history and identify clear indicators and overlapping points of intersection with the Latter-day Saint experience. The task is not overly simple given the spatial and chronological differences in the two stories and their contexts. However, despite such differences, there are important lessons to be learned by Latter-day Saints from Jewish successes and failures on this very question of accommodation within broader religious contexts.

The long history of Jews as participants in the many locales of diasporic experience provides a broad swath of useful examples and anecdotal comparisons, with complimentary stories of immense success and devastating loss. The experience of Jews as minority populations since the destruction of the Second Temple makes any comparison to Latter-day Saint history (a meager two hundred years old now) feel more than just a little inconsequential. However, there is an interesting jumping off point if we think more

---

1. Samuel Holdheim, "This is Our Task," in *Norton Anthology of World Religions*, 2nd ed., eds. David Biale, Lawrence S. Cunningham, and Jane Dammen McAuliffe (New York: W. W. Norton, 2015), 543. While Holdheim's sentiment firmly upholds the reform movement's anti-nationalistic sentiment, it does so through an appeal to the universal purpose of Judaism.

broadly about the claims made in Bell's piece about the nature of Jewish self-understanding. Bell correctly supposes that a useful methodology for examination is the dialectic between particularism and universalism.

In outlining the context for his investigation of the "unique" covenantal condition of Israelites, Bell suggests that there is an identifiable strand of thought that can be traced through rabbinic and Jewish contemplations through the Early Modern period. For Bell, the issue that derives from this covenantal condition is the reality of the "minority" position of Jews in "Western, Christian Europe." Citing Deuteronomy 7:8, Bell emphasizes the "minority" element, which is brought out most clearly in Robert Alter's recent translation of the Hebrew Bible, where "you are the fewest of all the peoples" provides the exceptionality of God's choice of Israel as the chosen people.[2] From the time of the declaration of "my chosen people," Israel has carried the burden of defending, explaining, and claiming this lofty title.

The Jewish philosopher Martin Buber depicted the challenge of this burden well in a follow-up examination of his concept of *Ich und Du* ("I and Thou") in his *The Eclipse of God*. Buber described a conversation with his host during one of his lectures in another "university city" in the following way:

> One morning I got up early in order to read proofs. The evening before I had received galley proofs of the preface of a book of mine, and since this preface was a statement of faith, I wished to read it once again quite carefully before it was printed. Now I took it into the study below that had been offered to me in case I should need it. But here the old man already sat at his writing-desk. Directly after greeting me he asked me what I had in my hand, and when I told him, he asked whether I would not read it aloud to him. I did so gladly. He listened in a friendly manner but clearly astonished, indeed with growing amazement. When I was through, he spoke hesitatingly, then, carried away by the importance of his subject, ever more passionately. "How can you bring yourself to say 'God' time after time. How can you expect your readers will take the word in the sense in which you wish it to be taken? What you mean by the name of God is something above human grasp and comprehension, but in speaking about you have lowered it to human conceptualization. What word of human speech is so misused, so defiled so desecrated as this!"[3]

Buber's response to this was pure and simple, yet juxtaposed the feelings of his interlocutor with the sense of responsibility Buber claimed was

---

2. Robert Alter, *The Hebrew Bible* (New York: W. W. Norton, 2018), 1:645.

3. Martin Buber, *Eclipse of God: Studies in the Relation between Religion and Philosophy* (London: Victor Gollancz, 1953), 16.

upon him as a Jew who sought divine relationship. As a phenomenologist, Buber could conceive of God only through human experience that sought relationship or dialogue with the divine within the muddy reality of social existence.[4] He noted:

> Yes, it is the most heavy-laden of all human words. None has become so soiled, so mutilated. Just for this reason I may not abandon it. Generations of men have laid the burden of their anxious lives upon this word and weighed it to the ground; it lies in the dust and bears their whole burden. The races of man with their religious factions have torn the word to pieces; they have killed for it and died for it, and it bears their finger-marks and their blood. Where might I find a word like it to describe the highest! If I took the purest, most sparkling concept from the inner treasure-chamber of the philosophers, I could only capture the presence of Him whom the generations of men have honored and degraded with their awesome living and dying. . . . But when all madness and delusion fall to dust when they stand over against Him in the loneliest darkness and no longer say "He, He" but rather sigh "Thou," shout "Thou," all of them the one word, and when they then add "God," is it not the real God to whom they all implore, the One Living God, the God of the children of man? Is it not He who hears them?[5]

The irreducibility of God beyond human social interaction bears potential to lessen the place and power of the divine, but not necessarily so. For Buber, the challenge of getting past the language was set, but this did not erase the need for individuals to seek such an encounter through dialogue and petition. For many in the world, the pursuit of the numinous is both eternally frustrating and perpetually rewarding—the journey remains central to the end result.

The Search for the Divine

The implications of a certain type of discomfort with the human condition and the necessary distance of relationship with God profoundly shape the nature of the questions that religiously minded individuals ask. In human attempts to define the relational complexity of human experience and anticipation of divine intervention in the world, both Jews and

---

4. Oliver Leaman, "Jewish existentialism: Rosenzweig, Buber, and Soloveitchik," in *History of Jewish Philosophy*, vol. 2, ed. Daniel H. Frank and Oliver Leaman (London: Routledge, 2003), 806. See also Norbert M. Samuelson, *An Introduction to Modern Jewish Philosophy* (New York: State University of New York Press, 1989), 185–86.

5. Buber, *Eclipse of God*, 17–18.

Latter-day Saints are left to sort through some of the complexity with a nod toward uncertainty. That uncertainty was productive for those whose search for God plays out on the pages of the Hebrew Bible as well as for the communities who still look to those pages with expectant hope for answers garnered from ancient pursuits in that same direction. Likewise, despite the constancy of the answers drawn from the sacred text where both Jews and Christians find their origins, both communities continue to search for and reframe their answers in light of new challenges posed by modernity. This effort to reanimate ancient wisdom is more than a mere positivist historical reading of modernity; it is rather a pursuit to unlock the keys of the divine mystery, albeit amidst the definitive boundaries posed by science and modern secular society. Rabbi Abraham Joshua Heschel recognized the complexity of this pursuit when he boldly declared:

> Human faith is never final, never an arrival, but rather an endless pilgrimage, a being on the way. We have no answers to all problems. Even some of our sacred answers are both emphatic and qualified, final and tentative; final within our own position in history, tentative—because we can only speak in the tentative language of man. Heresy is often a roundabout expression of faith, and sojourning in the wilderness is a preparation for entering the promised land.[6]

Religious pursuit of divine wisdom leads to the realization that the gulf between divine wisdom and human understanding is often far broader than the believer anticipated. The quotidian pursuits of human existence create a firm belief that we can speak definitively about things in the world. When this belief is overlaid with religious answers, religious adherents assert a confidence that is endearing but also fraught with possibilities to assume too much. Heschel showed the tendency of religious affiliation to produce claims of religious certainty. Often challenges arise when this certainty becomes rigid. The dangers of such rigidity and certitude are readily apparent in the history of religions in interaction with one another or when boundaries of orthodoxy become tightly controlled. Heresy becomes a possibility when maximalist claims define community—with the attached marginalization of those who operate on the boundaries of communally defined identity. Heschel pleads for openness partly out of experience, wherein he said religiously affiliated individuals opposed those who were entirely outside of their community or those who sought to expand contemporary thinking about communal existence.

---

6. Abraham Joshua Heschel, "No Religion is an Island," *Union Seminary Quarterly Review* 21, no. 1 (January 1966): 128.

Latter-Day Saint Navigation of Communal Ties

Members of The Church of Jesus Christ of Latter-day Saints occasionally perpetuate a belief that they possess a monopoly on truth in the world.
This claim, most fervently articulated in a comment from the Church's
founder, Joseph Smith Jr., serves as evidence for some Latter-day Saints of
God's providential intercession in the modern world. Wilford Woodruff,
an early Latter-day Saint apostle, wrote in his journal that "Joseph said the
Book of Mormon was the most correct of any Book on Earth and the key
stone of our religion and a man would get nearer to God by abiding by its
precepts than any other Book."[7] The notion that the Book of Mormon is
the most correct book rings familiar and clear for many Latter-day Saints.
From such a claim, erroneously understood, an exclusivist view is often
projected onto the Church that most directly engages with this book.[8]

Scott Esplin concludes that this phrase was given in dialogue among
Joseph Smith and members of the Quorum of the Twelve Apostles in
Nauvoo, Illinois, in 1843 upon the return of some members of that quorum from Britain.[9] In the early Latter-day Saint movement, the relationship of the Bible to the Book of Mormon, the context which gave rise to

---

7. Wilford Woodruff, *Journals*, ed. Scott G. Kenney (Midvale, UT: Signature
Books, 1983), 139. Since 1981, this statement, modified by B. H. Roberts in
the early twentieth century, found inclusion in the introduction to the Book of
Mormon. The modification transformed the statement from a third person to a
first person rendering. Such practices were common in Roberts's work. The revised
quotation, as contained in the Book of Mormon, reads, "I told the brethren that the
Book of Mormon was the most correct of any book on earth, and the keystone of
our religion, and a man would get nearer to God by abiding its precepts, than by any
other book." Beyond this, increased usage of this quotation by individuals like Bruce
R. McConkie and Ezra T. Benson transformed its usage to a sacrosanct reading.

8. The historical context that gave rise to this quotation by Joseph Smith is
reviewed thoroughly in Scott C. Esplin, "'Getting Nearer to God': A History of
Joseph Smith's Statement," in *Living the Book of Mormon: Abiding By Its Precepts*,
ed. Gaye Strathearn and Charles Swift (Provo, UT: Religious Studies Center
and Deseret Book, 2007), 40–54. Esplin shows quite clearly how this statement
gradually gained prominence among Latter-day Saints due to a shift in interpretation
and more ready use of it in discussion and teaching through the work of Church
leaders such as Joseph Fielding Smith and others. Hugh Nibley also modifies the
traditional understanding of the statement "most correct book" in *Since Cumorah*,
2nd ed., ed. John W. Welch (Salt Lake City and Provo, UT: Deseret Book and
Foundation for Ancient Research and Mormon Studies, 1981), 8.

9. Esplin, "Getting Nearer to God," 42–43.

the quotation above, was a topic of frequent discussion and debate both within the Church and by non-believers.[10] In modern usage, this phraseology "most correct" has taken on a life of its own. While traditional readings of this assertion of the Book of Mormon being the "most correct" book have morphed into meaning "perfect" in the finished sense, such notions are problematic in light of the historical development of the text. It is clear from the manuscript history of the Book of Mormon that the book underwent many revisions after its initial publication in 1830.[11] Thus, the development of a corrected correctness through emendation and editorial hand more properly reflects the process of textual production.

Such a view does not necessitate downplaying within the halls of faith claims to the book's "correctness," but it does require nuance. Latter-day Saints find their foundational religious identity in part through the Book of Mormon: it serves as the core of their claim to difference. It is a text that creates clearly identifiable boundaries of belief—there are those who reject it and its origins, and there are those who embrace it. Thus, those who embrace it find community in their belief of Smith's claims to its origins.

In recent years, a small effort has emerged to place this phrase— "most correct"—back within its context by Protestantizing its meaning. Robert Millet placed the need for such a phrase within the framework of a nineteenth-century definition (which Joseph likely understood) to be that of "setting right." Furthermore, Millet sees in this move an effort to protect the religious world of Mormonism (and broadly Christianity) from an attack of secularism. "Why work so hard to prove the truthfulness of the Bible?" he asked.

> Simply because a growing percentage of people in our world have begun to discount, belittle, or deny those elements of holy Scripture that make the Scriptures matter—divine intervention, miracles, and prophecy. And because the "quest for the historical Jesus" has retrogressed to the point of an outright rejection of our Lord's divinity and His bodily Resurrection from the dead on the part of people who still desire to be known as Christians.[12]

---

10. See Philip L. Barlow, *Mormons and the Bible: The Place of the Latter-day Saints in American Religion* (Oxford: Oxford University Press, 2013), 46–79.

11. For a description of these emendations, see Royal Skousen, *The Book of Mormon, The Earliest Text* (New Haven: Yale University Press, 2009), xxix–xlv.

12. Robert L. Millet, "'The Most Correct Book': Joseph Smith's Appraisal," in *Living the Book of Mormon Living the Book of Mormon: Abiding By Its Precepts*, ed. Gaye Strathearn and Charles Swift (Provo, UT: Religious Studies Center and Deseret Book, 2007), 57.

This notion of defending the Bible (and the Book of Mormon by extension) means that there is an expectation for Latter-day Saints that the
truths pasted upon its pages must exhibit a fideism, however rigorously or
naively construed.

This text leads members of the Church to seek their relation to the
ancient people who lived out their lives on the pages. In this way, the community of faith expands still further. When Latter-day Saints articulate
their usual definitive responses for this type of query, they tend at times toward confidence in their understanding of how they fit into the Abrahamic
covenant. Their understanding of belonging to this ancient familial line is
often framed with a type of what we might call adoption theology. Early
in Latter-day Saint theological development, Joseph Smith, the founder of
Mormonism, offered a "sacramental guarantee of salvation that was in its
essence communal."[13] Latter-day Saints cull their identity through partial
readings of Pauline thought (Rom. 8–11) combined with a sincerely felt
legitimization through patriarchal bestowal of lineage reminiscent of Old
Testament understandings. Through this appropriation of biblical themes,
Latter-day Saints develop a sense of belonging to a community that is
neither geographically nor chronologically bound.

The type of certainty that members of the community arrive at through
this form of adoption places them as willing conjoiners with the larger cos-
mological purposes of creation and thus imbues them with both authority
to act and purpose of mind. This sense of ownership that is derived from
biblical origins allows Latter-day Saints to strengthen connective tissues to
an Andersonian "imagined community" that spans the history of humankind.[14] In Christian thought, adoption places us in relationship because
we are "members of God's family" and thus are open to the benefits and
blessings of the covenant, broadly understood.[15] For Latter-day Saints, the
search for the divine leads to a quest for relational, physical belonging to

---

13. Samuel M. Brown, *In Heaven as It Is on Earth: Joseph Smith and the Early
Mormon Conquest of Death* (Oxford: Oxford University Press, 2012), 205.

14. Benedict Anderson, *Imagined Communities: Reflections on the Origins
and Spread of Nationalism* (London: Verso, 1991). Although Anderson uses
examples from a far different sort of sources, his broader theory about the place
of "literature" as a point of community identity formation and awareness seems
to resonate well within Latter-day Saint history.

15. Wayne Grudem, *Systematic Theology: An Introduction to Biblical Doctrine*
(Grand Rapids: Zondervan, 1994), 736.

community. The community spoken of in Latter-day Saint scripture is both here and now, historical (past), and anticipated (future).

This tangible collection of community past, present, and future is central to Latter-day Saint understandings of God's family. Doctrinally, Latter-day Saints look to several passages of scripture to reach this conclusion. During Smith's early ministrations by an angel named Moroni, the angelic visitor recast for Smith the passage from Malachi 3:24: "He shall reconcile parents with children and children with their parents, so that, when I come, I do not strike down the whole land with utter destruction."[16] According to Doctrine and Covenants 2:2, Smith learned that "he shall plant in the hearts of the children the promises made to the fathers, and the hearts of the children shall turn to their fathers." The transference of "hearts" and "promises" for Latter-day Saints suggests an essential generational bonding that intends to knit the promises in the hearts across the broadest possible spectrum of human history. Thus, the linkage to God's covenant is brought about by providing a form of lineal attachment to those original recipients of the promises.

For Latter-day Saints, the heart is both symbolically the receptacle for Godly truth and the mirror for one's belonging to the community. Because it is the heart of the children and the heart of the father that turn toward one another, Smith also connected the heart to the idea of "Zion" or God's community on earth. God's people are qualified because they are "pure in heart" (D&C 122:2)—even when one of Smith's major projects, that is, the establishment of physical Zion in 1830s Missouri, was determined to be in ruins in 1839 when Smith penned the words. Although the Latter-day Saint "Zion" in Missouri failed miserably, the idea of a people who were modeled upon the ancient people of Enoch remains firmly fixed definitionally as "Zion." In Smith's translation of Genesis, now contained in the Book of Moses in the Latter-day Saint canon, he suggested that the "Lord called his people Zion, because they were of one heart and one mind, and dwelt in righteousness; and had no poor among them" (Moses 7:18).

On February 9, 1831, Smith claimed revelation in Kirtland, Ohio, that regarded "the law of the Church" and that began the building blocks of the theological concept of "Zion" within Mormonism. Within a couple of weeks, the Saints were using "a working document" in which Smith

---

16. This translation is the JPS *Tanakh* rendition. In Latter-day Saint editions of KJV, this is Malachi 4:6.

worked to frame his understanding of divine law.[17] This came as the result of divine promises that when Smith and his followers arrived at "the Ohio," they would be given the "law of the Church of Christ" (D&C 38:32). "The law" that Smith was working on here encouraged his followers to adhere to a more strict form of social welfare that included care for the poor and needy along with expectations of communalism. However, in order to prevent this system from an abortive beginning, Smith found it necessary, through this revelatory experience, to instruct his followers regarding the patterns of minimal societal behavioral norms. He instructed them thusly:

> And again, I say, thou shalt not kill; but he that killeth shall die. Thou shalt not steal; and he that stealeth and will not repent shall be cast out. Thou shalt not lie; he that lieth and will not repent shall be cast out. Thou shalt love they wife with all thy heart, and shalt cleave unto her and none else. He that looketh upon a woman to lust after her shall deny the faith, and shall not have the Spirit; and if he repents not he shall be cast out. (D&C 42:18–24)

This passage precedes the further law that is established only after these basic behaviors are demanded. In other words, those who anticipate living a higher form of this "law" must be bound by these minimal expectations. The law that Joseph taught was meant to bring the religious community to a point where bonds were freely and firmly formed. The expectation, as Smith commented, was that members "remember the poor, and consecrate of thy properties for their support that which thou hast to impart unto them with a covenant and a deed which cannot be broken" (D&C 42:30). Thus, with security in knowing that those who bind themselves as a community do not need to worry about subversive actions by their neighbors, they are freely able to act in a more communal way. This notion of Zion was one that Joseph and the early Latter-day Saints sought after with varying degrees of success.

The concept of Zion, understood as outlined above, still resonates in Latter-day Saint communities today. Although for those affiliated with The Church of Jesus Christ of Latter-day Saints, the prospect of physical Zion in Jackson County, Missouri, has failed, the high hopes for a global community of believers who adhere to this ideal is actively sought for today. According to a revelation from August 1831, Smith learned that the future Zion, the one hoped for by members of the Latter-day Saint

---

17. "Revelation, 9 February 1831 [D&C 42:1–72]," 1, The Joseph Smith Papers, accessed May 15, 2021, https://www.josephsmithpapers.org/paper-summary/revelation-9-february-1831-dc-421-72/1.

movement today, is yet in the future.[18] This anticipated community of believers is modeled on ancient communities, but not without the ability to
adapt to modern frameworks. The "pure in heart" are to bind themselves
together in focus, effort, and desires for the kingdom of God.

This same sentiment was echoed by Brigham Young, the successor
to Smith, when in 1847 he called for the organization of companies to
make the march west. The "exodus" out of the United States at the time
was to move the community to a location where they could fully realize their religious expectations free from the persecutions of surrounding
communities. In the call by Young for the people to organize themselves
and prepare for their move west, he repeated similar calls for minimal
expectations before other expectations could be met. In this revelation and
instruction, the Saints heard:

> I am he who led the children of Israel out of the land of Egypt; and my arm
> is stretched out in the last days, to save my people Israel. Cease to contend
> one with another; cease to speak evil one of another. Cease drunkenness; and
> let your words tend to edifying one another. . . . Fear not thine enemies, for
> they are in my hands and I will do my pleasure with them. My people must
> be tried in all things, that they may be prepared to receive the glory that I
> have for them, even the glory of Zion; and he that will not bear chastisement
> is not worthy of my kingdom. (D&C 136:22–24, 30–31)

The similarity of the call to improve interpersonal relations by exact-
ing a rudimentary standard for human behavior seems to undergird the
Latter-day Saints' expectation to be a standard for others around them and
for their preparation to receive divine grace and blessing. This effort to
build a characteristically holy community was a central component of the
early Church of Jesus Christ from the time that the Church was officially
organized in 1830—most profoundly between the years 1831 and 1838,
when the Saints made their way to Nauvoo, Illinois.

In the context of this need for community in the physical sense now
and in the eschatological sense in the future, Latter-day Saints often see
these bonds as literal connectors to the idea of "Israel." The building of a
physical context of relationships among Latter-day Saints and operating
within the bounds of a constructed expectation of equality and communally minded society remain at the core of Latter-day Saint teaching in

---

18. Scott C. Esplin, "'Let Zion in Her Beauty Rise': Building Zion by
Becoming Zion," in *You Shall Have My Word: Exploring the Text of the Doctrine
and Covenants*, ed. Scott C. Esplin, Richard O. Cowan, and Rachel Cope (Provo:
Religious Studies Center, 2012), 139.

regards to interpersonal interactions. Today, these expectations also provide impetus for much of the Church's welfare and philanthropic work throughout the world. Further, in expanding the definition of community beyond locales and generational proximity, the Church fosters a form of generational linking through their temples and genealogical efforts. These programs are both symbolic of Latter-day Saint efforts to bring fulfillment of scriptural injunction into their lives and also tangible evidence that the linkage of generations remains central to their understanding of the covenantal relationship of God to the chosen people.

The Kingdom of God on Earth

It is just this kind of bold declarative conjecture that leads to the confidence of belonging that many Latter-day Saints have felt since the beginning of the Church's existence. As evidence of such boldness, the early efforts of some Latter-day Saints to strengthen their plea for establishing the "kingdom of God" on earth led them to incorporate language that was both inclusive of all religions while allowing for difference. Amasa Lyman, then a member of the First Presidency of the Church in 1844, connected the eventual Second Coming with the godly walk of the Saints in his own day by expanding the vision for what this effort might mean for the Latter-day Saints. In a meeting on April 11, 1844, Lyman was remembered to have alluded to the fact that:

> He looks for a full and perfect emancipation of the whole human race, that the sound of oppression should be buried in eternal oblivion. The paltry considerations of earthly gain and glory falls into insignificance before the glories we now realize. The object we have in view is not to save a man alone or a nation, but to call down the power of God and let all be blessed, protected, saved and made happy—burst the chains of oppression. This is a kingdom worth having. The political principles of this kingdom comes down from heaven and reaches down to the prisons of the dead. What we want of it is just enough to protect a man in his rights, but we never read of a government that would do that. Reference had been made to the government of Enock, but it went away. It was so like God and so unlike man that they could not bear it. He referred to the kingdom spoken of by Daniel as stone cut out of the mountain without hands which rolled until it filled the whole earth.[19]

---

19. "Minutes, 11 April 1844," 126, The Joseph Smith Papers, accessed June 3, 2021, https://www.josephsmithpapers.org/paper-summary/minutes-11-april-1844/33.

Lyman continued his connecting of Old Testament passages from Daniel 2, the life of Abraham, and the New Testament when he spoke of this future (an immediate future, he hoped) community. He argued:

> If God has appointed a man to rise to immortal glory he will rise with him, for he will hold on to the skirts of his garments. He has not reflected on the sacrifice we may have to make, for he does not think any sacrifice too great to make for this glories of this kingdom, even if it requires us to leave faster, mother, wives & children. He that will not leave these, cannot enjoy the kingdom, because he cannot attend to it. He referred to the excuses made at the marriage supper spoken of in the parable by the Saviour. It proves to us, that there is nothing so dear, no ties so great that we cannot part with for the kingdom even if the ties be as strong as existed in the bosom of Abraham toward Isaac. If a man will not sacrifice, the principle of a God is not in him.[20]

For Lyman, Smith, and many early Latter-day Saints, the reality of an expected millennial kingdom of God on earth presciently figured in the Mormon worldview.[21] For Latter-day Saints then, and even now, the call to heed God and build up "Zion" remains fervently intact. Joseph Smith declared through a revelation he believed came from God that "it shall come to pass that the righteous shall be gathered out from among all nations, and shall come to Zion, singing with songs of everlasting joy," and that they (i.e., the righteous) would gather at a "New Jerusalem" (located in Jackson County, Missouri) at a time when "Satan shall be bound" and that a "full restoration of the scattered Israel" would commence (D&C 45:17, 55, 66, 71). The reality of this anticipated moment for early Latter-day Saints was profoundly fixated upon the minds and hearts of those who heard Smith claim this as divine revelation that gave both purpose and structure to their gathering efforts.

Conclusion

As Church membership has continued to grow, these three elements— faith in the Book of Mormon as an avenue to Jesus, pursuit of blessings of the Abrahamic covenant, and the desire for a type of godly kingdom upon earth—become increasingly difficult to instill in all members of the movement. And yet, however frustrated believers may be at times because of the difficult task of continually seeking these three components of Latter-

---

20. "Minutes, 11 April 1844," 103.
21. Grant Underwood, *The Millenarian World of Early Mormonism* (Urbana: University of Illinois Press, 1999), 37.

day Saint faith, they remain the hallmarks of religious identity. While the forms of the religious community are perpetually reframed by global expansion and cultural development, the necessity of these pillars within that framing are absolute historical and theological imperatives. As The Church of Jesus Christ of Latter-day Saints continues to expand and grow, its relationship with these central elements will no doubt undergo shifts and turns. The ways in which Mormons develop their religious identity through these elements will likely reflect the growing pains of religious globalization. As Latter-day Saints look beyond their own day, they view the future through anticipated expectations that reflect but also expand the historical community from which this young church developed.

It's Funny, But Is It Jewish?
It's Jewish, But Is It Funny?
An Understated Overview
of Jewish Humor

Leonard Greenspoon

Introductory Jokes

As I see it, a discussion or analysis of humor should begin with a joke—or two, or even better three:

"My mother is the most annoying person on the face of the earth," Judy Gold jokes, "a miserable human being."

"You can say something to her and she cannot only make it negative, she makes it about herself. What are you having for New Year's, filet mignon? I'll be eating shit."

Her mother's just-published autobiography, she has quipped, is titled *I Came, I Saw, I Criticized*.[1]

Moses is standing at Sinai and God says to him, "You shall not boil a kid in its mother's milk."

Moses asks, "So are You saying that we shouldn't eat milk and meat together?"

God replies a little impatiently, "I said: You shall not boil a kid in its mother's milk."

Moses, still puzzled, says, "Do you want us to wait six hours after a meal before eating dairy foods? Is that what you mean?"

God, a bit more impatiently this time, reiterates, "I said: You shall not boil a kid in its mother's milk."

---

1. For more on this joke and its context, see Joyce Antler, "One Clove Away From a Pomander Ball: The Subversive Tradition of Jewish Female Comedians," in *Jews and Humor*, Studies in Jewish Civilization 22, ed. Leonard Greenspoon (West Lafayette, IN: Purdue University Press, 2011), 155–74.

Moses asks again, "Wait. You want us to use separate tablecloths for meat meals and dairy meals?"

God replies with resignation, "You know what? Have it your way."[2]

In this monumental synagogue in Łódź (which was located on the corner of Kościuszki and Zielona Streets before the Nazis destroyed it), the prayer services were held only on Saturdays and holidays. Because this house of worship was mainly used by the wealthy, it was necessary to obtain expensive entrance cards in order to enter it.

On Rosh Hashanah, a Jew in a caftan tries to enter the building. He is stopped at the door by the *shames* (a sexton in a synagogue). "Entrance card?"

"What card?! I have urgent business with factory owner Rosenblatt."

The *shames* says sarcastically: "I already know you, you thief! You have no business to do with Mr. Rosenblatt. You came here to pray!"[3]

All three of these jokes appear in the volume *Jews and Humor* that I edited. In this sense, each of them might qualify as "Jewish humor."[4] While we can disagree about how funny each one is, for our purposes here, the analysis focuses on how Jewish they are.

From any perspective I can imagine, the first joke is the least Jewish. In fact, despite its inclusion in the volume, many would deny that it's Jewish at all. According to them, a joke is not authentically Jewish if it could equally well apply to other ethnic, national, or religious groups. Surely, in fact, that is the case here. An overbearing, selfish mother is a stereotype that could equally well be applied to Italian women, for instance. Moreover, the toxic mother-daughter relationship this joke describes is by no means confined, in reality or in the popular imagination, to Jews.

The only certifiably Jewish element in this joke is the comedian, Judy Gold, who is being quoted here.[5] She is Jewish. Much of her humor is self-referential and more or less autobiographical. That said, full comprehension

---

2. For more on this joke and its context, see Eliezer Diamond, "But Is It Funny? Identifying Humor, Satire, and Parody in Rabbinic Literature," in Greenspoon, *Jews and Humor,* 33–53.

3. For more on this joke and its context, see Joanna Silwa, "Jewish Humor as a Source of Research on Polish-Jewish Relations," in Greenspoon, *Jews and Humor,* 67–82.

4. Full citation: Leonard Greenspoon, ed., *Jews and Humor,* Studies in Jewish Civilization 22, Proceedings of the Twenty-Second Annual Symposium of the Klutznick Chair in Jewish Civilization-Harris Center for Judaic Studies, October 25–26, 2009 (West Lafayette: Purdue University Press, 2011).

5. For more information on Gold, see Antler, "One Clove Away," 155–74.

of this joke requires no knowledge of Jews at all. As long as readers or hearers recognize the title of the mother's putative book as a play on Caesar's most famous, if putative, tripartite saying, they have "gotten" this joke.[6]

With the second joke, we are in an entirely different realm, as it were. Anyone who is going to react or interact intelligibly with this joke must first of all be aware that the thrice-stated expression, "You shall not cook a kid in its mother's milk," appears in the Hebrew Bible or Old Testament as a divine command. As a quick aside, it may be simply coincidence, or perhaps intention on the part of the person who developed this joke, that this expression appears three times here, exactly the number of its appearances in the Bible (Ex. 23:19, 34:26; Deut. 14:21).

Moses's first query to God, like his successive ones, depends on the rabbinic amplifications of the biblical expression in terms of the separation of milk and meat in their preparation as well as in their consumption. This first question is the most general; almost all Jews and a substantial number of non-Jews would be somewhat familiar with this separation.

In contrast, Moses's next concern—how long to wait between eating meat and milk products—presupposes a substantial degree of knowledge among those who hear or read the joke. While observant Jews can eat meat almost immediately after, say, drinking milk, the reverse, meat and then milk, requires the passage of a substantial amount of time. The six hours Moses brings forward are pretty much the standard among Jews who meticulously observe this practice, but even among Orthodox Jews there are some authorities who will allow for fewer hours.[7] To comprehend fully the nuances of this joke, the audience must take all this into account.

The use of different tablecloths, referred to in Moses's final riposte to God, is probably intended to encompass also different sets of dishes, silverware, pots and pans, and so forth.[8] The need for observant Jews to have at least two sets of everything food-related, one for milk and another for meat, may well be somewhat more widely known than the six (or fewer)

---

6. "Veni, vidi, vici"—"I came, I saw, I conquered." Plutarch (*Life of Caesar*) and Suetonius (*Lives of the Twelve Caesars*) attribute this phrase to Julius Caesar, who would have uttered or written it about 47 BCE.

7. For an accessible introduction to this issue, see "The Halachot of Waiting Between Meals," Orthodox Union Kosher, May 18, 2015, https://oukosher.org/blog/consumer-kosher/the-halachot-of-waiting-between-meals/.

8. For a how-to guide on making a home kosher, see "Your Kosher Kitchen," OK Kosher, accessed April 16, 2021, http://www.ok.org/consumers/your-kosher-kitchen/.

hours between meat and milk, but it is certainly less well known than the prohibition mentioned in Moses's first comment.

God's resignation in the face of Moses's continued elaborations may seem irreverent, perhaps even blasphemous, to some. But for the intended audience, who we've been identifying in these paragraphs, this is a familiar image of the Lord. In one of the most famous Talmudic passages, God is pictured as yielding to humans on the interpretation and application of Law, even though they are going against what God had intended.[9]

So, I think we can agree, for this joke to be understood and considered humorous, a considerable knowledge of Jewish law and practice is required. The same is true for the third joke, but it assumes or requires knowledge in a different aspect of Jewish life and practice.

The setting for this third joke is Łódź, a Polish city that was home to a sizable Jewish community before its occupation and partial destruction by the Nazis.[10] Its location in Poland is probably not crucial to follow this joke so long as the hearer or reader knows that the geographical context is Eastern Europe. Holding services only on Saturday and holidays is not an especially obscure reference, since most people know that Saturday is the Sabbath (or Shabbat) for Jews.[11]

The requirement to obtain and pay for an entry card before going into the synagogue for any service is not widely practiced today, if it is still practiced anywhere. But most Jews would be familiar with the still widespread need to obtain a ticket for the High Holidays, even if their synagogue has dispensed with this moneymaking procedure.

And, as it happens, the activity narrated in this joke takes place on Rosh Hashanah, the Jewish New Year and one of the High Holidays. In this context the term *shames* would be as unfamiliar to most Jews as it is to non-Jews; therefore, it is necessary to gloss it (here, sexton). Large number of Jews would, however, know the related term *shamash*, which designates the candle on the Hanukkah Menorah with which all of the other candles are lit.[12] Both of these terms come from the root meaning "to attend."

---

9. Bava Metzia 59a-b.

10. On this city, see Robert Moses Shapiro, "Łódź," The YIVO Encyclopedia of Jews in Eastern Europe, accessed April 16, 2021, https://yivoencyclopedia.org/article.aspx/%C5%81odz.

11. More precisely, from sunset Friday evening to sunset Saturday evening.

12. See the chapter of this holiday in Michael Strassfeld, *The Jewish Holidays: A Guide & Commentary* (New York: William Morrow, 1993).

The poor(er) man's plea to be allowed entry to the synagogue, although he lacks the requisite card, is buttressed by his argument that he needs to talk business with one of the wealthy men inside. In denying him access to the synagogue, the *shames* retorts that he doesn't believe this man—he doesn't have any business to conduct; he is going into the synagogue to pray, of all things! Alas it reflects a reality of traditional synagogues, where concerns for business or politics or gossip often occupy more time than does prayer among those in attendance.

But no matter how we look at it, the end of this third joke and of the proceeding one is surprising. Why should someone be castigated for praying in a synagogue? Why should God permit humans to take the lead in explaining and applying law? In both cases, we are looking at another characteristic of Jewish humor (the first being its references to Jewish beliefs and practices): its critical barbs are typically aimed inwardly, at members of their own community, rather than outwardly, at their enemies.

The creator and, I suspect, the teller of the third joke is critical of prayer's displacement by mundane concerns within the supposedly sacred confines of the synagogue. This joke invites us to be indignant at the appropriation of Judaism that the sexton and his employers embody. On the other hand, our feelings about the man seeking entry will probably vary depending on whether or not we take him at his word. To the extent we don't, we will probably sympathize with him all the more.

The direction of criticism in the second joke is not primarily upward. Yes, God could resolve matters of law in a decisive way, but he chooses not to. That's just God being God. But why have the rabbis, of the classical or Talmudic period as well as afterwards, exerted so much time and energy on small details of observance? Wouldn't they have been better occupied by promoting ethical behavior rather than adherence to laws that they render increasingly stringent and more difficult to comprehend or fulfill? From the point of view of this joke, the answer to the second question is a resounding yes.

The time frame these three jokes depict is very wide. Putting them in order, from earliest to latest, in terms of their respective time frames, the second joke (depicting Moses in conversation and negotiation with God) is from the biblical period. The third joke, from pre-Holocaust Poland, pictures Jewish society in the nineteenth or first half of the twentieth century. The first joke, reflecting the experience (real or imagined) of contemporary comedian Judy Gold, reflects life in the last decades of the twentieth or first decade of the twenty-first century.

Humor in the Hebrew Bible

The creation of this first joke and its telling were certainly close to each other chronologically. But the joke about Moses and God, set in the period of the Hebrew Bible, was certainly developed centuries, more likely millennia, after this setting. How about humor that dates from the biblical period? Is there humor in the Bible? If so, do humorous biblical passages constitute the beginning of Jewish humor? As I see, the answer to both of these questions is yes.

It is inherently difficult to discern humor in ancient documents. Not only do they lack explicit punctuation marks (like explanation points and question marks) and other indicators (e.g., all caps, underlining, and interjections) that accompany much humorous writing in the modern period, we cannot be certain that what they found funny (or may have found funny) is funny to us (and of course not everyone today has the same sense of humor). That said, there is really no serious doubt that intentionally funny things appear in the Hebrew Bible or for that matter in the Apocryphal books and New Testament, whose authors were also "Jewish."[13]

Plays on words are especially numerous in Sacred Writ. Since they depend on the Hebrew language, they often don't translate well, if at all, into a target language such as English. But for the original audience, they would attract attention whether they were read or heard.

Proper names are most commonly susceptible to word play. Take, for example, Nabal in 1 Samuel 25. The husband of Abigail and foe of David is exactly the "desiccated fool" that his name implies. When pleading that David spare her husband's life, Abigail says as much, "Please, my lord, pay no attention to that wretched fellow Nabal. For he is just what his name says: His name means 'boor' [better 'fool'] and he is a boor [better 'fool']" (v. 25). David relents, but Nabal could not escape his fate. Within two weeks, God struck down this drunken windbag (v. 38).

How about the appropriately named Midianite monarch Eglon, whom the Israelite judge Ehud slaughtered in this particularly grotesque way: "Reaching with his left hand, Ehud drew the dagger from his right

---

13. See among other recent studies, Leonard Greenspoon, "Humor in the Old Testament," "Humor in the New Testament," and "Humor in the Apocrypha," Oxford Biblical Studies Online, accessed April 16, 2021, respectively at https:// global.oup.com/obso/focus/focus_on_humor_ot/, https://global.oup.com/obso/ focus/focus_on_humor_new_testament/, and https://global.oup.com/obso/focus/ focus_on_humor_apocrypha/.

side and drove it into Eglon's belly. The fat closed over the blade and the hilt went in after the blade—for he did not pull the dagger out of his belly—and the filth came out" (Judg. 3:21–22). Grotesque but also appropriate—given that Eglon's name appears to come from the same root as the word used to designate a fatted sacrificial calf. Which is just what Eglon turned out to be!

Another example occurs earlier, in Genesis 4, in connection with the world's first murderer, Cain. As part of his divine condemnation for fratricide, Cain is to "become a ceaseless wanderer on earth" (v. 12). The root of the Hebrew word "to wander" is *n-w-d*, which appears also as the name of the area in which Cain is exiled, Nod. If the text spoke of Cain's wandering in the Land of Wandering, that would be a play on words of sorts. But what the text actually says adds an element of paradox to the narrative: "[Cain] settled in the land of Nod [Wandering]" (v. 16).

Of translators into English, only Everett Fox manages to establish a direct connection between the ancient text and the modern reader. Here is Fox's rendering of Genesis 25:30–31: "Esav said to Yaakov: Pray give me a gulp of the red-stuff, that red-stuff, for I am so weary! Therefore they call his name: Edom/Red-One." Another example characteristic of Fox is found at Genesis 37:36: "He [Esav] said: Is that why his name was called Yaakov/Heel-Sneak? For he has now sneaked against me twice."[14]

A second category of biblical humor is what I call "situational," in that the humor derives from the situation in which an action or occurrence takes place. Take, for example, the story of the Golden Calf as narrated in Exodus 32. Although this seems like an unlikely place to find humor, I am not alone in detecting it in Aaron's attempt to separate himself from the construction of this idol when confronted by his brother Moses: "You know this people [a.k.a. his fellow Hebrews] is bent on evil. . . . They gave it [the collected gold jewelry] to me, and I hurled it into the fire and out came this calf" (vv. 22–24). As if by magic with no help from Aaron himself! Such a self-serving explanation stretches the truth and, I'm pretty sure, Moses's credulity.[15]

A well-known example of biblical humor is found at Numbers 22, where Balaam, a non-Israelite prophet of renown, fails three times to see the angel of the Lord, who is clearly visible to the ass on which he is riding. Finally, in swift order, God opens the ass's mouth and Balaam's eyes (vv. 21–31).

14. Everett Fox, *The Five Books of Moses* (New York: Schocken, 2000).

15. For this and other occurrences of biblical humor, see Charles David Isbell, "Humor in the Bible," in Greenspoon, *Jews and Humor*, 1–11.

In my view, this is an inherently funny story. But it is made even more pointed when we recall that Balaam made his reputation (and presumably also his money) through the clarity of his (admittedly prophetic) eyes or eyesight. But here even a lowly ass is more aware than the supposed perceptive prophet.

We discern another example in Jonah 4, the last chapter of this book of one of the twelve minor prophets. Against his own volition but in accordance with God's command, Jonah succeeds in leading the residents of Nineveh, the great Assyrian metropolis, to repent of their sins—and thereby escape (at least momentarily) the punishment God had decreed for them.[16] After this the prophet withdraws to a spot outside the city, where God causes a plant—possibly a gourd—to sprout up in order to provide the prophet with shade during the heat of the day. But the following day God caused the plant to wither, and the sun beat down ever hotter on Jonah. He was "deeply grieved about the plant . . . so that [he] want[ed] to die" (v. 9). At this point the Lord observes: "You cared about the plant, which you did not work for and which you did not grow. . . . And should I not care about Nineveh, that great city, in which there are more than a hundred and twenty thousand persons" (vv. 10–11).

The image of a prophet sobbing over the loss of a single plant does not seem likely to elicit smiles, much less laughter—in most circumstances. But in the context of the book of Jonah, some such reaction is perfectly appropriate, inasmuch as this somewhat overwrought action on Jonah's part allows us to appreciate the depth and breadth of God's concern for all of his creation, from a small plant to a great city and beyond.

A third category consists of what I'd call vindictive humor, in which the biblical writer, presumably along with his (or her) community, takes what would appear to be unseemly pleasure in the defeat of Israel's enemies—actually the pleasure might well look unseemly from some perspectives, but not from the biblical one. If we are at all perceptive in our understanding of these passages, biblical writers and their communities felt fully justified in mocking the downfall of their foes, all of whom were mightier militarily than the supposedly puny Israelite forces.

Judges 3, which we looked at earlier, is a good example of what I'm terming vindictive humor. Other examples follow.

---

16. For rabbinic commentators, Nahum's prophecy, foretelling the destruction of Nineveh, demonstrates that the repentant Ninevites were either insincere or unable to pass on their contrition to later generations.

The first comes in the next two chapters of Judges: an Israelite victory over a coalition of Canaanites forces is narrated in prose (chapter 4) and poetry (chapter 5). It is to the latter that we turn. Judges 5:26–27 describes in excruciating detail how a woman named Yael killed the fleeing Canaanite general, Sisera: "She [Yael] struck Sisera, crushed his head// Smashed and pierced his temple//At her feet he sank, lay outstretched//At her feet he sank, lay still//Where he sank, there he lay—destroyed." This rhetorical overkill was bound to have been satisfying to Israelite audiences. But I don't think it's humorous.

On the other hand, the continuation of this poetic narrative would have elicited a broadening smile, if not more, from its intended audience. Sisera's mother is pictured as looking anxiously out of her window, wondering what could be keeping her son. She imagined that, after the Canaanite victory, he was spending time "with a damsel or two" (Judg. 5:30). Indeed, her son had been spending a bit of time with one particular damsel—Yael, by name—but, as a result of that encounter, he would not be returning home, as his mother imagined, loaded with treasure. Here, as on so many other occasions, God overturned the carefully laid out plans and expectations of humans. In this instance, divine intervention worked decidedly on Israel's side.

Nowhere are these ideas more fully and effectively developed than in the book of Esther. In effect, this book constitutes an extended reflection on the exquisite downfall of an enemy of the Jews. Many of the plots and subplots that fill this narrative are funny, some perhaps even hilarious.[17]

So, for example, the Persian king marries Esther, whose identity as a Jew is known to readers but not yet to the king. Her cousin Mordecai is a high official in the Persian court, but nonetheless outranked by the rancorous Haman, who is revealed as an implacable foe of the Jews. At one point in the story, the king learns of a good deed, as yet unrewarded, that Mordecai did on his behalf. Haman just happens to be around when the king is contemplating how to reward Mordecai. The monarch queries Haman, "What should be done for a man whom the king desires to honor?" (Esth. 6:5). Haman, who assumes the king is speaking of him, is over the top in describing what he imagines he will receive:

> For the man whom the king desires to honor, let royal garb which the king has worn be brought, and a horse on which the king has ridden and on

17. For this book and its place in Judaism, see Adele Berlin, *The JPS Commentary: Esther* (Philadelphia: JPS, 2001).

whose head a royal diadem has been set; and let the attire and the horse be put in the charge of one of the kings' noble couriers. And let the man whom the king desires to honor be attired and paraded on the horse through the city square, while they proclaim before him: This is what is done for the man whom the king desires to honor. (vv. 7–9).

Those in the know—including Jewish readers of this biblical book—are already laughing as Haman goes into such vivid detail to describe what he is sure is in store for him. Readers who aren't already in on the joke are not far behind, for they read—and Haman hears: "'Quick then!' said the king to Haman. 'Get the garb and the horse, as you have said, and do this to Mordecai the Jew, who sits in the king's gate. Omit nothing of all you have proposed'" (v. 10). This reversal of fortune is not lost on at least one of the characters in the story itself: Zeresh, Haman's wife, who declares: "If Mordecai, before whom you have begun to fall, is of Jewish stock, you will not overcome him; you will fall before him to your ruin" (v. 12). Haman ignores his wife's insight to his own peril.

Actually, there is a delicious paradox in Zeresh as spokeswoman of truth. Just a bit earlier she had urged her husband to construct massive gallows from which to hang Mordecai. After Haman falls out of favor, it is he, not Mordecai, who is hanged on these very gallows, along with his ten sons (Esther 7:9–10). Standing fifty cubits high (approximately 75 feet, the height of a six-story building), this would have constituted a very public execution of the once powerful villain. How the mighty have fallen![18] Or, in the words of the author of Judges 5, "So may all Your enemies perish, O LORD!" (Judges 5:31).

The Persian king, named Ahasuerus in the Hebrew Bible, is characterized more by his passivity and lack of attention than any evil motivation. But this does not entirely excuse him from criticism, which is encapsulated in withering remarks by Esther's author. A similar critique of Mesopotamian rulers is found in the first half of the book of Daniel. Yes, it is true, the Jews were not without power when they enjoyed the support of God. But within the real politics of the world they inhabited, the Jews were a distinct and vulnerable minority—often viewed and attacked as outsiders. In this world they would often fall short of the victories they envisioned in their literature. But they didn't lose the rapier sharpness of

---

18. From David's lament over Jonathan and Saul (2 Sam. 1:25).

their wit and would use it literarily to cut down to size enemies they could vanquish in no other way.[19]

I suggest that two elements of biblical humor are especially Jewish: first, a delight in words and word plays; second, a perspective deriving from a feeling of powerlessness and their status as outsiders with respect to the world at large. Added to the two elements adduced above—references to Jewish beliefs and practices and a self-critical, self-deprecatory stance— we have identified four characteristics that are generally connected with Jewish humor. It is worth reiterating the point that references to Jewish beliefs and practices that the joke teller and the audience share (or perhaps oppose) are crucial in establishing both a self-identity (we're the "insiders") and a demarcation between "us" and "them" (they are "outsiders"). For a minority group, such as Jews throughout most of their history, humor as a boundary marker assumes extraordinary significance with sometimes life-and-death implications.

Humor among the Rabbis

In what follows we analyze other examples of these characteristics and discern other characteristics. Humor from the rabbinic period (as record-ed in the Talmud and related material from Palestine and Babylonia [c. 300 CE – c. 600 CE]) displays a finely honed sensitivity to the multiple meanings of words. So:

Rabban Gamaliel married off his daughter. She said to him, "Father, bless me." He said, "May you never come back here." She gave birth to a son. She said to him, "Father, bless me." He said, "May 'Oy vey!' never cease from your mouth." She said to him, "Father, two happy occasions have come to me, and you have cursed me [on both]!" He said to her, "Both are blessings. Since you have peace in your house, you won't return here. And since your son will survive [infancy], 'Oy vey!' will never cease from your mouth: 'Oy vey that my son didn't eat!' 'Oy vey that he didn't drink!' 'Oy vey that he didn't go to shul!'" (Genesis Rabbah 26).

The daughter's response to her father's "blessings" explicitly alerts read-ers to an apparent incongruity: on two happy occasions, she asks for paternal blessings, but apparently receives admonitions that she classifies as curses. Is this rabbinic tough love? Bad parenting? Or something else entirely?

---

19. See Michael J. Chan, "*Ira Regis*: Comedic Inflections of Royal Rage in Jewish Court Tales," *Jewish Quarterly Review* 103, no. 1 (2013): 1–25.

We will probably breathe a collective sigh of relief if we're able to identify some other, more benign (and humorous) motivation for the father's
words. After all, I think we'd all feel better if fathers and daughters had
positive relations—or at least are pictured as having positive relations—in
this formative period of Judaism. And this in fact is the case. The father
looks forward to his daughter having a good marriage (the use of the
expression "peace in your house" here is something of a technical term for
ideal relations between husband and wife), with children (or at least one
child, a son) surviving infancy. To these the father adds, somewhat rue-
fully but also based on his own experience, the kinds of complaints any
parent (especially a Jewish one?) would have as their children grow up.

The father's explanation, which the daughter and subsequent readers
are probably likely to accept as valid, upends our expectations. And it
does so primarily through the introduction of a second, on the surface less
straightforward, level of meaning to expressions like "you're not returning
home" and "Oy vey."[20]

A second example (actually two examples embedded in the same passage) provides another demonstration (or two) of how true statements can
hide within them several meanings, which in the following instance are
intended to deceive:

"With this you shall be assured, by Pharaoh's life" (Gen. 42:15). When
Joseph wishes to swear upon a falsehood, he would say, "by Pharaoh's life."
R. Levi said,

> It is like the case of a goat that fled from the shepherd, and came upon a
> widow. What did she do? She slaughtered it, flayed it, put it in the bed, and
> covered it with a sheet. They [the officials] came inquiring about it from her.
> She said, "May I tear from the flesh of that one and eat, if I know anything
> about it." Thus, "by Pharaoh's life"! (Genesis Rabbah 91).

The officials quite naturally assume that it is the widow's husband who
is lying next to her in the bed. In order to demonstrate the seriousness of
her disavowal of any information about the escaped goat, so it goes, she
swears on her husband's life that she is telling the truth. As she knows, and
as readers we know, she is actually securing her oath not by a live husband
but a dead goat. Supplied with this information, we can affirm that in fact
the woman is telling the truth.[21]

---

20. See further David Brodsky, "Did the Widow Have a Goat in Her Bed?
Jewish Humor and Its Roots in the Talmud and Midrash," in Greenspoon, *Jews
and Humor*, 13–32.

21. Brodsky.

This kind of double message depends on an understanding of, and appreciation for, multivalent meanings inherent in language itself. As documented by several scholars, this rhetorical phenomenon is especially prominent in minority or oppressed communities, since it contains both a public transcript (for consumption by outsiders) and a hidden transcript (valuable, even crucial for community insiders).[22] Such double messages are not always humorous. When they are, as in this example from rabbinic literature, only members of the in-group are aware of the humor. Implicit or explicit criticism of the dominant, outside culture is bound up in the assertion that we're in on the joke, while they are not sufficiently clever to get it.

Jewish Joking in the Modern Period

As with other characteristics of Jewish humor, this love of language is not uniquely Jewish, but it does show up with some frequency in what we're likely to term Jewish jokes. Here are two other examples, both from the twentieth century. The first is set in the Soviet Union: Two brothers, Shmulik and Yosl, living in communist Russia, were

> attempting to emigrate to America. One day, Shmulik received permission to leave, but Yosl had to stay behind. At their tearful good-bye, they were concerned how they would be able to communicate freely in spite of the fact that the Soviet government would undoubtedly be reading their mail.
>
> "I have an idea," said Yosl. "If I write you in black ink, it will be the truth. If I use red ink, it will be false."
>
> Shmulik emigrated, and months passed with no word from Yosl. Finally, a letter arrived in black ink:
>
> My dear brother, life here in communist Russia is wonderful. We enjoy freedom and prosperity like never before. We have everything we could want. . . . In fact, the only thing we're lacking in all of Russia is red ink.[23]

In common with its rabbinic counterparts we looked at earlier, this twentieth century Jewish joke is about how minorities, oppressed in fact or living in fear of oppression, can communicate through hidden transcripts. Like these earlier examples, here too the humor comes from the recognition of multiple possibilities of interpretation. Taking a lead from Francophiles, we can also speak of this as double entendre.

In the world of Jewish humor, as is true of the world at large, especially the Western world, these days, double messages can explicitly depend on

---

22. Brodsky.
23. Brodsky.

nuances conveyed through punctuation rather than word choice. This is apparent in our second example. This joke is also set in communist Russia:

> During a gigantic celebration in Red Square, after Leon Trotsky had been exiled, Josef Stalin excitedly raised his hand to still the crowd: "Comrades! A most historic event! A cablegram—of congratulations—from Trotsky!" The hordes cheered, and Stalin read the historic cable aloud:
>
> STALIN
>
> > YOU WERE RIGHT AND I WAS WRONG. YOU ARE THE TRUE HEIR OF LENIN. I SHOULD APOLOGIZE
>
> > > > TROTSKY
>
> A roar of triumph erupted. But in the front row, a little tailor called, "Psst, Comrade Stalin. A message for the ages! But you didn't read it with the right feeling!"
>
> Whereupon Stalin stilled the throng once more: "Come, Comrade, read the historic communication!"
>
> The little tailor went up to the podium, took the telegram, and read:
>
> "Stalin, *You* were right, and *I* was wrong? *You* are the true heir of Lenin?! *I* should apologize?! Trotsky!"[24]

In this form of the joke italics are added for emphasis, but they are not necessary once the telegram has been "correctly" understood through insertion of the "proper" marks of punctuation. Because the joke ends where it does, we don't know the tailor's fate. We may suppose that it was anything but humorous.

And we also can't state unequivocally that the man on the front row was Jewish. But his description as a "little tailor" points in that direction, as does the chutzpah that he demonstrates in publically upbraiding and outshining Stalin himself. If, as the tailor asserts, he is (simply) reading the telegram as Trotsky intended, it is to Trotsky, or rather the Trotsky of this joke, to whom the double message should be attributed.

In our last example, which takes us from the Soviet Union to the United States, delight in language is also pressed into service, but primarily for entertainment value rather than any discernibly political purpose. Here we look at, and enjoy (for the first time or for the hundredth), the linguistic dexterity of Groucho Marx in a memorable scene from the memorable Marx Brothers movie, *Animal Crackers*, which first appeared in 1930:

---

24. Brodsky.

The principal animals inhabiting the African jungle are moose, elks, and Knights of Pythias. Of course, you all know what a moose is. That's big game. The first day, I shot two bucks. That was the biggest game around. . . . One morning, I shot an elephant in my pajamas. How he got into my pajamas I'll never know. . . . We took some pictures of the native girls, but they weren't developed, but we're going back again in a couple of weeks.

And so it went, and so it continues to go as younger generations of movie buffs "discover" Groucho for themselves. I think a strong case can be made for crowning Groucho as the king of double entendre. Credit goes to his gag writer (if he didn't write the jokes himself), to Groucho himself, whose delivery style, fashioned flawlessly, matched and enhanced the lines he threw out, and to the Jewish environment in which he was nurtured, which underlies (admittedly without explicit acknowledgment) the humorous words and actions of the Marx brothers. Individuals and families in even the most secular American Jewish communities of Groucho's youth were schooled in classical rabbinic texts, humor and all. Minnie Marx's family would have been no exception.[25]

My analysis, understanding, and appreciation of Jewish humor are all based on my sense of a long period of development, not necessarily linear, that ultimately connects instances of Jewish humor from biblical times to today's world. This development links communities across geographical and cultural expanses as well as different chronological periods.

Not all students of Jewish humor agree with my contentions on where and when Jewish humor originated. In particular, there are those who place its origins in the 1700s and associate it with Yiddish and the Eastern European communities in which that language and culture flourished.[26] With such individuals I more or less agree: yes, Jewish humor did begin in the 1700s; not the 1700s CE, but the 1700s BCE!

Fortunately, the scholars I admire and trust do not press the issue of origins. With equal wisdom and insight, they do not even attempt to construct a one-size-fits-all definition of Jewish humor by which specific texts or performances are accepted or rejected as authentic.[27] Instead, these researchers find, as I have, that identifying characteristic features of Jewish

---

25. See further Leonard M. Helfgott, "Groucho, Harpo, Chico, and Karl: Immigrant Humor and the Depression," in Greenspoon, *Jews and Humor*, 107–19.

26. Among the most prominent proponents of this view is Ruth R. Wisse, *No Joke: Making Jewish Humor* (Princeton: Princeton University Press, 2013).

27. See, among others, Wisse, *No Joke*, and Ted Cohen, *Jokes: Philosophical Thoughts on Joking Matters* (University of Chicago Press, 2001).

humor allows us to recognize and evaluate a wide, but not all-inclusive, number of examples that share a few or most of these traits in a mix that is unique even when its component parts are far more widespread. When we find some or all of these traits—a self-critical or deprecatory stance, a delight and marvel in language in all of its often ambiguous manifestations, reliance on insider knowledge and experience (here, Jewish knowledge and experience), pronounced self-recognition of the outsider status of an often-oppressed minority—expressed with humor that ranges from genial to abrasive, there we have come into contact with Jewish humor.

Why We'll Probably Never Have Grouchos of Our Own (But Maybe a Seinfeld)

Shawn Tucker

That title is supposed to be funny. Hopefully, if you got the joke, it was funny. But I'm guessing that at least some of you didn't get it, so let me explain. In 1888, Orson F. Whitney gave a speech about literature and Mormonism. He put forward the idea that one result of the Restoration would be a flourishing of the arts. He proclaimed, boldly, "We will yet have Miltons and Shakespeares of our own."[1] In a 1976 BYU fireside, Elder Boyd K. Packer quoted Orson F. Whitney and put forward that so far Mormons in the arts had not lived up to that great potential.[2] Michael Austin took this a step further. In a March 1999 issue of *Sunstone*, Austin wrote about the need for good Mormon satire. This satire, for Austin, would courageously "expose our faults and hypocrisies." In reference to the great satirist Jonathan Swift, Austin called his article "Swifts of Our Own."[3]

In this response to Leonard Greenspoon's excellent overview of Jewish humor, I want to examine why I believe Latter-day Saints will probably never have Grouchos of our own.[4] The "Jewishness" of Groucho Marx's humor is quite different from that of Latter-day Saint culture. There is and

---

1. First delivered as a speech by Bishop Orson F. Whitney at the Y.M.M.I.A. Conference, June 3, 1888, and published July 1888 in *The Contributor*, and then included in Brian H. Stuy's *Collected Discourses Delivered by President Wilford Woodruff, His Two Counselors, The Twelve Apostles, and Others. Volume 1 (1886–1889)* (Burbank CA, BHS Publishing, 1987), 154.

2. Boyd K. Packer, "The Arts and the Spirit of the Lord," BYU Devotional, February 1, 1976, https://speeches.byu.edu/talks/boyd-k-packer_arts-spirit-lord/.

3. Michael Austin, "Swifts of Our Own," *Sunstone*, March 1999, 64–66, available at https://www.sunstonemagazine.com/pdf/113-64-66.pdf.

4. For more on humor and laughter in Mormon culture, see Elisha McIntyre, *Religious Humor in Evangelical Christian and Mormon Culture* (New York: Bloomsbury Academic, 2018), and Shawn Tucker, "On Mormon Laughter," *BYU Studies* 15, no. 4 (2012): 141–54.

will be funny Latter-day Saints. There are standup comedians like Ryan Hamilton, Jenna Kim Jones, and Bengt Washburn. There are satirical books and blogs like the Mormon Tabernacle Enquirer. There are Calvin Gronhahl's cartoons about Latter-day Saint culture and beliefs. Latter-day Saints can be funny, but cultural differences make a Latter-day Saint Groucho difficult if not impossible to imagine. What I want to examine is why we will probably never have Grouchos of our own. And while we may never have Grouchos of our own, certain similarities between Latter-day Saint-ism and Judaism make it possible that we might, someday, have a Jerry Seinfeld of our own. I will explore that possibility as well.

To get at why Latter-day Saint culture will not produce a comic genius like Groucho Marx, I want to start with a poem that I think is an excellent example of Latter-day Saint humor.

Angels of Mercy

by Darlene Young

The Seventh Ward Relief Society
Presidency argued long and soft
Whether Janie Goodmansen deserved
To have the sisters bring her family meals.
It seems that precedent was vague—
No one was sure if "boob job" qualified
As a legitimate call for aid.
Janie herself had never asked for help—
A fault they found harder to forgive
Even than the vanity behind
The worldliness of D-cup ambition.
But in the end charity did not fail.
The sisters marched on in grim duty
Each evening clutching covered casseroles
(For, after all, it wasn't the children's fault).
More than once, though, by some oversight
The dessert came out a little short, as if
By some consensus they all knew
That Janie's husband, Jim, could do
Without a piece of pie that night.[5]

---

5. Young's poem is found in her collection, Darlene Young, *Homespun and Angel Feathers* (Salt Lake City: By Common Consent Press, 2019). The poem is included here with the poet's permission.

I hope that, as you read this, little bombs of knowing laughter and mirth exploded in your soul. This poem very humorously gets at many aspects of Latter-day Saint culture. Taking time to examine this poem, to see how it works, and to compare it with Greenspoon's insights about Jewish humor will make clear why Latter-day Saint will probably never have our own Grouchos.

Language and Wordplay

Young's poem plays with words. In the second line we are told that the Relief Society presidency argued "long and soft." We expect them to argue "long and hard," since that is the common phrase, but, of course, since these are kind Relief Society sisters, they would prefer to do it softly. Hardness is for wicked, stony hearts! But, beyond this, we can note that there is not a lot of play with words or language in the rest of the poem. And keep in mind that this is a poem. One of the most common features of poetry is to twist, stretch, and fool around with language.

This brings up the first point about why there will be no Latter-day Saint Grouchos: language and wordplay. Greenspoon provides strong, insightful examples of Jewish biblical humor. He notes the wordplay in Nabal, Eglon, and Cain's "wandering." Greenspoon even links this wordplay with the double entendres that we find in Groucho Marx's humor. The precision and ambiguity, the solidity and fluidity of language, are a paradox central to some Jewish humor, to elements of the rabbinical tradition, and to so many of Groucho's jokes.

That playfulness with language is not nearly as pronounced or important in Latter-day Saint culture. Latter-day Saints sometimes seek the Hebrew or Greek root of a Bible word or phrase, but not generally with the same linguistic zeal evident in the Jewish tradition. Latter-day Saints want to know the language to figure out what it might be saying; Jews love language for itself. There is a paradoxical Jewish playfulness and reverence for language that is not present with Latter-day Saints.

Another way to see this lack of linguistic laughter is to note that there does not seem to be any wordplay or even humor in the Book of Mormon. Somehow, in writing and translating a book that at least has one Jewish author, that humor is lost. But, honestly, Nephi doesn't seem like a jokester. He gets pretty riled up about rude dancing. And even though Joseph Smith was concerned at times with his "levity" and was known as a fun, social man, we do not see humor or witty wordplay in any of his revelations canonized in the book of Doctrine and Covenants. Groucho's double entendres emerge from a Jewish tradition that has no Latter-day Saint equivalent.

Outsider Status

The second element of Jewish humor that Greenspoon identifies, after the delight in words and wordplay, is what he calls "a perspective deriving from a feeling of powerlessness and their status as outsiders with respect to the world at large" (p. 253). I'm just going to come right out and say this: we Latter-day Saints still really, really, really want the world to like us! Sure, there was Haun's Mill, a governor who made it legal to kill us, and crossing the plains, but our almost overwhelming niceness combines with our missionary zeal in a people who are not content to bless the Mountain West alone, but who travel the world (and flood social media), anxious to bless the whole human race. When a Latter-day Saint runs for president and does not win, we don't feel like powerless outsiders. We feel glad to have had the opportunity, we feel optimistic that "we'll get it next time," and we are a little relieved that we do not have to be on our best behavior during his entire term in office. It is just hard to feel like outsiders when you are trying to get people to let you into their homes so you can talk about how we can all live with God in heaven forever. We even turn a filthy, satirical musical into a missionary opportunity.[6]

To see the distance between the "we want you to like us" element of Latter-day Saint humor and how Jewish humor may emerge from a feeling of powerlessness and outsider status, I want to mention something Greenspoon does not mention: laughter as a response to the Holocaust. There is a tremendous amount of scholarship about Jewish laughter as a response to evil and the Holocaust, but I just want to take the smallest bit of water off of this vast iceberg.[7] The insight is from Jacqueline Bussie

---

6. This is a reference to the Church's response to *The Book of Mormon* musical by sending missionaries to theaters and by using the lines "You've seen the play . . . now read the book" as an invitation to theatergoers to read the Book of Mormon.

7. For additional scholarship on Jewish humor as a response to the Holocaust, see Steve Lipman, *Laughter in Hell: The Use of Humor During the Holocaust* (Northvale NJ; Jason Aronson, 1991), John Morreall, "Humor in the Holocaust: Its Critical, Cohesive, and Coping Functions," Holocaust Teacher Resource Center, November 22, 2001, http://www.holocaust-trc.org/humor-in-the-holocaust/, and Whitney Carpenter, "Laughter in a Time of Tragedy: Examining Humor during the Holocaust," *Denison Journal of Religion* 9 (2010), https://digitalcommons.denison.edu/cgi/viewcontent.cgi?article=1066&context=religion.

who wrote *The Laughter of the Oppressed: Ethical and Theological Resistance in Wiesel, Morrison, and Endo*. In the chapter in Bussie's book on Elie Wiesel's novel *Gates of the Forest*, Bussie examines how Jewish laughter responds to the evil of the Holocaust, including how laughter shows the limits of language and storytelling and how it interrupts the oppressive system set up by the Nazis.[8] Laughter helps those who suffer to not give in and to not believe the terrible, dehumanizing lies that their oppression tries to impose on them. Laughter interrupts the system and even interrupts evil.[9] Laughter helps people avoid despair and doubt, and laughter honors conflict and paradox.[10]

On the other side of human experience from Wiesel's resistant and powerful laughter in the face of evil is Darlene Young's poem about compassionate service for someone who got a boob job. Not only do Latter-day Saints lack the history that informs Jewish humor, but they seem to use humor differently. Greenspoon notes that often Jewish humor establishes Jewish self-identity and marks them as insiders while creating a line between Jews and non-Jews. This is crucial in a world where anti-Semitic forces oppress, stigmatize, stereotype, bully, and murder Jews. Jews establish a viable sense of identity and worth in the face of that hatred and oppression. Latter-day Saints not only generally lack that experience and clearly lack that history, but Latter-day Saints want to make non–Latter-day Saints Latter-day Saint. Jews need the line to survive; Latter-day Saints want to blur and then erase it.

This effort to blur and then erase is somewhat clear in Young's poem. The poem's Latter-day Saints want to serve, but they feel a conflict. The conflict is their judgmental attitude and self-righteousness, flaws that the poem highlights and gently critiques. But even this very "Mormon" poem, addressing as it does common cultural elements, is okay for wider, non–Latter-day Saint reading and consumption. Latter-day Saints might not share it on social media with their non–Latter-day Saint friends, but they would not be embarrassed by it. Furthermore, this poem does not draw a clear, strong line between Latter-day Saints and non–Latter-day Saints. The poem, humorously, takes a long and soft look at an all-too-common cultural flaw. Latter-day Saints might understand it best, but others will not be put off by it.

---

8. Jacqueline Bussie, *The Laughter of the Oppressed: Ethical and Theological Resistance in Wiesel, Morrison, and Endo* (New York; T&T Clark, 2007), 31–32.

9. Bussie, 31–32.

10. Bussie, 31–32.

Reference to Beliefs and Cultural Practices

The way that Young's poem references Relief Society, traditions of compassionate service meals, casseroles, and even unhealthy lifestyles makes
it "Mormon." Some of those elements would need to be explained to
non–Latter-day Saints. In this respect this poem is like Jewish humor with
references to Jewish beliefs and practices. In addition, one of the things
that makes the poem funny is its "self-critical, self-deprecatory stance" (p.
253). The poem mocks the self-righteous, judgmental attitude of those
that reluctantly serve. In the end, they take food to the family, "for, after
all, it wasn't the children's fault." The final acts of compassion include the
not-so-subtle message: while charity never faileth, you are not getting the
full dessert.

In its relation to Latter-day Saint culture, "Angels of Mercy" is somewhat close to the joke Greenspoon tells about Moses's conversation with
God about the law. That joke, among other things, humorously explores
some of the conflicts of the rabbinical tradition. Young's poem explores
compassion, service, and communal censure for vain practices or tendencies. The poem uses humor to invite Latter-day Saints to examine how
they respond to service and how they respond to community members.
A similar poem could be about getting a tattoo, getting pregnant out of
wedlock, or a missionary returning home early. How Latter-day Saints
might communally censure is in tension with ideals of unfailing charity.
Yet while the poem humorously faces inward, examining cultural practices and religious ideals, it still seems to do so with an eye on the fact
that non–Latter-day Saints may be looking, may be listening in on this
discussion. Knowing that outsiders might be listening, it does not criticize
too harshly nor push those listeners away. It may be self-critical and softly
self-deprecating, but it does so with a smile.

The smile a reader gets from Young's poem is not a Groucho smile.
It is not a smile with linguistic double entendres. It is also not a smile of
people who have known oppression and who know how to use laughter to
maintain humanity in the face of evil. It is not the smile of those who use
humor with the hope of revealing their humanity to those who stereotype
and hate. It also is not Mordecai's smile at Haman's just desserts or Elijah's
mocking laughter at the priests of Baal. Young's poem inspires a smile that
seems younger, less experienced, and (perhaps naively) optimistic. Given
the complex and painful history behind Jewish humor, it is understand-

able that one might even hope that Latter-day Saints never have Grouchos of our own.

Observational Humor, or Could There Be a Mormon Seinfeld?

While I have so far argued the differences between Jewish and Latter-day Saint laughter, commonalities in the traditions can also provide insights. Those commonalities indicate that while Latter-day Saints may never have Grouchos, we may one day perhaps have Seinfelds of our own.

To get at those commonalities shared by Jewish and Latter-day Saint laughter, I begin with some of Immanuel Kant's insights about the nature of humor. Kant's insights come from his book *The Critique of Judgement*, where he describes humor thusly:

> *Humour* in the good sense means the talent of being able voluntarily to put oneself into a certain mental disposition, in which everything is judged quite differently from the ordinary method (reversed, in fact), and yet in accordance with certain rational principles in such a frame of mind. He who is involuntarily subject to such mutations is called a *man of humours* [launisch]; but he who can assume them voluntarily and purposively (on behalf of a lively presentment brought about by the aid of a contrast that excites a laugh)—he and his manner of speech are called *humorous* [launigt].[11]

Thus "humour" for Kant comes from being able to see and judge differently from how things are commonly seen and judged. Those who are humourous can draw upon this distanced mental disposition at will. Such a person can then point out or generate contrasts that evoke laughter.

Kant describes well a form of comedy popular today: observational humor. A contemporary genius in observational humor is, of course, Jerry Seinfeld. Some of Seinfeld's genius, to paraphrase Kant, is his ability to voluntarily enter a mental disposition where he sees and judges common, everyday experiences quite differently from the ordinary method. To listen to Seinfeld or to watch his famous and influential show is to be struck by the way everything makes sense, everything is in accordance with rational principles, but how everything nevertheless seems changed, twisted, and even reversed. An example of Seinfeld's observational humor is the bit of stand-up comedy used at the very beginning of an episode of *Seinfeld*. During this bit, which is in an episode called "The Cadillac" from season seven, Seinfeld says, "Old people in Florida, they drive slow and they sit

---

11. Immanuel Kant, *Kant's Critique of Judgement*, trans. J.H. Bernard, 2nd rev. ed. (London; Macmillan, 1914), 228.

low." He continues, "The state flag of Florida should be a steering wheel with a hat and two knuckles on it." Seinfeld develops more humorous observations when he describes such elderly drivers as having "that left-turn signal on from when they left the house that morning." He says that this signal marks a turn that is legal in the state of Florida and is known as "an eventual left."[12]

Not only is Seinfeld Jewish, but more than half the writers for *Seinfeld* were also Jewish.[13] Even the above joke connects with the common Jewish phenomenon of elderly Jews moving to Florida, something also present in the show. But I would argue that these are not the deepest or most insightful things about Jewishness and Seinfeld's observational humor. Observational humor can be a natural consequence for those who learn from their culture to not only question what they see and question the prevailing way of seeing things, but who are specifically taught to see things differently. Observational humor, to return to Greenspoon's insights, comes from a Jewish perspective that is derived from their "status as outsiders with respect to the world at large." Seinfeld's observational humor is that of a Jewish outsider who can voluntarily see things differently, even reversed.

The Jewish impulse toward voluntarily seeing things differently or even in reverse is evident when we again return to the Bible. Balaam, in the example Greenspoon used, can only see the common and the everyday, while the ass can see the world differently. Balaam sees a clear path; the ass, who sees the angel, sees quite the opposite. Haman sees his future success, with Mordecai on the massive gallows. Mordecai and Jewish readers see the opposite. Haman will see the opposite as well, but not for long. In addition to these examples, we note that Joseph saw many things that were quite different from what others saw. Joseph saw dreams of his future as well as the future of others. Joseph, when he was successful in Egypt, saw and recognized his brothers, while they did not recognize him. Joseph

---

12. *Seinfeld*. "The Cadillac," directed by Andy Ackerman, written by Larry David and Jerry Seinfeld. NBC Broadcasting, February 8, 1996.

13. J. Correspondent, "Critics Call Show Self-Hating: Was Seinfeld Good for Jews?" *The Jewish News of Northern California*, December 28, 2016, https://www.jweekly.com/1998/05/08/critics-call-show-self-hating-was-seinfeld-good-for-jews/. Jarrod Tanny explores the relationship between Judaism and *Seinfeld* in Jarrod Tanny, "Decoding Seinfeld's Jewishness," in *A Club of Their Own: Jewish Humorists and the Contemporary World*, ed. Eli Lederhendler and Gabriel N. Finder (New York: Oxford UP, 2016).

saw the years of plenty, but he also saw years of famine. The Lord was with Joseph, but how the Lord was with him would not be readily evident to those who only saw the given, everyday world. Finally, in one of the most dramatic examples of seeing something quite different from the common and every day, 2 Kings 6 describes how Elisha saw a mountain full of horses and chariots of fire, a vision which made the everyday, common view of the merely human Syrian army seem trivial.

This reversal of the norm, the expected, or the everyday that can give rise to observational humor is also present in writings of Jews as recorded in the New Testament. In fact, perhaps the most famous sermon in the New Testament has as its central feature an attempt to invite audiences to, in Kant's words, "judge quite differently from the ordinary method." The "Sermon on the Mount," as it is often called, encourages people to find righteousness beyond "the law." The sermon directly warns about the dangers and pitfalls of inaccurate judgement. But perhaps the sermon's greatest reversal is the Beatitudes. In a world dominated by martial Roman values or even the common experience of dog-eat-dog human competition for survival, Jesus sets up those who mourn, those who are meek, those who hunger and thirst for righteousness, the merciful, the pure in heart, the peacemakers, and the persecuted as those who are truly blessed. Living the life encouraged by this Jewish itinerate teacher means seeing and living quite differently from "the ordinary method." The view from the life Jesus encourages must make the common, worldly approach seem quite foolish, even comical.

There are no Latter-day Saint Jerry Seinfelds any more than there are Latter-day Saint Grouchos, but the distance between Seinfeld and Latter-day Saint comics is much shorter. As mentioned at the outset, there are successful Latter-day Saint stand-up comedians like Ryan Hamilton, Jenna Kim Jones, and Bengt Washburn. Like Seinfeld, those comics generally work in observational humor. Furthermore, the reason that there is less distance between a Latter-day Saint Seinfeld and a Latter-day Saint Groucho is because Latter-day Saints are also enculturated to "judge quite differently from the ordinary method" or from the manner that "the world" judges. Latter-day Saints draw upon the Jewish tradition for this distance, including the Old and New Testament elements previously mentioned. In fact, the Sermon on the Mount is repeated almost word for word in the Book of Mormon, reinforcing the cultural power of its many reversals. Latter-day Saints have also experienced some cultural marginalization, though, as already explored, not nearly to the magnitude of Jews.

Mormon Observational and Self-Critical Laughter

Observational humor developed from a distanced, outsider position would certainly be stronger with a culture that experienced such an outsider status in a longer, more sustained, and much more intense manner. Not only have Latter-day Saints not had nearly the sustained nor intense experience of being outsiders as have Jews, but, as explored earlier, Latter-day Saints work to blur the line between insider and outsider. But Latter-day Saints are still strongly encouraged to be "in the world, but not of the world." The culture encourages effecting positive changes in the lives and events in the broader world without being co-opted by "the world's" values.

Besides observational humor, there is one more point of contact between Latter-day Saint and Jewish laughter, a point closely aligned with observational humor. That point is self-critical laughter. Greenspoon provides an excellent example of this in his joke about Moses and the rabbinical dietary tradition. Greenspoon points out how the joke is critical of elements of the rabbinic tradition; it illustrates the "self-critical, self-deprecatory stance" that is characteristic of Jewish humor.

Observational humor, emerging from an ability to "judge quite differently from the ordinary method," and the self-critical and self-deprecatory stance can circle us back to Darlene Young's poem. We already explored how it is gently self-critical. It is also Kantian in how it recasts compassionate service and Latter-day Saint cultural anxiety over sexuality, sexual desire, the body, lust, vanity, and shame. In fact, one could almost imagine a Latter-day Saint version of an episode of *Seinfeld* dealing with the very issue Young explores. The episode could have a Latter-day Saint Jerry and a Latter-day Saint Elaine wondering about the compassionate service protocol for "boob jobs."

Young's poem illustrates some points of contact between Jewish and Latter-day Saint laughter, including observational humor with a self-critical and self-deprecatory edge. Of course that edge is not particularly sharp in Young's poem. To illustrate how that edge might be sharper in its critique of Latter-day Saint folk beliefs and in its critique of Latter-day Saint cultural anxieties, and to show how it might be possible for us Latter-day Saints to one day have Seinfelds of our own, I finish with two humorous examples from the satirical blog The Mormon Tabernacle Enquirer.

The first example, one which shows Latter-day Saint humor that takes aim at some common folk beliefs, is a post with the title "Recently Deceased Area Man Finds Spirit World is Two Long Lines of People Who

Want to Hug or Punch Him."[14] That satirical news article includes an interview with a man who, upon entering the Spirit World, is immediately punched by a former next-door neighbor. That neighbor is upset that the recently deceased Latter-day Saint "had never mentioned the gospel or even given him a pass along card." What is humorous about this is how it illustrates the common folk notion that a Latter-day Saint can anticipate being confronted in the Spirit World by those with whom they did not share the gospel. This man's experience is humorously exaggerated. What happens almost immediately for the same man is that a "really nice lady threw her arms around [him] so tightly, and she was shaking with tears of joy and gratitude." This woman, it turns out, had had her temple work done while the recently deceased man was a "13 year-old boy scout working in my genealogy merit badge." This instance enacts the other side of the folk belief, where here one is thanked for what they did to bring gospel blessings to others, especially the dead who are blessed by genealogy and temple work. The rest of the post alternates back and forth between people grateful for what the Latter-day Saint had done and people upset by what he failed to do, rendering the Spirit World two long lines of the appreciative and the enraged.

What is observational and Kantian about this post is how it places these two rather common yet contrasting folk beliefs about the Spirit World together. This juxtaposition in turn highlights some of the tension if not absurdity of both beliefs, providing a critique of the potentially inflated self-importance that those beliefs may inadvertently encourage. This post's critique is aimed more specifically at Latter-day Saint beliefs or at least folk beliefs than the way Young's poem examines cultural attitudes. Both the poem and the post bespeak the Kantian talent of "being able voluntarily to put oneself into a certain mental disposition, in which everything is judged quite differently from the ordinary method."

A final example is a Mormon Tabernacle Enquirer post with the title "Faithful LDS Teen Worried He Might Be Vegetarian."[15] The title itself seems to be intended as a surprise reversal, as one might expect that last

---

14. "Recently Deceased Area Man Finds Spirit World Is Two Long Lines of People Who Want to Hug or Punch Him," The Mormon Tabernacle Enquirer, February 25, 2013, https://motabenquirer.blogspot.com/2013/02/recently-deceased-area-man -finds-spirit.html.

15. Barley B. Bratt, "Faithful LDS Teen Worried He Might Be Vegetarian," The Mormon Tabernacle Enquirer, June 10, 2012, https://motabenquirer.blogspot .com/2012/06/faithful-lds-teen-worried-he-might-be.html.

word to be "homosexual" or "gay" instead of "vegetarian." Anxiety over homosexuality was very, very high in 2012, and, at current writing, still is. The "fear" that a young person would be "afflicted" with such a "sin or sinful disposition" was (and still is) very culturally pronounced. In fact, the entire post humorously plays with anxieties surrounding homosexuality. The young man, as the photo caption reads, "suffers from the appetite that dares not speak its name." This phrase is an allusion to Oscar Wilde's indecency trial where "the love that dare not speak its name" was understood as a euphemism for homosexuality. The young man's mother catches him watching "It Gets Better" videos, but instead of being videos about how adult homosexuals often find life better than when they were adolescents, these videos are by PETA. The young man notes his mother's disappointed hopes in the son's future marriage, but not because gay marriage was both illegal at the time and is still prohibited in the Church, but because the reception would not have "Vienna sausages, bacon wraps, and a full cutting station." One final parallel between the young man's vegetarianism and homosexuality comes when he overhears his father's arguments against vegetarianism. The father unambiguously asserts that God would not make a person who "only wants to eat artichokes, onions, sugar beets, peas, and carrots!" This statement recasts the traditional accusation of homosexuality's "unnaturalness" in humorous parallel with vegetarianism.

The writer of this post, who is identified only by the humorous pen name "Barley B. Bratt," a name that Latter-day Saints would quickly identify as a play on the famous Latter-day Saint Parley P. Pratt, engages in observational humor. What is being observed from a Kantian humorous position is Mormon cultural anxiety about homosexuality and vegetarianism. Vegetarianism is much, much less fraught with cultural anxiety, but creating this parallel casts homosexuality into a new, humorous, and rather absurd light. The post sets the crestfallen and deeply disappointed reactions of the youth's parents in light that makes them seem disproportionate and selfishly unloving. The youth's anxiety seems shame-driven if not baseless. Anxiety over homosexuality and vegetarianism are hereby drained of their intense cultural anxiety, making them appear petty and trivial, a move that may castigate a culture that would encourage or even sustain such anxieties.

This post, like Young's poem, isolates Latter-day Saint cultural attitudes and anxieties in such a way that it, to quote Kant again, "purposively" and with "the aid of a contrast" thereby "excites a laugh." The observations and contrasts serve to critique the attitudes. Such a criticism seems sharper and edgier in the post than in the poem, but that sharpness may have more to do with audience than the content itself. A Relief Society sister in charge of compassionate service may conclude that Young's poem is more pointed in its criticism than another sister whose child recently came out as gay. Both post and poem take aim at attitudes where the Mormon Tabernacle Enquirer post about the Spirit World addresses Latter-day Saint folk beliefs. The observational qualities of all three, the way that they address and then twist and even reverse common, everyday cultural beliefs or attitudes as well as their "self-critical, self-deprecatory stance" connect them most closely with the Jewish humor of someone like Jerry Seinfeld. And here again, the poem and posts could all three be the basis for episodes of a Latter-day Saint version of *Seinfeld*. While Latter-day Saints do not have Grouchos of our own, nor is Latter-day Saint laughter typified by the linguistic double entendres or an anguished smile in the face of horrific oppression, Latter-day Saints could, one day, have a Seinfeld of our own.

Contributors

Dean Phillip Bell, PhD, is President/CEO and Professor of Jewish History at the Spertus Institute for Jewish Learning and Leadership. He is the author or editor of ten books and dozens of articles in the field of early modern Jewish history.

Ashley Brocious is a doctoral student at the Jewish Theological Seminary in New York City. Brocious also received an MA in Hebrew and Jewish Studies from the University College London. Her research areas include the Bible and Its Interpretation, Jewish Studies, and literary criticism.

David C. Dollahite, PhD, is Professor of Family Life at Brigham Young University, where he teaches classes and conducts research on the links between religion and family life. He is Co-Director (with Dr. Loren Marks) of the American Families of Faith Project.

Leonard Greenspoon, PhD, holds the Klutznick Chair in Jewish Civilization at Creighton University, where he is also Professor of Theology and of Classical and Near Eastern Studies. Greenspoon is the editor of the 32-volume *Studies in Jewish Civilization* series. He has also written six other books, including his most recent one on Jewish Bible translations.

Peter Haas, PhD, is an ordained Reform rabbi who received his doctorate from Brown University in 1980. After teaching at Vanderbilt University for nearly twenty years, he moved to Case Western Reserve University in Cleveland, Ohio, where he served as chair of the Department of Religious Studies from 2003 to 2015.

Trevan Hatch, PhD, is the Religious Studies specialist in the Lee Library at Brigham Young University and an adjunct professor in the Department of Ancient Scripture. Hatch's expertise is in Bible and Jewish Studies, and he is the author of *A Stranger in Jerusalem: Seeing Jesus as a Jew* (Wipf & Stock Publishers, 2019).

Peter Knobel, PhD, received his rabbinic ordination from the Hebrew Union College and earned a doctorate in philosophy from Yale University. Before his death in August of 2019, Rabbi Knobel was emeritus rabbi at Beth Emet The Free Synagogue in Evanston, Illinois.

Ellen Lasser LeVee, PhD, is on the faculty of the Spertus Institute for Jewish Learning and Leadership and has published essays on the contemporary Jewish experience, women and Judaism, and on a variety of Biblical texts that highlight the distinctiveness of the Jewish cultural voice.

Loren D. Marks, PhD, is Professor of Family Life at Brigham Young University, where he teaches classes and conducts research on the links between religion and family life. He is Co-Director (with David C. Dollahite) of the American Families of Faith Project.

Camille Fronk Olson, PhD, is a Professor Emeritus of Ancient Scripture at Brigham Young University and former department chair. While at BYU, she engaged in interfaith dialogue and published on women of the Bible and Latter-day Saint doctrine.

Andrew C. Reed, PhD, is an assistant professor of Church History at Brigham Young University. He is a fellow of the Religious Outreach Council and co-editor of *Understanding Covenants and Communities: Jews and Latter-day Saints in Dialogue* (RSC and CCAR, 2020).

Gary A. Rendsburg, PhD, serves as the Blanche and Irving Laurie Chair in Jewish History at Rutgers University. His research areas include the Bible, the Dead Sea Scrolls, Judaism in late antiquity, the history of the Hebrew language, and medieval Hebrew manuscripts.

Byron L. Sherwin, PhD, was Professor of Jewish studies at the Spertus Institute of Jewish Studies in Chicago before his death in May 2015. He was trained at the Jewish Theological Seminary under Abraham Joshua Heschel and received his PhD at the University of Chicago. He authored numerous books on Jewish ethics, Jewish theology, and Jewish history.

Ben Spackman is a PhD candidate in American Religious History, with prior graduate training in ancient Near East and Semitics. He focuses on the twentieth-century interplay of hermeneutics, science, and fundamentalism.

Shawn Tucker, PhD, teaches Humanities at Elon University in Elon, North Carolina. In addition to his work on Laughter, he has conducted fruitful research on T.S. Eliot's *The Wasteland*, the virtues and vices in the arts, humility, Humanities pedagogy, Jasper Johns, and Radiohead.

Index

Also available from
GREG KOFFORD BOOKS

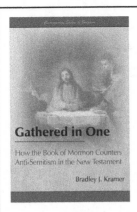

Gathered in One:
How the Book of Mormon Counters
Anti-Semitism in the New Testament

Bradley J. Kramer

Paperback, ISBN: 978-1-58958-709-0
Hardcover, ISBN: 978-1-58958-710-6

Since the Holocaust, a growing consensus of biblical scholars have come to recognize the unfair and misleading anti-Semitic rhetoric in the New Testament—language that has arguably contributed to centuries of violence and persecution against the Jewish people.

In *Gathered in One*, Bradley J. Kramer shows how the Book of Mormon counters anti-Semitism in the New Testament by approaching this most Christian of books on its own turf and on its own terms: literarily, by providing numerous pro-Jewish statements, portrayals, settings, and structuring devices in opposition to similar anti-Semitic elements in the New Testament; and scripturally, by connecting with it as a peer, as a divine document of equal value and authority, which can add these elements to the Christian canon (as the Gospel of John can add elements to the Gospel of Matthew) without undermining its authority or dependability.

In this way, the Book of Mormon effectively "detoxifies" the New Testament of its anti-Semitic poison without weakening its status as scripture and goes far in encouraging Christians to relate to Jews respectfully, not as enemies or opponents, but as allies, people of equal worth, importance, and value before God.

Praise for *Gathered in One*:

"His thesis is fresh, provocative, and rigorously argued. A signal contribution to Book of Mormon studies." — Terryl L. Givens, author of *By the Hand of Mormon: The American Scripture that Launched a New World Religion*

"Impressed by the book and its scholarship and attitude, I recommend it to all who are interested in the history of Christian attitudes towards the Jews, as well as those working towards interfaith reconciliation and mutual respect" — Yaakov Ariel, professor of religious studies at the University of North Carolina at Chapel Hill and author of *Evangelizing the Chosen People: Missions to the Jews in America, 1880–2000*

Re-reading Job: Understanding the Ancient World's Greatest Poem

Michael Austin

Paperback, ISBN: 978-1-58958-667-3
Hardcover, ISBN: 978-1-58958-668-0

Job is perhaps the most difficult to understand of all books in the Bible. While a cursory reading of the text seems to relay a simple story of a righteous man whose love for God was tested through life's most difficult of challenges and rewarded for his faith through those trials, a closer reading of Job presents something far more complex and challenging. The majority of the text is a work of poetry that authors and artists through the centuries have recognized as being one of--if not the--greatest poem of the ancient world.

In *Re-reading Job: Understanding the Ancient World's Greatest Poem*, author Michael Austin shows how most readers have largely misunderstood this important work of scripture and provides insights that enable us to re-read Job in a drastically new way. In doing so, he shows that the story of Job is far more than that simple story of faith, trials, and blessings that we have all come to know, but is instead a subversive and complex work of scripture meant to inspire readers to rethink all that they thought they knew about God.

Praise for *Re-reading Job*:

"In this remarkable book, Michael Austin employs his considerable skills as a commentator to shed light on the most challenging text in the entire Hebrew Bible. Without question, readers will gain a deeper appreciation for this extraordinary ancient work through Austin's learned analysis. Rereading Job signifies that Latter-day Saints are entering a new age of mature biblical scholarship. It is an exciting time, and a thrilling work." — David Bokovoy, author, *Authoring the Old Testament*

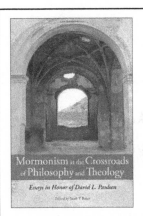

Mormonism at the Crossroads of Philosophy and Theology: Essays in Honor of David L. Paulsen

Edited by Jacob T. Baker

Paperback, ISBN: 978-1-58958-192-0

"There is no better measure of the growing importance of Mormon thought in contemporary religious debate than this volume of essays for David Paulsen. In a large part thanks to him, scholars from all over the map are discussing the questions Mormonism raises about the nature of God and the purpose of life. These essays let us in on a discussion in progress." —RICHARD LYMAN BUSHMAN, author of *Joseph Smith: Rough Stone Rolling*.

"This book makes it clear that there can be no real ecumenism without the riches of the Mormon mind. Professor Paulsen's impact on LDS thought is well known. . . . These original and insightful essays chart a new course for Christian intellectual life." —PETER A. HUFF, and author of *Vatican II and The Voice of Vatican II*

"This volume of smart, incisive essays advances the case for taking Mormonism seriously within the philosophy of religion–an accomplishment that all generations of Mormon thinkers should be proud of." —PATRICK Q. MASON, Howard W. Hunter Chair of Mormon Studies, Claremont Graduate University

"These essays accomplish a rare thing—bringing light rather than heat to an on-going conversation. And the array of substantial contributions from outstanding scholars and theologians within and outside Mormonism is itself a fitting tribute to a figure who has been at the forefront of bringing Mormonism into dialogue with larger traditions." —TERRYL L. GIVENS, author of *People of Paradox: A History of Mormon Culture*

"The emergence of a vibrant Mormon scholarship is nowhere more in evidence than in the excellent philosophical contributions of David Paulsen." —RICHARD J. MOUW, President, Fuller Theological Seminary, author of *Talking with Mormons: An Invitation to Evangelicals*

Authoring the Old Testament: Genesis–Deuteronomy

David Bokovoy

Paperback, ISBN: 978-1-58958-588-1
Hardcover, ISBN: 978-1-58958-675-8

For the last two centuries, biblical scholars have made discoveries and insights about the Old Testament that have greatly changed the way in which the authorship of these ancient scriptures has been understood. In the first of three volumes spanning the entire Hebrew Bible, David Bokovoy dives into the Pentateuch, showing how and why textual criticism has led biblical scholars today to understand the first five books of the Bible as an amalgamation of multiple texts into a single, though often complicated narrative; and he discusses what implications those have for Latter-day Saint understandings of the Bible and modern scripture.

Praise for *Authoring the Old Testament*:

"*Authoring the Old Testament* is a welcome introduction, from a faithful Latter-day Saint perspective, to the academic world of Higher Criticism of the Hebrew Bible. . . . [R]eaders will be positively served and firmly impressed by the many strengths of this book, coupled with Bokovoy's genuine dedication to learning by study and also by faith." — John W. Welch, editor, *BYU Studies Quarterly*

"Bokovoy provides a lucid, insightful lens through which disciple-students can study intelligently LDS scripture. This is first rate scholarship made accessible to a broad audience—nourishing to the heart and mind alike." — Fiona Givens, co-author, *The God Who Weeps: How Mormonism Makes Sense of Life*

"I repeat: this is one of the most important books on Mormon scripture to be published recently. . . . [*Authoring the Old Testament*] has the potential to radically expand understanding and appreciation for not only the Old Testament, but scripture in general. It's really that good. Read it. Share it with your friends. Discuss it." — David Tayman, The Improvement Era: A Mormon Blog

The Lost 116 Pages:
Reconstructing the Book of Mormon's Missing Stories

Don Bradley

Paperback, ISBN: 978-1-58958-760-1
Hardcover, ISBN: 978-1-58958-040-4

On a summer day in 1828, Book of Mormon scribe and witness Martin Harris was emptying drawers, upending furniture, and ripping apart mattresses as he desperately looked for a stack of papers he had sworn to God to protect. Those pages containing the only copy of the first three months of Joseph Smith's translation of the golden plates were forever lost, and the detailed stories they held forgotten over the ensuing years—until now.

In this highly anticipated work, author Don Bradley presents over a decade of historical and scriptural research to not only tell the story of the lost pages but to reconstruct many of the detailed stories written on them. Questions explored and answered include:

+ Was the lost manuscript actually 116 pages?
+ How did Mormon's abridgment of this period differ from the accounts in Nephi's small plates?
+ Where did the brass plates and Laban's sword come from?
+ How did Lehi's family and their descendants live the Law of Moses without the temple and Aaronic priesthood?
+ How did the Liahona operate?
+ Why is Joseph of Egypt emphasized so much in the Book of Mormon?
+ How were the first Nephites similar to the very last?
+ What message did God write on the temple wall for Aminadi to translate?
+ How did the Jaredite interpreters come into the hands of the Nephite kings?
+ Why was King Benjamin so beloved by his people?

Despite the likely demise of those pages to the sands of time, the answers to these questions and many more are now available for the first time in nearly two centuries in *The Lost 116 Pages: Reconstructing the Book of Mormon's Missing Stories*.

The End of the World, Plan B:
A Guide for the Future

Charles Shirō Inouye

Paperback, ISBN: 978-1-58958-755-7

Praise for *End of the World, Plan B*:

"Mormonism needs Inouye's voice. We need, in general, voices that are a bit less Ayn Rand and a bit more Siddhartha Gautama. Inouye reminds us that justice is not enough and that obedience is not the currency of salvation. He urges us to recognize the limits of the law, to see that, severed from a willingness to compassionately suffer with the world's imperfection and evanescence, our righteous hunger for balancing life's books will destroy us all."
— Adam S. Miller, author of *Rube Goldberg Machines: Essays in Mormon Theology* and *Letters to a Young Mormon*

"Drawing on Christian, Buddhist, Daoist, and other modes of thought, Charles Inouye shows how an attitude of hope can arise from a narrative of doom. The End of the World, Plan B is not simply a rethinking of the end of our world, but is a meditation on the possibility of compassionate self-transformation. In a world that looks to the just punishment of the wicked, Inouye shows how sorrow, which comes from the demands of justice, can create peace, forgiveness, and love."
— Michael D.K. Ing, Assistant Professor, Department of Religious Studies, Indiana University

"For years I've hoped to see a book that related Mormonism to the great spiritual traditions beyond Christianity and Judaism. Charles Inouye has done this in one of the best Mormon devotional books I've ever read. His Mormon reading of the fourfold path of the Bodhisattva offers a beautiful eschatology of the end/purpose of the world as the revelation of compassion. I hope the book is read widely."
— James M. McLachlan, co-editor of *Discourses in Mormon Theology: Philosophical and Theological Possibilities*

As Iron Sharpens Iron: Listening to the Various Voices of Scripture

Julie M. Smith

Paperback, ISBN: 978-1-58958-501-0

**2016 Best Religious Non-fiction Award,
Association for Mormon Letters**

Our scripture study and reading often assume that the prophetic figures within the texts are in complete agreement with each other. Because of this we can fail to recognize that those authors and personalities frequently have different—and sometimes competing—views on some of the most important doctrines of the Gospel, including the nature of God, the roles of scripture and prophecy, and the Atonement.

In this unique volume, fictionalized dialogues between the various voices of scripture illustrate how these differences and disagreements are not flaws of the texts but are rather essential features of the canon. These creative dialogues include Abraham and Job debating the utility of suffering and our submission to God, Alma and Abinidi disagreeing on the place of justice in the Atonement, and the authors Mark and Luke discussing the role of women in Jesus's ministry. It is by examining and embracing the different perspectives within the canon that readers are able to discover just how rich and invigorating the scriptures can be. The dialogues within this volume show how just as "iron sharpeneth iron," so can we sharpen our own thoughts and beliefs as we engage not just the various voices in the scriptures but also the various voices within our community (Proverbs 27:17).

Whom Say Ye That I Am?
Lessons from
the Jesus of Nazareth

James W. McConkie
and Judith E. McConkie

Paperback, ISBN: 978-1-58958-707-6

"This book is the most important Jesus study to date written by believing Mormons for an LDS audience. It opens the door for Mormons to come to know a Jesus most readers will know little about—the Jesus of history." — David Bokovoy, author of *Authoring the Old Testament: Genesis–Deuteronomy*

"Meticulously documented and researched, the authors have crafted an insightful and enlightening book that allows Jesus to speak by providing both wisdom and council. The McConkies masterfully weave in sources from the Gospels, ancient and modern scholars, along with Christian and non-Christian religious leaders." — *Deseret News*

The story of Jesus is frequently limited to the telling of the babe of Bethlehem who would die on the cross and three days later triumphantly exit his tomb in resurrected glory. Frequently skimmed over or left aside is the story of the Jesus of Nazareth who confronted systemic injustice, angered those in power, risked his life for the oppressed and suffering, and worked to preach and establish the Kingdom of God—all of which would lead to his execution on Calvary.

In this insightful and moving volume, authors James and Judith McConkie turn to the latest scholarship on the historical and cultural background of Jesus to discover lessons on what we can learn from his exemplary life. Whether it be his intimate interactions with the sick, the poor, women, and the outcast, or his public confrontations with oppressive religious, political, and economic institutions, Jesus of Nazareth—the son of a carpenter, Messiah, and Son of God—exemplified the way, the truth, and the life that we must follow to bring about the Kingdom of Heaven.

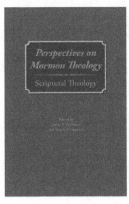

Perspectives on Mormon Theology: Scriptural Theology

Edited by James E. Faulconer and Joseph M. Spencer

Paperback, ISBN: 978-1-58958-712-0
Hardcover, ISBN: 978-1-58958-713-7

The phrase "theology of scripture" can be understood in two distinct ways. First, theology of scripture would be reflection on the nature of scripture, asking questions about what it means for a person or a people to be oriented by a written text (rather than or in addition to an oral tradition or a ritual tradition). In this first sense, theology of scripture would form a relatively minor part of the broader theological project, since the nature of scripture is just one of many things on which theologians reflect. Second, theology of scripture would be theological reflection guided by scripture, asking questions of scriptural texts and allowing those texts to shape the direction the theologian's thoughts pursue. In this second sense, theology of scripture would be less a part of the larger theological project than a way of doing theology, since whatever the theologian takes up reflectively, she investigates through the lens of scripture.

The essays making up this collection reflect attentiveness to both ways of understanding the phrase "theology of scripture." Each essay takes up the relatively un-self-conscious work of reading a scriptural text but then—at some point or another—asks the self-conscious question of exactly what she or he is doing in the work of reading scripture. We have thus attempted in this book (1) to create a dialogue concerning what scripture is for Latter-day Saints, and (2) to focus that dialogue on concrete examples of Latter-day Saints reading actual scripture texts.

Beholding the Tree of Life: A Rabbinic Approach to the Book of Mormon

Bradley J. Kramer

Paperback, ISBN: 978-1-58958-701-4
Hardcover, ISBN: 978-1-58958-702-1

Too often readers approach the Book of Mormon simply as a collection of quotations, an inspired anthology to be scanned quickly and routinely recited. In Beholding the Tree of Life Bradley J. Kramer encourages his readers to slow down, to step back, and to contemplate the literary qualities of the Book of Mormon using interpretive techniques developed by Talmudic and post-Talmudic rabbis. Specifically, Kramer shows how to read the Book of Mormon closely, in levels, paying attention to the details of its expression as well as to its overall connection to the Hebrew Scriptures—all in order to better appreciate the beauty of the Book of Mormon and its limitless capacity to convey divine meaning.

Praise for *Beholding the Tree of Life*:

"Latter-day Saints have claimed the Book of Mormon as the keystone of their religion, but it presents itself first and foremost as a Jewish narrative. *Beholding the Tree of Life* is the first book I have seen that attempts to situate the Book of Mormon by paying serious attention to its Jewish literary precedents and ways of reading scripture. It breaks fresh ground in numerous ways that enrich an LDS understanding of the scriptures and that builds bridges to a potential Jewish readership." — Terryl L. Givens, author of *By the Hand of Mormon: The American Scripture that Launched a New World Religion*

"Bradley Kramer has done what someone ought to have done long ago, used the methods of Jewish scripture interpretation to look closely at the Book of Mormon. Kramer has taken the time and put in the effort required to learn those methods from Jewish teachers. He explains what he has learned clearly and carefully. And then he shows us the fruit of that learning by applying it to the Book of Mormon. The results are not only interesting, they are inspirin: This is one of those books that, on reading it, I thought 'I wish I'd written th — James E. Faulconer, author of *The Book of Mormon Made Harder* and *F. Philosophy, Scripture*